D1533060

Production,
Work,
Territory

PRODUCTION, WORK, TERRITORY

The geographical anatomy of industrial capitalism

EDITED BY

Allen J. Scott and Michael Storper

University of California, Los Angeles

Boston
ALLEN & UNWIN
London   Sydney

Allen & Unwin Inc.,
8 Winchester Place, Winchester, Mass 01890, USA

Allen & Unwin (Publishers) Ltd,
40 Museum Street, London WC1A 1LU, UK

Allen & Unwin (Publishers) Ltd,
Park Lane, Hemel Hempstead, Herts HP2 4TE, UK

Allen & Unwin (Australia) Ltd,
8 Napier Street, North Sydney, NSW 2060, Australia

First published in 1986

British Library Cataloguing in Publication Data

Production, work, territory: the geographical
anatomy of industrial capitalism.
1. Industry—Location 2. Geography, Economic
3. Capitalism
I. Scott, Allen J.   II. Storper, Michael
338.09   HC79.D5
ISBN 0–04–338126–X
ISBN 0–04–338127–8 Pbk

Library of Congress Cataloging in Publication Data

Main entry under title:
  Production, work, territory.
Includes index.
1. Economic history–1971–   —Addresses, essays,
lectures.   2. Capitalism–Addresses, essays, lectures.
3. Regional economic disparities—Addresses, essays,
lectures. I. Scott, Allen John.   II. Storper, Michael.
HC59.P682 1986   330   85–20006
ISBN 0–04–338126–X (alk. paper)
ISBN 0–04–338127–8 (pbk. : alk. paper)

Set in 10 on 11 point Bembo by
Phoenix Photosetting, Chatham
and printed in Great Britain by
Mackays of Chatham Ltd, Chatham

Preface

This book is an attempt to elucidate the geographical underpinnings of modern industrial capitalism. With the recent maturation of research into the general processes of production and social development, it has become increasingly evident that these underpinnings are of major political and theoretical significance. The chapters that follow focus resolutely on this matter by providing a multifaceted overview of the production system of modern capitalism and its expressive effects on territorial organization and change. At the same time, it is shown how the territorial, as such, structures and restructures industrial capitalism as a definite system of social practices and relationships.

In this book, the economic geography of industrial capitalism is treated at several different levels. First, the broad structure and temporality of capitalism in its totality are examined. Second, the dynamics of production and work are looked at in considerable detail, with special attention being paid to the basic issues of industrial organization, technology, and local labor markets. Third, the implications of all of this are traced out in terms of the territorial development, reproduction, and transformation of complexes of human activity, from the local to the global scales. Throughout the book, concerted attempts are made to draw out the wider social and political meaning of these investigations.

As the title of our book makes clear, we explicitly reject the widespread idea that the contemporary world has now entered into a 'post-industrial' phase. On the contrary, capitalist society continues in fact to be stubbornly organized around the central processes of industrial commodity production. Those apparent manifestations of 'post-industrialism' in the modern world – for example, increasing white-collar representation in the labor forces of the developed nations, burgeoning information-processing activities, the growth of the service economy, and the like – are in reality no more than imbricated moments *within* the complex structure of modern industrial capitalism as a whole. This issue is dealt with at length in various of the chapters that follow.

The book is, of course, the collective effort of a wide variety of different authors. We, as editors, commissioned individual authors to write specific chapters within the context of the pre-defined theme of the book as a whole. This manner of proceeding has resulted in a book of considerable coherence and consistency, notwithstanding its multiple authorship. We have organized the chapters within a series of major divisions that capture the tripartite focus of the book on production, work, and territory. In addition, we have taken advantage of the conceptual gradient of the entire set of contributions by also arranging them in a single longitudinal flow. The book is introduced in an editorial essay that sets the scene and identifies the major problems to be dealt with. It is concluded with another editorial essay that reviews and systematizes the accomplishments of the book as a whole and attempts to identify the major tasks that still lie ahead. In both of these essays, we have self-consciously avoided the usual editorial strategy in collections of this sort of merely stringing together a series of abstracts of individual papers ('Smith says . . ., Jones says . . ., Black says . . . etc.'). Instead, in our editorial overviews we have tried to point out the major theoretical and empirical issues in their own right and on their own terms. Nevertheless, for readers' convenience and ease of reference, we have allocated a section at the front of the book to simple abstracts of the chapters that follow.

It is our conviction that the essays contained in this book constitute a major contribution to the emerging debate about the geographical anatomy of industrial capitalism. Further, as we indicate in our summing up, the book may also be seen as a stepping-stone to a proleptic theoretical human geography. We regard this theoretical human geography as a decisive moment in the growth of modern social theory, for it directly confronts the circumstance that territorially dependent processes are integral to the unfolding of social relations and human action. We accordingly offer this book as a critical condensation of a significant stage in the elaboration of the theory of capitalist development. As such, the book will be of crucial concern not just to academic geographers, but to social scientists, activists, and policy makers of all kinds.

ALLEN J. SCOTT
MICHAEL STORPER

Contents

Contents

Contents

List of tables

List of tables

Abstracts

1 *Production, work, territory: contemporary realities and theoretical tasks* (M. Storper and A. J. Scott)

In this chapter, the editors introduce the book as a whole. The new historical realities of capitalism are sketched out as a background to the theoretical and analytical tasks faced in the chapters that follow. The consequences of these new realities for contemporary theories of production and work are pinpointed. The organization of production and work within territorial complexes is shown to be an essential moment in any viable conception of capitalist society.

2 *New tendencies in the international division of labor: regimes of accumulation and modes of regulation* (Alain Lipietz)

Development analysis on the basis of core – periphery models can be criticized on the grounds of (a) current realities, and in particular the widely varying social and economic conditions of Third World nations, and (b) their methodological aberrations (functionalism, holism, etc.). An approach in terms of regimes of accumulation and modes of regulation sheds new light on the newly industrializing countries. Two stages of industrialization are recognized: bloody taylorization and peripheral fordism. Their characteristics depend on the forms of the international division of labor as well as on the internal regulating mechanisms of each social formation. The crisis of these processes in the early 1980s can be interpreted as an outcome of both inner social unrest and the shock of monetarism.

3 *Capitalist production, scientific management and the service class* (John Urry)

This chapter analyzes the comparative development of new forms of managerial control in a number of capitalist societies in the first three or four decades of this century. It is shown that developments in the USA were particularly advanced and that this had the effect of producing an extensive and causally powerful 'service class.' No such 'service class' developed to anything like the same degree in the UK and the consequences for this on the trajectory of British society are drawn out in detail.

4 *Technological imperatives and modern corporate strategy* (Edward J. Malecki)

Technology affects and is manipulated by corporate activity through both new products and more efficient, lower-cost production processes. To a considerable degree, these are very different in both their human resource implications and their geographical orientation. Product innovation strategies rely on technical workers to develop successful new products that can be produced in standardized production plants. Routine manufacturing in these plants is hardly a skilled task, however, and firms seek out the lowest-cost labor forces as an easy way to reduce costs. New processes also allow production labor to be reduced or eliminated. The geographical manifestation of technological change and firms' responses to it, then, is two-sided.

Technical labor is located in some places and low-cost labor is sought out in other places, although these may even be within a single urban region. The reduction of work skills in all regions has serious implications for regional development in the future.

5 *The organization and locational structure of production subcontracting* (John Holmes)

Until recently, subcontracting and other 'secondary' forms of production and employment were considered to be marginal or archaic features of advanced capitalist production which would eventually fade into history as a result of the progressive rationalization and centralization of production and capital. However, the persistence, and even resurgence, of subcontracting in both emerging as well as declining industrial sectors has led to the recognition that subcontracting is not an anachronism, but rather is one of a range of possibilities continually open to firms in organizing production. With this recognition has come the need adequately to theorize and understand the nature and dynamics of both subcontracting and the forms of labor market segmentation associated with it. After opening with a brief critique of the way interfirm linkages, such as subcontracting, have been dealt with traditionally in economic geography, the chapter identifies several different types of production subcontracting generated by different causal mechanisms. In particular, factors related to the nature of product markets, the technical organization of the labor process and the structure of labor markets which encourage the development of subcontracting are discussed. Finally, the chapter argues that while the spatial configuration of subcontracting is clearly important in understanding the locational structure of production, it is difficult to generalize about such spatial configurations due to the unevenness of capitalist development.

6 *Industrial location on a world scale: the case of the semiconductor industry* (Andrew Sayer)

This chapter develops an historical sketch of the changing geography of the international semiconductor industry in a way which exposes certain neglected issues of radical approaches to such subjects. The main failings are the neglect of product technology, the social and institutional character of capital and labor and the role and effects of nation-states in the internationalization of capital. In particular, the 'new international division of labour' thesis is shown to be seriously misleading, as are accounts which try to read off the uneven spatial development of a whole sector from a study of a few leading firms. Contrary to these orthodoxies, cheap labor and hence Third World production bases may be dispensable, proximity to markets is still important, technological complementarities or dependency still matter, and national (and other) differences in management and labor practices and policies are crucial for understanding the geography of production. Consequently a more flexible theory of industrial location is needed to appreciate the complexities of concrete patterns of capital accumulation.

7 *The crisis of the midwest auto industry* (Gordon L. Clark)

The midwest auto industry is undergoing a process of profound restructuring. Compared to the late 1970s, the region will have lost nearly 50% of its work-force in this industry by 1986. Understanding the crisis of the midwest auto industry involves two issues: the notion of crisis as a theoretical category, and the patterns of local class relations in this region and industry over the last 50 years. It is argued that the crisis is one of ossified class relations and inadequate adjustment to a competitive threat clearly recognized some years ago. However, it is also acknowledged that the present crisis has been borne by the many auto communities of the midwest. Future prospects for these communities appear bleak: the process of restructuring will pit communities against one another in a competition for investment and employment. Recent attempts at restructuring the class bargain of the local industry appear to have only narrowed the political base of workers; there is a real danger that local communities will be further fragmented as entry into the industry is denied to local residents.

8 *Labor demand, labor supply and the suburbanization of low-wage office work* (K. Nelson)

This locational analysis of 'back offices' (or large highly automated offices with low extramural contact needs) in the San Francisco Bay Area concludes that the distinguishing feature of the outer suburban area attracting this office type is an educated, stable and non-militant female labor supply associated with expanding single family housing districts. Automated clerical jobs are characterized by high job performance requirements and/or eroded working conditions, increasing the importance of such labor qualities. Back offices must be located nearby in order to recruit this labor supply, since the journey to work of these women is limited by low clerical wages and by household responsibilities. The resulting transfer of back office clerical jobs from central city, low-income, predominantly minority female work-forces to higher-income, predominantly white, suburban female work-forces is of concern due to the quantity and quality of the relocating jobs, and the dependence of many central city clerical workers on these jobs for the sole support of their families.

9 *Contesting works closures in Western Europe's old industrial regions: defending place or betraying class?* (Ray Hudson and David Sadler)

In contrast to the preceding two decades, the latter years of the 1970s and the initial ones of the 1980s in northeast England were the occasion for a series of campaigns to contest works closures or major employment losses. These anti-closure campaigns were characteristically organized around the threatened works and the community reliant upon it for employment and wage income. Furthermore, it became clear that such campaigns were by no means confined to northeast England as similar ones developed or revived in the 'old' industrial regions elsewhere in the European Community. In several of these other cases protests became generalized within an industry at regional – even national – level, or throughout particular regions across a wide spectrum of social groups. In these cases attachment to place and class became contingently conjoined so that these became complementary rather than competitive bases for social organization in defence of place. In this chapter the issues of place and class, and the implications of and reasons for their conjunction, are explored.

10 *Regional production and the production of regions: the case of Steeltown* (M. J. Webber)

This chapter analyzes the processes of regional growth and decline, using as an example the case of Hamilton, Ontario. Accumulation occurs in only a few regions which offer particular advantages to capitalists, but these advantages turn to disadvantages as labor gains power, mechanization proceeds and fixed capital becomes obsolete. Capital can offset these disadvantages by being relocated to new regions where new forces and relations of production can be established. Hamilton exhibits many of the characteristics of an obsolete social structure and fixed capital stock, and recent investment decisions by its major employer show both how to avoid these difficulties and how to begin the process of modifying them.

11 *Integration and unequal development: the case of southern Italy* (M. Dunford)

Since the mid 1950s the structure of the Italian Mezzogiorno has been transformed by a process of industrialization. Yet the gap in levels of development between the North and South has not been narrowed. In this study the new types of inequality and dependency that have come to characterize the Mezzogiorno are outlined. It is suggested that the new problems of the South are related in part to the dominant role played by large chemical and steel projects in southern industrial development, and to the impact of an externally controlled process of industrialization in the social and economic fabric of the region. The development of these industries in the South along with the more recent investments in engineering is in its turn related to the economic strategies of the public and private groups concerned. But it is also argued that they form part of a wider model of national economic and political development whose trajectory can be explained with the help of what is called the theory of regulation.

12 *Unequal integration in global fordism: the case of Ireland* (Diane Perrons)

This chapter is concerned with the way in which Ireland has been integrated into the international division of labor that was established in the period of growth following World War II. This growth has been characterized by the development of a regime of intensive accumulation, or fordism. The chapter begins by examining the nature and origins of the economic and social conditions prevailing in Ireland in the 1940s and 1950s. These conditions are contrasted with those emerging in other industrial economies which followed a fordist growth path. An outline of the character and determinations of fordism is given. This is followed by a discussion of how Ireland was drawn into and transformed by this regime of growth, initially perhaps as a peripheral part of the growth process but subsequently, it is argued, playing a very specific role as the regime of growth at the center went into crisis. The nature of the transformation of Ireland is then examined more critically by focusing on the problems of the industrial sector and its contribution to development and on the ability of the state to finance the current pattern of development. This discussion is intended to support the main argument that, although substantial changes have taken place in Ireland, it has been the nature or form of unequal development and not unequal development itself that has changed as a consequence of Ireland's revised role in the international division of labor.

13 *The state, the region and the division of labor* (R. J. Johnston)

The increasing international mobility of capital is producing a substantial alteration in the context of regional problems and of government regional policies. This, in turn, is leading to a new set of crises for the state apparatus as it seeks to promote both capitalist accumulation and worker legitimation, *in places*. Two opposing policy directions are suggested to counter these crisis: one argues for a closed economic system, insulated from the world–economy, as a means of promoting local prosperity, whereas the other argues that economic success will only come if the national economy becomes more efficient. These policies are considered in the light of the British case.

14 *The spatial strategies of the state in the political-economic development of Brazil* (Pedro P. Geiger and Fany R. Davidovich)

In Brazil, a late developing country, the state has had a leading role in economic development. It has used, implicitly and explicitly, a series of spatial strategies involving the location of activities and populations. These strategies follow the logic of accumulation in the capitalist process, but adjust this logic to the political interests of the groups in power. The paper describes the larger phases of the Brazilian economy in the last 50 years and the different spatial strategies adopted by various governments. In general these strategies shifted from strong spatial concentration of urban activities to diffusion of modernization of the administration and tertiary activities and to industrial deconcentration.

15 *Industrial change and territorial organization: a summing up* (A. J. Scott and M. Storper)

In this concluding chapter, the editors draw out the consequences of all the previous chapters for the theory of territorial organization. The social division of labor is shown to be a central mechanism in the process of industrial complex formation. Various processes of organizational, technical and financial restructuring create tendencies to locational dispersal from centralized complexes. The geographical meaning of the new international division of labor is investigated. Problems of class and community in territorial production systems are then highlighted. The chapter ends with a claim to the effect that production, work, and territory must now be accorded a central position on the agenda of theoretical human geography.

Part I

*Overview:
production, work,
territory*

1

Production, work, territory: contemporary realities and theoretical tasks

M. STORPER and A. J. SCOTT

This book represents an attempt to develop an understanding of the economic geography of contemporary capitalism. The task is urgent because, since the second half of the 1970s, capitalism in America, Western Europe, and the world at large seems to have embarked on a radically new course in comparison with the economic and political structures that were set in place in the decades immediately following World War II. This gives rise to two intertwined imperatives: the need for a factual account of recent geographical and historical developments; and the need for a theoretical *cum* ideological debate about the meaning and significance of these developments.

In this introductory chapter we survey briefly the changing face of international capitalism and we attempt to identify some of the more important theoretical tasks and agendas raised by the current conjuncture. We begin with an overall review of the genesis of these realities taken as a whole. We then investigate their meaning for questions of production, work, and territory and describe how the chapters in this book intersect with and illuminate these questions.

The new historical realities of capitalism

In the 1970s and 1980s, a number of significant new historical realities of capitalism have made their appearance. These realities have had major impacts on the development of industries, regions and cities, for it is within the overarching forces and influences of capitalism that real agents in actual territorial systems deploy their behavioral strategies. Equally, territorial outcomes have decisive effects on the shape and form of capitalist development itself.

The new realities of capitalism have their roots in the end of the postwar economic boom in the late 1960s and early 1970s. Most analyses of the new realities center on its most spectacular outcome, namely, the internationalization of social and economic relations to an extent never before known. This forms a central element in our analysis, too, but it must be rooted in, and seen as a consequence of, strategies that have been undertaken to reorganize

3

investment, production, and work, and not just as some independent and abstract structural imperative.

The sustained economic growth of the Western world in the immediate postwar decades was led by the United States where accumulation was based on accelerated housing construction and the production of associated consumer durables (including, of course, the private car), and a deepening commitment to Keynesian macro-economic policy. The long boom of the 1960s was also based on these additional circumstances: capital goods exports to other countries, oligopolistic pricing policies, an emerging military-industrial complex, and a cold war ideological climate that helped to hem in the activities of organized labor.

Once it was set in motion, the boom was prolonged by a series of intervening events. By the mid 1960s, the United States was becoming ever more deeply embroiled in the Vietnam War, and this encouraged large increases in arms expenditure by the federal government. For a time, the military–Keynesian policy pursued by the United States government during the Vietnam War, combined with increases in social welfare spending, maintained high levels of aggregate demand. A further extension of the boom was secured by the opening up of many new investment opportunities in the NICs (newly industrializing countries) such as Brazil, Mexico, Chile (after the fall of Allende in 1973), Taiwan, Singapore, Hong Kong, and Korea. With strong state industrialization policies aimed at fostering the growth of internal markets and export opportunities through investment by multinational corporations, these countries provided an outlet for much investment capital during the early 1970s.

Ultimately, however, nothing seemed able to prevent the eventual end to the boom. As early as the mid 1960s, the very success of the boom was creating conditions which were starting to undercut its further advance. Markets were already becoming saturated and industrial overcapacity was pervasive. International penetration of American and European markets rose steadily over the 1960s. In the meantime, Japan had reindustrialized via exports, first in low-value goods, and then increasingly in high-quality, high-value durables coordinated through a central industrial planning authority. This had the immediate effect of aggravating the industrial overcapacity problem in the United States and Europe. The precise point at which the profitability of capital began to decrease depended very much on sector and nation. Britain was one of the first major capitalist economies to show signs of the crisis, followed by the United States. These two countries had an aging capital stock (some of it dating from before World War II), and their major industries, such as steel and cars, had enjoyed various forms of protection and support for a long time. France and Italy followed by Germany and the NICs began to experience economic stress between 1974 and 1978; and finally even Japan's economy started to falter in the early 1980s. These trends have not been a simple echo of the events of the 1930s. Rather, the 1970s has been a period of multiple recessions and recoveries, with the recessions becoming each time more severe, and the recoveries more shallow in terms of employment, personal income, and profitability increases.

Even before the end of the boom, many large-scale industries were undergoing some locational reorganization. As early as the 1930s the US textile industry had largely relocated to the South, and in the 1950s both US and European companies had started to locate production units in selected overseas areas (for example, apparel and shoe plants in Southeast Asia). During the 1960s, this outflow of foreign direct investment capital accelerated rapidly. At the same time, General Motors in the USA adopted its so-called 'southern strategy' and located branch assembly plants in the southern and southwestern states in order to take advantage of low wage levels and an anti-union atmosphere.

Most migrant plants (as in apparel, shoes, and textiles) brought few developmental advantages to their host countries, and so many nations, especially in Latin America, reacted with strong import substitution policies in the 1960s and 1970s. This induced multinational corporations to arrange much of their foreign direct investment in a way that served (at least in part) the domestic markets of the NICs. The celebrated 'miracles' in Brazil, Mexico, and Korea were largely due to this type of policy. Thus, much of the most visible investment in the NICs during the 1960s and early 1970s was something other than a simple transfer of fixed capital from developed countries or regions for the purposes of producing for export back to the developed world.

At the end of the boom, infrastructural and labor resources were already in place in the Third World, because of prior import substitution strategies followed in countries such as Mexico and Brazil, or because of aggressive industrialization in the production of low-value export goods, as in Singapore and Korea. These resources have now attracted to the Third World the production facilities of industries that find themselves in crisis, and the facilities of newer, growing industries.

Massive rationalization of production systems in the old industries of the developed countries is now occurring: production processes are being combined and divided into new units of production, new process technologies are being deployed, and the search continues for new kinds of industrial labor relations.

Both old and new industries seem to have embarked on a period of experimentation in locational behavior and production organization. For example, both the new electronics industry and the old apparel industry have located phases of their production processes in low-wage regions and countries. In addition, revolutionary organizational and spatial strategies are being experimented with on the part of automobile manufacturers. Ford, for example, has created the 'World Car', which involves international integration of very large-scale production units with standardized output, many parallel plants, and the provision of product variety by creating different interchangeable components which are combined with core products to make possible great variety at high levels of output. By spreading the production process over many different areas, the company faces diminished risk of blockages created in any one plant or region. This permits a great increase in company bargaining power with labor forces and governments. But it remains to be seen whether the integrated world production system is a durable locational tendency or merely a transitional response to crisis conditions while longer-term rationalization of technologies and facilities is accomplished. For example, General Motors is experimenting with precisely the opposite system to Ford's, based on just-in-time parts delivery and flexible automation, with a tendency toward locational agglomeration and a focus on corporatist labor relations. Which of the approaches and which spatial pattern will prevail remains to be seen.

The majority of international investment flows continue to be between the highly developed countries. Japanese auto companies are building assembly plants in the United States, while American and Japanese companies are constructing branch plants for assembly and research and development in Europe. Both new and old industries, moreover, are forming international production consortia (involving either national or multinational corporations) consisting of project-by-project alliances around particular lines of production. These permit a rationalization of the use of capital at the international level without actually denationalizing the corporations themselves or raising the policitical problem of excessive foreign ownership (e.g. the Renault–American Motors and GM–Toyota deals in the USA; the General Electric and SNECMA partnership to produce jet turbines in Europe; and the Franco-British Concorde project). These patterns can be viewed, in one sense, as an expression of the long-term tendency toward the centralization of industrial capital, in the context of international rationalization and integration.

The Third World, faced with the demands of the international financial system (to which we will come in greater detail shortly), has been forced to re-emphasize production of industrial goods and agricultural commodities for export in place of the developmentally oriented import-substitution strategies of the late 1960s and 1970s. Thus, many nations, such as Brazil and Mexico, are again welcoming low-wage industries and phases in the production process even though they had earlier played down these activities in their attempts to diversify their economies.

Whatever its extent and durability, the internationalization of production is only one facet of the current reorganization of industrial capitalism. The internationalization of finance capital is an equally important event of the last two decades. Its effects on the physical structure of production, the use of labor, and location in all the major capitalist economies are at least as great as those that emanate from the actual reconstruction of production systems and labor markets across international boundaries. Too often, however, the genesis of financial internationalization is treated as if it were independent of the internationalization of production. Financial internationalization is an outcome of the profitability crisis to which we have alluded above. It has been provoked, in part, by the internationalization of production and it encourages further internationalization and competition on the basis of international productivity and price standards. Four basic, interrelated aspects of the latest wave of financial internationalization should be noted.

First, when declining profitability and overcapacity, combined with Vietnam War spending, created runaway inflation in the early 1970s, the dollar suffered a massive devaluation relative to gold and other international currencies. This made imports much more expensive and yet did not advance the position of American exports in most industrial markets (with the exception of specialized capital goods) because their high costs were still not offset by the declining value of the currency. When imports continued to erode domestic market shares in many industries, the underlying weaknesses of American industries were revealed, and this suggested the need to rationalize production. Later, in the mid 1970s, when overcapacity and international penetration had increased, a series of major studies of productivity growth revealed that there had been a significant aging of the US industrial capital stock and a general failure on the part of industrial corporations to pay attention to new process technologies.

Secondly, the rise in OPEC oil prices severely damaged the financial and export positions of those countries lacking domestic petroleum resources. Among the heavy petroleum importers, Japan was least injured, suggesting the benefits of higher productivity in weathering international price fluctuations. Moreover, the same event caused an immense swelling of the eurodollar market, further weakening the control of the United States over international exchange rates and investment.

Thirdly, much of the industrialization of the Third World has been financed by private banks in the United States and Europe. Even though serious debt crises have been created in many NICs by unprecedentedly high interest rates combined with the global recession of the 1980s, it is clear that the banks will not force Third World economies to default on their debts. Rather, these countries will be treated leniently, in order to encourage them to remain industrial powers so that they can continue to make payments on their debts and participate in world trade.

Fourthly, with the failure of any country or currency to control the international financial system during the 1970s and early 1980s, a period of rapidly fluctuating exchange rates was ushered in. These fluctuations provided an additional incentive for international trade and investment, for if firms are organized as multinational production systems, they can alter the flow of shipments and payments to take advantage of transitory financial opportunities.

As a consequence of all of this, the now highly articulated international system provides immediate information to each national economy on its international performance through the most spatially and temporally mobile form of capital – money itself. Even though most production continues to serve purely regional and national markets, and though labor supplies and labor market conditions vary greatly according to sector and region, pressure has been created for whole economies to shape themselves according to international conditions. This is especially true of class relations and state economic policies. The currently observable pressures on European social democracies are a significant case in point and, as the examples of France and Britain make clear, they have found it extraordinarily difficult to maintain their integrity in the face of the new international realities of capitalism. Even the United States is not free from such pressure, and especially since so much of the economic recovery in the early 1980s has been financed by foreign capital inflows seeking the high interest rates engendered by the ballooning federal deficit.

Ironically, the militancy of labor, the poor, women, blacks, and other groups reached a peak just as the long post-war boom was running out and recessionary pressures were conferring new bargaining powers on capitalists. In the advanced industrial nations, social conflict intensified after May 1968 in France, the 'Hot Autumn' of 1969 in Italy, and the black riots and anti-war protests of the late 1960s and early 1970s in the United States. Militancy peaked somewhat later in the NICs, as exemplified by the near-general strike of São Paulo in 1977–8. In short, just as demands for redistribution and social justice were starting to make themselves felt, the race to rationalize production systems and international finance and terms of trade started to accelerate. This tendency to rationalization has encouraged the creation of new labor processes, helped to redefine occupational and remuneration structures, and spurred deep changes in capital–labor relations in most of the capitalist countries. It has also seemed to be associated with major shifts in the complexion of national electorates and it correlates with a resurgence of political conservatism and attacks on the welfare state in almost all of the advanced capitalist economies.

As we have seen, the new historical realities of capitalism began with a crisis of profitability in production in the developed nations. This same crisis created a deepening internationalization of production and financial systems. Through the interaction of industrial production and money capital, internationalization has now emerged as a relatively external pressure on the organization of production, work, and territory in all countries. The global economy consists of a set of interdependent commodity, labor, and financial flows. It is within this articulated but decentralized international system that the concrete forms of production, work, and territory documented in this book are situated.

Theory and the new realities

Much economic and geographic theory has hitherto failed to grasp these new macro-economic realities and thus the potential diversity of capitalist development. For example, in the 1950s and 1960s, the evolution and performance of the large corporation were described in terms of oligopolistic control. The economy was said to have entered a 'monopoly capital' phase of development in which competition was no longer the rule. The existence of corporate bureaucracies was assumed to mean that capitalism itself had entered a stage in which development was rationally planned by corporate technocrats. Geographers and regional scientists accordingly documented the rational spatial expansion of the corporate production system, and regional development theorists advanced notions of stages of modernization and developmental 'turning points.' The existence of oligopolies did not, however, imply any such control. Oligopoly itself is merely a condition of an industry in which there are technological discontinuities that affect freedom of entry, but this does not give oligopolists the ability to control entry permanently, or by the same token, to control the evolution of the sector via oligopolistic pricing practices.

Indeed, many of the theories invoked to explain economic structure, even those that have significantly departed from neoclassical models, have missed the openness of development processes. Cumulative causation theory, for example, extended the concept of agglomeration mechanically and statically, and so could not foresee the eventual decline of many old industrial cities in the United States and Western Europe. This, together with other core–periphery theories (including product cycle theory), missed the potential for new industrial complexes to grow up in totally new places, and instead focused on semi-theorized processes of incubation in and diffusion from major metropolitan centers.

In contrast to hierarchical, diffusionist concepts of development (whether of the city systems, interregional convergence, or modernization varieties), which overemphasize the potential for smooth growth and universal increases in living standards under capitalism, marxist theorizing on development has tended to stress interregional disparities, uneven development and the potential for critical breakdowns in regional systems. Much marxist work has also exhibited something of a fixation on backward and dependent regions to the exclusion of the more developed ones. Capitalism, however, has proven itself to be more technically dynamic and socially creative than has been anticipated in marxist crisis theory. For example, capital-saving technologies, the cheapening of constant capital inputs, and the increases in the rate of exploitation of labor made possible by the internationalization of production have radically counteracted the tendency for the rate of profit to fall. Similarly, development of Third World nations has also often defied the predictions of marxian theory, for many of them have gone beyond their initial roles as cheap labor depots and (as the cases of Brazil, Singapore and Hong Kong make clear) have started to develop more complex patterns of industrialization.

Recently, the new realities of capitalism have begun to be reassessed by theorists. In contrast to much of the work of the 1960s and 1970s, the research emerging in the late 1970s and early 1980s is concerned just as much with developed as it is with underdeveloped areas. The new work has many different currents, though a few overall themes dominate. For example, there is much concern with the problem of corporate behavior. Corporate behavior is embedded in the organizational web of production, which in turn is deeply structured by the capital–labor relation. This is the context in which technological choices and production rationalization occur. A good deal of work has also been concerned with the redefinition of labor demand and the evolution of the employment relation as a basic condition of production. Much of this analysis builds upon recently developed ideas about labor market segmentation. There has also been a pouring forth of new work on technological change and the dynamics of industrial organization, which considers the problem of how production processes are established, divided technically and in space, and how the social and detailed divisions of labor change over time as a consequence of technological change.

Macro-economics too is now rapidly changing its theoretical colors. As noted, questions about the long-run potentials of capitalist development have moved back to the center of the intellectual stage. Even though the old orthodoxies continue to be debated within and outside of marxism, there is now considerable interest in non-teleological conceptions of capitalist macro-economic evolution in which *contingency* plays a significant role, as for example in the work of the French Regulationist School (see Chapter 2 below). By no means has any new broad synthesis of capitalism's tendencies emerged; rather, there has been a marked backing away from the notion that there is any pre-determined developmental path of all. Attention is now being increasingly focused on the details of class relations, technological change, and political struggles, as the concrete and contingent determinants of history.

Lastly, we should note here that much of the recent work on cities and regions draws on and contributes to debates in social theory about the differential roles of human agency and social structure in the formation of historical outcomes. The nature of social practice itself is being re-examined, and in particular the roles of reason, discourse, and daily habit in contributing to the grand currents of history and geography. While there continues to be much debate about the merits of structuralist versus post-structuralist modes of reasoning, there is strong agreement that functionalist, mechanical, and pseudo-biological metaphors for human social history are to be rejected. Much of the work reported on in this book draws on and contributes to these debates by exploring the time–space constitution of social action and its expression in the form of geographical economic systems.

The new realities of production

As already indicated, many of the basic theoretical assumptions of the 1960s and 1970s about the evolution of capitalist economies and their overall developmental possibilities are being increasingly called into question by recent events. The same is true for the organization of production. Overly mechanistic conceptions of the nature of industrial organization and behavior are being challenged by current realities.

A prime motive force behind the contemporary reorganization of production is the introduction of new process and product technologies. The switch from inert merchanical systems to programmable electronic technologies is significant not only for the macro-economic reasons we noted previously, but also because it introduces an array of organizational possibilities not attainable with mechanical systems. It should be noted, in passing, that there is as yet no single really viable theory of technological change. Technological change remains largely an historical puzzle, exogenous to most economic theory, and considered only in the most general historical terms in the remainder of the social sciences. As in the cases of oligopoly and cumulative causation noted above, in the past there has been a strong tendency to take a given state of technology and generalize from its empirical characteristics to the overall possibilities for industry organization and locational behavior. In light of the recent major changes, not only are the empirical realities of production organization being reconsidered, but the problem of the basic logic of industry organization (given a set of technologies) is now again open to question. This, combined with better theories of technological change, promises an industrial geography that can theorize the rich palette of organizational possibilities in historical time. Let us now consider some of the dimensions of production organization in the current period that have spurred these theoretical efforts.

First, there are powerful trends in the direction of disintegration of the production processes of many once vertically integrated industries. In numerous industries, it appears that an increasing proportion of transactions is conducted in the market between technically and financially separated units. This represents a reversal of the trend toward integration of production and ownership along final output lines that tended to characterize the development of capitalist industry in the first decades of this century in the drive to mass production and mass consumption. Newly disintegrated functions will have different locational possibilities and limitations from their (integrated) predecessors. Holmes deals explicitly with this process in his description of vertical disintegration and subcontracting activity (Ch. 5).

Secondly, the rapid growth of the office-based economy, which is devoted principally to managerial control, business services, and information processing, is also an outcome of vertical and spatial disintegration (either institutionally, by the creation of new business service industries, or technically, by the separation of packets of existing office work from blue-collar production activities). Nelson's study of back offices in the San Francisco Bay Area (Ch. 8), Urry's analysis of the growth of managerialism (Ch. 3) and Malecki's chapter on research and development (Ch. 4) explore this phenomenon. Nelson and Urry demonstrate the falseness of the 'post-industrialism' view by pointing out that these new branches are clearly in the service of commodity production. At the same time, they demonstrate that the historical evolution of the division of labor within commodity production at some point generates tasks which appear in the form of qualitatively new branches of production and labor processes (and not merely as physical and financial fragmentation of pre-existing tasks and their re-combination into new units of production). Both processes are part of the same tendency, but the qualitatively different aspect of the new generic functions, such as are now found in management and information circulation, must be acknowledged.

Thirdly, the simple concept of a sector as a collection of establishments producing homogeneous outputs is increasingly being called into question. Typically, it is assumed that units of production with similar outputs have technically and socially similar production processes, from which flow similar measurable economic, geographical, and social consequences. With the shift from inert mechanical production systems to programmable electronically controlled robots of immense versatility and flexibility, it can no longer be assumed that an establishment is devoted to the same mix of outputs over even the short run. Moreover, the relationship of level of output to scale economies is being radically altered by programmable machinery. Firms may employ a much richer mix of strategies than was ever possible with inert mechanical technology. The variety of these strategies is alluded to in Holmes' treatment of subcontracting (Ch. 5) and in Sayer's chapter on the

11

international semiconductor industry (Ch. 6). As a result of these developments, it has become increasingly difficult to accept traditional definitions of
an industry or sector, such as the American SIC or British MLH conventions.
These sectoral definitions often result in arbitrary designations that hinder the
tasks of understanding industrial organization by diverting attention from
the new possibilities that are appearing on the historical stage.

Fourth, all these observations suggest the need to reconsider theoretically
the dynamism of industrial organization in capitalist economies. In contrast
to attempts to impose rigid and closed conceptions of production organization, as in theories of the product cycle, oligopolistic competition, or
monopoly capital, this book suggests the need for an *enriched conception of
capitalist competition* in which diversity is fully and directly dealt with. Sayer's
chapter on the semiconductor industry raises this issue directly. This theory
of competition must account not only for choices under particular productivity, price, and profit conditions, but also for the variety of responses that
active agents make to these conditions, and in so doing create new historical
possibilities. This does not lead back to behavioral analysis of industrial
systems, but resolutely forward to historical approaches in which behavior
itself (within the dialectic of agency and structure) becomes a subjacent
element of the whole process of historical eventuation.

The new realities of work

Production is carried out on the basis of organized work, and to speak of
production without also speaking of human labor is to abstract a technical
and functional logic from its necessary social context. Work has been the
subject of considerable academic attention for several decades ranging from
Elton Mayo's writings in the 1930s, through the researches of the Tavistock
Group on shop floor organization, to the dramatic increase in attention given
to the labor process following the publication of Braverman's *Labor and
monopoly capital* in the early 1970s. Work in modern capitalism has taken on
forms not anticipated in much prior theory and empirical research. This book
suggests some important contemporary directions in which work has been
evolving.

To begin with, Braverman's prediction about the massive deskilling of
work has turned out to be only partially correct. Along with deskilling there
has been considerable reskilling as a result of the development of new
branches of production and new fractions within the division of labor. Urry,
for example, finds that managerial skills were at one time a qualitatively new
kind of labor attribute (Ch. 3), and Malecki writes about the emergence of
specialized research and development skills in the American industrial system
(Ch. 4). Notice that skill is always a relative category. One is skilled to the
degree that one possesses an ability that is differentiated and not ubiquitous.
As certain skills become fully socialized they lose their special meaning. Thus
in a society of illiterates, literacy is a considerable skill, but as everyone learns
to read and write, it becomes simply an undifferentiated norm.

New labor processes are consequences of both technical change and new social arrangements within production. Production technologies, when embodied in a workplace, create particular domains for capital–labor interactions, and it is within these domains that social relations in production are formed. Concrete patterns of labor demand and the arrangement of work go beyond abstract profit-maximizing calculations to 'qualitative efficiency', i.e. personnel management strategies undertaken at given conjunctures of the capital–labor relation. The chapters by Malecki, Holmes, Clark, and Nelson examine this problem (Chs. 4, 5, 7 & 8).

The chapters below also demonstrate the importance of spatial milieu for the production of particular kinds of human attributes which are important components of labor demand (Chs. 7–10). The future of regional economies depends critically on the processes by which local social reproduction occurs, for it is in the domain of social reproduction that such characteristics as the willingness to work under a given set of conditions and tolerance for particular relations of distribution are formed. In this respect, labor supply conditions *qua* concrete cultural circumstances (going far beyond the simple issue of reservation wages) may have an ultimately decisive role in determining the outcomes of industrial restructuring. This remark obviously puts the problem of regional politics and place-specific processes of reproduction in the forefront of theoretical inquiry (Chs. 7 & 10).

In the final analysis, all of this points to a continued critical examination of our notions of class, class-consciousness, and class behavior. With the diversity of labor processes noted above, we are perhaps observing the end of the 'mass collective worker.' Not only is labor demand differentiated by industry, occupation, skill, age, gender, and race, but also by geographical affiliation. Add to this the often complex loyalties that individuals have to their communities, and the ways in which experience and world-views cut across these social divisions within specific regions, and an extremely complex mosaic of social life in capitalism suggests itself. It is not necessary to depreciate the reality of these divisions before the structural reality of class. We should rather seek to understand the intersections between the two as a way of understanding the reproduction of the class power upon which capitalism rests. These issues point to the need for detailed analytical investigations of specific regional forms of industrialization relative to these concrete forms of labor supply. While it may still be legitimate in some quarters simply to reaffirm class categories as undifferentiated objective phenomena, this view seriously denatures the local forms of social life within which real production, work, and capital accumulation take place.

Geographical anatomy: its methodological and theoretical significance

The various contributions in this book begin the task of correcting the bias in social analysis toward time and away from space. Put simply, the historical dynamics of socioeconomic systems can only be fully comprehended in geographical context, for the possibilities and limitations of human action are intrinsically constructed in spatially specific circumstances. This methodological prescription, however, presupposes its own qualification: territorial analysis cannot be constituted as a science in itself, since the basic forces of locational activity are themselves expressions of the wider system of the social and property relations of capitalism.

In order to carry out the project of a geographical analysis of industrial capitalism, this book goes far beyond the kind of macro–micro problematic that seeks on the one hand to explain detailed social outcomes in terms of broad structural logic, and on the other hand to account for overall social developments in terms simply of an aggregation of small-scale events. Here, we focus insistently on the interactions between these two distinctive levels of analysis via the mediations of what we refer to as a *meso* level of theory and empirical inquiry. Two main points need to be made.

First, the emerging human geography presented in this book subsumes micro-level adjustment processes and decision-making dynamics within an historical and structural framework (Chs. 2, 7, 10 & 13). This subsumption does not lose sight of the significance and integrity of the micro-level, but neither does it lose sight of the circumstance that micro-economic and micro-sociological analysis has little to say about broad social currents. Micro-analysis can never fully penetrate into the architectonics of social organization.

Secondly, the converse of these propositions must also be taken seriously. The macro-economy and the long run are built up from time- and space-differentiated outcomes at extremely detailed levels of resolution. In particular, the reproduction of the broad structural constitution of capitalist society is posited upon the peculiar behavior and practices of the innumerable individuals who compose that society. Macro-analysis, in its turn, has little to say about this central problem of the role of agency.

The micro and macro levels must thus be simultaneously and actively present in any really viable analysis of capitalist development. But at the same time, it is necessary to keep to the forefront the intermediating meso level to which we have alluded above. Territorial analysis is intrinsically such a case where, as we move from the dynamics of the mode of production down to the specifics of community and place (and back again) it is necessary to invoke a complex series of intermediate variables dealing with such issues as industrial organization, the division of labor, technology, labor market processes, international capital flows, and all the rest. This is also, it need hardly be said, a domain that is especially strongly touched by contingency and open-endedness so that as we move analytically through this domain to the micro-level we arrive at an extremely varied and often quite unexpected set of outcomes, however stable and uniform the generalized structures we may start out with.

This contingency and open-endedness is nowhere more apparent than in the developmental characteristics of territorial complexes of production and social activity. As capitalism opens out from a broad general structure into a system of geographically differentiated units of organization it takes on the form of an extraordinarily varied mosaic of socio-spatial relationships. In turn, the re-totalization of capitalism in a way that incorporates this mosaic provides us with a dramatically widened conception of historical and social

14

change. Precisely how the territorial foundations of capitalism operate, are reproduced and transformed through time, and come together in functionally compatible ways is the subject of the chapters that follow.

2

New tendencies in the international division of labor: regimes of accumulation and modes of regulation

ALAIN LIPIETZ

Some 20 years ago, the case seemed to be settled, although the judges did not all deliver the same verdict. An international division of labor set the industrialized nations in opposition to the others. The former exported manufactured goods whereas the latter exported mineral and agricultural raw materials or human labor. For the dominant group of liberal economists (such as Rostow 1963 with his stages of economic growth model), the non-industrialized nations lagged behind the industrialized nations as children lag behind adults. They would soon take off and economic exchange would contribute to this. On the other hand, various heterodox, marxist, 'dependentist', 'third worldist' lines of thought suggested that relations between the core and the periphery (i.e. between the North and the South) were indeed obstructing any possibility of 'normal' development in the South.

The argument of the dependentists was approximately as follows: the North needed the South as an outlet for the export of its surpluses. Also, the wealth produced in the primary sector of the South was transferred to the North through unequal exchange. Any industrial emancipation of the South would have represented an aggression against the North, and the North possessed the military means to avert such an outcome.

This proposition had an immense advantage over the liberal argument. It focused research on the links between economic spaces in the world system. It had the weakness of not being concerned with the concrete conditions of capitalist accumulation, whether in the core or the periphery. As a result, it could see neither the transformations going on in the logic of accumulation in the core, nor the parallel transformations within the countries of the periphery.

The dogma of the inescapable development of underdevelopment was dealt a blow by the emergence during the 1970s of a real capitalist industrialization in some countries of the periphery. In the face of this, some marxists rallied to the rostovian thesis and even sang the praises of imperialism as the pioneer of capitalism and as promoter of the development of productive

16

forces and the unification of humanity (Warren 1980). Others simply rejected the novelty of the event (Frank 1982).

Despite the undeniable advantages of the imperialism/dependency approach it seems that (as with the stages of development approach) it had fallen into an ahistoric dogmatism. Two stopped clocks gaze upon the movement of history. Is the South stagnating? The dependentist clock gives the exact time. Is a new industrialization emerging? It is take off time.

In order to overcome this blockage, it is obviously necessary to take into account the historic and national diversity of the forms of capitalist accumulation in each nation-state, whether in the core or in the periphery.

However, it is not my intention in this paper to present *the* true theory of the international division of labor as it has evolved from the imperialist period. On the contrary, I want to advance a few cautious methodological remarks and to warn against certain misuses of terms and concepts. These misuses partly explain the blockages referred to above. In a later section we shall see that changes in the pattern of central capitalism had strong impacts on the 'old' division of labor. Accordingly, there appeared a 'peripheral fordism' whose origins and logic will be the focus of a yet later section of the paper.

Questions of method

I want to begin by warning against two errors: first, the deduction of concrete reality from immanent laws, themselves derived from a universal concept such as imperialism or dependency; and, second, what is essentially the same thing, the analysis of the internal evolution of each national social formation as though it were a partita executed under the direction of a global maestro.

Imperialism or the Beast of the Apocalypse

In *The name of the rose*, Umberto Eco (1980) shows us a Franciscan Sherlock Holmes, William of Baskerville, untying the knot of a mysterious series of crimes in a medieval monastery. The crimes seem to be linked together like the maledictions of the Apocalypse. Following this lead, William finds the assassin and the motive, and realizes that each crime has its own reasons and causes which, naturally, have nothing to do with the Antichrist. However (and this is the supreme cleverness of the novel), (a) the culprit convinces himself that he is following the plan of the Apocalypse; (b) at least one of his crimes is staged in consequence; and (c) in the last resort, the assassin actually plays the role of the Antichrist.

Thus, William (who is the spokesman of the great English Franciscan philsopher of the Middle Ages, William of Occam, as well as of the founder of semiotics, the American C. S. Peirce) deduces the emptiness of general laws and the richness of single events.

This novel gives us a wonderful story and a lesson. Have we not invented many Beasts of the Apocalypse by over-schematizing, generalizing, dogmatizing our thinking? Have we not deduced from these Beasts and their properties the future unfolding of concrete history? Have we not affirmed, in the 1960s, that the immutable laws of imperialism would widen the gap between nations, polarizing wealth on one side, poverty on the other? Have we not deduced the implacable succession of stages of development or underdevelopment? Have we not predicted the impossibility of industrial development in dominated countries? Then, in the 1970s, when England's downfall accelerated, when the US was in relative decline, and when the NICs took off from the 'backyard' of imperialism, what did we have to say? Some tried more theory, and (falling back on yet more verses of the Apocalypse) continued to predict an inevitable future. Thus Warren (1980) retrieved the old text of Marx on the Indian railways that were supposed to develop capitalist relations as surely as productive forces were supposed to cause the disruption of relations of production.

The basic issue is that, as Lenin said, 'History possesses infinitely more imagination than we do.' That is, history of the human variety, history of that 'objective subject' (Kosik 1970) which creates its own history, not as a subject gifted with foresight, but as a vast body composed of millions of subjects struggling against one another, with their victories and defeats.

Marx himself cautioned us too, with very nominalist terms, against the idea that to know the Particular it is sufficient to have seized upon the Universal. This Universal, in any case, is only our mental systematization of real practical experience. As he stressed in *The holy family*: 'Just as it is easy to create the abstract representation of *the* fruit starting from real fruits, so is it as difficult to create real fruits from the abstract idea of fruit.'

The habits of history

Is it to be said then that in view of the freedom of history no rational knowledge is possible? No universal law, no necessity, therefore no science, no generalization, no concept? To speak like William: since any law limits the freedom of God, is it possible to conceive of a necessity woven out of the possible? To this question, William (the real one: Occam) answered in the affirmative. Because, on the one hand, as God in his freedom is still subject to the principle of non-contradiction, not everything can happen. On the other hand, the power of God is materialized in creation that is reified as a 'conditioned power,' a created habit of nature.

Do not be alarmed, I am not about to conduct a course in theology. Henceforth, if we restrict ourselves to this dialectical materialism, there exists a scientific project for the science of history: (a) the study of the regularities that occur in the relations between human beings and that were produced in past struggles; (b) the study of crises in these regularities, due to contradictions that are only temporarily resolved; (c) the study of changes in these regularities, due to current struggles of human beings, for or against their freedom.

This means that the concepts we use should not simply come out of thin air. On the contrary, they are the product of partial systematizations of a reality

18

that only partially constitutes a system. They are then used to recognize general features in other concrete situations. From there, either they are pertinent and can help the liberation of humans oppressed by the 'habits of history,' or they are inadequate and must therefore be modified and, if necessary, rejected.

Let us take the case of the capitalist mode of production. It is a very rich concept that marks out a certain system of relations between human beings in some areas, at a certain time. We know its trends and countertrends, some by observation, others by logical deduction. One of the biggest contradictions of this mode of production derives from its market aspect. That is, even though capitalists know how to organize production in their firms and (with the help of habit and calculation) how to establish 'the iron law of proportionality' (Marx 1867, Ch. XIV), they still behave with respect to the rest of society like private gamblers. Their products will or will not be bought at a price making production profitable (the celebrated problem of realization). Still, the system works – except when there is a crisis. To study how it works necessitates the production of new concepts. Along with several French colleagues I have proposed the concepts of 'regime of accumulation' and 'mode of regulation.' I will specify them below, but I should say a few words here to clarify their methodological status.

The *regime of accumulation* describes the stabilization over a long period of the allocation of the net product between consumption and accumulation; it implies some correspondence between the transformation of both the conditions of production and the conditions of the reproduction of wage earners. It also implies some forms of linkage between capitalism and other modes of production. Mathematically, a regime of accumulation is describable by a schema of reproduction. A system of accumulation exists because its schema of reproduction is coherent: not all systems of accumulation are possible. At the same time, the mere *possibility* of a regime is inadequate to account for its existence since there is no necessity for the whole set of individual capitals and agents to behave according to its structure. There must exist a materialization of the regime of accumulation taking the form of norms, habits, laws, regulating networks and so on that ensure the unity of the process, i.e. the approximate consistency of individual behaviors with the schema of reproduction. This body of interiorized rules and social processes is called the *mode of regulation*.

It should be noted that not any mode of regulation can govern any regime of accumulation; besides, a single mode can present itself as different combinations of forms of partial regulation. For instance, the indirect wage does not have the same importance in the USA that it has in Northern Europe.

Above all – and this is the essential point – the emergence of a new regime of accumulation is not written into the fate of capitalism even if it does correspond to some tendencies that can be observed. Regimes of accumulation and modes of regulation are outcomes of the history of human struggles: outcomes that have succeeded because they ensured some regularity and permanence in social reproduction. Thus, there is no sense in trying to comprehend any concrete social formation (even the currently dominant one) as a standardized, inevitable pattern.

The functionalism of the worse

We have just touched on the precariousness of contemporary capitalism, the amplitude of the contradictions that must be resolved for its reproduction to proceed, and the necessity of harnessing it within a regime of accumulation and a mode of regulation. However, we should not simply assume that the mode of regulation has the 'function' of making the regime of accumulation work (e.g. that social security was invented to make mass production churn more smoothly). Rather, a regime of accumulation and forms of regulation get stabilized together, because they ensure the crisis-free reproduction of social relations over a certain period of time. At most, it is possible to practice an *a posteriori* functionalism as in the metaphoric: 'everything works as if . . .' (for example, the underdevelopment of the periphery has purpose for the functioning of capitalism in the core).

Undoubtedly tendencies to functionalism (even to intentionalism) are nowhere more evident than in the theory of international relations. We are not talking here about Ricardo and the proponents of the so-called Hecksher–Ohlin–Samuelson theorem, for whom the international division of labor seems to be the result of some world conference which, after having measured relative productivities, evaluated collective preferences and considered the initial endowments of factors, computes the optimal allocation of production; each conference participant then returns home convinced not only of the virtues of free exchange but also of the legitimacy of each country's fate as a result of the law of comparative costs.

The great achievement of the theorists of imperialism or dependency is to have swept away the apologetics of this fable. They have pointed out that the empirically indisputable differences between economic spaces consist in differences of wealth and power, and that those who take advantage of this situation have more faith in maintaining or imposing it forcibly than in the invisible hand of the market.

Basing their views on Adam Smith rather than on Ricardo, the marxists and dependency theorists showed correctly that the existence of an unequal development of capitalism between nations, followed by the stabilization of structures of exchange, favored fast accumulation in the advanced countries. There seems to exist, in brief, a regime of accumulation on the global scale with respect to which core/periphery polarization plays a regulating role.

From here it is only one step to the proposition that this regime was imposed on dominated countries because it was necessary that some areas take on the function of resolving the problems of capitalism, or worse still that these relations of domination were imposed *with the intent* of resolving those problems. It is only a matter of style whether we speak of the presence of a conscious subject imposing the demands of the core, or of an immanent global reality separating the core from the periphery for the purposes of its own operation.

However, we should not confuse *results* with *causes*: nor an ensemble of partial systematic regularities with the full deployment of a system. Among the reasons why we should not think in this way of the international division of labor are the open-endedness of history, the class struggle, and capitalist competition. The reality of the autonomy of national social formations and the sovereignty of states must also be kept clearly to the fore.

The state is indeed the archetypal form of any regulation: it is at this level that the struggle of classes is regulated; it is the institutional form which embodies the compromise without which the different groups that compose the national community would be consumed in endless struggle. To declare that world capitalism has been instituted from the start as a unique regime of accumulation with its forms of global regulation would be to suppose that, on the global scale, economic exchange, social norms, codified procedures guaranteed by a unique sovereignty and eventually delegated to local states, have been instituted at the same time. It would be to suppose that each compromise or each shift of power relations at a given place on Earth corresponds to the necessary adjustments of a cybernetic system endowed with perfect homeostasis.

This picture is as bleak as it is unrealistic. The development of capitalism in each country is principally the result of internal class struggles, producing outlines of regimes of accumulation that are consolidated by forms of regulation sustained by the local state. Within these national social formations, it can happen that their external relations turn out to be useful and take on decisive importance in the regime of accumulation; and eventually the national social formation may no longer be able to function without these relations because they resolve some of the contradictions of its mode of production. From then on these relations *appear* to be there expressly for that purpose. In reality certain compatible relations become combined with each other, and that is all. Had it happened with other kinds of relations, the story would have been different.

Thus the goal is to study for itself each national social formation, to observe the succession of its regimes of accumulation and modes of regulation, to analyze its expansion, its crises and the role therein of its external relations. This is regularly done for the countries of the core but the features of the functioning of the periphery are generally treated as pure *consequences* of the demands of the core.

Can it be said that there is no malevolent intervention in the underdevelopment of some countries of the periphery and that regimes of accumulation are merely spatially juxtaposed without forming a system? We are returning to William's questions when he faced the wrongdoings of the mysterious Antichrist. In the end, he unties the knots of the intrigue because he looked for the links between the causes, the relations between the signs: and each situation is unique.

In capitalism, there are general contradictions, and if imperialism can resolve them, even temporarily, then it is legitimate to say that imperialism developed by resolving the general contradictions to the benefit of specific national capitalisms. Imperialism was not specifically created to resolve these contradictions, but it continued to exist; it developed because, in fact, it resolved them. It could disappear, be modified, or hold on 'by habit' if other solutions were found to these contradictions, or if other contradictions developed. Only in that sense can it be said, things being what they are and history having its habits, that imperialism's function is to resolve these contradictions.

Certain class alliances in some countries have been constrained by force or have believed it would be to their advantage to adopt international relations that reduce their country to the function of a periphery. And indeed we can say that, from the moment when core/periphery relations are stabilized, there exists a global regime of accumulation (or an international division of labor) with its specific forms of regulation (expeditions, wars, international treaties, subcontracting agreements, and international financial system, etc.).

How do we reconcile national regimes of accumulation and global regimes of accumulation? As in the wave/particle duality, they are two aspects of the same thing depending on the perspective we take. Thus, the Trade Triangle characterized certain features of the Spanish regime of accumulation as well as certain features of the world economy in the mercantilist era; and what I will call 'peripheral fordism' characterized some NICs and some aspects of the global economy of the 1970s. But in reality, struggles and institutional compromises take place mainly in the national framework, and thus methodological priority should be placed on the study of each particular social formation together with its external linkages.

Can we exclude the possibility that some agents, states or companies, knowing that imperialism would resolve certain problems, may have deliberately created or maintained imperialist relations? Of course we cannot. There have been, there are, there will be wars and *coups d'état* fomented to keep markets open, to get raw materials, to keep control of cheap labor sources. But to limit ourselves to cases of the open intervention of dominant groups in central countries in order to explain the fate of dominated nations is to confuse a particular form for the general case. On the contrary, these interventions were actions whose aim was often extra-economic and often contradictory. They resulted in a more or less coerced consensus in favor of a given regime of accumulation.

An approach in terms of the exigencies of central capitalism tells us nothing about the successes of North America, Japan or Prussia, or about the failures of Latin America; it tells us nothing about the relative fates of Australia, Canada or Argentina; it undoubtedly misleads us very much, on Argentina as well as on Canada.

Obviously, things are rather different in the case of colonies, those territories subjected to the policies of the metropolitan power. Their functionality relative to the dominant metropolitan group is evident (even though Spain undoubtedly never realized what its colonies would cost it). So it is with regions. Where we must be alert to the peculiarities of the local situation is in regard to those states with formal independence and with relatively autonomous class struggles. Such is the case with the ex-colonies of Latin America from the beginning of the 19th century, and also with some British dominions, particularly Canada and Australia, at the end of the century. However, it is very significant that, when Frank (1979) poses the question, he initially uses the language of the Apocalypse: 'From about 1820, both Canning and Bolivar were giving expression to the historical process that, if not providence, world capitalist development held in destiny for Latin America.' Then he argues in more concrete terms, detailing for us the key role of the defeat of the internal bourgeoisie (oriented toward manufacturing development) by the liberal bourgeoisie dependent on the import–export sector. What would

22

have happened if the struggle had turned to the advantage of the former? There would perhaps be a Prussia or Japan in Latin America. But what is world capitalist development doing in this story? It is simply a stunning concept that theoretically summarizes the *result* of concrete processes. It is in no circumstances the cause of destiny.

In conclusion: beware of the international division of labor, and of labels

It is the case that, even if no immanent destiny ordains a certain nation to hold a certain position in an international division of labor, the immanent contradictions of capitalism find (I insist on the notion of 'find') a temporary solution in certain types of differences in the regimes of accumulation of different national social formations. Even if the positions are not foreordained, the *field* of available positions (that is, the range of mutually compatible national regimes of accumulation) exists nevertheless. The dominant classes of different countries have 'models' in view, some (dominant) dreaming of holding the others (dominated or even autonomous) in a peripheral status, while the latter develop strategies that lead them to dependence or autonomy. But not all can be dominant at the same time.

We are not trying here to let the ghost of global capitalism come in by the window when we have chased it out through the door. Once again, what happens to be making up a system and what our intellect can identify as a system because of its temporary stability should not be conceived of as a finalized structure, an order put in place in view of its coherence. This coherence is only an effect of the interaction between several relatively autonomous processes, an effect of complementarity and of temporarily stabilized antagonisms between various national regimes of accumulation. The core/periphery relation is not directly a relation between states or territories within a unique process. Rather, it is a relation between processes, between more or less autonomous or extroverted regimes of accumulation. This relation between processes obeys constraints of compatibility like those that rule the process of valorization of capital in a reproduction schema: the world production of capital goods must be equal to the world demand for the same goods. As we know, the useful schemas for solving the contradictions of capitalism are not ones in which every country produces and exchanges the same thing. But the actually existing international division of labor constitutes once again a 'find.'

Indeed, we will see that some economic-financial monopolistic groups attempt to deploy themselves over the checkerboard of unequally developed nations (or regions). They do this by dividing labor processes in their sector and then spreading the segments out over different labor pools with varying employment relations. They consciously organize a geographical division of labor, and the generalization of these practices consolidates a new international division of labor. However, it should not be concluded that this new international division of labor is the product only of the organizing activity of multinational firms. In reality, the objectives of these multinational firms articulate with the ambitions of the dominant classes of some national economies who want to play the card of what we may call 'the strategy of export-substitution;' we will see that this corresponds to several internal regimes of accumulation ('bloody taylorization,' 'peripheral fordism'). The studies gathered together by Michalet (1980) show that the creation of a new international division of labor was not, in general, the real purpose of the delocalization of segments of productive processes by multinational firms. More often, it simply happens that capitalists in the core try to avoid a customs barrier erected by a country in the periphery, and thus try to sell manufactured goods according to the logic of the old division of labor.

A last word on the objective nature of positions in the 'field' of the unequal development of national social formation: it is rather easy to give a stylistic description in such terms as 'center of the world-economy,' 'developed country,' 'underdeveloped country', 'exporter of raw material' or 'self-centered or extraverted countries,' 'NICs' and so on. It is much more difficult and often harmful to attribute one of these labels to a given country, or worse to describe the country on the basis of a label attributed to it. The field itself varies as the regime of accumulation in different countries varies (and thus also as the dominant international regime varies). This does not mean that one replaces the other, that the center of the 'world-economy,' to speak as Wallerstein (1974) and Braudel (1980) do, moves from one country to another. It is the very texture of the field that varies: the 'core' was formerly a city (Venice, Amsterdam), and then a country (England, USA), but why would there not be several centers, why would the system not be organized on a network basis rather than around a center? Why should we necessarily look for a predecessor to England or a successor to the USA?

But even more importantly, in reality, the field presents itself as a quasi-continuum of situations, that is, of local regimes and modes of insertion within the global economy. Some countries appear to typify certain internal regimes of accumulation and modes of insertion; by comparing individual countries with these typical cases, we will spontaneously tend to classify nations. Once this classification is made (although there could never be an agreement as to the exact distribution of nations between the different categories), there will be a tendency to consider the abstract category as the determinant of the specific features of each country. We will put Argentina in the same category as a banana republic of the Caribbean because it mainly exports raw materials, and we will be quite puzzled by Canada. However, national situations are not definable by classificatory barriers, according to characteristics that reveal the essence of their position in the international field. Once again, there exist typical cases, 'cores' and 'peripheries' above all, and similarities revealed by theoretical and empirical studies or by self-designation as in the cases of OPEC or the NICs. But disaster begins when the classification becomes convention and thereby induces us to forget concrete analysis, and when metaphysical debates are started about such and such a country in such and such a case under the pretext that it is already 'sufficiently externalized,' that it 'exports enough raw material' or 'too little capital equipment.' The disaster is ultimate when we deduce the essential characteristics of a country from the typical case, when we deduce a policy from this case, and so on.

Beware of these labels, beware of the 'international division of labor;' or

24

rather, let us see how every country functions, what it produces, for whom, how, what the forms of wage relations are, what successive regimes of accumulation developed and why. And let us be very cautious when we attempt to throw a net over the world so as to catch the established relations between the regimes of accumulation of various national social formations.

From the old to the new international division of labor

With all these caveats in mind, we now attempt to detect new trends in the international division of labor.

Right away, we must go beyond the methodological precautions stated in the first section. To understand the new trends in the evolution of a mode of production that has become hegemonic on the planet implies an understanding of the principal mutations this mode has gone through in the social formations where it first developed. Here, we must resign ourselves to abstraction and to starting from the core.

Accumulation and regulation in the core

Over the last several years in France, economic studies of the long run have shed light on the great diversity of regimes of accumulation (Aglietta 1976, Boyer & Mistral 1978, Lipietz 1979). A regime of accumulation can be either extensive (i.e. given to the extension of the scale of production on the basis of identical norms), or intensive (i.e. given to the continuing reorganization of work and the real subsumption of labor to capital). Further, as Palloix (1973) has noted, capitalist production has been successively focused on luxury goods, capital goods, and wage goods. Besides, even in the earliest capitalist countries, the capitalist mode of production articulated with other modes of production, and this articulation formed the matrix of the internal inter-regional polarization of these countries (Lipietz 1977).

Briefly, until World War I, an extensive regime of accumulation focused on the widened reproduction of capital goods dominated in the big capitalist countries, and since World War II this has given way to a mainly intensive regime focused on mass consumption. Regimes of accumulation are not satisfied with just any mode of regulation. Thus, we can analyze the crisis of the 1930s as the first crisis of intensive accumulation or the last crisis of 'competitive regulation.' This mode of regulation was effectively characterized by an *a posteriori* adjustment of quantities to prices, by a strong sensitivity of price movements to demand, and by an adjustment of wages to price movements, which resulted in the stability (or slow growth) of the direct real wage. Such a mode of regulation was relatively adequate for extensive accumulation.

In such a mode of regulation, the tentative search for outlets by different capitals which could not correctly anticipate their collective growth was a persistent problem, and sectoral or generalized overproduction was a major risk. And at the end of World War I, the progressive generalization of new forms of the labor relation was about to create unprecedented productivity gains. Competitive regulation failed to induce a growth of final demand compatible with these productivity gains. The boom created by the enormous rise of relative surplus-value ended up in a formidable overproduction crisis (Boyer 1982).

After World War II, the intensive regime of accumulation, focused on mass consumption, could be generalized because a new monopolistic mode of regulation encouraged a growth of popular consumption compatible with productivity gains. It is this regime of growth that (following Gramsci's intuition) we call today *fordism*, thereby indicating two historically and theoretically linked but relatively distinct phenomena.

The first is fordism as a mode of capital accumulation, based on the constant upheaval of the labor process by the incorporation of workers' know-how into the automatic system of machines. This intensive regime of accumulation is characterized by joint growth of the productivity of labor and of the volume of fixed capital *per capita*. The precondition of this type of accumulation is the systematization of the actions of craftsmen by methods of the 'Scientific Organization of Labor.' This stage, called 'taylorism' (after its theorist), intensifies the separation between conception and execution, and the polarization between technicians and unskilled workers. Even so, within 'taylorized' and then 'fordized' segments of the economy, the presence of skilled workers is essential at every level, and above all in upstream labor processes: those constituting the core of the production system – capital goods, machine tools, and the like (CEPREMAP 1980).

The second phenomenon is fordism as a mode of regulation, of continual adaptation of mass consumption to productivity gains caused by intensive accumulation. This adaptation has caused an enormous mutation of workers' life-styles and their normalization and integration into capitalist accumulation. It has taken the form of a network of institutions helping to stabilize the growth of workers' nominal income and to create monopolies in a productive structure that allows the big firms of leading sectors to administer their prices independently of the fluctuations of demand. All this supposed a modification of the role of the state and of the forms of money management, including the substitution of credit money for gold-based currency (Lipietz 1983).

Toward the end of the 1960s and the beginning of the 1970s, fordism as a mode of capital accumulation based on the upheaval of the labor process seemed to reach technical and social limits (Coriat 1979), and the productivity gains accompanying mechanization seemed to slow down: this created the conditions of a profitability crisis. The monopolistic regulation of the wage relation ended up in a dilemma: any reduction of popular buying power resulted in direct recession; any increase resulted in a decrease of the rate of profit. The concern to avoid a recession seemed to be still prevalent in big capitalist countries during the 1970s. But the accession of monetarism to hegemony in Great Britain, then the USA, proclaimed the open crisis of this mode of regulation. It was a mode that had given capitalism a 25-year golden age.

As we see, permanent as they may be, the celebrated contradictions of capitalism take on varying forms depending on the prevailing regime of accumulation and mode of regulation (Boyer 1979). Since international relations are derived from the same contradictions, we must also inquire into the duration of core–periphery relations and the forms of the international division of labor.

The old international division of labor

If it is true, as we have tried to show, that capitalism has seen a succession of regimes of accumulation and modes of regulation, then it is pointless to attempt to derive a general theory of core–periphery relations deduced out of the fundamental tendencies of the mode of production. Such a theory would simply hit against the dead-end of the specificity of these regimes and modes of regulation.

In the 19th century, the emergence of relatively complex forms of manu-facturing cooperation permitted by the capitalist wage system immediately gave it an absolute advantage – from the point of view of productivity – over any other mode of production. But the extensive accumulation of capital in countries experiencing this mode of growth was not accompanied by a parallel extension of social demand (because of a lack of monopolistic regula-tion of the wage). Because this demand was missing it *had* to be sought out externally, and it could be elicited precisely because of the absolute advantage.

At that time – and in the theorizations of that period from Lenin to Rosa Luxemburg – 'the exterior' is first an *outlet* for the products that cannot be sold on the markets of the core. As soon as market production and the wage systems are developed sufficiently there, it becomes an outlet for capital investment. The only differences between marxists on this issue relate to the urgency of finding such outlets given that the exterior of *capitalism* is not necessarily the exterior of the *country*.

Let us add that the exterior is also a pool where capitalism picks up what it cannot create but can only transform (raw materials) and reproduce (the labor force). This was not stressed by theorists at the beginning of the century, since these two problems had no urgency. Industrial capitalism could still find essential resources internally (although already the industrial reserve army formed from the peasantry transcended international boundaries). From then on, it was possible to speak of an international division of labor (the South producing raw materials at low prices, the North producing manufactured goods) allowing transfers of value from the South to the North.

Under this set of relations between a core and a periphery, the role of the periphery is effectively that of a thermostat. The capitalist machinery of extended reproduction cannot be closed off at the core. The exterior brings to it a warm source (labor and raw materials) and a cold source (outlets). Accordingly, we can understand the low level of theoretical interest that theorists of imperialism assign to the concrete analysis of social relations inside the periphery. Very often, these relations are 'primitive' and 'pre-capitalist' (forced labor, pseudo-slavery, quasi-feudal agriculture etc.), and they are destined for dissolution. Nothing is expected from them but what is required by the functioning of the core. Depending on circumstances local manpower will be exploited according to capitalist forms or else according to rickety pseudo-precapitalist forms. Capital itself will be central or local, but this scarcely changes anything in the character of the periphery. We simply calculate that on balance there is a flow of value from the periphery to the center, and this then helps to prop up the rate of profit in the center.

It must be stressed that these core–periphery relations appear first as a process (of the diffusion of outlets for capitalist manufacturing centers, of the widening of the manpower pool, of the scattering of plants that depend on central capitalism) before they are consolidated in a *structure* of unequal relations. Or, more exactly, if there is a structural relation, it is a relation between two types of processes. In the core, capitalism is developed in depth; in the periphery it is developed on the surface, as Lenin (1899) wrote cryptically but significantly. That is, what characterizes the core is the growing interconnection of production processes in regimes of accumulation that are more and more clearly defined, whereas units of capitalist production develop in a purely external way in the periphery.

We have already insisted on the importance of the analysis of class conflicts in the periphery; these qualify the 'irreversibility' of the path to peripheralization. In the apocalyptic view, however, the Beast is already there: the 'first' international division of labor between the core which produces manufactured goods, and the periphery which exports raw materials and labor.

Of course, at a certain stage in this process, the extroversion of the nation-state can no longer be easily reversed, and this deeply affects its social relations. From there, it is easy for dependency theorists to conclude that its socioeconomic structure is only a function of the needs of the core (in a way, this is the case with colonization) and that its ills reside in its dependency. Long-run history and the failure of the first attempts to break away from dependency by import substitution call for a more nuanced judgment.

Successes and failures of autocentered capitalist development

Naturally, we may wonder why, during the period of extensive accumulation, so few autocentered spatial structures were established. We should notice first that several spaces of this type were constituted by the scattering of European capitalism (to the USA and much later Australia) or by the acclimatization of this model within protectionist zones, as in the case of Japan.

With the depression of the 1930s, populist regimes in Latin America followed in the 1950s by other countries such as South Korea inaugurated import-substitution strategies. The object was to accumulate primary export incomes in consumption goods industries by buying capital goods in the core and by protecting these fledgling industries by customs barriers. The hope was that it would then be possible to move upstream toward the production of capital goods.

After initial successes, failure became obvious in the 1960s. This model of industrialization of the periphery, by adopting the central model of production and consumption, but without adopting the corresponding social

28

relations, failed to insert itself into the virtuous circle of central fordism. There were three main reasons for this.

First, with regard to labor processes, technology is not a transferable resource that grows in the forests of the North. The importation of machines is not enough. The corresponding social relations of labor must be built. However, these countries did not have the experienced working class and the management personnel necessary for the functioning of these fordist modes of operation (which, even when they derive from an expropriation of workers' know-how by means of capital intensification, can never totally do without that know-how). Thus, the theoretical productivity of imported forms of production was never reached. On the contrary, once the phase of easy substitution is overcome – a phase that necessitates little fixed capital – the cost of investments (of capital goods imports) increases very rapidly with mechanization. There is then a decrease in the profitability of capital, which can be masked for a time by the imposition of inflationary price policies by domestic monopolistic firms.

Secondly, with regard to outlets, the characteristics of monopolistic regulation are reduced to the administered management of profit margins and credit money. There was significant extension of the workers' and peasants' buying power only under Peronism, and later, under Christian Democracy and Chilean Popular Unity. The outlets remained limited to the dominant and middle classes engendered by the export economy, which constitutes a limited market, and one that is very stratified sociologically and not inclined to mass consumption of standardized goods; and the exterior, that is, the core. However, because of a lack of productivity and in spite of differences in wages, peripheral production was not competitive.

Finally, with regard to external trade, the process of import substitution required a very rapid growth in the volume of investments, and hence imports. These imports could not be paid for by growth in raw materials exports. Thus, the policy of import substitution could only collide with the barrier of external trade and debt, and with internal inflation (as was the case in Chile) – unless the model dies stillborn (as was the case in the Philippines).

Nevertheless, these experiments have encouraged real social transformations, with the development of a modern working class, middle strata and industrial capital. We can speak of a 'sub-fordism,' that is, a *caricature* of fordism, an attempt at industrialization with fordist technology and models of consumption but *without* the social conditions, i.e. neither the forms of the labor process nor the norms of mass consumption.

The responsibility of dependency for this failure is real, though less so than vengeful slogans would have us believe. The missing link is to be sought in *internal* social structure. This structure is consolidated by the maintenance of the raw materials export sector and by the redistributive failure of agrarian reforms, as well as by an inability to extend the manufacturing sector and to integrate popular consumption within the regime of accumulation. The presence of the core makes itself strongly felt by the success of its own self-centralizing tendencies: i.e. the diffusion of the regime of intensive accumulation, and the widening competitiveness between the center and the periphery forcing the latter out of international trade in manufactured goods.

However, it is by means of the very success of the fordist revolution that the core diffused its model of production and its consumption norms, thereby leading to the trap of the early import-substitution policies.

This diffusion was not accomplished anywhere in one day. The unequal diffusion of intensive accumulation (Mistral 1982) has brilliantly swept away continental Northern Europe, Japan, Australia, Canada, New Zealand. But Britain, because of the resistant strength of its working class and the weight of its financial capital, which is too internationalized to be given over to this internal revolution, has partially missed the boat of fordism, therefore initiating a process of its own eviction from the core. Argentina, one of the richest and most developed countries in 1945, also missed it because of workers' resistance and the tendency of its dominant class to fall back on agricultural exports. The failure of the diffusion of fordism in the import-substitution countries in the 1950s and 1960s has contributed to a belief in the eternity of the old international division of labor. However, what fails with Latin American *desarrollismo* has succeeded more or less in Italy (with the exception of the south). Indeed, fordist models and norms took off in France and Italy after 1945 *with* the help of the USA, but not in Latin America *despite* the help of the USA.

Toward a globalization of fordism?

The emergence of the NICs showed that this exclusion from the virtuous circle of intensive accumulation was in no way final. Even so, it must be stressed that at the zenith of central fordism, in the middle of the 1960s, the importance of the periphery in global trade in manufactured goods was reduced to almost nothing. It is toward that period that the proportion of exports in the GNP of the developed countries reached its minimum. These were essentially exports to other core countries. The proportion of exports of manufactured goods to the periphery has fallen, to 2% of GDP for the EEC and 0.8% for the USA! If the search for outlets was the *cause* of imperialism and of the blockage imposed on the periphery, then the core no longer needed the periphery.

At the same time, the proportion of manufactured imports coming from underdeveloped countries is negligible (less then 0.2%) for all industrialized countries.

A limited international extension of fordism

The historical process of diffusion-integration of capitalist relations was ignited again in the 1960s by a combination of two factors.

The first factor relates to the logic of fordism and its latent crisis. It allowed a division of the production process into three levels:

(a) conception, the organization of methods, and engineering;
(b) qualified manufacturing requiring skilled workers;
(c) deskilled execution and assembly.

The possibility of geographically separating these three levels provided an opportunity to articulate the productive cycle of fordist sectors with three types of labor pools differentiated mainly by skills and social conditions. First developed within the internal regions of the core, the delocalization of work tasks spread, in the 1960s to countries of the immediate external periphery where hourly wages were considerably lower and the working class less organized (Spain, Korea, Mexico and even Eastern Europe).

Thus, on top of the old horizontal division of labor, between sectors (primary agricultural and mining/secondary manufacturing), a second vertical division was superimposed between levels of qualification within industrial sectors. This redistribution of industrial tasks was a form of reorganization of the regime of accumulation and not a relation between the regime and its exterior.

The reason for this reorganization was twofold. The object was to extend the scale of production of central fordism and, consequently, of the markets it supplied; but the customs barriers whose aim was to encourage import substitution often forced the implantation of final assembly establishments in certain countries. Moreover, fordism did not suffer so much from the absence of outlets as from increasing pressures on the rate of profit; countries with abundant cheap labor permitted fordist plants to produce at low cost, and this included production for core area markets.

Then again, these countries had to satisfy an internal condition, which is the second factor: the existence of authoritarian political regimes selecting that economic strategy. This outcome presupposed very strong autonomy of the state, not only with regard to overexploited classes but even to leading classes linked to traditional exports or to the internal market (Salama & Tissier 1982). We should notice that these authoritarian regimes are not necessarily identified with the traditional image of the repressive state (e.g. Mexico or Hong Kong).

Without getting into the details of specific national social formations, two typical schemes can be distinguished, 'bloody taylorization' and 'peripheral fordism.'

Bloody taylorization

This is a case of the delocalization of precise and limited segments of sectors in social formations with very strong rates of exploitation (in wages, duration and intensity of labor etc.), the products being mainly re-exported toward the core. In the 1960s, the free zones and the workshop states of Asia (Singapore, Hong Kong) were the best illustration of this strategy, which is widespread today. We may think of it in terms of a strategy of export-substitution.

This delocalization revolves essentially around textiles and electronics. Two characteristics of this strategy may be noted. First, the activities are mainly taylorized but relatively non-mechanized. The technical composition of capital in these firms is particularly low, much lower than in firms producing for the local market. Hence, this pattern of industrialization gets away from a disadvantage of import-substitution: the cost of importing

31

capital goods. On the other hand, since it mobilizes a largely female work-force, it incorporates into itself all the know-how acquired through domestic patriarchal exploitation.

Secondly, it is bloody in Marx's sense when he speaks of 'bloody legisla-tion' at the dawn of central capitalism. To the ancestral oppression of women it adds all the modern arms of anti-worker oppression (managed union-ization, absence of social rights, imprisonment and torture of opposition).

From the standpoint of the theory of accumulation and regulation, the production processes in question must be considered as productive deloca-lized segments of the central regime of accumulation; their impacts on the growth of global social demand are negligible. Regulation is induced directly by monopolistic transnational firms, by direct investments, and especially by subcontracting to local, often tiny firms. All this requires at least the consent of the dictatorial states in question.

Such a model is quite fragile. Social tensions rapidly become explosive. Local dominant classes, pushed to make wage concessions, must rapidly turn to more sophisticated forms of socioeconomic regulation. This implies in general some ascension in the hierarchy of the international division of labor, with subcontracting of abandoned segments to a new generation of even poorer and more dictatorial countries.

Besides, the accommodation of these low-wage segments in the regime of central accumulation competes with equivalent segments previously existing in the core, causing sectoral and regional crises in the old industrial countries. These countries react by protectionism: this is the case of the Multifiber Agreement whose third version now puts the textile industry of Hong Kong in crisis. The cases described below are much more complex.

Peripheral fordism

In the 1970s, there appeared in some countries the conjunction of local autonomous capital, a large urban middle class and significant elements of an experienced working class. This conjunction provided certain states with the opportunity of a new strategy that we will call peripheral fordism. We must insist again on the *political* aspect of this choice.

Why peripheral fordism? It is an authentic fordism, based on the coupling of intensive accumulation and the growth of markets. But it remains *peri-pheral* in the sense that in the global circuits of productive sectors, qualified employment positions (above all in engineering) remain largely external to these countries. Further, its markets correspond to a specific combination of local middle-class consumption, along with increasing workers' consump-tion of domestic durables, and cheap exports toward the center.

Peripheral fordism as a regime of accumulation can therefore be analyzed from two perspectives: as a regime of internal accumulation for each NIC; and as a regime of accumulation coupling the core and the NICs within a *total* process of production and marketing.

The case of the automobile is typical. The establishment of factories in peripheral countries was initiated in order to penetrate markets protected in the first period of import substitution, and it rapidly acquired a double goal:

A. Lipietz

local market penetration and the re-export of vehicle parts toward the center (from the Iberian peninsula or Eastern Europe to north-west Europe, or from Mexico to the USA). In exchange for these re-exportations, protectionism against other manufactured goods was reduced.

The extreme variability of the regimes of accumulation collected together here under the term 'peripheral fordism' must be insisted upon. Thus, the ratio of manufactured exports to internal demand varies from 4.1% for Mexico to 25.4% for Korea (in 1978), and in each concrete regime of accumulation, the mixture of growth of internal final demand/import-substitution/industrial re-export is evidently not the same. That in turn reflects big differences in the mode of regulation, especially in the employment relation, the forms of hegemony of dominant classes and so on. Significantly, Mexico is relatively democratic – at least in the urban sector – and Korea is dictatorial.

However, we can only talk of peripheral fordism when the growth of the internal market (for manufactured goods) plays a real role in the national regime of accumulation. In this regard, it must be pointed out that Korea, which some persist in qualifying as a workshop country (because of bloody taylorization in some delocalized labor-intensive industries), long ago transcended this state of affairs which characterized its growth in the 1962–72 period. After 1973, industrial growth was refocused on the domestic market: export shares fell, then stabilized, and an active policy of import-substitution caused imports to fall from 27% to 20% of the domestic market. Real wages, which grew more slowly than productivity, took off after 1976 (and this will undoubtedly compromise the competitiveness of Korea relative to Taiwan (Benabou 1982)).

South–South relations

The emergence of these countries of peripheral fordism, just as the accumulation of monetary assets in some OPEC countries, caused an explosion of the periphery, and a complete reshuffling of the hierarchy. The periphery itself has never been homogeneous, and a new element is the growth of exchange (similar to the *old* division of labor) between the NICs and those countries that have remained exporters of raw materials. The NICs are now competing with the center in these countries in regard to ordinary fordist goods. A triangular system of exchange (raw materials–emigration–manufactured products) is developing within the South.

Very significantly, what characterizes the exports of the NICs to the South is the fact that they are more sophisticated and more capitalistic than the exports of the NICs to the core. Thus, from year to year, the old international division of labor is recreated, but now within the periphery. For example, in its industrial trade with the South, the export/import ratio of Brazil went from 153% in 1973 to 555% in 1980 with an excess balance of $3.2 billion (the corresponding amount for Korea being $4.5 billion). The structure of this trade is quite different from that which characterizes exports from the NICs to the center. Capital goods make up 41% (compared with 31%) while clothing makes up 5% (compared to 21%). Capital-intensity is twice as high.

33

Finally, on these markets, the NICs are starting to become technologically dominant, for their import substitution activities permit them to export cheap capital goods.

We can even observe a sort of duplication of the new international division of labor, this time within the nations of the South. The wage increases in the first wave of NICs makes them less competitive in the framework of a strategy of re-export/delocalization based on pure bloody taylorization; also, with stronger import quotas in the core, these countries are organizing (in competition with multinational firms) a second stage of bloody taylorization. This is what a November 1982 report of the *OECD Observer* calls the 'second wave of developing countries which export manufactured goods,' such as Malaysia, the Philippines, Thailand, and China.

This duplication of the division of labor does not constitute a global economy organized around a hegemonic center – far from it. The Third World today appears as a constellation of particular cases with vague regularities constituted out of fragments of the logic of accumulation (which proceeds well or badly depending on local circumstances) and tendencies that rise and fall over a few years without establishing any stable mode of regulation.

Financing and regulation

In the 1970s, the development of peripheral fordism was mainly financed by the borrowing of external banking capital. This financing was secured against future income from traditional exports (including oil); the promise of work (Palloix 1979), itself dependent on the establishment of new processes of production in the NICs as well as upon the existence of future outlets for this production; and the near-mandatory recycling of borrowed capital used for the purchase of capital goods from the core.

This regime was judged unanimously to be feasible by the international community of lenders, and all the more so as (after the first oil shock) they faced an explosion in the volume of disposable money. The surpluses of OPEC, deposited in private banks, were crying out for borrowers at any price.

We should note that, concerning the transfer of value from the periphery toward the core, the new system is as effective as the old one. Not only do the exports of the NICs fail to pay for their imports, but a growing proportion of income is dissipated in debt interest charges. Thus, to the repatriation of profits by multinationals is added heavy debt service.

In the context of this element of global regulation by the private banking system, various NICs adopt the most varied internal modes of regulation; some go with liberalism, others with protectionism and rigorous planning. Moreover, different models can co-exist in the same country. Thus Mexico exports oil and manpower, makes available to the USA a border zone of sweatshops where bloody taylorization runs free, develops peripheral fordism, and so on. But the global availability of capital to finance fordist industrialization remains subject to the state of international financial markets and their profitability; and these are factors that totally escape national sovereignty.

Success and crisis of peripheral fordism

The spectacular success of Brazil, Korea and Mexico during the 1970s has contradicted the thesis of the development of underdevelopment. Indeed, the periphery can be industrialized, grow, win in competition with the core for markets in manufactured goods. The average growth of the manufactured product of the NICs during the years 1970–8 ranges from 4.6% for Portugal (an early case) and 6.5% for Mexico (which is closer to import substitution) to 18.3% for Korea. The GNP per capita of this latter country went from $70 to $2,281 between 1960 and 1979. The success of peripheral fordism seems overwhelming.

The conjuncture of success

In fact, peripheral fordism could only be developed in a very particular context. In the core, the golden age of fordism was ending. Productivity gains were no longer sufficient to allow continuing increases in popular consumption norms, thus plunging the economies of the core into a dilemma: either an increase of the wage cost per unit of output or a stagnation of internal demand.

Whereas stagnation was spreading in the core, the NICs (which were now attaining mass consumption, with growth rates reaching 7% to 10%) offered a respite to world fordism in the 1970s. But we must also point out the limited success of the NICs on a world scale. Nigeria, Iran and Turkey were for a time expected to play a sub-imperialist role, but either became spectacularly bogged down or have exploded internally. The year 1980 saw the increase of workers' struggles and the breakdown of growth in Korea, Brazil, and Poland. And in 1982, financial bankruptcy was declared in Mexico: like an avalanche, suspensions of payment are spreading.

This is because the factor of the global and local crisis of fordism is added to the internal crisis factors of the periphery. Let us consider the latter point. With regard to the labor process, we find problems that are similar to those of the first period of import-substitution, for example, the difficulty of attaining the productivity norms of the core, and above all, the rising cost of investment goods. As for labor-intensive industries, we see reversals of the delocalization process. Techniques with low capital intensity located in the periphery are threatened by highly automated techniques in the core. This is very clear in the textile industry (where mass production is now in some circumstances more profitable in the core) and the situation is uncertain in electronics.

With regard to demand, its growth is near zero in the core (typically in the automobile industry) and the only new mass production demands come from wage increases in the periphery. Certainly, the labor force is increasing, but the wage is restricted by the need to remain competitive. As for the socio-political regulation of the whole system, it is characterized by a rapidly increasing chaos of social relations. Authoritarian structures necessary for the continuation of high rates of exploitation in the export sectors co-exist with the rise of urban middle classes and independent unionization in factories which then encourages democratization. This encouragement is either repressed and the repression destabilizes the regime (Korea, Poland) or it explodes uncontrollably (Iran); or it more or less results in a precarious democratization (Spain, Portugal, Brazil) opening the gates to workers' claims that break the competitiveness of export-substitution.

From a strictly economic point of view, peripheral industrialization remained possible as long as the rise in capital intensity implied by import-substitution was translated into increasing imports of capital goods made feasible by easy international credits and excellent re-exportation prospects. If we take into account the fact that the NICs remain for the most part dependent on raw materials, some of which they export, the stability of the model over a decade appears miraculous.

Among other international circumstances, the necessary conditions were the slowing down of fordism in the core (so that productivity in the periphery could catch up with the productivity of the core), but the continuation by governments of the core with the practice of moderate Keynesianism to ensure growth of global demand; and the maintenance of investment in the periphery by means of international credit.

These two conditions are now disappearing with the access of monetarism to hegemony in the core.

Peripheral fordism in the trap of central monetarism

In the 1970s central fordism survived its crisis as best it could, a crisis which was latent since the end of the 1960s but fully open since the first oil shock. It was able to do this by maintaining forms of monopolistic regulation. On the one hand, the subsistence and often the progression of the buying power of the mass of wage earners prevented a cumulative collapse of demand, despite deindustrialization. On the other hand, the monetization of debt, principally the debt held by the OPEC countries, increased credit on the basis of petro-dollars, and delayed devalorization of capitals affected by the crisis; it also allowed the financing of new investments on the simple speculation that enlarged global intensive accumulation would continue. We have seen that global fordism is founded on this speculation, and, as is the rule in any regime of accumulation, the speculation partly contributes to its own actual realization.

Monetarism consists essentially in a denial of this speculation and in an attempt to keep the crisis open; thus the questioning of the sharing of value added between capitalists and workers, and the refusal to continue to finance non-profitable enterprises. All this is done in the name of a mythical 'cleansing' as if by deliberately tearing apart the safety nets which prevented the collapse of the regime of fordist growth, a new regime of growth could be mirac-ulously unleashed by the market's invisible hand.

The attack against workers' income in Britain and then in the USA, and the increase in the interest rate with the purpose of slowing the creation of credit money, were the two principal levers of this policy. By contrast, the regula-tion of international money creation depends crucially on the 'base' (US money held by non-residents, or xeno-dollars) and on interest rates on the

American market (Lipietz 1983). In 18 months, Thatcherism wiped out all the industrial growth of the Callaghan Labour government (−15%) and in three financial quarters Reaganism wiped out the growth of the Carter presidency (−10%). What was left of growth in the core was smashed, even in the most social-democratic countries and even in Japan, the most competitive exporter.

From then on, the crisis of the NICs was inevitable. On the one hand, their external markets are contracting when at the same moment they have to pay back the loans that had financed their investments. Since 1980 all the NICs have been floating on short-term credit to ensure the repayment of their long-term debt. On the other hand, at exactly the same moment, because of the drying up of OPEC surpluses and the increases in interest rates, the global overliquidity of the 1970s was transformed into a shortage of capital: xeno-dollars became rare and expensive.

The crisis has reached a dramatic level that evokes the depressive chain of events of the 1930s, in spite of the strength of monopolistic regulation under the blows of monetarism. Over three successive years, growth has stopped in the North and for the first time since the beginning of the 1970s it has also stopped in the South, including the NICs. In the summer of 1982, this madness reached its peak with the bankruptcy of Mexico. Then, the US administration abandoned monetarism and re-opened the way to the creation of world credit-money. However, the cost of these maneuvers will be defrayed over a long period of time by the peoples of the South.

Conclusion

I wish to sketch out some political conclusions: not about strategies for dealing with bloody taylorization or peripheral fordism in the underdeveloped countries (that is the responsibility of militant workers, peasants and intellectuals in those countries). But what ought to be the attitude of militant unionists and intellectuals in former imperialist metropolitan powers in regard to the recent competition from the NICs over markets for manufactured goods? On the basis of the analysis that has just been presented, it seems possible to me (from a European viewpoint) to put forth the following arguments.

The old international division of labor has been revealed as being less rigid than was at first thought. Even though capitalism in industrial countries always needs manpower and raw materials from backward countries, it no longer needs to maintain this exterior in a state of industrial non-development in order to sell its products there. Since World War II, fordism has taught capitalism to create its own outlets. The relative failure of the first import-substitution policy was not attributable to an imperialist will to break the competition of new producers but to their temporary inability to insert themselves into the virtuous circle of intensive accumulation.

It is just when this regime started to develop weaknesses that central capitalism had to look for help in the periphery, not in order to find outlets, but to produce at low cost there. And there, it also linked up with the ambitions of the dominant strata who were able to impose on their countries this new form of industrialization. A new division of labor was superimposed on the old without replacing it entirely. This was manifest in the development of productive circuits and sectors appropriate to the different skill and wage levels of each country.

As long as this consisted simply in the delocalization of purely labor-intensive industrial segments, their markets remained in the developed countries, as bloody taylorization did little to increase the standard of living of its victims in the periphery. But with the development of peripheral fordism, the global regime of accumulation found an opportunity to expand just as it was burning out in the core. A true industrial growth in some countries of the South offered to the North outlets for its advanced technologies, and its capital goods, in exchange for consumption goods or low-priced manufactured parts.

This ultimate stage of growth (which was moderate in the core, rapid in a few countries, and negative for the mass of rural dwellers) was by no means checked by rising petroleum prices. This latter phenomenon, in any case, was no more than a simple redistribution of global surplus value. Nor was it checked by the competition of cheap products based on the exploitation of peripheral workers. In the final account, this competition was more than compensated for by the creation of new jobs in the North in order to supply capital goods to the South. Growth was checked through the choice of the dominant classes and conservative majorities of certain core countries (above all the USA) who broke its momentum by making their workers pay for the crisis while at the same time dismantling the international credit economy.

The possibility for an economic recovery in the old industrial countries, notably in Europe, must therefore be developed internally, but in any case not by stifling new competition from the periphery. We should define this argument further. No one (except those firms that have delocalized the most labor-intensive segments of their productive apparatuses) has an interest in maintaining the exploitation conditions of the last century in the countries of bloody taylorization. Their miserable wage levels exert a depressive effect on the normal wages of the central fordist countries. The acceptance of free trade in such conditions would bring about a re-alignment of norms of exploitation of the labor force on the basis of the worst-paid segments of the working class. But a clear decision (at the European level if possible) not to accept the exports of countries that do not respect minimal rules in matters of social protection and union rights not only would stop the breakdown of some old industries in the core but would also put pressure on dictatorial states. The latter would have to choose between improvement of the conditions of life of their working masses and their exclusion from important central markets.

By contrast, co-development agreements with some countries of the Third World that respect such rules would secure to mutual benefit the advantages of industrialization in the periphery. This presupposes at least a general cancellation of the Third World debt.

However, we should not expect miracles. As Massiah (1982) notes, the projects of global Keynesianism and the 'Third World Marshall Plan' are subject to the general constraints of the crisis of fordism. In particular, the problem of financing is in itself unsolvable. All the OPEC surpluses would not have sufficed to re-establish full employment in the European Community alone.

In fact, we must invent a new model of industrialization, new modes of production and new social relations in both the North and the South, the two being necessarily linked together. Whatever the extent of these social changes, the failure of the revolutionary attempts of the 1960s (from Cuba to China) suggests that there is not likely to be in the 1980s a radical rupture with the capitalist mode of production. At the most (beyond avoidance of nuclear annihilation), we can hope for progress on some of the elements of a neo-social-democratic 'new deal.'

Where will each country be situated within this new deal? It is my hope to have shown that no exterior destiny, no general law of capitalism dictates to any nation its place within an implacable division of labor. Unless, that is, 'exterior destiny' means simply the weight of the past, inscribed in social structure; or unless it signifies the interiorization of the norms of some development model (one, perhaps, that has been eminently successful elsewhere); and unless we simply interpret the idea of coercive laws of motion to mean the deliberate acceptance of the rules of free exchange, i.e. the free play of market forces. For even on the basis of given conditions, inherited from the past, we make our own history.

Note

This paper is a summary of a series of recent conference presentations at Sfax (1981), Modena (1982), Ottawa (1983), and Paris (1983). The author expresses his gratitude to his co-participants in these conferences for their many helpful comments. He also wishes to thank Kipham Kan and Allen Scott who translated the paper from French into English.

References

Aglietta, M. 1976. *Régulation et crises du capitalisme*. Paris: Calmann-Lévy.

Benabou, R. 1982. La Corée du Sud ou l'industrialisation planifiée. *Economie Prospective Internationale* **10** (August).

Boyer, R. 1979. La crise actuelle: une mise en perspective historique. *Critiques de l'Economie Politique* **7–8** (April).

Boyer, R. 1982. Origine, originalité et enjeux de la crise actuelle en France: une comparaison avec les années trente. In *La crise economique et sa gestion*. Montreal: Boréal-Express.

Boyer, R. and M. Mistral, 1978. *Accumulation, inflation et crise*. Paris: Presses Universitaires de France.

Braudel, F. 1980. *Civilisation matérielle, économie et capitalisme*. Paris: A. Colin.

CEPREMAP. 1980. *Redéploiement industriel et espace économique*. Report to DATAR by J. Lafont, D. Leborgne, and A. Lipietz. *Travaux et recherches de Prospective* **85**.

Coriat, B. 1979. *L'atelier et le chronomètre*. Paris: Bourgois.

Eco, U. 1980. *Le nom de la rose*. Paris: Bernard Grasset.

Frank, A. G. 1979. *The development of underdevelopment.* New York: Monthly Review Press.

Frank, A. G. 1982. Asia's exclusive models. *Far Eastern Econ. Rev.* (Hong Kong), June.

Kosik, K. 1970. *La dialectique du concret.* Paris: Maspéro.

Lenin, V. I. 1899. *Le developpement du capitalisme en Russie.* Paris: Editions Sociales.

Lipietz, A. 1977. *Le capital et son espace.* Paris: Maspéro.

Lipietz, A. 1979. *Crise et inflation: pourquoi?* Paris: Maspéro.

Lipietz, A. 1983. *Le Monde enchanté. De la valeur à l'envol inflationniste.* Paris: La Découverte–Maspéro.

Marx, K. 1867. *Le capital.* Paris: Editions Sociales.

Massiah, G. 1982. Les enjeux de la politique française de coopération. Paper presented to the colloquium Politique Economique de la Gauche (Paris, November 20–1), mimeograph.

Michalet, C. A. 1980. *Banques multinationales, firmes multinationales, et économie mondiale.* CEREM, University of Paris X (mimeograph).

Mistral, J. 1982. La diffusion internationale inégale de l'accumulation intensive et ses crises. In J. L. Reiffers (ed.), *Economie et finance internationale.* Paris: Dunod.

Palloix, C. 1973. *Les firmes multinationales et le procès d'industrialisation.* Paris: Maspéro.

Palloix, C. 1979. L'economie de crédit international. In *La France et le Tiers Monde.* Grenoble: Presses Universitaires de Grenoble.

Rostow, W. 1963. *Les étapes de la croissance économique.* Paris: Seuil.

Salama, P. and P. Tissier. 1982. *L'industrialisation dans le sous-développement.* Paris: Maspéro.

Wallerstein, I. 1974. *The modern world system.* New York: Academic Press.

Warren, B. 1980. *Imperialism, pioneer of capitalism.* London: New Left Books.

PART II

Industrial production systems

3

Capitalist production, scientific management and the service class

JOHN URRY

Changes in the organization of production in capitalist societies have been understood in recent years as resulting from either the needs of capital accumulation, or from the dialectic of capital *and* the resistance of labor. In this chapter I do not wish to dispense with the insights that such formulations have generated. However, both such formulations ignore one particular set of developments which concern what has been discussed in the USA under the term the 'professional-managerial class' thesis (see Walker 1979); or in Britain, the thesis of the 'service class' (see Goldthorpe 1982, Abercrombie & Urry 1983). In the next section I shall argue that changes in the organization of capitalist production in the USA in the first third of this century partly resulted because 'management' was able to wrest control away from 'capital.' I shall consider what it was that made this possible. What was it that enabled new forms of management to develop, particularly the one known as scientific management? Why were there fewer constraints upon the development of management in the USA compared with countries in Western Europe, and in particular Britain?

Furthermore, the initial growth of scientific management, and of more complex managerial hierarchies generally, had a number of important consequences: to increase the size and powers of social groupings intermediate between capital and labor; to expand the number and influence of occupational professions; and to enlarge the systems of higher education and more generally of credentialism. In short, I shall suggest that the initial development of scientific management was a catalyst that provoked a major restructuring of capitalist America in which an extremely powerful professional-managerial or service class transformed the basic structuring of class relations. The USA, which is often taken to be the paradigmatic capitalist society, is paradoxically that society in which a profoundly significant third force (or 'class') gradually came in a sense to make itself, to realize some of its causal powers and thus to develop organizational and cultural resources separate in part from capital and labor. The particular features of the capital/labor relationship in the USA provided the context in which the 'service class' gradually came to make itself.

In the final section I shall consider the British experience over the same period. I shall show that management was not able to wrest control away from capital, that scientific management was implemented much less quickly and in a less thoroughgoing form, that its general effects were much more limited, and that there was nothing like the same growth of a 'service class' before World War II. Class structures are thus to be viewed as geographically specific. Variations in such class structures have, moreover, profoundly significant cumulative consequences. The contrast between Britain and the USA demonstrates that changes in technology and production cannot be separated from the wider social structures and that these vary considerably.

Management, the service class, and American society

It is now commonplace to note that the growth of the factory had a profound effect in changing people's work habits and experiences. There was some shift from an orientation to task toward an orientation to time (see Thompson 1967). However, it is also clear that the growth of the factory did not result in a direct increase in the social control that capital exercised over labor. What Marx called the 'real subsumption' of the laborer was not simply brought about by the factory system. There is widespread evidence that before the development of 'scientific management' in its various forms the laborer was not generally placed under conditions of real subsumption by *capital*. There were three alternative bases of control: first, that exercised by skilled craft workers – as Nelson says, 'the factory of 1880 [in the USA] remained a congeries of craftsmen's shops rather than an integrated plant' (1975: 4; and see Braverman 1974, Montgomery 1979: Ch. 1 on union rules and mutual support); second, that effected by 'foremen,' especially through 'driving' the workers via authoritarian rule and physical compulsion (see Nelson 1975: Ch. 3 on the 'Foreman's Empire'); and third, that produced through 'internal contracting' by which contractors hired and fired their own employees, set their wages, disciplined them and determined the production methods to be used (see Larson 1980: Ch. 3, Stark 1980, Littler 1978, 1982b: Ch. 11).

There was of course great variation between different industries and areas as to which of these different forms of control were found; and indeed there was often a combination of such forms within a single enterprise. Littler suggests that internal contracting was important in the period up to 1914 in the following industries: iron and steel, foundries, coal, engineering, armaments, arsenals, potteries, glass, newspaper printing and clothing (1982b: Table 11.3, and see Clawson 1980: 74–9). Internal contracting was more common in the traditional industrial areas on the east coast, and was often structured along lines of ethnic division as waves of immigrants settled in the USA beginning in the east (1982b: 165–71, Buttrick 1952, Soffer 1960). It was also in certain cases, such as clothing, structured along lines of gender division (see Benenson 1982: 70). Thus, as Clawson points out, inside contracting was an importantly non-bureaucratic form of control since the contractor 'did production work as well as supervision, there were no set qualifications, no levels of authority, essentially no written documents or files were kept, and there were no codified rules (or very few rules)' (1980: 73). For the growth of 'management' and hence of managerial bureaucracies, this power of the inside contractor had to be substantially broken (see Stone 1974, Montgomery 1979, on how this constituted a form of 'workers' control,' and see Clawson 1980: Ch. 3).

It was a basic premise of all such systems of control in 19th-century America that workers knew more than anyone else about how to do the detailed work and that they possessed the knowledge relating to the relevant labor process. Capitalist control was effected but only indirectly. It rested upon the power of skilled workers, foremen, or inside contractors, who exercised dictatorial control over labor, often of a patriarchal or racist form. Control was overwhelmingly 'personalistic' rather than bureaucratic. In general, as Hobsbawm argues, 19th-century capitalism operated 'not so much by directly subordinating large bodies of workers to employers, but by subcontracting exploitation and management' (Hobsbawm 1964: 297). Within about 30 years, however, much of this was to change in the USA. In the following discussion of the emergence of scientific management, I shall consider what it was that transformed the American social structure. In the mid-19th century there were no middle managers in the USA; while the number of 'administrative employees' within American industry increased four and a half times between 1899 and 1929, from 7.7% to 18.0% of total employment (Chandler 1980: 11, Bendix 1956: 214). The growth of 'management' and what I elsewhere term the 'socialization of unproductive labor' ('Abercrombie & Urry 1983: Ch. 6) occurred in the USA because of a struggle waged in part against both labor and capital. It is necessary to explain how and why this struggle was successful. Why was it that in at least parts of the USA labor lost its monopoly on the knowledge of the day-to-day organization of work, and why did the form of capitalist control which had persisted during the 19th century collapse? Part of my approach here will be to try to examine the issue posed by Stark when he says of the growth of management that 'the occupants of the new positions did not simply "fill in" a set of "empty places" created by forces completely divorced from their own activity, but actually participated, within a constellation of struggling classes, in the creation of these positions themselves' (1980: 101). In particular, the development of a large-scale management involved overcoming two particular forms of resistance: on the one hand, from the work-force itself, especially from the skilled craftsmen; and on the other hand, from the owners and existing managers who believed that 'scientific' management was an unnecessary and dangerous expense (on the details of scientific management, see Taylor 1947, Littler 1982b). Montgomery argues that the basic principles of scientific management had been very widely accepted by the 1920s. These principles included the centralized planning and integrating of the successive stages of production; the systematic analysis of each distinct operation; and detailed instruction and supervision of each worker in the performance of each discrete task; and the designing of wage payments to induce workers to do what they were told (1979: Ch. 5, Littler 1982b: 179–83).

The main conditions which facilitated this growth of scientific management in the USA, a development which had profound effects on the structure of American society, were (a) technological changes which outstripped the capacity of craftsmen trained in traditional techniques to organize production in the way they had in the past (see Chandler 1980: 16–23); (b) growth in the size of enterprises and plants after 1865 (see Chandler 1980: 23–6, Herman 1981: 188, 388); (c) declining rate of profit and merger boom especially around the turn of the century (see Nelson 1959, Littler 1982b: Ch. 2); (d) dramatic growth of immigration, especially from 1897, which segregated and fragmented the labor force (see Foner 1955, Montgomery 1979: Ch. 2); (e) the growing strength of organized labor, especially between 1894 and 1919, and the perceived need by capital to deal with this (see Foner 1955, Montgomery 1979, Brech 1982, Dubofsky 1983); (f) the impact of World War I and the growth of standardized product lines and corporatist state strategies (see Bendix 1956: 284–5, Stark 1980, Dubofsky 1983); (g) the growth in the numbers and influence of industrial engineers and their increasingly symbiotic relationship with corporate capital (see Noble 1979); and (h) the growth of progressivism between 1890 and 1920, which particularly involved the movement for 'improved efficiency' (see Kolko 1963, Palmer 1975, and on all of these points Urry 1986).

These conditions should be viewed as constituting an appropriate context within which 'management' began to challenge existing capital. The movement for scientific management not only emerged out of these conditions but also began to change them, as it provided the basis for the appearance of a fully fledged service class in the USA in the interwar period. The term 'service class' here refers to all those places in the social division of labor which are involved in the management and supervision of the functions of capital (of control, reproduction and reconceptualization), to the extent to which these are separated from capitalist ownership (see Renner 1978, Abercrombie & Urry 1983: Ch. 7, Goldthorpe 1982). The service class thus 'serves' capital as ownership and control become divorced; but as its own forms of intra-class organization develop (universities and colleges, bureaucracies and careers, professions and credentials), it gradually comes to make itself a separate class, a class-in-struggle, opposed in part to both capital and labor.

The 'causal powers' of the service class are considerable. They are to restructure capitalist societies so as to maximize the divorce between conception and execution and to ensure the elaboration of highly differentiated and specific structures within which knowledge and science can be maximally developed. They are thus to deskill productive laborers and to maximize the educational requirements of places within the social division of labor. This implies the minimizing of non-educational/non-achievement criteria for recruitment to such places; and the maximizing of the income and resources devoted to education and science, and more generally to the sphere of 'reproduction.' The service class will thus possess powers to enlarge the structures, whether private or public, by which they can organize and 'service' private capitalist enterprises.

I shall try to show below that certain of these powers were realized in the USA in the interwar period. They were in a sense set in motion by the early growth of scientific management, which led to the elaboration of the intra-class organization central to the 'service class.' It is also important to note that the very movement for scientific management was well organized. The viewpoint was represented particularly strongly in the *Engineering Magazine* and the *Transactions of the American Society of Mechanical Engineers*, and various organizations were formed, such as the Efficiency Society, the Taylor Society and the Society for the Promotion of Scientific Management (see Copley 1923: vols. 1 and II, Palmer 1975: 34–5). Crucial meetings were held, especially the 1903 meeting when Taylor read his paper on 'Shop management' to the American Society of Mechanical Engineers. And although the 'movement' was characterized by considerable discussion (for example, over the importance of 'motion' studies), by 1912 and the hearings before the House of Representatives special committee there was widespread public awareness, and some acceptance, of the broad objectives of the new scientific managers (Nadworny 1955: Ch. 4). I shall now consider some aspects of their emergence, in particular that they were located in struggle with both labor *and* capital, and that to succeed they had to undermine resistance from both the work-force and from capitalists and existing foremen and managers who generally believed that a growth in 'scientific' management was an unneccessary expense that would undermine their own prerogatives (see Nelson 1975: 75–6, Clawson 1980: 68–9, Stark 1980: 91, Abercrombie & Urry 1983: 101). I will consider first the resistance of labor to the growth of scientific management.

The first struggle can be examined initially by reference to Braverman's *Labor and monopoly capital* (1974). In this he argues that the development of scientific management involves the separation of conception and execution, the former coming to reside with capital, the latter with labor. However, as Burawoy argues, this is strictly speaking not correct: 'Rather than a separation of conception and execution, we find a separation of workers' conception and management's conception, of workers' knowledge and management's knowledge' (1978: 277). Partly as a result, he argues, workers showed great ingenuity in opposing, outwitting, and defeating the agents of scientific management before, during and after the 'appropriation of knowledge.' However, up to about 1910 there was in fact relatively little union opposition to 'scientific management,' partly because it had not been introduced into strongly unionized plants; while for the next ten years or so there was widespread opposition. This came initially through the American Federation of Labor (AFL) which was particularly important in attempting to protect the 'secrets of the craft' (Nadworny 1955: Ch. 4). Sam Gompers well realized how scientific management would 'reduce the number of skilled workers to the barest minimum' (quoted Nadworny 1955: 53), and the costs for labor were strongly emphasized in Professor Hoxie's report on scientific management prepared for the US Commission on Industrial Relations (see Nadworny 1955: Ch. 6). Apart from the opposition at the Watertown Arsenal (Aitken 1960), perhaps the most impressive opposition of labor to new forms of management was to be seen in the strike of the Railroad Carmen on the Illinois Central and Harriman lines, which lasted for nearly four years and involved about 30000 workers (see Palmer 1975: 42). The carmen maintained an extraordinarily determined opposition to the transformation of their skilled trades which resulted from the attempt to introduce piece work and bonus systems, speed-ups, and time and motion studies. In the course of the strike, 533 strikers were jailed, 91% of strikers were forced to move to cheaper housing, and 16 men committed suicide (Palmer 1975: 42).

However, for all the sustained and militant opposition of some groups of craft workers to scientific management, such workers were generally unwilling to develop broad-based industrial alliances with semi-skilled and unskilled workers, especially immigrants, blacks or women workers. Benenson suggests that where the very earliest industrial unions were established, these were to be found in industries where skilled workers were not threatened by displacement by the less skilled (as in coal and garment-making; Benenson 1982: 73 and generally on the organization of different industries). The organization of labor during this period was not simply the result of craft workers responding to the degradation of skill (as in Braverman's analysis), but was much more varied, geographically, industrially and historically, and involved differing and complex alliances of workers, not only struggling against specific 'deskilling' but much more generally over the forms of control, both within the workplace and the community (see Foner 1955, Palmer 1977).

By 1919–20 the opposition of labor to scientific management had partly subsided, although as Palmer points out this was much more true of the official union leadership than of all groups of workers (1975: 41f). This reduced opposition resulted from a number of conditions. First, there were various semi-corporatist arrangements established in wartime, which ensured, as Person put it, 'labor's interest in good management and increased productivity' (1929: 20). Secondly, there was the more conciliatory and accommodating attitude of the engineers themselves. Thus, in 1917, C. B. Thompson argued that 'scientific managers have been freely advised to recognize more fully the necessity of cooperation with the unions' (1917: 269). And thirdly, after 1919 and the following year when up to 20% of the American labor force went on strike, labor was decimated in the early 1920s. One and a half million members were lost by the AFL, and the union advocated a new doctrine of labor–management cooperation (see Brody 1980: 44–6).

I will now consider scientific management's other struggle, with capital and existing management. The starting point here is to recognise Burawoy's claim that 'one cannot *assume* the existence of a cohesive managerial and capitalist class that automatically recognises its true interests' (1978: 284). Indeed, the very growth of 'scientific management' in the USA in a sense reflects not so much the strength of capital and its ability to deskill labor but rather its relative weakness in the early years of this century, in particular to prevent the appropriation of effective economic possession by a new class of 'managers.'

This opposition from existing capital and management was well recognized at the time. C. B. Thompson described scientific management as a 'veritable storm-center' (1917: 211), while H. Person talked of the general reluctance of most existing managements to undertake theoretically 'revolutionary improvements' rather than to continue existing opportunistic practices which were, according to Litterer, 'increasingly chaotic, confused and wasteful' (Person 1929: 1–12, Litterer 1963: 370). Taylor himself stated in his testimony in 1912 to the Special House Committee to Investigate the Taylor and Other Systems of Shop Management that:

> nine-tenths of our trouble has been to 'bring' those on the management's side to do their fair share of the work and only one-tenth of our trouble has come on the workman's side. Invariably we find very great opposition on the part of those on the management's side to do their new duties . . . (1947: 43)

This is confirmed in Nelson's survey of 29 taylorized plants where he found that opposition came both from foremen and supervisors (see Litterer 1982b: 181), and more generally from existing management. Nelson concludes that 'the experts encountered more opposition from managers than workers' (1975: 75). For example:

> Gantt encountered serious opposition from the management at the Sayles Bleachery and Joseph Bancroft & Sons, and less formidable problems at the Canadian Pacific shops; Barth antagonized his employers at the S. L. Moore Company and lost the confidence of the Yale & Towne officers; Gilbreth alienated the managers of the Herrmann, Aukam Company; C. B. Thompson complained bitterly of the opposition he encountered from the supervisors at the Eaton, Crane & Pike Company; Cooke reported a similar experience at Forbes Lithograph; Sanford Thompson noted the suspicions of the managers at Eastern Manufacturing; Evans faced substantial opposition from certain superiors and many foremen; and the experts who worked at the Pimpton Press and Lewis Manufacturing Company found Kendall, Taylor's friend and admirer, a highly critical observer of their work. (Noble 1979: 75)

One reason for the opposition of existing management was that Taylor attempted, as he put it, to substitute 'exact scientific investigation and knowledge for the old individual judgement or opinion, either of the workman or the boss' (1947: 31). This involved giving considerable autonomy to the industrial engineer. Layton argues that the effect was that 'Taylor has opened the possibility of an independent role for engineers in an area in which their position had been that of bureaucratic subordinates' (1971: 139).

The first and most obvious effect of the development of scientific management, or of complex managerial hierarchies more generally, was to produce a substantial change in the American occupational structure. Thus the ratio of administrative to production employees in manufacturing industry increased from 7.7% to 17.9% in the first third of this century (Bendix 1956: 218). Furthermore, over the same period the proportion of American workers in the tertiary or service sector increased from one-third to almost one-half (Sabolo 1975: 9). These changes were particularly important within the chemical and electrical industries which formed the vanguard of modern technology in the USA. The development of new innovations in these industries fostered the gradual 'electrification' and 'chemicalization' of older, craft-based industries which thus rapidly acquired 'scientistic' features, partly through the recruitment of chemical and electrical engineers (Noble 1979: 18–19). This led to the growth of technical education, which was well summarized by Professor J. B. Turner's call to replace the 'laborious thinkers' produced by the classical colleges by the 'thinking laborers' necessary for industry (Noble 1979: 21). The emergent, technically trained, electrical and chemical engineers were predominantly employed within large corporations and promotion mainly consisted of movement within the corporation into management (see Layton 1974). Professional advancement consisted of promotion *within* the corporate hierarchies of the science-based industries. These professional engineers were particularly significant in effecting a number of major changes in the USA, in the period 1860-1930: standardizing weights and measurements, modernizing patent-law in favor of science-based industrial corporations, developing large industrial research laboratories with a heightened division of labor, integrating industrial and university-based research, ensuring an appropriate industry-based curriculum within the dramatically expanding university system, and encouraging the general development of modern management and related techniques (see Noble 1979: Part 2).

Thus, the development of engineers/managers helped to weld science and technology into the growing corporate structure, and this had the effect of further separating engineers/managers from the directly productive workers (see Noble 1979, Stark 1980, Abercrombie & Urry 1983: 149). This was in part because their growth served to generate an 'ideology of technical expertise' which then served other occupations as they systematized cognitive categories and developed new organizational forms in, as Stark puts it, 'their attempts to define and maintain their privileged position over and against the working class and struggled to increase their autonomy from the capitalist class in the schools, the universities, and the state' (1980: 118; but see Burrage 1972, Larson 1977 on why they did not develop a full professional identity). The engineers thus provided a model of how education and industry were to be integrated over the course of the 20th century as one occupation after another sought to strengthen its market-power by connecting together the production of knowledge with the production of the producers via the modern university. Schools of business administration had already been established, the first (the Wharton School of Finance and Commerce) in 1881, with others at Berkeley and Chicago following in 1898, at Dartmouth and New York University in 1900, and at Harvard as early as 1908 (Touraine 1974: 29). There was a structural linkage effected between two sets of elements, specific bodies of theoretical knowledge on the one hand, and markets for skilled services or labor on the other hand (see Larson 1980: 141–2, and 1977 more generally). Thus higher education became the means for bringing about professionalization and for the substantial transformation of the restructuring of social inequality. As Noble puts it, 'the integration of formal education into the industrial structure weakened the traditional link between work experience and advancement, driving a wedge between managers and managed and separating the two by the college campus' (1979: 168, and see Chs. 7 and 8 on the changing engineering curriculum). He goes on to note that in emphasizing the role of formal education as a vital aspect of their professional identity, engineers at the same time laid the foundations for the educationally based system of occupational stratification that characterizes the USA (1979: 168, and see Abercrombie & Urry 1983: 147–9). Thus the very process of professionalization contributed to the restructuring of the patterning of social inequality, to a system based on the salience of occupation, to legitimation via achievement of socially recognized expertise, and to a heightened concentration on education and the possession of credentials (see Wiebe 1967: 121f, Disco 1979: 179, Abercrombie & Urry 1983: Ch. 6).

This set of developments led to an extraordinary expansion of higher education in the half century after 1880. By 1930 the USA possessed more institutions of higher education than France possessed academic personnel and its university and college population was ten times larger than the secondary school population in France (see Debray 1981: 43–4, Mulhern 1981:49; the population in the USA was only three times that of France in 1930). It would also seem plausible to suggest that this especially large increase in both the size of the middle classes and of the mobility into them in the USA (their proportion increased from 12 to 22% between 1900 and 1930; see Kocka 1980: 19) was one factor which prevented the development of strong work, market and political divisions between such employees and the working class in this period. Kocka talks of the 'indistinctness and relative insignificance of the collar line in industry' (1980: 117 and *passim*), although it should be noted that he attributes this to the lack of bureaucratic and corporate structures in pre-industrial America (compared particularly with Germany up to 1933).

One important reason for the development of a large number of occupations all pursuing a program of professionalization through colleges and universities was that the development of industrial engineering had raised but left unanswered a whole series of questions and issues concerned with the nature of work and the worker. Bendix summarizes:

> When Taylor and his followers proposed that the selection and training of workers be put on a scientific basis, they opened the way not to the promotion of industrial harmony on the basis of scientific findings, but to the involvement of industrialists in intellectual debates for which their training and interests had not prepared them. (1956: 288)

Especially during the 1920s and 1930s a large-scale debate developed as to what workers were really like and how they could be appropriately motivated. A resulting battery of tests and testers emerged to investigate their typical attitudes and aptitudes (Bendix 1956: 289f). This was associated with the more general bureaucratization of industry and the realization by management that the exercise of control would ideally involve the elaboration of rules, the delegation of authority, the specialization of administrative functions and the development of complex systems of personnel investigation and management (Bendix 1956: 298, Baritz 1960: Ch. 4). Each of these developments presupposed new occupations, especially various branches of organizational psychology and sociology, which literally became in Baritz's term 'servants of power' and which copied the professionalization strategy employed by the industrial engineers (see Baritz 1960, Nelson 1975: Ch. 10, Church 1974, on the development of 'economists as experts'). And this was part of a general movement which Wiebe summarizes:

the specialized needs of an urban–industrial system came as a godsend to a middle stratum in the cities. Identification by way of their skills gave them the deference of their neighbours while opening natural avenues into the nation at large. Increasingly formal entry requirements into their occupations protected their prestige through exclusiveness. (1967: 113)

He also points out that each of these groups, making up a 'service class,' appeared first in the older, larger and more industrially developed cities in the northeast. Wiebe talks of the development of 'an aggressive, optimistic, new middle class' sweeping all before it from about 1900 onward (1967: 166). This was then reflected in a further development of the 'helping professions,' a process which should not be seen as simply one which involved responding to certain clearly defined 'social needs' (see Wiebe 1967, Bledstein 1976). But such professions should not be seen as purely autonomous since as Lasch argues we should not ignore 'the connection between the rise of modern professionalism and the rise of professional management;' or more critically 'American professionalism has been corrupted by the managerial capitalism with which it is so closely allied' (1977: 17). Lasch points out the considerable similarities between the appropriation of knowledge, centralization and deskilling in the industrial and in the non-industrial spheres of social activity, especially within the American health service (see Brown 1980). Hence, a powerful and wide-ranging 'service class' developed in the USA and its emergence weakened labor not merely in the sphere of work, but within most areas of social and political life.

Britain and the 'scientific management' movement

In this section I shall explore some implications of what Littler has illuminatingly termed the 'Ambrit' fallacy (1978: 187, 1982a: 145). By this he means the continual tendency to conflate the history and culture of two very different societies, namely the USA and Britain, and the attempt to draw significant sociological conclusions on the basis of this conflation between the two. Littler maintains that it is necessary to investigate the precise conditions and circumstances under which scientific management was introduced in each society, rather than to presume that there is almost a natural history of 'the deskilling of the capitalist labor process' (as is argued, for example, in Braverman 1974, and in rather different terms in Bendix 1956). In particular, Littler argues that scientific management was introduced into parts of American industry before World War I during a period of economic expansion; in Britain by contrast scientific management, where it was introduced, occurred later, in the 1920s and 1930s during a period of profound economic depression (1982a: 145). Furthermore, the 'rationalization' of work was not something which affected all industries to anything like the same degree. In the USA we have already seen that the transformations of the metal-working, electrical and chemical industries were particularly important (see Noble 1979). In Britain, the movement to scientific management primarily affected the food, drink, tobacco, chemical and textile industries (Littler 1982a: 145; 1982b: 114).

In the following I shall, first, show that the 'Ambrit' fallacy is indeed a fallacy, since British developments did lag far behind the Americans. I shall also show that they also lagged considerably behind developments in certain other countries in Europe. In this I shall follow what has now been fairly clearly established in much of the literature, both by commentators at the time, like Cadbury, Devinat and Urwick, and by contemporary historians of economic and social change, such as Levine, Maier, and Wiener. My main purpose here will be to establish just why British industry failed to adopt new forms of managerial control and hierarchy and I shall argue that existing explanations are unsatisfactory. In particular, it is necessary to examine the particular balance of social forces. Far from scientific management being something that would be introduced unless resisted, it is rather the case that such innovations would *not* be introduced unless they are very specifically struggled for *and* unless undoubtedly widespread opposition can be effectively neutralized. Hence, although such developments are broadly 'functional' for capital, it does *not* follow that such functions explain either the growth of, or the persistence of, scientific management as a form by which capital controls labor. In particular, it is necessary to investigate the industrial and spatial variations involved in order to explain how and why struggles to 'scientize' management were only variably successful, and in general were less successful in Britain than in the USA, Germany and Japan. Hence, in order to explain just why managerial change was particularly developed in the USA, it is necessary to show why the existing social forces there were not able to prevent change, whereas in the UK they were.

First, however, I shall briefly detail the restricted uptake of scientific management in the UK. Although, as Littler shows, some changes did occur in the period up to 1914 (development of piece work and other bonus systems, the gradual and variable replacement of internal contractors with a directly employed supervision system, and revived forms of paternalism; see 1982b: Ch. 7, Burgess 1980: Ch. 4), systematic schemes of scientific management aroused little or no interest amongst engineers and managers in this period and were very rarely implemented. Charles Maier summarizes:

> Not merely did this reflect an industrial leadership set in its ways; an underlying satisfaction with decentralized production, with the premises of a liberal regime in a country where the middle classes felt little anxiety about the social order, postponed real interest until the economic difficulties of the 1920s and 1930s. (1970: 37)

In 1911 the journal, *Engineer*, objected to American notions of scientific management with the comments that 'there are fair and unfair ways of diminishing labor costs . . . We do not hesitate to say that Taylorism is inhuman' (quoted in Wiener 1981: 143, and see Urwick & Brech 1946: Ch. 7). Urwick summarized the reaction of capital by claiming that only a few employers here and there had given serious attention to Taylor's work and this was because the industrial *milieu* presented an infertile soil because of skepticism and apathy. There was an incapacity to understand that anything other than technology was of any consequence (1929: 58). He goes on to suggest that where employers did take up aspects of Taylor's work (even during and after World War I) they tended to over-emphasize one particular aspect (such as 'Welfare and Psychology on Costing or Technical Research') and as a result their 'business suffered the usual penalties of lack of balance' – as a result they then revised scientific methods, when what they needed was more science (Urwick 1929: 70).

Other contemporary commentators reinforced this interpretation. A. Shadwell, for example, the author of the monumental *Industrial efficiency* (1906), maintained in 1916 that in British industry:

> Very often there is no planning at all; it is left to the operative and rule of thumb. Generally there is planning of a rough and ready kind, but some of the most famous workers in the country are in such a state of chaos that the stuff seems to be turned out by accident. (1916: 375–6)

Similarly critical comments were developed by J. A. Hobson in *Incentives in the new industrial order* (1922, but see 1913), and Sidney Webb in *The works manager today* (1918), while Edward Cadbury pointed to the potential dehumanising consequences of the implementation of scientific management (1914a, although see 1914b). Levine details the specific lack of attention devoted to Taylor's seminal papers in the British engineering journals – for example, his 'Shop management' was ignored by all four of the major British engineering journals (Levine 1967: 61). Levine classifies the reaction to scientific management into three types: the humanitarian, as in the quote from *The Engineer* above; the economic, as in the claim that scientific management was unnecessary in Britain because labor costs were lower; and the anti-scientistic, as in another leader from *The Engineer* in which it is claimed that 'too much science . . . is likely to lead to a decrease of efficiency rather than an increase' (April 25, 1913: 443), or in E. T. Elbourne's view that 'golden rules' or organization *per se* 'can never be a substitute for good men' (1914: 169).

Finally, we might note that in C. B. Thompson's survey conducted in 1917, he claimed to have found 201 factories where taylorist schemes of management had been introduced – yet only four of these were in Britain (1917: 39, and see Levine 1967: 67). Likewise Levine, in his survey of the related development in mass production, maintains that there were very few traces in Britain in the period up to World War I, particularly because of the failure to develop the characteristics of specialization, standardization and interchangeability (Levine 1967: 52–4).

There is some controversy as to when any widespread implementation of scientific management actually did occur in Britain. Certain commentators see the period of World War I as marking some kind of watershed. Burgess, following Pollard, maintains that it 'was one of the major long-term effects of the War that it marked the widespread implementation in Britain of the methods of "scientific management"' (1980: 166, Pollard 1969: 53–6, 81–2). However, he cites no contemporary evidence for this and it seems more plausible to suggest that while the war did produce a number of significant effects, such as increased standardization, advances in mass production techniques in government arsenals, and some erosion of skill differentials, the most important innovations in Britain did not take place until considerably later (see Littler 1982b: 99-100). Littler has most recently drawn attention to the importance of the Bedaux system for the understanding of changes in management in Britain in the interwar years (see Bedaux 1917, Livingstone 1969, Layton 1974, as well as Littler 1982a: 139–43; Littler 1982b: Chs. 8 & 9).

The Bedaux consultancy firm was begun in 1918 in Cleveland, Ohio, and within a few years Bedaux was the owner of two networks of consultants, one American, one international. His extraordinarily rapid financial success was particularly due to his salesmanship. As Littler points out, while Taylor was keen to justify his system intellectually, Bedaux simply set out to sell himself and his system to engineers and managers (1982b: 107). Moreover, while Taylor's system took a long time and was difficult to install (see Layton 1974), Bedaux's was quick and easy and involved relatively little change to the existing management structure. Indeed, the main innovation of Bedaux was to appear to have solved the problem the solution to which had eluded Taylor, namely the nature of the relationship between work and fatigue (see Layton 1974: 382). Bedaux claimed to be able to determine the exact proportions of the two necessary for the fulfillment of any task. Moreover, it was then possible to compare all the different tasks within the factory; they would all be based on particular combinations of work and rest. They could all be reduced to the same measuring grid and hence subject to a systematic control and monitoring system. At the same time, Bedaux built a fairly crude reward system into his proposals which is summarized by Livingstone:

> If a man earned £3 a week for producing 40 articles, Bedaux offered him £4 a week if he produced 80. Put in these terms, the confidence trick is too obvious, but the logic was confused by jargon . . . For instance, Bedaux always started from the premise that the man should have been producing 60 articles for his £3, and thus if he produced a third more – 80 – he got a third more pay – £4. What could be fairer? (1969: 50)

An investigation of the Bedaux system by the AFL concluded that beneath its pseudo-scientific jargon it was basically a means of speeding up the work done with little consideration being paid to other aspects of good and efficient management (see Brown 1935). In other words, it enhanced the existing power of management at the expense of the workers and it gave managers an illusory sense of being able to understand and control efficiency (see Layton 1974: 382). Bedaux was in fact frequently criticized for not doing enough to improve methods of working and indeed for thrusting all the burden of increasing output on to the workers (see Littler 1982b: 112). Indeed the Taylor Society itself, fearful of the charge that they were concerned merely to 'speed up,' struggled to dissociate itself from the Bedaux system (see Nadworny 1955: 134).

This system was widely adopted in Britain. In 1937, of the 1100 or so firms using it, 500 were American, over 200 British and 150 French (Littler 1982b: 113). The firms involved in Britain included many of the new and expanding firms of the 1930s – food processing (Huntley and Palmers), light engineering (GEC (Coventry)), motor components (British Goodrich Rubber Co. Ltd.), chemicals (Boots Pure Drug Co.), and services (Vernons Ltd.), as well as certain older industries, particularly textiles (Wolsey Ltd) (see Littler 1982b: 114, and 1980: Appendix A). There are two important aspects of the implementation of the Bedaux system in the UK. First, in very few cases did its introduction involve the destruction of some long-established craft skill. Most of the industries in which it was introduced depended on semi-skilled or unskilled labor, not on craft labor. Even where there was some craft deskilling involved this seems to have occurred *before* the implementation of the Bedaux system (Littler 1982b: 128–30). Second, the introduction of this system activated considerable opposition and antagonism in the work-force. This was both because it brought about increases in unemployment during periods of already very high national and local unemployment, and because of the obvious resentments about being spied upon, and speed-ups at work. However, much of the opposition was unsuccessful so that strike action quickly evaporated (Littler 1982b: Ch.9). Nevertheless, the effect of such resistance was that the unions often became *active* participants in creating and sustaining effort norms, a process reflected in the generally accommodatory response of the national unions and the TUC to Bedaux by the 1930s (as reflected, for example, in the TUC report 1933: 16).

These developments during the 1930s did not involve the simple pattern of craft deskilling as suggested by Braverman. As Littler argues, the pattern of craft deskilling mainly occurred in a 'non-confrontational' manner through changes in occupational/industrial structure, that is, the growth of new industries, the emergence of new firms with different technologies, the development of new production processes, and the spatial relocation of industries, firms and plants both within the UK and abroad (see Littler 1982b: 141). The introduction of Bedaux mainly occurred within these new industries and firms, where there were not well-established craft skills waiting to be 'deskilled.' Changes were nevertheless brought about in the 'confrontational' manner but these did not involve the simple destruction of craft skills – indeed the main effects of Bedaux were to 'legitimize' the speeding of work and of the introduction of new forms of control and payment, but not to 'restructure' management and its relationship with labor in anything like the fashion effected in the USA (through more thoroughgoing taylorist systems). There was considerable worker resistance to the introduction of such schemes in the UK (also from foremen and supervisors; see Littler 1982b: 142–3) but this was not generally successful in preventing their implementation, only in modifying it.

So far, then, we have seen that management was restructured in the UK both later and in a far less thoroughgoing fashion than in the USA. Before analyzing why this was the case I shall briefly consider what happened in the rest of Europe during this period (on related developments in Japan, see Wood & Kelly 1982: 80, and Littler 1982b: Ch. 10, and in the USSR, see

Wood & Kelly 1982: 81; for a contemporary account see Devinat 1927, and a general survey Maier 1970).

The country which most rapidly copied American innovations in this area was Germany. According to Kocka, 'scientific management' first appeared in the workshops of large enterprises at the turn of the century (1978: 574; see Devinat 1927: 80–3). Partly this stemmed from the fact that German entrepreneurs and managers took study trips to the USA in order to investigate the 'Taylor' system at first hand. But it also derived from pre-existing features of German society, namely the bureaucratic tradition which led to written instructions, precision and formalization within organizational structures. Kocka maintains that from fairly early on a clear division was established within large engineering workshops between the preparations for and control of production on the one side, and the execution of production on the other. There was also the widespread growth of offices including paperwork and card index systems, some standardization of production, and reduction in the power of foremen, the growth of 'organizational specialists, and an increased devotion to science, technology and technical training' (also see Levine 1967: 46, 75, 147). Such developments were moreover given a heightened impetus during World War I (see Pichierri 1978).

Considerable interest in scientific management was also found in France before World War I. In the 18th and 19th centuries French engineers had been in the vanguard of technological change and so they were among the first to study and attempt to implement taylorist systems of management. Particularly important were Henry le Chatelier and Henri Fayol (see Devinat 1927: 30–2, Maier 1970: 37–8, Layton 1974: 379–80). The main industry where such theories were applied was the rapidly growing one of automobile production, especially at Renault and Pankard (Layton 1974: 380). Fayol was important in developing the idea that parallel with already recognized functions of management there was also something he termed the 'administrative function' which covered forecasting, organization, direction, coordination and supervision (Devinat 1927: 31). Generally it would seem that the *overall* impact of scientific management was less marked than in Germany, although it is interesting to note that in 1918 Clemenceau was suggesting that it was neccessary to establish taylorite planning departments (Copley 1923: vol. I, xxi).

There was no substantial international exchange of scientific management ideas until after World War I. The first international congress was held in Prague in 1924 and attended by delegates from six European countries from the USA. Further congresses were held in 1925 and 1927 when 1400 delegates heard over 170 papers (for details, see Urwick 1929: 75f). In 1927 the ILO established at Geneva the International Management Institute to collate, classify and disseminate all known schemes of scientific management.

So far, then, I have established that scientific management was established considerably later and in a weaker form in the UK compared particularly with the USA and partly with Germany and France (and incidentally Japan). There are a number of causes for this which I will discuss below. However, these causes should be viewed in a rather different light from the customary one. That is to say, their importance lies in the fact that they prevented the substantial realization of the 'causal powers' of the service class in Britain to anything like the degree to which they have been realized elsewhere, especially in the USA. These causal powers were not realized in the UK because there were other entities sufficiently strong and organized which were able to prevent the 'service class' emerging in the UK to restructure the society, particularly strong capitalist and working classes. Moreover, in Britain there was not the same development of appropriate 'collectivities-in-struggle' specific to the service class. Stark summarizes the contrasting situation in the USA:

> In attempting to defend their claims to technical expertise or to maintain the currency value of their certified degrees, the members of these new occupations stand not with one foot in the working class and one foot in the capitalist class but with one foot in a professional association and one foot in a bureaucratic (corporate or state) organization. The constellation of relations of conflict and alliance between these associations and other organizations arising from work, community, and political life must be the object of study in the analysis of class relations in the current period. (Stark 1980: 119; see also Abercrombie & Urry 1983: 132–3)

I shall now try to summarize just why the service class in the UK was never able to realize its powers in a fashion remotely similar to that achieved in the USA in the first third of this century, a process under the leadership, as we have seen, of the industrial engineers. Four important features of the economic structure should initially be noted: first, family firms remained of much greater significance in Britain than elsewhere and there was little tendency for ownership and control to become divorced (Chandler 1976: 40); second, there was relatively little increase in the overall level of industrial concentration until after World War I when the 1920s merger booms brought about substantial increases (Hannah 1976: 105f); third, even in these industries where increases in industrial concentration did take place the owners did not try to construct an integrated and centralized administrative system (see Littler 1982b: 103, on the Calico Printers Association founded in 1899 which possessed 128 directors and 8 managing directors!); and fourth, there was an extraordinarily high rate of capital export in the years up to 1914, so much so that in that year British investments accounted for over one-half of the world's total (see Burgess 1980: 113, and see Rubinstein 1977 and Wiener 1981: 128–9 more generally). The consequence of these features was that industry remained relatively unchanged and subject to continuing forms of familial control. Alfred Marshall wrote in 1903 that '[Many] of the sons of manufacturers [were] content to follow mechanically the lead given by their fathers. They worked shorter hours, and they exerted themselves less to obtain new practical ideas than their fathers had done' (Marshall 1938: 21). And at the same time there was an expanding and increasingly profitable development of finance-capital. The latter, as opposed to industrial-capital, 'was decidedly richer, more powerful, and possessed of a more distinguished historical pedigree . . . the City, with its centuries-old traditions, its location near the heart of upper-class England, and its gradually woven, closely knit ties to the aristocracy and gentry, enjoyed a social cachet that evaded industry' (Wiener 1981: 128). As a consequence, the financial institutions within the City of London did not greatly contribute to the financing of British industry, especially the new industries of electrical engineering and automobile production which in the USA were particularly significant sites for the implementation of taylorism and fordism (Wiener 1981: 129). Moreover, the enormous rewards from such overseas investment and the secure imperial markets both cushioned the British economy so that the pressures to restructure management were less intense (see Wood & Kelly 1982: 42; more generally, see Ingham 1982).

The effects of this were moreover particularly important because of the fact that Britain had been the first to industrialize and that broadly speaking its capital stock was of an older vintage compared with other economies (see Levine 1967: 122–3, on differences with the USA). New schemes of management would have been more likely to be introduced either where the latest technology was to be found, or where new capital investment was about to be implemented. Two examples where this restriction seems to have been an important factor preventing the development of new management structures in the UK were, first, in the high levels of existing investment in steam and gas in Britain which militated against the widespread development of electrification and hence of electrical engineering; and second, existing investments in iron and steel were so enormous that this fact in itself constituted a formidable barrier to change (see Levine 1967: 123–4). This problem was further exacerbated because of the essentially 'interconnected' nature of industrial organization so that it was impossible to introduce any particular innovation without in effect restructuring the whole industry (see Frankel 1955). This was a particular problem in Britain for two reasons: first, because of the highly fragmented pattern of ownership in most of the leading industries; and second, because unlike the USA Britain was a national social and political entity which meant that it was much more difficult for new investments to be developed hundreds of miles away from those already established (see Littler 1982b: 183–5).

It is also widely claimed that the level of wages were not high enough in Britain for them to provide a major incentive to introduce new management schemes. The share of wages in the national income, for example, fell steadily from the peak in 1893 so that by 1913 they constituted a smaller share than in 1907 (Pollard 1965: 101). Moreover, both money and real wages rose more slowly in Britain than in the other advanced economies after 1890 and indeed real wages fell in Britain 1895–1913 (Brown & Browne 1968: 67). The coal mining industry was a good example of where employers were able to recruit labor at very low wage-rates before World War I (see Levine 1967: 77). However, Levine convincingly shows that this is by no means a sufficient explanation (Levine 1967: 76–8). We have to consider both why managers and engineers could not force through appropriate changes and why workers, even if low paid, were able to resist. One reason for this is that according to Burgess 'there is substantial evidence to support the argument for increasing working-class "solidification" since the late 1870s, both at the workplace and in the community' (1980: 97). This is related to the growth in trade-union membership from one million in 1889 to four million in 1913.

Particularly if labor resisted it was much more difficult to invest elsewhere. Moreover, employers in Britain were unwilling to encourage their workers to share in the productivity gains that would result from a transformed managerial structure (see Littler 1982b: 95). British capital simply sought to keep wages as low as possible rather than to develop a high wage, high productivity economy. As a result it is hardly surprising that the rapidly unionizing, community-organized labor movement was able to mount fairly effective and sustained opposition to any attempts to effect substantial managerial restructuring.

This was also true for another reason. As J. A. Hobson put it, the country's 'great business men' appear to have carved out their niche in the world without science or 'trained brains in others' (1922: 62, Levine 1967: 70). He points to their 'contemptuous scepticism of science and all that science stands for' (1922: 81). Alfred Marshall likewise maintained that England could not 'maintain her position in the world, unless she calls science to her aid in a much more thorough way than hitherto' (quoted Levine 1967: 70). Particular deficiencies were noted with regard to the failure to apply the fruits of scientific knowledge and to develop the field of chemical engineering (Wedgwoods in 1884 claimed, for example, not to employ any chemists; Wiener 1981: 201). These problems moreover were effected in the general failure to develop anything like the same 'progressive' ideology which characterized the USA in the early years of this century. As Maier argues: 'Rationalization in Europe, therefore, was only a stunted offspring of the American productive vision as originally conceived' (1970: 59). Indeed, the USA provided a very distinctive negative example, especially during the later years of the 19th century and the early years of the 20th. Disparagement of the American way of life – one centered on idolizing technology and wealth – became commonplace. Indeed Wiener suggests that the industrial revolution itself became redefined as a characteristically un-English event (1981: 88–90).

This in turn was related to the development of two preferred agents of management within British industry, agents that do not have the same significance in the USA. These two agents were the educated amateur, the 'gentleman,' on the one hand, and the 'practical man,' on the other (Wiener 1981: 138–9). The latter was in effect the defensive ideal of those who were excluded from functioning as the former, especially through the absence of an elite education. For them training on the job was central and they disparaged the value of education or formal training for their work. The twin cults of the two models, the educated amateur and the practical man, mutually reinforced opposition within management and industry to science, technology and to formal education. Coleman summarizes: 'Economics, management techniques, industrial psychology: all were frequently looked upon with grave suspicion, for they represented attempts to professionalize an activity long carried on jointly by "practical men" and gentlemanly amateurs' (1973: 113). Management was typically not regarded as something to be pursued simply for itself but rather more as the *means* to something else, to politics, land-ownership, culture, or a position in the City (see Shanks 1963: 62). Management did not develop in Britain as a relatively autonomous set of interrelated professions, able to force through further widespread educational, technical and organizational reforms.

I have so far sought to establish that (a) the service class is a potentially powerful social entity within 20th-century capitalist societies; (b) the service class has substantially realized its powers within the USA – a process activated by, but not reducible to, the early and wide-ranging scientization of management; and (c) for a number of reasons the service class did not realize its powers to anything like the same degree in the UK, where scientific management was introduced somewhat later and in a less far-reaching form, and where this class did not develop anything like the same institutional and organizational structures. I shall now mention certain of the consequences for British society which follow from point (c). Incidentally, these are not consequences which follow simply from the absence of a 'service class consciousness' because that was substantially absent in the USA. Rather, the service class in Britain before World War II did not possess sufficient organizational and cultural resources to produce a substantial restructuring of British society (on the importance of analyzing a class's organizational and cultural resources, see Lash & Urry 1984). Although Goldthorpe (1982) most interestingly investigated this service class concept he does not examine two points being emphasized here; namely, that the service class is of variable significance in different periods in different capitalist societies, and that a class (especially this one) can exert powers whether or not that class develops a distinctive 'socio-cultural identity' (Goldthorpe 1982: 172).

Briefly, then, the consequences for British society of a weak 'service class' were, first, that the rapid development of the professions occurred before the growth of scientific management and thus much more under the sway of the landed-aristocratic class – the gentry model of 'status professionalism' rather than the bourgeois one of 'occupational professionalism' (see Elliott 1972, Larson 1977: 103, Wiener 1981: 15). Rubinstein summarizes, particularly noting the spatial significance of London for this process of status professionalization:

> The process of incorporation, acquisition of an expensive and palatial headquarters in central London, establishment of an apprenticeship system, limitations on entries, and scheduling of fees, are all manifestly designed to 'gentrify' the profession and make it acceptable to society. This aspect of professionalization is profoundly anti-capitalist, and hence at odds with much of the rest of nineteenth-century British society. (1977: 122; for further details, see Perkin 1961–2: 128–9).

Second, neither industrial engineers in particular nor managers in general became professionalized over this period in Britain. This is well demonstrated by the survey conducted by Nichols in the early 1960s – he concluded that the managers he interviewed

> cannot be regarded as professionals. They lack professional management qualifications and were seldom members of professional bodies. They have a low level of participation in such bodies. And, most important, they deny the legitimacy of such bodies and very rarely accept even the *existence* of a body of management theory. (1969: 88–9)

Moreover, of those few managers identifying themselves as professionals, none of them considered that they were professional *managers*.

Third, there was a much slower and less marked development of non-productive workers in British industry (compared with the USA or Germany). Thus in 1930 while the ratio of non-productive to productive workers was 17.9% in American manufacturing industry, it was only 11.3% in Britain (see Sargent Florence 1948: 143, although see Burgess 1980: 203–4).

Fourth, educational qualifications continued to play a relatively less important role in British industry – in particular, Nichols maintained that there was only a 'limited and late development of institutions concerned with higher management education' (1969: 90). By contrast Kocka suggests that in Germany even by 1930 formal education was especially important for the recruitment of salaried entrepreneurs (1978: 583).

Fifth, the labor movement was not weakened in Britain in the way in which it was in the USA through the early deskilling effected through scientific management. At the same time there was a slower development of a successful industrial economy in Britain which could generate the high wages necessary to convert the trade unions into the kind of business unionism characteristic of the USA.

Sixth, formal educational qualifications played a less significant role in the UK as compared with the USA. Education in Britain remained far more tied to the pre-existing elite structures and was characterized by 'sponsored' rather than the 'contest' pattern as found in the USA (see Turner 1961).

Finally, there was much less development of the range of social sciences associated with assessing the output and characteristics of industrial workers. These were not seen as aspects which could be assessed scientifically; and as a consequence the social sciences did not develop to the same degree as in the USA or in such close harmony with the processes of occupational professionalization as found in American universities.

The most telling summary of the differences between the UK and the USA can perhaps in this respect be found in Oscar Wilde's *The importance of being earnest*. Lady Bracknell says of education in Britain:

> I do not approve of anything that tampers with natural ignorance. Ignorance is like a delicate exotic fruit; touch it and the bloom is gone. The whole theory of modern education is unsound. Fortunately in England, at any rate, education produces no effect whatsoever. If it did, it would prove a serious danger to the upper classes, and probably lead to acts of violence in Grosvenor Square.

References

Abercrombie, N. and J. Urry 1983. *Capital, labour and the middle class*. London: Allen and Unwin.

Aitken, H. G. J. 1960. The economy, management and foreign competition. In G. Roderick and M. Stephens (eds), *Where did we go wrong? Industrial performance, education and the economy in Victorian Britain* 13–32. Lewes: Falmer.

Baritz, L. 1960. *The servants of power*. Westport, Conn.: Greenwood Press.

J. Urry

Bedaux, C. 1917. *The Bedaux efficiency course for industrial application*. Bedaux Industrial Institute.

Bendix, R. 1956. *Work and authority in industry*. Chichester: Wiley.

Benenson, H. 1982. The reorganization of US manufacturing industry and workers' experience, 1880–1920: a review of bureaucracy and the labour process by Dan Clawson. *Insurgent Sociologist* **11**, 65–81.

Blau, P. and O. D. Duncan 1967. *The American occupational structure*. New York: Wiley.

Bledstein, B. J. 1976. *The culture of professionalism*. New York: Norton.

Braverman, H. 1974. *Labor and monopoly capital*. New York: Monthly Review Press.

Brech, J. 1982. *Strike*. Boston: South End Press.

Brody, D. 1980. *Workers in industrial America*. Oxford: Oxford University Press.

Brown, E. H. and M. H. Browne 1968. *A century of pay*. London: Macmillan.

Brown, E. Richard 1980. *Rockefeller medicine men*. Berkeley: University of California Press.

Brown, G. C. 1935. AFL report on the Bedaux system. *American Federationist* **42**, 936–43.

Burawoy, M. 1978. Towards a Marxist theory of the labour process: Braverman and beyond. *Politics and Society* **3–4**, 247–312.

Burgess, K. 1980. *The challenge of labour*. London: Croom Helm.

Burrage, M. 1972. Democracy and the mystery of the crafts. *Daedalus* (Fall), 141–62.

Buttrick, J. 1952. The inside contract system. *J. Econ. Hist.* **12**, 205–21.

Cadbury, E. 1914a. Some principles of industrial organization: the case for and against scientific management, *Sociol. Rev.* **7**, 99–125.

Cadbury, E. 1914b. Reply to C. B. Thompson. *Sociol. Rev.* **7**, 266–9.

Chandler, A. D. 1976. The development of modern management structures in the US and UK. In L. Hannah (ed), *Management strategy and business development*, 23–51. London: Macmillan.

Chandler, A. D. 1980. The United States. Seedbed of managerial capitalism. In A. D. Chandler and H. Daems (eds), *Managerial hierarchies*, 9–40. Cambridge, Mass.: Harvard University Press.

Church, R. L. 1974. Economists as experts: the rise of an academic profession in the United States, 1870–1920. In L. Stone (ed), *The university in society*, vol. 2, 571–610. Oxford: Oxford University Press.

Clawson, D. 1980. *Bureaucracy and the labour process*. New York: Monthly Review Press.

Coleman, D. C. 1973. Gentleman and players. *Econ. Hist. Rev.* **26**, 92–116.

Copley, F. B. 1923. *Frederick W. Taylor*, 2 vols. New York: Harper & Row.

Debray, R. 1981. *Teachers, writers, celebrities*. London: Verso.

Devinat, P. 1927. *Scientific management in Europe*. Geneva: ILO.

Disco, C. 1979. Critical theory as ideology of the new class. *Theory and Society* **8**, 159–214.

Dubofsky, M. 1983. Workers movement in North America, 1873–1970. A preliminary analysis. In I. Wallerstein (ed), *Labor in the World Social Structure*, 22–43. Beverly Hills: Sage.

Elbourne, E. T. 1914. *Factory administration and accounts*. London: Longman.

Elliott, P. 1972. *The sociology of the professions*. London: Macmillan.

Foner, P. S. 1955. *History of the labour movement in the United States*, vol. 2. New York: International Publishers.

Frankel, M. 1955. Obsolescence and technical change in a maturing economy. *Am. Econ. Rev.* **45**, 296–319.

Goldthorpe, J. 1982. On the service class, its formation and future. In A. Giddens and G. Mackenzie (eds), *Social class and the division of labour*, 162–85. Cambridge: Cambridge University Press.

Haber, S. 1964. *Efficiency and uplift: scientific management in the progressive era, 1890–1920.* Chicago: Chicago University Press.

Hannah, L. 1976. *The rise of the corporate economy.* London: Methuen.

Herman, E. S. 1981. *Corporate control, corporate power.* Cambridge: Cambridge University Press.

Hill, S. 1982. *Competition and control at work.* London: Heinemann.

Hobsbawm, E. 1964. *Labouring men.* London: Weidenfeld & Nicolson.

Hobson, J. A. 1913. Scientific management. *Sociol. Rev.* **6**, 197–212.

Hobson, J. A. 1922. *Incentives in the new industrial order.* London: Parsons.

Ingham, G. 1982. Divisions within the dominant class and British 'exceptionalism'. In A. Giddens and G. Mackenzie (eds), *Social class and the division of labour,* 209–27. Cambridge: Cambridge University press.

Kocka, J. 1978. Entrepreneurs and managers in German industrialisation. In P. Mathias and M. M. Postan (eds), *Cambridge economic history of Europe,* vol. 7, 492–589. Cambridge: Cambridge University Press.

Kocka, J. 1980. *White collar workers in America, 1890–1940.* London: Sage.

Kolko, G. 1963. *The triumph of conservatism.* New York: Free Press.

Larson, M. S. 1977. *The rise of professionalism: A sociological analysis.* Berkeley: University of California Press.

Larson, M. S. 1980. Proletarianisation and educated labour. *Theory and Society* **9**, 131–75.

Lasch, C. 1977. The siege of the family. *New York Review of Books* **24**, 15–18.

Lash, S. and J. Urry 1984. The new marxism of collective action: a critical analysis. *Sociology* **18**, 33–50.

Layton, E. 1971. *The revolt of the engineers.* Cleveland: Press of Case Western Reserve University.

Layton, E. 1974. The diffusion of scientific management and mass production from the US in the twentieth century. *Int. Cong. Hist. Sci.* **4**, 377–86.

Levine, A. L. 1967. *Industrial retardation in Britain, 1880–1914.* London: Weidenfeld & Nicolson.

Litterer, J. 1963. Systematic management: design for organizational recoupling in American manufacturing firms. *Business Hist. Rev.* **37**, 369–91.

Littler, C. 1978. Understanding taylorism. *Br. J. Sociol.* **29**, 185–202.

Littler, C. 1980. *The bureaucratisation of the shop-floor: the development of the modern work-system.* PhD thesis, University of London.

Littler, C. 1982a. Deskilling and changing structures of control. In S. Wood (ed), *The degradation of work,* 122–45. London: Hutchinson.

Littler, C. 1982b. *The development of the labour process in capitalist societies.* London: Heinemann.

Livingstone, P. 1969. Stop the stopwatch. *New Society* 10 July, 49–51.

Maier, C. 1970. Between taylorism and technocracy: European ideologies and the vision of industrial productivity in the 1920s. *J. Contemp. Hist.* **5**(2), 27–61.

Marshall, A. 1938. *Principles of economics.* London: Macmillan.

Montgomery, D. 1979. *Workers' control in America.* Cambridge: Cambridge University Press.

Mulhern, F. 1981. 'Teachers, writers, celebrities', intelligentsias and their histories. *New Left Review* **126**, 43–59.

Nadworny, M. J. 1955. *Scientific management and the unions, 1900–1932.* Cambridge: Mass.: Harvard University Press.

Nelson, D. 1975. *Managers and workers, origins of the new factory system in the United States, 1880–1920.* Madison, Wis.: University of Wisconsin Press.

Nelson, R. 1959. *The merger movement in American industry 1895–1956.* Princeton NJ: Princeton University Press.

Nichols, T. 1969. *Ownership, control and ideology*. London: Allen & Unwin.

Noble, D. 1979. *America by design*. Oxford: Oxford University Press.

Palmer, B. 1975. Class, conception and conflict: the thrust for efficiency, managerial views of labour and the working class rebellion, 1903–22. *Rev. Radical Polit. Econ.* **7**, 31–49.

Perkin, H. 1961–2. Middle class education and employment in the nineteenth century: a critical note. *Econ. Hist. Rev.* **14**, 122–30.

Person, H. 1929. *Scientific management in American industry*. The Taylor Society, New York: Harper.

Pichierri, A. 1978. Diffusion and crisis of scientific management in European industry. In S. Giner and M. Archer (eds.), *Contemporary Europe*, 55–73. London: RKP.

Pollard, S. 1965. Trade unions and the labour market, 1870–1914. *Yorks. Bull. Econ. and Soc. Research* **17**.

Pollard, S. 1969. *The development of the British economy, 1914–67*. London: Edward Arnold.

Renner, K. 1978. The service class. Repr. in T. Bottomore and P. Goode (eds.), *Austro-Marxism*. 249–52. Oxford: Clarendon Press.

Rubinstein, W. D. 1977. Wealth, elites and class structure in Britain. *Past and Present* **76**, 99–126.

Sabolo, Y. 1975. *The service industries*. Geneva: ILO.

Sargant Florence, P. 1948. *Investment, location, and size of plant*. Cambridge: Cambridge University Press.

Shadwell, A. 1906. *Industrial efficiency*, 2 vols. London: Longman.

Shadwell, A. 1916. The welfare of factory workers. *Edinburgh Rev*. October, 375–6.

Shanks, M. 1963. The comforts of stagnation. In A. Koestler (ed.), *Suicide of a nation?* 51–69. London: Hutchinson.

Soffer, B. 1960. A theory of trade union development: the role of the 'autonomous' workman. *Lab. Hist*. **1**, 141–63.

Stark, D. 1980. Class struggle and the transformation of the labour process. *Theory and Society* **9**, 89–130.

Stone, K. 1974. The origin of job structures in the steel industry. *Rev. Rad. Polit. Econ.* **6**, 113–73.

Taylor, F. W. 1947. *The principles of scientific management*. New York: Harper.

Thompson, C. B. 1917. *The theory and practice of scientific management*. Boston: Houghton Mifflin.

Thompson, E. P. 1967. Time, work-discipline, and industrial capitalism. *Past and Present* **38**, 56–97.

Touraine, A. 1974. *The academic system in American society*. New York: McGraw Hill.

TUC Report 1933. *Bedaux Report*.

Turner, R. H. 1961. Modes of social ascent through education: sponsored and contest mobility. In A. H. Halsey, J. Floud and C. A. Anderson (eds.), *Education, economy, and society*, 121–39. New York: Free Press.

Urry, J. 1986. The growth of scientific management: transformation in class structure and class struggle. In N. Thrift and P. Williams (eds.), *The making of urban society*. London: Routledge & Kegan Paul (forthcoming).

Urwick, L. 1929. *The meaning of rationalisation*. London: Nisbet.

Urwick, L. and E. F. L. Brech 1946. *Management in British industry*. London: Management Publications Trust.

Walker, P. (ed.), 1979. *Between labour and capital*. New York: Monthly Review.

Webb, S. 1918. *The works manager today*. London: Longman.

Wiebe, R. H. 1967. *The search for order*. London: Macmillan.

Wiener, M. J. 1981. *English culture and the decline of the industrial spirit, 1850–1980.* Cambridge: Cambridge University Press.

Wood, S. and J. Kelly 1982. Taylorism, responsible autonomy and management strategy. In S. Wood (ed.), *The degradation of work?* 74–89. London: Hutchinson.

4

Technological imperatives and modern corporate strategy

EDWARD J. MALECKI

The prominence of technology in the economic competitiveness of firms and nations is one of the more striking and visible phenomena of recent years. At the corporate level, the established practice of corporate strategy increasingly includes technology in an important, and often central, role. It is difficult, if not impossible, to address issues of regional change without explicitly focusing on the corporate activities that take place within a region. These activities may range from headquarters and administrative functions, to research and development, production of products at small or large volumes, and distribution. Each activity faces a different degree of external pressure to change, and responds in ways that directly affect regional development. In particular, the mobility of most production and the relative immobility of non-production activities greatly influences the ways in which regions can adapt and change in response to rapid global economic change.

This chapter begins by setting a context, common in the business and management literature, that stresses the competitive environment in which firms (and nations and regions) must operate. The corporate response to competition in recent years has centered around a 'corporate strategy' framework that includes dimensions of choices that a firm can make. The role that product and process technology plays in these decisions is reviewed, and the context is transferred to that of corporate location decisions for manufacturing and for research and development activity. Finally, the regional development implications are reviewed in terms of the evolution of regional markets in response to technological change.

Corporate strategy

The topic of corporate strategy now holds a hallowed place in the education and literature of business and management, although the concept originated only in the early 1960s (Chandler 1962). Strategy is the determination of long-term goals for an enterprise, the adoption of courses of action, and the allocation of resources needed to meet the firm's goals. Nearly all the early work on corporate strategy focused on growth via a set of firm-expanding strategies: expansion of volume, geographical dispersion, vertical integration, and product diversification (Chandler 1962: 14). Most of Chandler's work and the body of research based upon it has focused on the necessary changes in corporate structure associated with growth from a single product firm to a multiproduct, multiplant, and multinational firm. The end-product of the evolution of the typical corporation is a multidivisional (or global) firm that must coordinate the activities of each of its rather distinct product-line divisions (Galbraith & Nathanson 1978).

Much, perhaps most, of the corporate strategy literature is concerned with the firm's portfolio of activities and its diversification into new lines of business (Day 1975, Sutton 1980, Yavitz and Newman 1982). Two sources of external influence are important in this view: the product life cycle and the competitive environment (the activities of other firms). The product life cycle incorporates the monopoly power allowed an innovator, who can reap a high level of profits even when sales are quite small (Markusen 1982, Von Hippel 1983). Imitators may chip away slowly at the market and its profits as the market grows and sales increase. Alternatively, the imitators can quickly usurp the market with a radically better product design or a process technology that permits production at a very low price. The activities of competitors pose a threat primarily through behavior that can change the basis of competition, either from product to process or from process to product (Williams 1983). In the management literature, firms generally are thought to specialize in either process technology or new product innovation, but are rarely successful at both. Process technology, especially standardized production and minor modifications, is concerned primarily with cost reduction. Product innovation serves to differentiate products, whether by their quality or innovativeness or by their focus on particular market niches (Hayes & Wheelwright 1979, Hall 1980, Porter 1980, Williams 1983).

The managerial literature on corporate strategy has shifted in recent years to accommodate the technological capability of firms, either for product or for process innovation. This capability is usually embodied in and measured by the amount of organized research and development (R & D) activity undertaken (Kantrow 1980). Most R & D is for new products and product improvements, whether on short-term, low-risk projects or long-term, high-risk projects (Mansfield 1981). Interfirm variations in R & D levels (such as the percentage of sales devoted to R & D) are partially explainable in terms of sectoral characteristics that make innovation easier, for example, in newer industries such as electronics and more difficult in an older industry such as paper products[1]. Where these inter-industry variations do not account for observed differences, a 'corporate culture' that influences strategy is currently considered to explain intra-industry differences. This culture is either pro- or anti-technology, and reflects the degree of risk and the speed of feedback (e.g. profits) from decisions (Deal and Kennedy 1982, Frohman, 1982). Taken together, then, industry characteristics and corporate culture are utilized by the managerial perspective to impose constraints or boundaries around potential corporate strategies. The level of financial commitment to R & D is somewhat independent of the strategy chosen, and is perhaps more a function of peer pressure (industry norms) and inertia (corporate culture). However, the strategy of the firm with respect to innovation and change will somewhat influence the way in which its resources are spent (Freeman 1982).

The plethora of writing on corporate strategy has led to attempts to impose order on the diverse array of ways in which firms respond to competition. Two principal types of strategies focus on the extreme ends of the product life cycle and emphasize the alternative strengths that a firm may wish to emphasize. *Overall cost leadership* requires high levels of capital investment, process engineering skills, and the design of products for ease of manufacturing (Hayes & Wheelwright 1979, Porter 1980). Cost leadership, because it stresses minimization of production costs, makes use of standardized production processes that permit mass production (Abernathy & Utterback 1978, Utterback 1979). The second general type of strategy may be termed *differentiation*, to encompass novelty and uniqueness both through genuine innovativeness and through perhaps minor differences in product characteristics, such as design, flavor, or quality[2]. A corporate emphasis on product differentiation is typically thought to depend on R & D capability, coordination between R & D and marketing, and amenities to attract skilled and creative people (Porter 1980: 41)[3].

The distinction between cost leadership and product differentiation is, of course, difficult to make in all cases. Some product designs may facilitate lower cost production, thereby confounding the conventional distinction between product and process technology (Porter 1983a). Porter (1983b), for example, attributes Japanese success in the television set market to a design based on integrated circuits and related changes that facilitated automated assembly and testing. In other industries, such as machine tools or chemicals, efforts toward product innovation are continuous, although perhaps not at the same level as in electronics or pharmaceuticals. In addition, the products of these industries are used as inputs by firms in other sectors, and may be utilized as manufacturing process improvements in the latter.

A further feature is the level of corporate R & D associated with different strategies. Kay (1982) concluded that, at the industry level, firms are more diversified as the rate of technological change in the industry increases. In low technology industries, strategies favor specialization, and most diversification is in highly related areas. The work of Soukup and Cooper (1983) on the electronic components sector supports this as well, finding that firms which have large market shares in older products also tend to develop broad lines in newer technologies. In a sense, we are back to the 'corporate culture' notion, wherein firms either emphasize R & D or not and, if they do, tend to keep abreast of developments by competitors and to respond relatively quickly to those threats. The continual development of new products aimed at specific niches has also shortened the customary product life cycles to which firms have responded. A constant and high level of innovation and marketing effort is thought to be needed to keep sales curves rising (Goldman 1982, Swan & Rink 1982, *Business Week* 1983b).

Corporate strategy can be summarized at one level as the choice among different general paths to growth, including diversification, vertical integration, and market expansion (Caves 1980). These paths are primarily based

on the patterns of growth of a hypothetical firm, and are useful for understanding the impacts of merger and acquisition (Leigh & North 1978),
rationalization of production (Watts 1974), and plant closures (Healey
1982). However, these traditional categories of growth strategies may not
be very informative concerning the responses of firms to technological
pressures such as shorter product life cycles, decreasing benefits from long
production runs, and the need for a constant, high level of innovation.
These pressures have shifted current emphasis in some firms to niche-
product development and marketing strategies, for which the competitive
basis of standardized large-volume production is less important (*Business
Week* 1983b).

Corporate strategy and location

The literature on corporate strategy as it concerns corporate location and
regional impact is rather homogeneous. It takes the sequential model of firm
growth and puts it in the context of geographic expansion from a single
location to global activity (Krumme & Hayter 1975, Erickson & Leinbach
1979, Hakanson 1979, Watts 1980). Growth, both organizational and spatial,
comes about largely through a combination of market growth (and spatial
spread), acquisitions and mergers, diversifications, and product development. By far the greatest amount of interest has been on diversification and
mergers and acquisitions, because their spatial effects are most easily
observed (Hakanson 1979, Watts 1980). The patterns observed are by now
well known: the two previously separate corporate networks are consolidated; redundant headquarters and R & D facilities are closed, as are the least
competitive plants and other establishments (Leigh & North 1978, Watts
1981, Smith & Taylor 1983). New branch plants are established in areas that
promise favorable labor conditions, such as low wages and avoidance of
unionization (Cobb 1982, Schmenner 1982).

To an extent not noticed until recently, the location decisions of firms are
clearly divided into two principal types, defined by the labor force needs of
the firm for a given establishment. Production workers, data entry operators,
and others whose work is standardized and routine are available in a large
number of locations. Some firms, such as Emerson Electric, have made
location in rural, non-union areas part of their explicit strategy of low-cost
production (*Business Week* 1983a). Lower wages and benefits are demanded
by workers in small towns and rural areas of developed countries and, for
routine work tasks, the availability of even lower wages in most Third World
countries is associated with the global dispersal of manufacturing
employment (Ross 1983). The mobility of firms and the knowledge that
other low (or lower) wage sites are available allow firms to have a ready
supply of acceptable locations (Goodman 1979, Cobb 1982). The lack of
unionization, a good 'business climate,' and the availability of female labor
represent the package of low-cost, flexible labor desired for routine production (Browning 1980, Schmenner 1982, Harrison 1984). (The 'objective'
management concern for labor cost minimization of authors like Browning

and Schmenner avoids mention of tactics that manipulate unskilled labor, emphasized by Harrison 1984 and Storper and Walker 1984.)

At the same time, corporate activities requiring professional and technical labor are constrained in different ways. Unlike unskilled labor which is rather immobile, educated workers are able generally to choose the locations where they work, given the relative scarcity of technical skills. This is especially true of scientists and engineers, whose availability is the most important location factor for corporate R & D location (Browning 1980). Recruiting and retaining engineers and capable managers is typically the overriding concern in the location decisions of high-technology companies, and the phrase 'quality of life' is used to represent the combination of good educational, cultural, and recreational amenities desired by these workers (Schmenner 1982: 134–5, Riggs 1983). Only metropolitan area sites tend to be considered, at least in part because of the rise of two-career families for whom occupational alternatives and residential stability are a desirable combination.

Competitive pressure has produced two sets of technological responses by firms: a dependence on product innovation, even in more mature industries, and more rapid development of standardized production, which can often be accomplished with automated equipment even at relatively low volumes. The focus on product innovation has sparked a large amount of R & D activity in large corporations and, in innovative industries, among small competitors as well. The locus of competitiveness, however, lies not only on R & D and product development, but also on process technology that can manufacture products of high quality at competitive cost. It is here that the automated plants of Japanese firms have become the model for other firms in electronics and related sectors (Ferguson 1983, Porter 1983b).

The growing sophistication of automated processes itself has two important effects on the labor needs of firms. First, the pressure to reduce costs through some degree of automation, even for products with relatively short lives, means that process-related R & D must take place alongside product design. Thus automated plants tend to be 'closer to home' (e.g. Albuquerque, Fort Lauderdale, or Portland rather than overseas) for electronics and computer firms, and in urban areas rather than small towns because of the increased need for engineers on site. As automation reduces the need for unskilled labor, the advantages of low-wage rural and Third World plants are diminished. R & D of some type therefore takes place at a large number of the automated facilities; large-scale basic research and product-innovation effort are still very concentrated in a few facilities within each firm. Second, process automation has greatly reduced the level of skill required in production tasks. 'Deskilling' of work tasks by automation has eliminated the need for many of the skilled craftsmen of earlier industrial times. This has resulted in a 'vanishing middle' of the skill spectrum, eliminating skilled workers entirely at many plants while increasing the proportion both of unskilled workers and of professional-technical workers (although the absolute number of the latter remains small; Massey 1979, Weiss 1983, Harrison 1984). Although skilled craftsmen remain important in some sectors, such as aircraft and instruments, their dominant role in manufacturing is past. The norm now is to standardize tasks to the greatest extent possible, in order to reduce the costs and the geographic immobility imposed by a dependence on scarce skill. This is a high priority in the computer software industry, which is especially dependent on educated, skilled workers. Firms in the industry are attempting to standardize programming to some degree so that work can be decentralized away from the high-cost San Francisco and Los Angeles regions preferred by 'supertech' workers on whom the firms still rely for software design (Hall *et al*. 1983).

Technological change, corporate strategy, and regional development

The prospects for regional development in nearly all nations have decreased as our understanding of the regional implications of corporate actions grows. Stöhr (1982) provides a long list of qualitative and structural variables or side-effects that describe regional conditions, but which have been ignored in most regional research. To a large degree these qualitative issues (such as external control, innovative ability, and the mix of jobs) are avoided merely because of lack of published data (Mercer 1984), thus necessitating extensive fieldwork and case study (Sloan 1981, Markusen 1983, Harrison 1984). However, it is more likely that the nature of locational decisions is so contradictory that no single pattern exists (Storper & Walker 1983, 1984). Further, even with detailed research, the outsider will be unable to identify the crucial strategies or cultures of firms concerning location, although it may be possible to deal reasonably well with individual location decisions or with broad patterns (Bluestone & Harrison 1982, Harrison, 1984).

The two corporate concerns of product differentiation and cost control largely define the range of corporate actions. Cost control has led primarily to the global dispersal of branch manufacturing plants to areas of low wage labor. It has also led to well-located automated plants in areas where R & D and engineering workers are willing to live. For other places, such as industrial cities whose labor forces have traditionally demanded high wages and working conditions, the short-term prospect (unemployment) is poor and the long-term prospect (low-paying jobs mainly in services) is also not very attractive (Harrison 1982, 1984).

Product differentiation, including product innovation and improvements, has two sets of implications. The first is the inevitability of replacement by a newer, better, or cheaper product. This means that plants and areas where a product is produced face a constantly changing product mix as part of corporate strategy (Healey 1981). Secondly, it also means that places where R & D and product innovation take place are those best suited for surviving cyclical downturns, rationalization, and plant closures that result from cost minimization strategies. As Thwaites (1983) has shown for Britain, employment decline occurred at all types of plants, but least of all at establishments where R & D was one of the firm's activities. This simple empirical finding could result from a number of separate, but related, factors. Industries with high levels of R & D are more likely to be producing products for which demand is growing at all plants in the industry. More attractive is the possibility that, in large, multi-locational firms, employment gains are largely restricted to sites where newer products are developed and produced (Thwaites 1982).

The spatial effect from these two dominant corporate strategies is a 'spatial division of labor' that appears to be pervasive in contemporary regional development (Storper & Walker 1984)[4]. The phenomenon is well documented for France (e.g. Aydalot 1978, Lipietz 1980, Savey 1983) and the UK (Hamilton 1978, Goddard 1979, Massey 1979). In what appears to be a persistent and global regional problem, regions are acquiring distinctive specializations, based not on industrial sectors, but on the different corporate activities and labor forces present. Savey's (1983) three-way categorization is useful in this regard. She distinguishes not only central areas or zones where R & D and administrative activities are found, and low-wage, mainly rural zones, but also a third type of zone where highly skilled labor and technical sophistication are declining but still persist. The decline of skilled-labor zones is taking place through two processes observed elsewhere as well: (a) technological sophistication, which allows a replacement of skilled by unskilled workers; and (b) geographical transfer to other parts of the world or to the low-wage rural zones. Skilled labor regions will always be needed by firms in those sectors where mass production is not possible because of product characteristics, but it would seem that there are relatively few regions in any country that contain these essential pools of skilled labor (Hekman 1980, Oakey 1981), just as there are not many 'world cities' of economic control (Friedmann & Wolff 1982) or R & D regions (Malecki 1980). There are, on the other hand, many places where low-wage jobs are considered improvements over conditions of unemployment or seasonal employment.

One issue that is raised by these observations on corporate regional specialization or division of labor pertains to the prospects for growth and development of regions. Growth may occur in a region, providing jobs and general economic expansion, at the same time as its long-term development potential is declining. Those are the concerns raised by Stöhr's (1982) proposal to look at the 'side-effects' of conventional growth patterns. Koch et al. (1983) make the seldom-mentioned observation that the phenomenal growth in the US Sunbelt is almost exclusively in branch plant activities, whereas few R & D or innovative activities have either been moved in by corporations or grown up locally. The fear (also not often expressed in the US) is that this recent growth is in many instances probably only short term and will not survive the next round of corporate cost-cutting, when a large number of plants will be vulnerable to the attraction of even low wages in the Third World countries.

Even in 'high-tech' regions, massive changes in the labor market are casting shadows on bright long-term regional prospects. Harrison (1982, 1984) has vividly shown that the Boston region's growth is associated with a widening schism between well-paid, administrative and technical jobs on the one hand and low-paying, low-skill jobs on the other. Markusen (1983) and Weiss (1983) note similar processes at work in the San Francisco Bay ('Silicon Valley') area. Noyelle (1982) contends that in those few urban areas where decision making is a major part of the economic base future growth prospects are best. Other, production oriented centers face long-term decline. A recent German study by Pfaff and Hurler (1983) reinforces this view even in the short term. They found that regional labor markets characterized by high percentages of primary (managerial, technical, professional) workers had lower unemployment rates from 1967 to 1977.

The resulting dualism within regions, then, is a complex phenomenon. At the same time that some regions are growing, attracting or creating new businesses, and withstanding cyclical downturns fairly well, they are also witnessing the proliferation of dead-end jobs in which upward mobility is slight (Noyelle 1982, Harrison 1984). This may well be the set of ideal conditions for regional growth in the short term. The creation of new jobs through local R & D might mean a small number of professional-level or primary jobs and a large number of low-level service and production jobs. However, we really have very little knowledge about the actual multiplier effects of R & D or decision functions.

Global corporations best illustrate the explicit incorporation of location into strategies for competitiveness. In the automobile industry, for example, components for manufacture are now frequently made in a set of locations where labor costs can be controlled (Holmes 1983). Reich (1984) maintains that Japanese automobile firms such as Toyota are now quite willing to undertake production and to purchase high percentages of parts in countries that require it, because they are retaining in Japan the knowledge-based and sophisticated components and portions of production (such as design) on which their distinctiveness depends.

Conclusion

The focus on corporate strategy as a perspective on regional development has both advantages and disadvantages. Among the advantages is the fact that it helps to explain the dualistic nature of corporate activity as it ultimately affects places and regions. The two-pronged nature of competition, based on low cost production and innovativeness, serves to condense the range of corporate activities into two distinctive categories of activities. The techno-logical and management functions concerned with decision making, new products and product differentiation comprise a set of choices and behaviors that are fundamentally different from cost-reduction functions. Competition based on cost pressure involves a variety of production-related decisions that include capital investment, plant modernization, production relocation and consolidation, and bargaining to reduce labor costs.

The impact of labor on the location of corporate activity in these two functions is considerable. Professional workers operate in a national, even international, labor market in which they have considerable mobility and in which they can exert locational preferences. Firms must locate where the workers live or are willing to live. Unskilled workers for routine production tasks in branch plants are typically immobile and tied to local labor markets. Consequently, firms need only seek out sites with the most attractive set of labor market conditions (Clark 1981, Cobb 1982, Cooke 1983, Harrison

E. J. Malecki

1984). The skilled labor needed in some industries (e.g. aircraft, instruments) is similar to professional labor, but tends to be somewhat less mobile. Firms depend on their skills and must locate themselves where a sufficient agglomeration is located. This has been true in instruments (Oakey 1981) and in the machine tool industry as it evolves into robotics (Berry 1984). The trend toward niche markets and smaller production volume, however, is not likely to require skilled workers to the extent that it once did, because of the trend toward automated production (*Business Week* 1984a).

Regional prospects for development are different from the potential for job growth in the short term. As branch-plant economies without significant innovative or decision making activities proliferate, more regions essentially find themselves moving toward the periphery of economic life, with similar downward movement for labor in those regions. There will still be jobs in these places, but a markedly lower level of job than was the norm during earlier times of industrial prosperity. The places where decision making and R & D jobs agglomerate are themselves internally dualistic, since they rely on both the primary labor force and on a large number of low-wage production and service workers (Noyelle 1982, Saxenian 1983). Even though all jobs cannot be in high value-added products, activities, or sectors, a local mix focused in such specialties might be the best possible in the current situation (Malecki 1984). How might corporate strategies and their effects change in the future? The prospects are either very dim, where virtually all human production labor will be replaced by automated machines (Leontief 1983), or very rosy, as we rise up on the next Kondratiev wave (Norton & Rees 1979, Rostow 1983). The actual future is likely to be somewhere in between, with geographically and socially uneven consequences.

Notes

1 R & D spending as a percentage of sales ranges from an average of 7.4% for software firms to 0.6% in the steel industry, 0.4% in the tobacco industry, and 0.8% in textiles and apparel (*Business Week* 1984b).
2 The minor nature of most new products has prompted Haustein and Maier (1980) to call them 'pseudo-innovations.'
3 The amenities that are attractive to technical workers comprise principally *urban* amenities – the range of goods, services, entertainment and recreational opportunities generally found to a greater extent in large urban regions. It should not be confused with climate or warm temperatures frequently used in migration studies.
4 Cooke (1983) refers to this phenomenon as 'labor market discontinuity.'

References

Abernathy, W. J. and J. M. Utterback 1978. Patterns of industrial innovation. *Technol. Rev.* **80** (June–July), 40–7.
Aydalot, P. 1978. L'aménagement de territoire en France: une tentative de bilan. *L'Espace Géographique* **7**, 245–53.
Berry, B. J. L. 1984. *Robotics, the labor force and regional development*. Paper presented at

the Symposium on Technology and Regional Development: The Policy Issues, Syracuse University, April 1984.

Bluestone, B. and B. Harrison 1982. *The deindustrialization of America*. New York: Basic Books.

Browning, J. E. 1980. *How to select a business site*. New York: McGraw-Hill.

Business Week 1983a. Emerson Electric: high profits from low tech. April 4, 58–62.

Business Week 1983b. Marketing: the new priority. November 21, 96–106.

Business Week 1984a. The revival of productivity. February 13, 92–100.

Business Week 1984b. A deepening commitment to R & D. July 9, 64–78.

Buswell, R. J. 1983. Research and development and regional development: a review. In *Technological change and regional development*, A. Gillespie (ed.), 9–22. London: Pion.

Caves, R. E. 1980. Industrial organization, corporate strategy, and structure. *J. Econ. Lit.* **18**, 64–92.

Chandler, A. D. 1962. *Strategy and structure*. Cambridge, Mass.: MIT Press.

Clark, G. L. 1981. The employment relation and spatial division of labor: a hypothesis. *Ann. Assoc. Am. Geog.* **71**, 412–24.

Cobb, J. C. 1982. *The selling of the South: the southern crusade for industrial development 1936–1980*. Baton Rouge: Louisiana State University Press.

Cooke, P. 1983. Labour market discontinuity and spatial development. *Prog. Human Geog.* **7**, 543–65.

Day, G. S. 1975. A strategic perspective on product planning. *J. Contemp. Business* **4**, 1–34.

Deal, T. E. and A. A. Kennedy 1982. *Corporate cultures: the rites and rituals of corporate life*. Reading, Mass.: Addison-Wesley.

Erickson, R. A. and T. R. Leinbach 1979. Characteristics of branch plants attracted to nonmetropolitan areas. In *Nonmetropolitan industrialization*, R. E. Lonsdale and H. L. Seyler (eds.), 57–78. New York: Winston/Wiley.

Ferguson, C. H. 1983. The microelectronics industry in distress. *Technol. Rev.* **86** (Aug.–Sept.), 24–37.

Freeman, C. 1982. *The economics of industrial innovation*, 2nd edn. Cambridge, Mass.: MIT Press.

Friedmann, J. and G. Wolff 1982. World city formation: an agenda for research and action. *Int. J. Urban and Regional Research* **6**, 307–43.

Frohman, A. L. 1982. Technology as a competitive weapon. *Harvard Business Rev.* **60** (Jan.–Feb.), 97–104.

Galbraith, J. R. and D. A. Nathanson 1978. *Strategy implementation: the role of structure and process*. St. Paul: West Publishing.

Goddard, J. B. 1979. Office development and urban and regional development in Britain. In P. W. Daniels (ed.), *Spatial patterns of office growth and location*, 29–60. New York: Wiley.

Goldman, A. 1982. Short product life cycles: implications for the marketing activities of small high-technology companies. *R & D Management* **12**, 81–9.

Goodman, R. 1979. *The last entrepreneurs: America's regional wars for jobs and dollars*. New York: Simon & Schuster.

Hakanson, L. 1979. Towards a theory of location and corporate growth. In *Spatial analysis, industry and the industrial environment*. Vol 1: *Industrial systems*, F. E. I. Hamilton and G. J. R. Linge (eds.), 115–38. New York: Wiley.

Hall, P., A. R. Markusen, R. Osborn, and B. Wachsman 1983. The American computer software industry: economic development prospects. *Built Environment* **9**(1), 29–39.

Hall, W. K. 1980. Survival strategies in a hostile environment. *Harvard Business Rev.* **58** (Sept.–Oct.), 75–85.

Hamilton, F. E. I. 1978. Aspects of industrial mobility in the British economy. *Regional Studies* 12, 153–65.

Harrison, B. 1982. The tendency toward instability and inequality underlying the 'revival' of New England. *Pap. Regional Sci. Assoc.* 50, 41–65.

Harrison, B. 1984. Regional restructuring and 'good business climates': the economic transformation of New England since World War II. In *Sunbelt/snowbelt: urban development and regional restructuring*, L. Sawers and W. K. Tabb (eds.), 48–96. New York: Oxford University Press.

Haustein, H. D. and H. Maier 1980. Basic improvement and pseudo-innovations and their impact on efficiency. *Technol. Forecasting and Social Change* 16, 243–65.

Hayes, R. H. and S. C. Wheelwright 1979. Link manufacturing process and product life cycles. *Harvard Business Rev.* 57 (Jan.–Feb.), 133–40.

Healey, M. J. 1981. Product changes in multi-plant enterprises. *Geoforum* 12, 357–70.

Healey, M. J. 1982. Plant closures in multi-plant enterprises – the case of a declining industrial sector. *Regional Studies* 16, 33–51.

Hekman, J. S. 1980. Can New England hold onto its high technology industry? *New England Econ. Rev.* (March–April), 35–44.

Holmes, J. 1983. Industrial reorganization, capital restructuring and locational change: an analysis of the Canadian automobile industry in the 1960s. *Econ. Geog.* 59, 251–71.

Kantrow, A. M. 1980. The strategy–technology connection. *Harvard Business Rev.* 58 (July–Aug.), 6–21.

Kay, N. M. 1982. *The evolving firm: strategy and structure in industrial organization*. London: Macmillan.

Koch, D. L., W. M. Cox, D. W. Steinhauser, and P. V. Whigham 1983. High technology: the Southeast reaches out for growth industry. *Econ. Rev. Federal Reserve Bank of Atlanta* 68 (Sept.), 4–19.

Krumme, G. and R. Hayter 1975. Implications of corporate strategies and product cycle adjustments for regional employment changes. In *Locational dynamics of manufacturing activity*, L. Collins and D. F. Walker (eds.), 325–56. New York: Wiley.

Leigh, R. and D. J. North 1978. Regional aspects of acquisition activity in British manufacturing industry. *Regional Studies* 12, 227–45.

Leontief, W. 1983. Technological advance, economic growth, and the distribution of income. *Pop. and Devel. Rev.* 9, 403–10.

Lipietz, A. 1980. Inter-regional polarization and the tertiarisation of society. *Pap. Regional Sci. Assoc.* 44, 3–17.

Malecki, E. J. 1980. Corporate organization of R and D and the location of technological activities. *Regional Studies* 14, 219–34.

Malecki, E. J. 1984. High technology for local economic development. *J. Am. Plann. Assoc.* 50, 262–9.

Mansfield, E. 1981. How economists see R & D. *Harvard Business Rev.* 59 (Nov.–Dec.), 98–106.

Markusen, A. R. 1982. *The sectoral differentiation of regional economies*. Paper presented at the North American Regional Science Association Meetings, Pittsburgh, November.

Markusen, A. R. 1983. High-tech jobs, markets and economic development prospects: Evidence from California. *Built Environment* 9(1), 18–28.

Massey, D. 1979. In what sense a regional problem? *Regional Studies* 13, 231–41.

Mercer, D. 1984. Unmasking technocratic geography. In *Recollections of a revolution*, M. Billinge, D. Gregory, and R. Martin (eds.), 153–99. London: Macmillan.

Norton, R. D. and J. Rees 1979. The product cycle and the spatial decentralization of American manufacturing. *Regional Studies* 13, 141–51.

Noyelle, T. J. 1982. The implications of industry restructuring for spatial organization in the United States. In *Regional analysis and the new international division of labour*, F. Moulaert and P. W. Salinas (eds.), 113–33. Boston: Kluwer-Nijhoff.

Oakey, R. P. 1981. *High technology industry and industrial location*. Aldershot: Gower.

Oakey, R. P. 1983. New technology, government policy and regional manufacturing employment. *Area* **15**, 61–5.

Pfaff, M. and P. Hurler 1983. Employment policy for regional labor markets. *Environment and Planning C: Government and Policy* **1**, 163–78.

Porter, M. E. 1980. *Competitive strategy*. New York: Free Press.

Porter, M. E. 1983a. The technological dimension of competitive strategy. In *Research on technological innovation, management, and policy*, R. S. Rosenbloom (ed.), vol. 1, pp. 1–33. Greenwich, Conn.: JAI Press.

Porter, M. E. 1983b. *Cases in competitive strategy*. New York: Free Press.

Reich, R. B. 1984. Collusion course. *The New Republic*, February 27, 18–21.

Riggs, H. E. 1983. *Managing high-technology companies*. Belmont, Calif.: Wadsworth.

Ross, R. S. J. 1983. Facing Leviathan: public policy and global capitalism. *Econ. Geog.* **59**, 144–60.

Rostow, W. W. 1983. Technology and unemployment in the Western world. *Challenge* **26** (March–April), 6–17.

Savey, S. 1983. Organization of production and the new spatial division of labour in France. In *Spatial analysis, industry and the industrial environment*. Vol. 3, *Regional Economics and Industrial Systems*, F. E. I. Hamilton and G. J. R. Linge (eds.), 103–20. New York: Wiley.

Saxenian, A. 1983. The urban contradictions of silicon valley: regional growth and the restructuring of the semiconductor industry. *Int. J. Urban Regional Res.* **7**, 237–62.

Schmenner, R. W. 1982. *Making business location decisions*. Englewood Cliffs, NJ: Prentice-Hall.

Sloan, C. 1981. A good business climate: what it really means. *The New Republic* (Jan.) 3–10, 12–15.

Smith, I. J. and M. J. Taylor 1983. Takeover, closures and the restructuring of the United Kingdom ironfoundry industry. *Environ. Plann. A* **15**, 639–61.

Soukup, W. R. and A. C. Cooper 1983. Strategic responses to technological change in the electronic components industry. *R & D Management* **13**, 219–30.

Stöhr, W. 1982. Structural characteristics of peripheral areas: the relevance of the stock-in-trade variables of regional science. *Pap. Regional Sci. Assoc.* **49**, 71–84.

Storper, M. and R. Walker 1983. The theory of labour and the theory of location. *Int. J. Urban Regional Res.* **7**, 1–41.

Storper, M. and R. Walker 1984. The spatial division of labor: labor and the location of industries. In *Sunbelt/snowbelt: urban development and regional restructuring*, L. Sawers and W. K. Tabb (eds.), 19–47. New York: Oxford University Press.

Sutton, C. J. 1980. *Economics and corporate strategy*. Cambridge: Cambridge University Press.

Swan, J. E. and D. R. Rink 1982. Fitting market strategy to varying product life cycles. *Business Horizons* **25** (Jan.–Feb.), 72–6.

Thwaites, A. T. 1982. Some evidence of regional variations in the introduction and diffusion of industrial products and processes within British manufacturing industry. *Regional Studies* **16**, 371–81.

Thwaites, A. T. 1983. The employment implications of technological change in a regional context. In *Technological change and regional development*, A. Gillespie (ed.), 36–53. London: Pion.

Utterback, J. M. 1979. The dynamics of product and process innovation in industry. In *Technological innovation for a dynamic economy*, C. T. Hill and J. M. Utterback (eds.), 40–65. New York: Pergamon.

E. J. Malecki

Von Hippel, E. 1983. Increasing innovators' returns from innovation. In *Research on technological innovation, management and policy*. R. S. Rosenbloom (ed.). Vol. 1, pp. 35–53. Greeenwich, Conn.: JAI Press.

Watts, H. D. 1974. Spatial rationalization in multi-plant enterprises. *Geoforum* **17**, 69–76.

Watts, H. D. 1980. *The large industrial enterprise*. London: Croom Helm.

Watts, H. D. 1981. *The branch plant economy*. London: Longman.

Weiss, M. A. 1983. High-technology industries and the future of employment. *Built Environment* **9**(1), 56–60.

Williams, J. R. 1983. Technological evolution and competitive responses. *Strategic Mgmt. J.* **4**, 55–65.

Yavitz, B. and W. H. Newman 1982. *Strategy in action*. New York: Free Press.

5

The organization and locational structure of production subcontracting

JOHN HOLMES

. . . it is premature to assign this method of organizing the labour process to the dustbin of anachronistic forms.
(Rubery & Wilkinson 1981: 118)

The subcontracting of production continues to be an important feature of the organization and locational structure of a number of industrial sectors in the advanced capitalist economies. Take, for example, the automotive industry in Canada. The industry consists of two major subsectors which have significantly different organizational structures: the automobile assembly sector and the automotive parts and components sector. The former is characterized by marked concentration and centralization of production. Assembly is carried out in very large-scale foreign-owned plants, using archetypal fordist techniques of production and a highly organized and unionized work-force. On the other hand, the parts and components sector is characterized by a large number of firms of varying size. Plants in this sector range from small workshops employing less than half a dozen people to large factories employing over 700 workers, and there is considerable variation in the degree of sophistication of the technology and technical organization of production used. Many of the plants are owned and operated by small independent Canadian companies. Complex and extensive linkages, including a variety of subcontracting relationships, exist between the large 'primary sector' multinational firms in the assembly sector and what at first glance appear to be small independent competitive firms (so called 'secondary sector' firms) in the parts and components sector.

Similar arrangements have been noted in the automotive industries of other countries and in other sectors such as electronics, metal-working and textiles (Watanabe 1971, Friedman 1977, Taylor & Thrift 1982). In fact, 'secondary' industrial sectors and 'secondary' forms of production and employment such as subcontracting and outwork appear to be far more prevalent and persistent in advanced industrial economies than had been thought previously. Until recently, conventional wisdom (in both neo-classical and marxist economic analysis) had considered such phenomena to be marginal or archaic features of advanced capitalism which would eventually disappear through the continued and progressive rationalization and centralization of production and capital[1]. Therefore, subcontracting and outwork were viewed as being of little material importance or theoretical interest and consequently have been largely ignored by economic theory. However, such 'secondary' forms of production organization and employment not only have persisted but, in the context of the current restructuring crisis in the world economy, appear to have taken on a new significance and to be playing an important role in the restructuring of certain industrial sectors at both the international and intranational scale. For example, international subcontracting linked to the development of free trade and export processing zones has become an important element of the international development strategies advocated by agencies such as UNIDO and the World Bank (UNIDO 1974, UNCTD 1975, UNCTD 1979, Berthomieu & Hanaut 1980). Empirical evidence suggests that over the last decade and a half there has been a significant decentralization of production and corresponding increase in the number of 'secondary' sector firms and in the use of subcontracting and outwork in advanced industrial countries such as France and Italy (Berger & Piore 1980, Mattera 1980, Berger 1981, Sabel 1982, Murray 1982, Brusco 1982), and a resurgence of homeworking and 'sweatshop' operations in the heart of major metropolitan areas such as New York, Los Angeles, London and Toronto (Wolin 1981, Ross & Trachte 1983, Harrison 1983, Johnson & Johnson 1983).

Therefore, the persistence and even expansion in the use of a wide range of marginalized labor combined with evidence of a vertical disintegration of production in advanced as well as declining sectors of industrial production calls for a reappraisal of the material and theoretical significance of different forms of production and labor organization such as subcontracting and outwork. The objective of this chapter is to examine the role that the subcontracting of production and related labor market segmentation plays in the organization of industrial production in advanced capitalist economies, and the implications of these forms of production organization for the locational structure of industry.

The chapter falls into two major sections. The first section begins with a brief review and critique of the way in which interfirm linkages (of which subcontracting relationships are clearly but one subset) have been dealt with traditionally in economic geography. It goes on to develop a working definition of subcontracting and to identify and describe briefly a number of different forms of subcontracting. The second section of the chapter attempts to analyze the form, causes and dynamics of production subcontracting. This analysis is based on an extensive review of the existing literature on subcontracting and labor market segmentation and an initial exploratory empirical analysis of subcontracting relationships in three specific sectors of the Canadian economy: the automotive, electronics and clothing industries. The chapter concludes that a full and adequate explanation of production subcontracting will require multicausal explanations and, in all likelihood, will include considerations of the structure of technology and work organization, the nature of product markets, control over the labor process and labor supply conditions.

Interfirm linkages, subcontracting and location theory

Linkage analysis in economic geography

Subcontracting relationships comprise one subset of a myriad of interrelationships which exist between firms and which are often manifested in an observable pattern of material and information flows and linkages between pairs of firms. Such linkages have been the focus of a significant amount of research in industrial geography over the last decade and a half. It is not the intention of this chapter to provide an exhaustive review and critique of the literature on industrial linkage analysis. The literature is voluminous and good critical reviews exist elsewhere (Taylor & Thrift 1982, Scott 1983a). However, it is pertinent to provide a brief characterization of the problematic within which the majority of linkage studies in economic geography have been conducted and to raise a number of criticisms which can be levelled against this genre of study[2]. While reviews identify a number of different types of linkage study (Taylor & Thrift 1982), this discussion is framed in the context of microlevel studies of material linkages between firms, since these are most relevant to our ultimate interest in subcontracting.

The form and content of much of the research on linkages between industrial firms have been shaped by a number of common underlying methodological and theoretical presuppositions. The latter include a heavy reliance on the conceptualization of the market economy and of the nature of the firm provided by neo-classical economic theory, a view of the nature of economic geography which abstracts and focuses upon the spatial aspects of industry and industrial organization as its principal object of study, and the adoption of a positivistic approach to scientific explanation.

Notwithstanding a number of serious and damaging critiques, the ahistorical models of the market economy and of the firm derived from neo-classical economic theory continued to exercise considerable influence on contemporary industrial location theory throughout the 1970s. In neo-classical economic theory, with its emphasis on the individual firm and household and on the analysis of market exchanges between individual economic actors, it is assumed that firms engage in cost-rational decision making independent of each other. These assumptions, in combination with others, imply that interactions between firms occur through the market place where individual firms meet as equals. Thus, in this view, linkages occur either between different plants and divisions of a single firm or as the result of arm's-length transactions between a manufacturer and independent suppliers regulated by the market. As several writers have pointed out, one consequence of incorporating such a model into the locational analysis of interplant linkages is that such analyses tend to ignore the unequal relationships of power and dependence which lie behind those linkages that result from arrangements such as subcontracting, franchising, licensing and trade credit (Fredriksson & Lindmark 1979, Taylor & Thrift 1982). Furthermore, although in reality there exists a large number of permutations for the organization of the production of any one product, both between and within firms, conventional economic theory has commonly only focused upon the two alternative modes for the organization of production hinted at above: internal organization through vertical integration, or external organization by arm's-length transactions between firms regulated by the free market (Friedman 1977). Sheard succinctly summarizes this position and its limitation:

> for any input to the production process a firm has two options – to produce the input in its own factories or purchase it from other firms via the free market. Profit maximising firms are presumed to choose the least cost method of these two alternatives. However, between the two extremes of internal organization (in house production) and free market transactions lies a spectrum of intermediate interfirm arrangements including production through a subsidiary or affiliate, subcontracting, and monopsonistic power over suppliers. Most of these intermediate modes are not treated explicitly by economic theory but may in fact be more typical than the polar modes of internal organization and free market transactions. (Sheard 1983: 51)

Thus subcontracting relationships have been consistently under-emphasized in both neo-classical economic theory and the location theory which is derived from it.

A large proportion of the geographical research on industrial linkages has sought to correlate the geographical dimensions of linkage structures (both static and dynamic) with various measures of industrial organization such as plant size and ownership characteristics. In general, the results of this research suggest that both the size of establishment and external ownership are positively correlated with the magnitude and spatial extent of the firm's linkages. In reviewing this literature both Scott and Taylor and Thrift emphasize the sparsity of the generalizations that have been yielded by the considerable volume of research conducted on industrial linkages, and also the ambiguity of many of the findings (Taylor & Thrift 1982, Scott 1983a). The paucity of the findings of this research stem from two features of the problematic within which it is couched. First, the research focuses almost exclusively on the spatial dimensions of linkages as the object of study. Secondly, much of the research reflects a positivist commitment to seeking generalizations in the form of regular relationships that are found to exist between observable phenomena, in this instance the search for regular relationships between the spatial extent of linkages and various independent measures of industrial organization. Consequently, the concept of 'linkage' in much of this literature is a classic example of what Sayer has called a 'chaotic conception' (Sayer 1982)[3]. The over-riding research question of 'what are the spatial effects of linkages?' has focused the analysis on the geographical dimensions of linkages while ignoring the causal processes which have produced the linkages. If we want to understand the nature of a particular class of linkages we must understand the conjuncture of processes and circumstances which have generated those linkages. However, the linkage research literature is replete with instances where the spatial characteristics of very different types of linkages drawn from a wide range of very different types of industries and firms are indiscriminately abstracted and lumped together for the purposes of analysis. It is no wonder that this research has yielded little in the way of substantive insights and/or unambiguous findings.

Therefore, the aim of this chapter is to attempt to make the concept of 'linkage' a little less chaotic by focusing upon one 'species' of interfirm linkage, namely those linkages which result from production subcontracting relationships, and by stressing the need to understand such linkages in terms of the underlying mechanisms and processes which produce them. Subcontracting arrangements are clearly linked to the organization of production processes and, more particularly, to the decomposition of specific labor processes. Consequently, the analysis presented in the latter half of the chapter seeks to understand the nature and causes of subcontracting in the context of a theoretical understanding of the tendencies inherent in the capital accumulation process and the evolving nature of the labor process and the firm under capitalism.

The nature of subcontracting

'Subcontracting' is itself something of a 'chaotic conception'! The term is used loosely and often ambiguously in the literature, and several writers have distinguished a number of identifiable 'subspecies' of subcontracting relationships between firms (Houssiaux 1957a, Sallez & Schlegel 1963, Watanabe 1971, Sharpston 1975, Chaillou 1977, Friedman 1977). However, it is generally agreed that formally the term 'subcontracting' refers to a situation where the firm offering the subcontract requests another independent enterprise to undertake the production or carry out the processing of a material, component, part or subassembly for it according to specifications or plans provided by the firm offering the subcontract. Thus, subcontracting differs from the mere purchase of ready-made parts and components from suppliers in that there is an actual contract between the two participating firms setting out the specifications for the order. However, in some industries, such as the automotive and electronics industries, this distinction between 'supplier' and 'subcontractor' is indeed an extremely fine one. Furthermore, the distinction between subcontracts and contracts is also vague and ill defined. Once again, this is certainly the case in the automotive industry. Some writers would argue that work done by a direct supplier of parts and components for a manufacturer should be classified technically as either a straightforward market transaction or as contracted out work, but not as subcontracted work. However, as Friedman points out, amongst suppliers to the automotive industry the term 'subcontracting' is often used to refer to relations such as those noted above which might be more narrowly defined as simply contracted out relations. This leads Friedman and others to use the term subcontracting 'loosely to refer to situations when suppliers produce parts and components to specifications set out in advance by the large manufacturers, whether materials are issued or not and whether the contract is directly with the large manufacturer or through some intermediary contract with another supplier' (Friedman 1977: 119). In the subsequent discussion we will adopt this 'loose' definition and (following Sheard) will simply refer to the firm issuing the subcontracted work as the 'parent firm' and that undertaking the work as 'the subcontractor.'

The first major distinction between different types of subcontracting can be drawn on the basis of whether the parent firm is either a wholesaler or retailer on the one hand or a manufacturer on the other. Watanabe has labelled these two types of subcontracting commercial and industrial subcontracting respectively (Watanabe 1971: 54)[4]. The focus in this chapter is on studies of industrial subcontracting, but it must be emphasized that commercial subcontracting is an important feature of the organization of a number of retail sectors and particularly those involving clothing, food and appliances[5]. In these sectors large chain retailers satisfy their demands for their own brandname lines of merchandise by subcontracting the production of the merchandise to a number of relatively small and economically far less powerful manufacturers. Rainnie provides an excellent account of such relationships in the UK clothing industry (Rainnie 1984). He notes, for example, that one chain retailer, Marks and Spencer, purchases approximately one-fifth of the total output of the UK clothing industry and is supplied by over 800 firms, many of whom 'sell their soul to St. Michael (the M & S brandname) on the basis of no more than batch by batch contracts' (Rainnie 1984: 149).

Even within the category of industrial subcontracting various writers have attempted to differentiate further between different types of subcontracting arrangements. Such differentiation has been attempted, for example, on the basis of the technical character of the subcontracted work (Sharpston 1975), the source of materials required for the subcontracted work (Taylor & Thrift 1982), the durability and stability of the relationship between parent and subcontractor (Sharpston 1975), and the nature and form of the business relationship between parent and subcontractor (Sharpston 1975). One of the most rigorous and comprehensive attempts to develop a typology of subcontracting is that of Chaillou (1977). This typology is developed around three considerations. He begins by evaluating the degree to which decisions about the conception, design and specification of the subcontracted part, the design of the labor process to produce the part, and the actual fabrication of the part reside with the subcontractor or with the parent firm. At one exteme, if all these decisions are the prerogative of the parent firm then one is faced with a situation akin to vertically integrated production. At the other extreme, where the subcontractor makes all these decisions, the situation is that of an independent supplier. Therefore, at the two extremes one is considering a situation which does not strictly involve subcontracting, but between the two extremes lie a variety of subcontracting arrangements. Secondly, Chaillou considers the structure of the market for the subcontracted part, whether the market is strictly competitive, monopolistic or tending to oligopoly. Finally, he considers whether or not the parent firm is fabricating the part in one of its own plants at the same time as putting out some of the production of the part to the subcontractor. Although Chaillou's typology identifies and describes seven distinct subcategories of subcontracting, for simplicity he collapses them into three major categories which are referred to frequently in the French literature on subcontracting (Houssiaux 1957b,

Sallez 1972, Bayle–Ottenheim *et al*. 1973, Vennin & de Banville 1975, Lafont *et al*. 1982), and have equivalents in the English language literature. These three major categories are as follows:

(a) Capacity subcontracting (*sous-traitance de capacité*, also sometimes referred to as *sous-traitance conjuncturelle* (Vennin & de Banville 1975), concurrent subcontracting (Scott 1983b), or cyclical subcontracting (Watanabe 1971)). In this case only the fabrication of the subcontracted part is carried out by the subcontractor according to a detailed set of plans and specifications set down by the parent firm, and usually the parent firm will also be manufacturing a proportion of its total requirement for the part within one of its own plants. In effect, concurrent subcontracting 'involves the farming out of overflow work that could normally be done in house except for a current excess of orders relative to installed operating capacity' (Scott 1983b: 242). The parent firm and the subcontractor thus engage in similar work and are mutually competitive by nature, in the sense that once demand slackens they must compete with each other for orders.

(b) Specialization subcontracting (*sous-traitance de spécialité*, also sometimes referred to as *sous-traitance structurelle* (Vennin & de Banville 1975), complementary subcontracting (Scott 1983b) or vertical quasi integration (Blois 1972)). In this case the decisions about both the method of fabrication and fabrication itself are usually taken by the subcontractor and the part is not produced in house by the parent firm. Therefore, the parent firm and the subcontractor are engaged in different but complementary production, and whereas capacity subcontracting represents a horizontal disintegration of production, specialization subcontracting represents a vertical disintegration of production (Scott 1983b: 242). Some authors suggest that specialization subcontracting often utilizes more technologically sophisticated labor processes as compared with the simpler and more labor-intensive labor processes which characterize capacity subcontracting. It appears that capacity subcontracting is far more common in West European countries such as Italy and France while specialization subcontracting is the predominant form of subcontracting in North America (Watanabe 1971: 58, Berger & Piore 1980: 106).

(c) Supplier subcontracting (*sous-traitance fourniture*). The third of Chaillou's categories has received relatively little attention from other authors[6]. It refers to a situation where the subcontractor is in many respects an independent supplier with full control over the development, design and fabrication of its product, but is willing to enter into a subcontracting arrangement to supply a dedicated or proprietary part to the parent firm. This form of of subcontracting is particularly prevalent in the automobile, aerospace and certain segments of the electronics industries.

The explanation and dynamics of production subcontracting

Having sought in the first part of this chapter to identify and describe the principal types of production subcontracting relationships that exist between firms, our attention now turns to a search for explanations for the existence of such relationships. This section also contains brief discussions of the temporal dynamics and locational structure of subcontracting relationships.

Explanations of production subcontracting

The subcontracting relationships that exist between large and small firms raise some interesting theoretical questions. Why do large manufacturers tolerate the existence, and even actively encourage the creation, of small firms and enter into subcontracting arrangements with them? There is now fairly general agreement that these relationships are a persistent and structural, rather than ephemeral, feature of advanced capitalist production, but the reasons for their existence are disputed. For example, with respect to the European auto industry some writers have argued that the subcontracting of some parts production provides assembly firms with increased managerial flexibility to adjust output to marked fluctuations in product demand (Friedman 1977, IWC 1978). However, other writers have reported that they have found no empirical evidence to support this thesis and argue that the subcontracting relationship hinges instead upon the high levels of internal efficiency which can be achieved within relatively small parts firms (Fredriksson & Lindmark 1979).

In fact, a survey of the literature on production subcontracting reveals numerous explanations for the phenomenon. These explanations encompass a wide variety of factors and circumstances which are identified by different writers as being of prime 'causal' importance in explaining the existence of subcontracting. However, despite the diversity of explanations, it is possible to identify three broad sets of explanatory hypotheses: those based on (a) the structure and temporal stability of product markets, (b) the fixed capital requirements of the production process and the nature of the production technology used in the labor process, and (c) the structure and nature of labor supply conditions and, in particular, the questions of labor cost minimization and control over the labor process (Rubery & Wilkinson 1981: 115). These three major sets of factors interact in determining the extent to which production is 'subcontracted' in any particular industrial sector or region, and 'in doing so they give form to the structure of the labour market and the structure of production' (Brusco & Sabel 1981: 103). The latter is an extremely important point since many analyses tend to view subcontracting as either one element of labor market segmentation or as one aspect of industrial organization. Rarely are the links made between these two generally discrete bodies of theory. Therefore, in order to understand the nature of subcontracting fully it is necessary to consider together the results of research into both the structure of industrial organization and the structure of labor markets.

Many of the individual analyses of subcontracting tend to consider only one or two factors as the prime causes of subcontracting. However, although the origins of all forms of subcontracting can be explained with reference to the uneven dynamics of capitalist development, the more specific causes of subcontracting are both multiple and interrelated. Consequently, an under-standing of the full range of circumstances under which production subcon-tracting becomes a feasible strategy for capital in the organization of production systems must be multicausal in nature.

There are two recurrent themes which run through much of the literature on subcontracting. First, the idea that the primary benefit accruing to parent firms from their subcontracting relations is flexibility and, secondly, that the relationship between parent and subcontractor is one of unequal economic power. The latter situation enables the parent to exercise and benefit, to the detriment of the subcontractor, from the flexibility afforded it by subcontracting.

There are clearly some benefits to the subcontractor of entering into a subcontracting relationship with a large parent firm. Such benefits include a guaranteed market for its product, assistance and economies in securing raw materials for the subcontracted work, and the provision of technical and managerial assistance to the subcontractor by the parent firm (Watanabe 1971). However, the overwhelming consensus is that usually the relationship is a very unequal and that the relatively strong position of parent firms enables them to benefit at the expense of their subcontractors. In their study of artisan production in Italy, Brusco and Sabel do identify a group of small firms engaged in subcontracting which appear to stand in a very different relationship to their parent firms (Brusco & Sabel 1981). They label this phenomenon 'independent decentralization' and describe it as follows:

> in contrast to the clients of dependent small firms who place precise orders, often supplying tools, raw materials, special machines and detailed blueprints themselves, the customer of an independent, small firm typically comes with a problem to solve . . . he needs, for example, a gear shift for a new kind of small tractor . . . even if the customer has a blueprint he is much more likely to pose the problem than answer it. The job for the small firm is to find some technically and economically feasible solution to the problem thus creating a new product and defin-ing the customer's needs at the same time. (Brusco & Sabel 1981: 106)

Clearly, there are some similarities between the situation described by Brusco and Sabel and Chaillou's category of supplier subcontractor which we noted in the first part of the chapter.

Much of the literature that the following discussion draws upon tends to analyze subcontracting almost exclusively from the point of view of the flexibility it affords to larger capitals in their organization of production. Thus there is a danger of viewing subcontracting as being simply 'functional' for large capital. However, it should be stressed that subcontracting also creates the possibility for the existence of small independent entrepreneurial capital. For example, Sabel points out that in Italy a number of the owners of small firms involved in subcontracting in the metal-working industry had formerly been militant workers:

> near Modena, in Emilia-Romagna, many beneficiaries of the decen-tramento produttivo [in the 1970s] were Socialist and Communist

artisans who had gone into business for themselves in the early 1950s after a series of bitter strikes at the Officine Meccaniche Reggiane, a large engineering firm; near Turin, many shops were founded by skilled workers expelled from the factories during the political purge of the 1950s. (Sabel 1982: 221)

Similarly Scase and Goffee stress the opportunities opened up to small entrepreneurs by subcontracting in the building industry (Scase & Goffee 1982).

Each of the three sets of explanatory hypotheses identified above will now be discussed in more detail.

THE STRUCTURE AND TEMPORAL STABILITY OF PRODUCT MARKETS

There are a number of circumstances related to the structure and temporal stability of product markets which favor the development of subcontracting. These include the situation where the parent firm is engaged in manufacturing a product for which demand is uncertain or irregular because of cyclical or seasonal variations in demand; secondly, the case where sufficient demand to permit the continuous mass production of a particular product line simply never exists; and, thirdly, the market conditions that exist at the beginning and end of a particular product cycle.

In the first instance, subcontracting becomes one means of 'production smoothing' for the parent firm which enables it to reduce production costs directly with output. One of the better-known and more rigorous analyses of 'dualism' in product markets is provided by Piore (Berger & Piore 1980). Piore's analysis is based upon the premise that firms, faced with cyclical demand for their products, decompose the total demand for the product into a stable and an unstable component. The former is determined by the demand at the bottom of the troughs in the cyclical demand curve and the unstable component is equal to the difference between actual demand and the stable component of demand. Sabel summarizes Piore's model as follows:

> according to the model, not peak or average demand, but that demand for a product that persists at the lowest point in the industries' business cycle determines the degree of development of the division of labour. Progress in the division of labour depends on increased investment in product-specific equipment and forms of organization. Because they are more product-specific, the new techniques cannot be put to alternative use during downturns as easily as the old. To ensure that expensive machinery and workers with narrowly defined skills are always sufficiently employed, production capacity must therefore keep step with changes in the stable component of demand . . . the model thus suggests that each branch of industry or group of firms producing related goods can be divided into two sectors. The primary sector (or core) . . . will employ the technologically most advanced division of labour and will satisfy the stable component of demand. The secondary sector, composed of competitive, peripheral firms, will use less-refined and less-product-specific techniques of production; it will principally satisfy the fluctuating component of demand. (Sabel 1982: 35)

A number of writers, but most notably Friedman (1977), have argued that this type of mechanism is the principal cause lying behind the subcontracting of parts production in the automotive industry. They argue that the automotive industry has traditionally been faced with a highly cyclical pattern of demand, in response to which the large automobile assembly firms have developed in-house capacity to produce parts to meet the stable component of demand and have subcontracted the unstable component to a variety of smaller parts procedures. Thus during downturns in demand the auto assemblers avoid the responsibility and costs for idle specialized fixed capital and the lay-off of workers which are borne by the small subcontracting parts firms[7]. A similar arrangement has been noted in the North American electronics industry by Susman and Schutz, who write: 'competitive firms are explicity used as an employment buffer by IBM. This helps IBM maintain a 100% employment policy in which its employees are guaranteed jobs at their salary level' (Susman & Schutz 1983: 174). However, this arrangement depends critically on the continued presence of subcontractors ready to meet expanded levels of production once demand picks up again. Therefore, subcontractors cannot be allowed to fail *en masse* during downturns. Parent firms employ a number of strategies to guard against this eventuality. For example, Susman and Schutz note that IBM has a rule that a supplier may not do more than 30% of its business with IBM. The purpose of this rule is to try and ensure that competitive subcontracting firms remain viable during IBM market downturns and are able to resume production on short notice (Susman & Schutz 1983: 174). In their study of the Swedish car industry Fredriksson and Lindmark remark that 'in the majority of cases the transactions between buying companies and contractors were designed so that the volumes of the flows of material were largely regulated by the turnover of the buying companies. Production was not 'taken home' to any great extent even during recessions, since the buying company was anxious to remain in contact with its contractors pending the expected economic upswing' (Fredriksson & Lindmark 1979: 168).

The use of subcontracting to achieve 'production smoothing' is clearly an instance of capacity subcontracting and can be expected to increase in scale during periods of rapid market expansion and to be significantly curtailed during downturns in demand.

Firms also use subcontracting where the demand for the product is simply insufficient to engage in large-scale capital-intensive mass production using fordist techniques. For example, Piore suggests that in the garment industry the stable portion of demand is comprised of such items as work clothes and jeans which are largely factory produced, whereas the unstable component of demand such as quality ladies' and children's fashionware, for which demand is both limited in scale and highly volatile because of fashion changes, is unsuited to factory production and is largely contracted out (Berger & Piore 1980: 68). Similarly, in the electronics industry the assembly and testing of unstandardized printed circuit boards is often subcontracted (Scott 1983c: 360).

A third instance where the structure of the market clearly influences the degree of subcontracting occurs towards the beginning and end of so-called product cycles. Two examples will illustrate the point. Currently, in the microelectronics sector, technical product innovation as much as cost minimization is a key competitive strategy pursued by firms (Sayer & Morgan 1983). The speed with which a new product moves from the design stage to production is crucial to its success or failure on the market. Therefore, the firm developing the product will often subcontract its initial production to firms who have already installed capacity to produce the product, or at least its major subcomponents, in small batches. As soon as the product is established in the market and a certain minimum volume of demand has been attained, then the parent firm will take the production of the product in-house. At the other end of the product cycle, cost minimization is often crucial to firms seeking to retain a toehold in a declining market and again such firms may well resort to subcontracting in order to survive. This in large measure explains the resurgence and proliferation of subcontracting and homeworking[8] in the North American apparel industry where, in the face of intense international competition from low-wage offshore producers, many firms would be forced out of business if they had to pay the capital costs, overhead, and higher labor costs associated with in-factory production (Johnson & Johnson 1983, Ross & Trachte 1983, Harrison 1983).

PRODUCTION TECHNOLOGY AND LABOR PROCESS ORGANIZATION

The second major group of hypotheses which have been advanced to explain subcontracting are related to the technical characteristics and fixed capital costs of the production technology used in the production process. Here one of the prime reasons for the development of subcontracting is that different stages of the production process may have different levels of minimum efficient scale. For example, if one part of a firm's production process requires an efficient scale of production considerably greater than the firm's own requirements for the part, subassembly or process, this 'part' tends to be separated off from the main production process and put out to a subcontractor. The latter, by working for a number of parent firms, can achieve a larger and more efficient scale of operation than any individual parent firm could have achieved for that particular process or part. In many of these instances the subcontractor will utilize highly sophisticated production technology.

This type of subcontracting is clearly an example of what was defined as specialization subcontracting earlier in the chapter. It is prevalent in the automotive sector where the minimum efficient scale for many parts is far in excess of the demands of any one assembly plant. In his study of the printed circuit board industry in Los Angeles, Scott reports that many firms subcontract out such specialized operations as drilling, multilayer laminating and solder fusing which involve relatively heavy expenditures on fixed capital goods, and that 'subcontracting is then a means of collectivizing work tasks so as to avoid the heavy cost penalties incurred in the partial or inefficient use of capital' (Scott 1983c: 359). Rubery and Wilkinson also identify this form of subcontracting in the shoe industry, where the minimum efficient scale for cutting the leather uppers is much higher than for sewing the uppers together (Rubery & Wilkinson 1981: 121).

A similar but slightly different form of specialization subcontracting is characteristic of those sectors where it is possible to fragment the production process without having to resort to inferior process technology or any loss in productivity. In particular, this occurs in processes where economies of scale can be attained at the level of the individual machine rather than the factory; for example, sewing in the garment industry. As Brusco stresses, 'economies of scale should be calculated in the first instance for phases of production and the economies which result from the juxtaposition of similar operations are often negligible' (Brusco 1982: 172).

It has also been suggested that a shortage of capital, or the need to save capital, on the part of parent firms will encourage the development of specialization subcontracting. This is one of the reasons frequently cited to explain the complex development of specialized subcontracting hierarchies in Japanese industries. For example, Sheard writes of the Japanese automotive industry:

> small and medium sized engineering firms in the 1950s and 1960s represented a pool of potential subcontractors which the auto makers could control with minimum capital outlay . . . developing a subcontracting relationship with a medium sized engineering firm was in most cases a more cost efficient method of obtaining a supply of a particular part than takeover of the firm or inhouse production. Scarce financial and managerial resources could then be used to secure the most modern and efficient plant and equipment for final vehicle assembly. (Sheard 1983: 57)

Similarly the parent firm may be able to conserve its own productive capital by reducing its own inventory of parts to a minimum and forcing the subcontractor to absorb the cost of circulating capital needed to maintain an adequate buffer level of stocks.

Underlying each of the above strategies is the desire by the parent firm to segment capital in order to benefit from the enhanced economies and flexibility that such segmentation affords.

THE STRUCTURE AND NATURE OF LABOR SUPPLY CONDITIONS

Four interrelated but distinct aspects of the structure and nature of labor supply have been posited as influencing the extent to which subcontracting will take place in a particular sector. In addition to the relatively straightforward questions of the cost and availability of labor there are questions about the nature of labor relations and the attempt by management to retain as much flexibility and control as possible with respect to the organization of the labor process.

Subcontracting to minimize and control labor costs   Subcontracting provides an important means of minimizing the costs of variable capital to the parent firm since it acts as both a mechanism ensuring wage discipline and as a method for segmenting the labor force (Friedman 1977, Berger & Piore 1980, Rubery & Wilkinson 1981, Sabel 1982, Scott 1983c). If labor supply is not homogeneous and if variable capital can be purchased at different prices then subcontracting can be used to exploit supplies of the cheapest labor (Rubery &

Wilkinson 1981: 123). Thus in those industrial sectors where wage differentials between large and small firms are relatively large it might be expected that subcontracting relationships would be more widespread and that there would be a tendency to subcontract the most labor-intensive portions of the production process.

The wage discipline forced upon the competitive subcontracting sector is discussed by Gouverneur (1982: 142–3). He argues that:

> the price of the subcontracted commodity can be kept very low through the unequal relation prevailing between the two enterprises: the large enterprise is in a position to impose not only the norms of production but also the price; the small enterprise is obliged to accept these conditions, all the more since subcontracting is generally a matter of its elimination or survival. But the small enterprise, in order to survive as a capitalist enterprise, must enjoy a minimal rate of profit. Because of the low prices imposed by the large enterprise, it will be under pressure to reduce its variable capital per unit through imposing lower hourly wage rates on its workers . . . Both lower wages and longer labour time are indeed usual in small-scale subcontracting enterprises, which means a higher rate of exploitation. (Gouverneur 1982: 143)

Thus Gouverneur argues that subcontracting has a two-fold effect on rates of profit in that it increases the average rate of surplus value through a higher rate of exploitation of the workers employed by the subcontractor, and it creates the potential for a transfer of surplus revenue from the subcontractor to the parent firm through the low regulated price imposed by the latter on the former[9].

Where trade unions are strong in parent firms, employers seek to avoid the homogenization of work conditions and rates of pay throughout the plant. A plant which employs workers of diverse types is particularly dangerous from the point of view of capital since it creates the possibility that a strong union may be able to establish the wages and conditions of the best of workers as the standard for all. In such cases the parent firm through the careful use of subcontracting can homogenize the labor force within the parent firm and thus control the cost of variable capital (Sabel 1982). In some cases this process will lead to marked spatial divisions of labor within the industry (Storper & Walker 1983, Holmes 1983). Interviews with purchasing managers in automotive assembly plants suggest that this is a prime motive behind the subcontracting of much lower skilled parts production in the North American automotive industry, given the relatively generous compensation and benefits packages won by the United Automobile Workers' Union (UAW) for workers employed by the large automakers, both on the assembly line and in in-house parts production.

Subcontracting to retain flexibility with respect to variable capital
Parent firms may not only use subcontracting to capture the benefits of differences in the price of labor but also to be able to treat labor as a variable cost of production. Although capital costs are usually viewed as being relatively fixed and labor costs relatively variable, as Sabel emphasizes, what

a variable cost is depends on the structure of capital and labor markets (Sabel 1982: 48). The effect of strong worker organization is to create 'a differentiated wage structure and to establish property rights in jobs through agreements to increase job security and establish seniority systems, guaranteed wages and hours or [sic] work, sickpay, holiday pay and the like . . . these measures reduce flexibility in the use of labor and capital seeks to evade them by resorting to the subcontract system' (Rubery & Wilkinson 1981: 123). Again this is clearly a concern in the North American automotive industry where the UAW through the development of the SUB (Supplementary Unemployment Benefits) system ensures that its members receive 95% of their normal take-home pay during periods of lay-off[10].

Subcontracting to maintain managerial control over the labor process
Subcontracting can also be used by capital to counter union encroachment on the prerogative of managers to manage the labor process. Normally, it is easier for unions to organize worker resistance in large plants than in small. Therefore, the decentralization and subcontracting of work into smaller plants or to plants in areas with less militant labor organizations can be used to undermine the basis for union power and restore managerial control over the labor process (Rubery & Wilkinson 1981: 123). Several authors suggest that this was a prime motive which lay behind the dramatic decentralisation of production in the automotive and metal-working industries of northern Italy during the 1970s (Amin 1985, Murray 1983). Thus, subcontracting and the concomitant segmentation of the labor market can be 'both the medium *for* and the result *of* the struggle for control over the labour process between capital and labour' (Rubery & Wilkinson 1981: 129). Subcontracting to multiple vendors can protect the parent firm from disruptions caused by strikes or other interruptions to production among subcontractors or at in-house parts production plants (Friedman 1977). Depending upon the minimum efficient scale for the subcontracted 'part,' the parent firm may have to trade off the loss of cost savings, attributable to economies of scale, which could be gained if the part was single sourced, in order to ensure a continuous supply of the part by 'multisourcing'. Certainly auto assemblers in both North America and Western Europe adopted a strategy of multisourcing parts in order to ensure an uninterrupted supply when faced with an increase in the incidence of 'wildcat' strikes in the mid 1960s (Friedman 1977: 122, IWC 1978).

Subcontracting to ensure an adequate supply of labor If labor in general, or specific types of labor, are in short supply, subcontracting may be used by parent firms to mobilize sources of labor not normally available for direct wage labor owing to location or other factors. For example, the recent resurgence of homeworking in a number of sectors such as clothing and electronics has enabled firms to 'tap' sources of very cheap female labor by employing women tied to the home by family commitments. In her study of homeworking in the Toronto garment industry, Johnson points out that many women resorted to homeworking because they were unable to secure adequate or affordable childcare for their pre-school children and homeworking allowed them to both care for their children themselves and work for wages at the same time (Johnson & Johnson 1983).

Thus, although ultimately all rooted in the uneven nature of capitalist development and the exigencies of the processes of capitalist competition and accumulation, the 'causes' of subcontracting are clearly both multiple and interrelated. The relative importance of factors related to the market, technical organization of production, and labor supply in explaining the extent to which work is subcontracted will vary from industry to industry and from country to country. The structure of capital and labor markets and forms of production organization depend crucially on historically specific political and institutional factors. It is highly probable that any particular concrete instance of subcontracting will require a multicausal explanation. Two brief examples will serve to illustrate the point.

First, take the example referred to at several points in this chapter, of subcontracting in the form of homeworking in the North American garment industry. The structure of competition in this sector is such that in the last ten years domestic firms in North America have come under extreme pressure to lower production costs and, particularly, labor costs if they are to survive the competition from cheap offshore producers in Asia and Latin America. Given the nature of technology in the garment industry and, particularly, the fact that in the 'making up' phase of garment production economies are fixed at the level of the individual sewing machine, and given the 'availability' (in or close to the traditional garment-making districts in the central areas of cities such as New York, Los Angeles, Toronto, Montreal and Winnipeg) of labor (often female and immigrant and sometimes illegal) willing to work for very low wages, the subcontracting of sewing and finishing to homeworkers became a viable strategy for capital to pursue.

Secondly, an adequate explanation of the development in the 1950s and 1960s of the extensive and sophisticated systems of subcontracting in the Japanese automotive industry must take account of several factors. These include the shortage of capital available to the automotive assembly firms, the desire to overcome some of the rigidities of the *nenkō* system of employment in the parent firms, and the availability of low-wage labor owing to widespread underemployment, which, coupled with a bias against small firms in an already tight capital market, was responsible for the survival of many small labor-intensive firms (Yoshino 1968, Paine 1971).

The temporal dynamics of subcontracting

Although some subcontracting relationships do remain stable over relatively long periods of time it is probably more correct to view the relationships as being much more fluid and dynamic. Clearly levels of subcontracting will ebb and flow with the rhythm of business cycles. However, it is important once again to emphasize the need to distinguish between different types of subcontracting on the basis of their 'causes,' since the same economic conditions may well lead to the levels of different types of subcontracting moving in quite opposite directions. For example, in discussing subcontracting resulting from the need to segment labor in order to reimpose market discipline on wages, Scott suggests that 'a strong overall hypothesis that emerges is that subcontracting tends to decrease in times of economic improvement when manufacturers can absorb some degree of internal wage drift, but that it increases again as economic conditions deteriorate and strong cost cutting measures become imperative' (Scott 1983b: 244). On the other hand, Friedman's analysis of capacity subcontracting suggests the reverse pattern, with subcontracting increasing during boom periods and being curtailed during downturns in the economy (Friedman 1977: 126).

But beyond these relatively short-run cyclical variations in the level of subcontracting there is some evidence to suggest that there are also qualitative shifts in the scale and nature of subcontracting associated with shifts from one phase of capitalist accumulation to another[11]. For example, in the machinery factories of New England and the Middle Atlantic states of the USA the internal contract system (in effect a system of subcontracting internal to the factory) was an important form of industrial and labor market organization from the 1860s through to World War I (i.e. during the regime of extensive accumulation). Under this system skilled workmen became managers as well as workers. The firm provided tools, material, power and a factory building. The skilled employee – the 'contractor' – in turn agreed to manufacture a particular product or component in a given quantity, at a designated cost and by a specific time. Otherwise they retained virtually complete control over the production process, hiring other workers – 'subcontractors' – and directing their work and setting their wages (Nelson 1975, Clawson 1980). The internal contract system disappeared with the rise of taylorism and fordist techniques of production (Littler 1982). In turn, the latter seems to have been associated with the renewed use of external subcontracting. This is a highly speculative point and needs much more detailed empirical investigation. There is mounting, although still fragmentary, evidence that the industrial restructuring and reorganization which is occurring in the context of the current economic crisis involves the emergence of new subcontracting relationships and the recasting of old relationships (Lafont *et al.* 1982: 24–6, Lipietz 1984: 33–6). In this context let us briefly consider some of the changes underway in the North American automotive industry.

In the late 1970s the switch to the production of smaller cars and the tendency to overcapacity in the world automotive industry brought North American auto producers, for the first time, into direct competition with Japanese and European producers for the North American (and the world) mass market. The issue that currently overrides all others for the North American automotive industry is the differential that exists in labor productivity and unit cost between it and the Japanese automotive industry. For example, in the period 1978–9 Japanese production required an average of 80.3 person-hours per vehicle, while US production required 144 person-hours (Perry 1982: 31). Perry estimates that in 1979 combination of lower hourly compensation and superior productivity of both direct and indirect labor yielded a US landed cost advantage to the Japanese producers of US $1650 per vehicle[12]. Faced with such differentials North American producers have embarked on a round of massive new investments and the emphasis in the restructuring process is on cutting unit production costs by increasing labor productivity and engaging in other cost cutting measures (Holmes 1984).

How is this restructuring affecting the structure and nature of subcontracting arrangements in the industry? A number of tendencies are discernible. First, since the auto assemblers have been hard pressed to raise the enormous amounts of working capital which are needed to reorganize their own internal assembly and production processes, they have tried to pass more of the costs of the design, development and production of parts to the subcontractors in order to conserve their own working capital. Secondly, since a significant proportion of the value of the final assembled car is attributable to value embodied within the parts supplied by subcontractors, the latter are being urged and encouraged to adopt more technologically sophisticated labor processes in order to increase labor productivity and hence lower the unit costs of parts produced in their plants.

One facet of this drive to increase the labor productivity of subcontractors has involved a distinct move away from the multisourcing of parts, which developed in the 1960s to guard against interruptions in production caused by labor relations problems in the subcontractors plants, toward single sourcing. The latter, coupled with the promise of longer-term contracts, enables individual subcontractors to attain the benefits of longer production runs and to lower the unit price of parts. However, it increases the vulnerability of assembly plants to interruptions in the supply of parts from the subcontractor.

Another factor aimed at cost reduction, which will also add to the vulnerability of the parent firms, is the move towards tighter inventory control similar to the Japanese *kanban* system (sometimes called just-in-time delivery systems) which was pioneered by Toyota (Sugimori 1977, Lee & Schwendiman 1982, Sheard 1983)[13]. Timing and coordination of the delivery of parts from the subcontractor to the parent plant plays an integral role in the functioning of auto production systems in Japan. To quote from the excellent discussion of the *kanban* system provided by Sheard:

> automakers have eliminated to a large degree the need for stocks of parts at their plants by requiring their subcontractors to make frequent deliveries in small batches as they are required at the assembly plant. In the ideal case the only stocks at the assembly plant would be those being fitted at any one time. Immediately upon depletion these would be replaced by the subcontractor concerned, such replacement occurring as a continuous process. Although unattainable in practice zero stock level is the goal for which auto-makers strive. (Sheard 1983: 60–1)

The ability to exercise such tight inventory control has been facilitated through the development of advanced telecommunication and computer technologies which enable the continuous monitoring and exchange of data on inventory levels and stock requirements between parent firm and subcontractor. By reducing to a minimum the inventory levels for the production system as a whole, the *kanban* system can result in significant improvements in the rate of accumulation by reducing the amount of required circulating capital and thus reducing the turnover time of capital. For example, Sheard notes that a recent Japanese study estimated that in one year Toyota saved Aus \$40 million, or 10% of net profit, through the operation of its *kanban* system (Sheard 1983: 62).

Sheard also makes the observation that the *kanban* system is simply the extension of fordist principles of intraplant production organization to the regional production system of assembly plants and subcontractors, and its effect is 'for the production lines of the subcontractors to be integrated with that of the parent firm and spatially the tendency for subcontractors to locate near the assembly plant is strengthened' (Sheard 1983: 61). In North America most assembly plants are placing a maximum limit of 100 miles on how far their major subcontractors can be located from the parent plant.

In sum, the result of these tendencies is fewer suppliers, located closer to the assembly plant and with much closer and more formal ties between parent and subcontractor (Clifford 1984)[14].

The locational structure of subcontracting

Perhaps surprisingly, little has been said in this chapter about the locational structure of subcontracting. In part, this is because there is very little in either the theoretical or empirical literature on subcontracting which addresses this question directly. More importantly, it is because I believe, on the basis of my initial research, that very few, if any, non-trivial *general* theoretical tendencies concerning the spatial configuration of subcontracting relationships can be identified. It appears that in most cases the actual spatial configuration of subcontracting linkages is highly dependent upon a host of contingent relationships which can only be uncovered and understood through concrete empirical research.

However, mention must be made of a very recent series of important and interesting papers written by Scott on industrial organization and location at the intra-urban scale (Scott 1983b, 1983c, 1984). In these articles Scott first derives a number of hypotheses concerning the locational structure of inter-firm linkages in general, and subcontracting relationships in particular, from a rigorous theoretical analysis of the phenomena. He then tests these hypotheses with reference to the printed circuit board industry and the women's clothing industry in Los Angeles. Specifically, Scott argues as follows:

(a) 'networks of subcontracting relationships are likely to be more intimately and intensively developed where plants are clustered tightly together in geographical space; conversely, they are likely to be more sparsely developed where plants are widely scattered' (Scott 1983b: 242);
(b) locational clustering of activities is very characteristic where the connections are small in scale and where parent–subcontractor relationships are impermanent; conversely, where connections are large in magnitude and reasonably stable, locational dispersal will tend to take place (Scott 1983b: 243).

Certainly it is true that Scott's empirical data, although sparse, tend to confirm these hypotheses. However, the question remains as to how far they can be generalized to other sectors and to other geographical scales and settings. For instance, in the case of the Japanese *kanban* system discussed earlier in this section, although the connections are large in magnitude and extremely stable, the subcontractors are clustered close to the parent because of the crucial necessity to deliver parts to the assembly plant punctually. In the case of the clothing industry, recent crackdowns by the authorities on illegal activities connected with subcontracting and homeworking in the Quebec garment industry have revealed a network of subcontracting which, although centred on the inner city of Montreal, extends well beyond the metropolitan area into the Eastern Township of Quebec.

In some cases subcontracting is carried out over considerable distances. The development of international subcontracting, particularly in the clothing and electronics industries, is clearly a case in point. In their discussion of contemporary subcontracting in France, Lafont *et al.* argue that, due to reductions in transportation costs and technological developments in the field of telecommunications, in general distance is no longer an important factor governing the parent firm's choice of subcontractor for most forms of subcontracting (Lafont *et al.* 1982: 25). They suggest that, while the subcontractor must still maintain close contacts with the head offices of parent firms in order to win contracts, the actual production facilities within which the subcontracted work is performed can be widely dispersed: 'sur le continent européen la distance maximale entre usines des sous-traitance et des donneurs d'ordre est considérée comme celle permettant à un technician l'aller et retour en avion dans la journée' (Lafont *et al* 1982: 26).

This is not to suggest that the spatial configuration of subcontracting is unimportant, or that subcontracting is not important in understanding the locational structure of production in certain sectors and regions, but simply that it is difficult, if not impossible, to generalize about such configurations. Clearly, it is possible to derive spatial/locational corollaries for subcontracting relationships in specific contexts. Take, for example, Sheard's argument about the tendency toward spatial clustering in the Japanese automotive industry, which can be derived directly from an understanding of the aspatial nature and functioning of the *kanban* system; or the hypotheses derived by Scott about the locational structure of subcontracting in two Los Angeles industries. However, it seems to me that it is highly unlikely that such generalizations about the locational structure of subcontracting will hold over time or across sectors at any greater scale due to the very unevenness of capitalist development.

Conclusion

The purpose of this chapter has been to examine the organization of production subcontracting and the role that it plays in the organization of industrial systems. Until relatively recently subcontracting was considered by both orthodox and marxist theorists to be an anachronistic feature of advanced capitalism, being confined to the traditional or declining manufacturing sectors and expected eventually to disappear altogether. However, the resurgence of subcontracting and other forms of outwork in the past 15 years has led to the recognition that subcontracting is not an anachronism but rather that it forms one of a range of possibilities continually open to firms in organizing production. With this recognition has come the need to theorize adequately about the nature and dynamics of subcontracting. One of the most appealing aspects of the study of 'secondary' forms of production such as subcontracting is that it draws together on the one hand work on industrial organization and, on the other, work on labor market structure and segmentation. All too often these two theoretical endeavors have existed in solitary isolation from each other.

Throughout the chapter we have emphasized the importance of not treating the linkages between firms, or even the more narrowly defined set of linkages which are generated through subcontracting relationships, as a 'chaotic conception.' In fact, several different types of production subcontracting generated by different causal mechanisms have been identified. In particular, factors related to the nature of product markets, the technical organization of the labor process and the structure of labor markets which encourage the development of subcontracting were discussed. There is a growing consensus in the literature that 'the search for one explanation of outwork [subcontracting] applicable to all advanced countries and all industries is misplaced and that the structure and causes of segmentation will depend on a country's and industry's specific historical experience' (Rubery & Wilkinson 1981: 129). A corollary to this is that the use of subcontracting is likely to vary temporally between industries and regions as the economic, technical and social conditions of production and the balance of class forces with respect to control over the labor process changes.

Implicit throughout the paper is the belief that an understanding of interplant subcontracting relations is essential to the development of a broader understanding of the geography of production and industrial systems. However, it is likely that in most instances the spatial configuration of subcontracting linkages will be dependent upon a host of contingent relationships and hence few empirical generalizations concerning the spatial structure of such linkages will be forthcoming. Clearly what is urgently needed is detailed concrete research on subcontracting relationships in a number of industrial sectors in order to enhance our understanding of the organization and dynamics of contemporary capitalist production. This is particularly pertinent since it appears that one common response of capital in the current economic crisis has been to marginalize at least some part of the labor force through a variety of 'secondary' forms of production such as subcontracting.

Notes

The Queen's University Advisory Research Committee provided financial support for the research from which this paper is drawn. This is a revised version of a paper presented to the 'Symposium on the Structure and Dynamics of Industrial Systems' held at Nébian, France in August, 1984 under the auspices of the IGU Commission on Industrial Systems. Funding to attend the Symposium was provided by the Social Sciences and Humanities Research Council of Canada. I would like to acknowledge the helpful comments made on the original paper by participants at the Symposium and by the editors of this book, and to express my thanks to Tod Rutherford who has been an invaluable sounding board for many of the ideas contained in the paper.

1 Take, for example, debates over the development of the labor process. Non-marxist writers such as Landes argue that the driving force behind the development of the factory system of internalized production was the increasing technological complexity and sophistication of mechanized production (Landes 1969). On the other hand, marxists such as Braverman argue that the factory system cannot be explained solely by the requirements of technical efficiency but also involve the need of capitalists to establish control over labor and the labor process by determining the length and pace of the working day (Braverman 1974). However, as Rubery and Wilkinson emphasize, 'despite these differences both schools agreed that non-factorised production would diminish and would be found if at all in technological and economic backwaters' (Rubery & Wilkinson 1981: 118). Thus, for example, Braverman considers labor subcontracting as a 'transitional form' which is 'incompatible with the overall development of capitalist production and survives only in specialized instances' (Braverman 1974: 63). In part, this stems from Braverman's assumption that the real subordination of labor by capital was unproblematical and that the struggle by workers for control of the labor process ceased with the development of deskilled factory production, a view that has been roundly criticized in more recent marxist writing on the labor process (Lazonick 1983). It is worth noting that in his chapter on modern industry Marx emphasizes that modern industry incorporates older systems of production rather than superseding them. Rubery and Wilkinson also point out that 'the criticism that students of the labour process have overstated its unidirectional development applies with equal force to the main strands in the labour market segmentation debate, which place great emphasis on the modernity of the primary and the backwardness of the secondary sector' (Rubery & Wilkinson 1981: 139). Similarly, recent work in British economic history has stressed that outworking and subcontracting in several industries were not replaced by the centralized factory system nearly as fast as previously assumed (Bythell 1978) and that 'the persistence and resurgence of domestic and workshop industry provoke scepticism about viewing changes in the organization and concentration of industry as the major index of fundamental economic change' (Berg *et al.* 1983: 31). The *History Workshop Journal* commented, in an editorial published in 1977, on the tendency within economic history 'to present the relationship between leading sectors and small scale production as if it were a relationship between the essential and the contingent . . . For, as long as the mid Victorian economy is thought of in terms of a division between "a modern industrial sector" and an array of "preindustrial survivals" (always on the point of extinction, but still miraculously there a generation later) the effect will be to marginalize the latter' (*History Workshop Journal* 3 (1977), 2).

2 It should be emphasized that this characterization is of the type of linkage analysis which is typical of the brand of location theory and locational analysis which dominated Anglo-American economic geography from the late 1950s through to the late 1970s. As noted by Scott, earlier analyses of interfirm linkages in fact did stress (albeit in a largely descriptive manner) the changing technical and institutional features of productive activity and particularly stressed the process of the

division of labor and its manifestation in the spatial structure of industrial systems (Scott 1983b).

3 Sayer describes the notion of a 'chaotic conception' as follows: 'in place of a theory of abstract elements of a situation and how they combine to compose concrete phenomena, there is an acceptance of unexamined, largely commonsense definitions of these *empirical* objects, and a *generalization* of the features of these "chaotic conceptions" . . . these unities of diverse aspects are treated as single objects which can be used as a basis for aggregation or else added up for manipulation in statistical analyses' (Sayer 1982: 75).

4 Watanabe suggests that 'if manufacturers lack financial and marketing capacity these are sufficient conditions for commercial subcontracting to develop, while they are necessary but not sufficient conditions for industrial subcontracting. For the latter, an additional technological condition is required; the product and the production process must be divisible and every part or process need not be produced or performed on one spot continuously' (Watanabe 1971: 55). While this is an interesting point it is based on a partial view of the parent–subcontractor relationship, focusing exclusively on the subcontractor's side.

5 It should be noted that subcontracting is also increasingly important in the service sector and historically has been at the root of the organization of the production process in the building industry (Scase & Goffee 1982).

6 Exceptions being Friedman (1977) and Brusco and Sabel (1981).

7 As we shall see subsequently, in some industries labor costs are also fixed because of particular institutional and political factors related to the control of the labor market and the labor process. This is certainly the case in the North American automotive industry.

8 Homework is the ultimate extension of decentralized production since all costs are variable to the parent firm because *all* tools and plant are owned by the worker (Sabel 1982: 48).

9 Note that the first effect increases the rate of profit for industrial capital as a whole, whereas the second effect is limited to the rate of profit of the parent firm.

10 It is generally agreed that the existence of the *nenkō* system of industrial labor relations in large Japanese companies which provides lifetime job security to 'primary' sector workers has contributed to the highly developed system of subcontracting that exists in Japan (Yoshino 1968, Paine 1971).

11 Here the phrase 'phase of capitalist accumulation' is used to refer to the kind of periodization of capitalist development suggested by the French regulation school's concept of 'regime of accumulation' (Aglietta 1979, Lipietz 1982, 1984, De Vroey 1984) and by Gordon *et al.*'s concept of 'a social structure of accumulation' (1982). Gordon *et al.* define the latter as 'the specific institutional environment within which the capitalist accumulation process is associated with a distinct social structure of accumulation . . . these social structures of accumulation define successive stages of capitalist development,' and they argue that two of the constituent institutions of a social structure of accumulation are the organization of work (i.e. the labor process) and the structure of labor markets. Thus it is likely, and there is some evidence to suggest this, that another constituent feature of a social structure of accumulation is the form and role that subcontracting assumes within the organization of production.

12 Some caution should be exercised with respect to the accuracy of these figures. For a good discussion of the difficulties involved in estimating productivity and cost differentials between North American and Japanese auto producers see National Academy (1982). Nevertheless, despite disputes over the magnitude of the absolute figures there is agreement that the differentials are substantial and in favor of Japanese producers.

13 The increased vulnerability of assembly plants to interruptions in supplies of parts as a result of recently instituted just-in-time delivery systems has been graphically demonstrated by the 1984 strikes against General Motors in both the USA and Canada.

14 Sheard suggests that in Japan this system has resulted in subcontracting being firm specific rather than industry specific – subcontractors 'belonging' to a parent first and to a particular sector second – and for many subcontractors to be partially, if not fully, integrated into the production system of the parent firm so that they almost assume the character of branch plants (Sheard 1983: 52).

References

Aglietta, M. 1979. *A theory of capitalist regulation: the US experience.* London: New Left Books.

Amin, A. 1985. Restructuring in Fiat and the decentralization of production into Southern Italy. In *Uneven development in Southern Europe*, R. Hudson and J. Lewis (eds.). London: Methuen (forthcoming).

Banville, E. 1982. La sous traitance pour l'automobile et le poids lourd: constatations et hypothèses. *Revue d'Economie Industrielle* **19**, 34–40.

Bayle-Ottenheim, J., A. LeThomas and A. Sallez 1973. *La sous traitance.* Paris: Chotard.

Berg, M. *et al.* (eds.) 1983. *Manufacture in town and country before the factory.* Cambridge: Cambridge University Press.

Berger, S. 1981. The uses of the traditional sector in Italy. In *The petite bourgeoisie*, F. Bechofer and B. Elliot (eds.), 71–89. London: Macmillan.

Berger, S. and M. J. Piore 1980. *Dualism and discontinuity in industrial societies.* Cambridge: Cambridge University Press.

Berthomeiu, C. and A. Hanaut 1980. Can international subcontracting promote industralisation? *Int. Lab. Rev.* **119**(3), 335–49.

Blois, K. J. 1972. Vertical quasi integration. *J. Indust. Econ.* **20**, 253–72.

Braverman, H. 1974. *Labour and monopoly capital.* New York: Monthly Review Press.

Brusco, S. 1982. The Emilian model: productive decentralisation and social integration. *Camb. J. Econ.* **6**, 167–84.

Brusco, S. and C. Sabel 1981. Artisan production and economic growth. In *The dynamics of labour market segmentation*, F. Wilkinson (ed.), 99–113. London: Academic Press.

Bythell, D. 1978. *The sweated trades: outwork in nineteenth century Britain.* New York: St Martin's Press.

Chaillou, B. 1977. Definition et typologie de la sous traitance. *Revue Economique* **28**(2), 262–85.

Clawson, D. 1980. *Bureaucracy and the labor process: the transformation of US industry, 1860–1920.* New York: Monthly Review Press.

Clifford, E. 1984. Automotive: companies seek support of unions to continue their recent recovery. *Report on Business 1000* June 22, 50–2. Toronto: Globe and Mail.

Contini, B. B. 1981. Labour market segmentation and the development of the parallel economy: the Italian experience. *Oxford Econ. Pap.* NS **33**(3), 401–12.

De Vroey, M. 1984. A regulation approach interpretation of contemporary crisis. *Capital and Class* **23**, 45–66.

Fredriksson, C. G. and L. G. Lindmark 1979. From firms to systems of firms: a study of interregional dependence in a dynamic society. In *Spatial analysis, industry and the industrial environment*, F. E. I. Hamilton and G. Linge (eds.), 155–86. Chichester: Wiley.

Friedman, A. L. 1977. *Industry and labour: class struggle at work and monopoly capitalism.* London: Macmillan.

Goldberg, M. 1965. La sous traitance dans l'industrie métaux. *Cahiers de l'Institut d'Aménagement et d'Urbanisme de la Région Parisienne* **2**, 1–67.

Gordon, D. M., R. C. Edwards, and M. Reich 1982. *Segmented work, divided workers: the historical transformation of labour in the US.* Cambridge: Cambridge University Press.

Gouverneur, J. 1983. *Contemporary capitalism and marxist economics.* Oxford: Martin Robertson.

Harrison, P. 1983. *Inside the inner city.* Harmondsworth: Penguin.

Holmes, J. 1983. Industrial reorganization, capital restructuring and locational change: an analysis of the Canadian automobile industry in the 1960s. *Econ. Geog.* **59**(3), 251–71.

Holmes, J. 1984. *The contemporary restructuring of Canadian industry.* Paper presented to the Workshop on Development in the 1980s, Queen's University, Kingston, Canada, May 1984.

Houssiaux, J. 1957a. Le concept de quasi intégration et le rôle des sous traitants dans l'industrie. *Rev. Econ.* **8**, 221–47.

Houssiaux, J. 1957b. Quasi intégration, croissance des firmes et structures industrielles. *Rev. Econ.* **8**, 385–411.

IWC (Institute for Workers' Control) 1978. *A worker's inquiry into the motor industry.* London: CSE Books.

Johnson, L. C. and R. E. Johnson 1983. *The seam allowance: industrial home sewing in Canada.* Toronto: Women's Press.

Lafont, J., D. Leborgne and A. Lipietz 1982. Rédeploiement industriel et espace economique. *Travaux et Recherches de Prospective* **85**. Paris: Documentation Française.

Landes, D. S. 1969. *The unbound Prometheus.* Cambridge: Cambridge University Press.

Lazonick, W. 1983. *Class relations and the capitalist enterprise; A critical assessment of the foundations of marxian economic theory.* Paper presented to the Marx Centennial Conference, Marxism: the next two decades', Winnipeg, March, 1983.

Lee, S. M. and G. Schwendiman (eds) 1982. *Management by Japanese systems.* New York: Praeger.

Lipietz, A. 1982. Towards global fordism? *New Left Review* **132**, 33–147.

Lipietz A. 1984. *L'audace ou l'enlisement: sur les politiques économiques de la gauche.* Paris: Editions La Découverte.

Littler, C. R. 1982. *The development of the labour process in capitalist societies.* London: Heinemann.

Mattera, P. 1980. Small is not beautiful: decentralized production and the underground economy. *Radical Am.* **14**(5), 67–76.

Murray, F. 1983. The decentralization of production – the decline of the mass collective worker. *Capital and Class* **19**, 74–99.

National Academy 1982. *The competitive status of the US auto industry.* Washington, DC: National Academy Press.

Nelson, D. 1975. *Managers and workers: origins of the new factory system in the United States, 1880–1920.* Madison: University of Wisconsin Press.

Paine, S. H. 1971. Lessons for LDC's from Japan's experience with labour commitment and subcontracting in the manufacturing sector. *Bull. Inst. Econ. and Stat.* **33**(2), 115–33.

Perry, R. 1982. *The future of Canada's auto industry.* Toronto: James Lorimer.

J. Holmes

Rainnie, A. F. 1984. Combined and uneven development in the clothing industry: The effects of competition on accumulation. *Capital and Class* **22**, 141–56.

Ross, R. and K. Trachte 1983. Global cities and global classes: the peripheralization of labour in NYC. *Review* **6**(3), 393–431.

Rubery, J. and F. Wilkinson 1981. Outwork and segmented labour markets. In *The dynamics of labour market segmentation*, F. Wilkinson (ed.), 115–32. London: Academic Press.

Sabel, C. F. 1982. *Work and politics: the division of labour in industry*. Cambridge: Cambridge University Press.

Sallez, A. 1972. *Polarisation et sous-traitance*. Paris: Evrolles.

Sallez, A. and J. Schlegel 1963. *La sous-traitance dans l'industrie*. Paris: Dunod.

Sayer, A. 1982. Explanation in economic geography. *Prog. Human Geog.* **6**(1), 68–88.

Sayer, A. and K. Morgan 1983. *The international electronics industry and regional development in Britain*. Working Paper 34, Urban and Regional Studies. Brighton: University of Sussex.

Scase, R. and R. Goffee 1982. *The entrepreneurial middle class*. London: Croom Helm.

Scott, A. J. 1983a. Location and linkage systems: a survey and reassessment. *Ann. Regional Sci.* **17**(1), 1–39.

Scott, A. J. 1983b. Industrial organization and the logic of intra-metropolitan location. I: Theoretical considerations. *Econ. Geog.* **59**(3), 233–50.

Scott, A. J. 1983c. Industrial organization and the logic of intra-metropolitan location. II: A case study of the printed circuits industry in the Greater Los Angeles region. *Econ. Geog.* **59**(4), 343–67.

Scott, A. J. 1984. Industrial organization and the logic of intra-metropolitan location. III: A case study of the women's dress industry in the Greater Los Angeles area. *Econ. Geog.* **60**(1), 3–27.

Sharpston, M. 1975. International subcontracting. *Oxford Econ. Pap.* **27**, 94–135.

Sheard, P. 1983. Auto-production systems in Japan: organisational and locational features. *Aust. Geog. Stud.* **21**(1), 49–68.

Shinohara, M. 1968. A survey of the Japanese literature on the small industry. In *The role of small industry on the process of economic growth*, B. F. Hoselitz (ed.), 1–113. The Hague: Mouton.

Solinas, G. 1982. Labour market segmentation and workers careers: the case of the Italian knitwear industry. *Camb. J. Econ.* **6**, 331–52.

Storper, M. and R. Walker 1983. The spatial division of labor: labor and the location of industries. In *Sunbelt/snowbelt*, W. Tabb and L. Sawers (eds.). New York: Oxford University Press.

Sugimori, Y. *et al.* 1977. Toyota production system and kanban system: materialization of just-in-time and respect-for-human system. *Int. J. Prod. Res.* **15**(6), 553–64.

Susman, P. and E. Schutz 1983. Monopoly and competitive firm relations and regional development in global capitalism. *Econ. Geog.* **59**(2), 161–77.

Taylor, M. J. and N. J. Thrift 1982. Industrial linkage and the segmented economy: I. Some theoretical proposals. *Environ. Plann. A*, **14**(12), 1601–13.

UNCTD 1975. *International subcontracting arrangements in electronics between developed market economy countries and developing countries*. New York: UN.

UNCTD 1979. *Transnational corporation linkages in developing countries: the case of backward linkages via subcontracting*. UN Centre on Transnational Corporations ST/CTC/17. New York: UN.

UNIDO 1974. *Subcontracting for modernizing economies*. Vienna: UN.

Vennin, B. and E. de Banville 1975. Pratique et signification de la sous-traitance dans l'industrie automobile en France. *Rev. Econ.* **26**(2), 280–306.

Watanabe, S. 1970. Entrepreneurship in small enterprises in Japanese manufacturing. *Int. Lab. Rev.* **102**(6), 531–76.

Watanabe, S. 1971. Subcontracting, industrialization and employment creation. *Int. Lab. Rev.* **104**(1–2), 51–76.

Wolin, M. L. 1981. Sweatshop: undercover in the garment industry. Los Angeles: Herald Examiner.

Yoshino, M. Y. 1968. *Japan's managerial system: tradition and innovation.* Cambridge, Mass.: MIT Press.

6

Industrial location on a world scale: the case of the semiconductor industry

ANDREW SAYER

Great strides have been made in recent years in the study of industrial geography. Two major developments stand out as particularly important, one theoretical, the other a matter of empirical focus: the former involves the adoption and adaptation of marxist theory of industrial capital and uneven development; the latter a shift of focus from the study of individual plant location decisions to an approach which considers such location decisions, together with other significant changes in plants, in the context of industrial sectors and the wider economy, and – as is increasingly appropriate – in the context of international systems of production organized by multinational companies. There has therefore been a convergence between studies of imperialism and the internationalization of capital on the one hand (e.g. Mandel 1975, Radice 1975, Lipietz 1982, 1984) and studies of industrial location on the other. Particularly useful has been the conceptual distinction between different types of internationalization – of commodities (exports), of money capital (portfolio investment), and of production (foreign direct investment) (Palloix 1975). But the explanatory power of such ideas needs to be tested through concrete studies of particular industries, as well as through more macro-level analyses of concrete patterns of development (e.g. Dunford & Perrons 1983, 1984). Although we have found radical theories of the geography of production invaluable we have also found through studies of particular industries that they are deficient in important respects. In this chapter, I will review the changing geography of production in the semiconductor industry and discuss some critical implications for our understanding of industrial geography and uneven development.

I will begin by briefly setting out some criticisms of certain popular radical views, although their significance will become clearer when we move on to look at the empirical case study. (These criticisms are developed in Sayer 1985.)

First, concrete patterns of uneven development are often wrongly treated as an unmediated outcome of the tendencies of capital accumulation in the abstract. But the tendencies always work through specific mediating technical and social forms, such as particular technologies, types of labor and management systems (i.e. ways of combining labor, materials and machinery). Ignoring or belittling these mediations produces a misinterpretation of certain trends (e.g. the runaway industry phenomenon) as having epochal significance, so that it becomes difficult to appreciate how they could be reversed as the mediating processes change. It also encourages the belief that new developments are just the playing out of possibilities within the same old repertoire of responses and radically underestimates the options open to capital. As we shall see the New International Division of Labor thesis, particularly as it is argued by Fröbel *et al.* (1980), which relates de-industrialization in the West to the rise of manufacturing industries in cheap labor countries, is the main culprit as regards this problem.

Secondly, there are also some rather restricted views of competition in the radical literature. Apart from the extraordinary view that big (or 'monopoly') capital is not competitive, there is a tendency to see competition only in terms of price competition for a largely fixed stock of goods, thereby underestimating the importance of product innovation and technological complementarities in competition. Falling costs per unit are also seen simply as a function of speed-up, automation and scale economies rather than also as a function of quality improvements within the production process which reduce costs incurred by wastage.

Thirdly, there is also a tendency to underestimate the significance of the social and institutional characteristics of capital and labor, for example, the striking differences between Japanese and British capital. The former is notable for its long-term profit horizons, its obsession with quality in both product and process, the intense involvement of management on the shop floor, company unions, its trading companies facilitating exports and its caution regarding direct overseas investment: the characteristics of British capital are virtually the opposite of these. Such differences have spatial implications, not only directly through their differing locational strategies, but more indirectly through their differential consequences for the competitive strength of capitals and hence for global patterns of uneven development.

Lastly, there is a common tendency to underestimate the role of the nation-state as an 'actor' affecting uneven development, as if multinational firms played out their locational strategies in a *laissez-faire* world economy. In fact, through tariffs, import quotas, technical standards, policies on inward investment and the transfer of technology, support for domestic producers and for R & D, regional policy and government procurement policies, national governments can influence the internationalization of capital, and of course other economic variables specific to individual countries, such as company taxation and currency exchange rates, are important.

Actually, the last three problems might alternatively be treated as instances of the first in terms of a problematic application of abstract theory to concrete research; the abstract theory of capital accumulation quite reasonably abstracts from such mediations, but concrete studies cannot afford to do so.

While I hope that the case of the semiconductor industry will illustrate the significance of these neglected mediations, I do not of course want to go to the opposite extreme of ignoring what is being mediated, that is, the underlying tendencies of capital. It is emphasized that what follows is just a sketch of the industry; readers seeking a more detailed and definitive account are referred to Sciberras (1977), Dosi (1981), Ernst (1981), Rada (1982), and especially UNCTC (1983).

The semiconductor industry

Semiconductors are a particular category of electronic component, embracing discrete components such as valves and transistors, and the more recent integrated circuits (i.c.'s) which embody hundreds or even thousands of transistors and other functions on tiny chips. Although this sector is small, with less than 300000 employees worldwide, its strategic importance is enormous for it is the basis of the microelectronics revolution, which looks set to dominate technical change for the next few decades. Not surprisingly, despite the heavy costs of involvement, few advanced capitalist countries lack a support program for microelectronics in general and semiconductors in particular.

It is common in radical research to try to 'read off' the form of uneven development from the corporate hierarchies and locational strategies of leading firms on the grounds that the economic characteristics of places come to reflect the place of their industries in the international corporate division of labor. While there is a certain logic to this approach it also has its pitfalls (cf. Sayer 1985). For example, we could take a supposedly typical US producer of standardized chips and look at its internal geography of production, which would probably be something like this:

(a) research and development and other pre-production activities needing skilled scientific, and managerial labor: Silicon Valley, California;
(b) 'wafer fabrication', a capital-intensive process involving etching micro-circuits on to silicon wafers: as this needs highly skilled process engineers and semi-skilled operators, it is likely to be located in a rich country, e.g. the USA or, in Europe, Britain;
(c) assembly, i.e. dicing wafers into individual chips, mounting them on carriers and soldering wires to them, and testing: this is a labor-intensive stage of production, and given the portability of the product it can be done in cheap labor locations in the Third World, e.g. Taiwan, Malaysia or the Philippines.

However, this is just one type of locational strategy and one which is becoming outdated, for reasons which we will explain shortly. Recently, advanced countries have been more favored for assembly and the 'captive' US producers, firms like IBM which produce semiconductors for their own use rather than for sale, have never used offshore assembly. Also the internal geographies of European and Japanese semiconductor firms differ again from that of the 'typical' US merchant chip producer. Consequently, it is no surprise that the spatial structure of the latter is a poor guide to the geography of the industry as a whole; in particular, it is not clear why there are so many low-skilled operatives in the industry in Silicon Valley (more than any other category of worker), why so much production is concentrated in Europe and

Japan, and why, despite the high degree of internationalization, the lines of competition have a distinctively national character.

In order to make sense of this situation, it is necessary first to understand a few basic technical characteristics of the industry which are relevant to its geography, and secondly to take a broader and more historical view of the industry. As regards the technical side, the distinction between discrete components and the more recent integrated circuits is important, the European firms having strength primarily in the former until recently, the American firms having strength in both. Within i.c.'s, memories and microprocessors are particularly important. The latter, performing the function of the computer's central processing unit, are the most research-intensive products and the ones most dominated by American firms. Since the introduction of i.c.'s in the late 1960s/early 1970s, the degree of miniaturization or 'integration' of circuitry on each chip has increased exponentially. The effect of this has been rapidly to lower the cost of each chip while increasing its power. But as the industry moves from LSI (large-scale integration) to VLSI (very large-scale integration), the chips become less like components and more like systems (UNCTC 1983: xix) which would formerly have consisted of hundreds of thousands of separate components. This has had two important effects: first, it has lowered the cost of hardware relative to software, with the latter now exceeding the former, particularly in the case of standardized chips; and secondly, it has produced a convergence between the component, computer and software industries.

The growth and pace of technological advancement in the industry has been exceptional. Against the background of the world recession, demand for chips has grown at about 30% per annum, although employment growth has been very modest by comparison. Despite this rapid growth, the industry has already suffered three crises of overproduction in its short life (1970–1, 1974–5 and 1981–2). In the last of these the El Dorado image of California's Silicon Valley was somewhat tarnished by shutdowns and lay-offs, relocations to areas with cheaper labor, and by the introduction at Intel – perhaps the best-known chip producer – of a 50-hour week without extra pay. This apparently strange combination of characteristics arises from the rapidly increasing economies of scale of production and consequently of costs of entry, particularly for R & D. Over a quarter of sales revenue usually goes on investment and research (Ernst 1981). The UNCTC report estimates that the capital investment costs of producing a 16K memory chip in 1981 were five times those of a 4K chip in 1977 (UNCTC 1983).

Despite the rocketing costs of production of each successive new type of chip, the possible gains (or losses) are considerable. Where prices fall by 25% per year, the profit gains/losses of being a year ahead/behind competitors in the technological race are potentially huge. The characteristics of the product are also important; not only do learning curve and scale economies lower the price of chips, but technological advances increase the power of each chip, so that a given level of demand can be met by fewer chips (Duncan 1981, Rada 1982). It is for these reasons that competition is so fierce and overproduction so common in a market which is growing so rapidly. As we shall see, the Japanese producers, with their long-term profit horizons and aggressive pricing strategies, were able to increase their market share rapidly by keeping production up during the slumps and prices down during the intervening 'chip famines.'

Throughout the short history of the industry (about 35 years for semiconductors in general, 15 years for integrated circuits), international competition through exports and direct overseas investment have been integral formative processes. American firms have been dominant throughout, although European producers have fallen back drastically and Japan has made rapid inroads into the industry, overtaking Europe's share of world production in the late 1970s (see Table 6.1).

Part of the reason for the national character of the competition derives from the fact that firms of the same nationality are significantly affected by a common institutional, cultural environment and relationship with their home state. (The EEC might itself be considered as equivalent to a state rather than as a transcendence of the state.) The lead of the American firms originates in the unique environment of the 1950s and 1960s in the USA, with state expenditure on military and space applications – in which the technology was chiefly developed – far in excess of other countries, and also a

Table 6.1 World semiconductor production by home base of producing firms, 1978–83 (millions of US dollars)

Location	1978	1979	1980	1981	1982	1983
United States						
i.c. merchant	3 238	4 761	6 360	6 050	6 300	7 000
i.c. captive	1 344	2 020	2 695	2 900	3 000	3 450
i.c. total	4 582	6 681	9 055	8 950	9 300	10 450
Discretes	1 540	1 944	2 080	1 950	1 875	1 970
total semiconductor	6 122	8 625	11 135	10 900	11 175	12 420
Western Europe						
i.c. total	453	600	710	790	790	855
discretes	960	1 050	910	750	710	720
total semiconductor	1 413	1 650	1 620	1 540	1 500	1 575
Japan						
i.c. total	1 195	1 750	2 450	2 590	3 130	3 910
discretes	1 295	1 180	1 390	1 580	1 520	1 640
total semiconductor	2 490	2 930	3 840	4 170	4 650	5 550
rest of world						
i.c. total	482	675	130	160	160	190
discretes	985	1 025	190	200	190	200
total semiconductor	1 467	1 700	320	360	350	390
total i.c.	6 712	9 706	12 345	12 490	13 380	15 405
total discretes	4 780	5 199	4 570	4 480	4 295	4 530
total worldwide semiconductor	11 492	14 905	16 915	16 970	17 675	19 935

Source: UNCTC 1983: 34.

favourable institutional structure which encouraged a high degree of inter-action between industry and the scientific establishment (e.g. the Bell labora-tories). In Britain, although R & D expenditure on defense is high in relative terms, it is small in comparison to US expenditure, and it has been notably lacking in links between military and civilian production. By contrast Japan, of course, lacked this military basis, although as we shall see it was to make up for it later by other means.

Until the mid/late 1960s, American semiconductor firms like Texas Instru-ments and ITT either merely exported to Europe or used their European subsidiaries only for making mature products, reserving new, 'state of the art' technologies for the more advanced US markets. With the major European firms they formed a stable electromechanical oligopoly, which had lasted several decades (cf. Teulings 1984). The European companies were able to maintain their position by imitating the more advanced American products. The break-up of this situation began with the introduction by existing and new American firms of integrated circuits, which suddenly widened the tech-nology gap and hence the imitation lag in Europe. The US firms then began to produce and sell new products much earlier in Europe, thereby cutting their European imitators out of the market. The situation deteriorated for the European producers because many i.c.'s replaced rather than supplemented the discrete components in which they have had considerable strength – a classic example of the power of product innovation as a competitive strategy. Then in 1971, in response to a slump in demand, American firms started a price war in Europe, though not in the USA, which further advanced their position. Also, whereas the European firms were inhibited by their inheritance of a fragmented production base, with each country being supplied by a separate plant producing according to national technical standards and marketing constraints, the American firms, with the new products, were able to establish new pan-European technical standards and use a new set of plants geared to producing for several countries (*Financial Times*, October 26, 1982). In other words, the small size of the European national markets compared to the American market was itself a disadvantage to the European firms.

The reaction of most of the European firms was to withdraw from the fiercely competitive mass markets for standardized chips into the more specialized markets for custom chips and also in-house production, chiefly for defense uses where they were to a certain extent insulated from the law of value by the special pricing conditions attaching to government defense procurement. While such products might be sophisticated, process innovation takes a very poor second place to product innovation and their production requires wholly different types of organization from that for low-cost mass production and marketing. Government telecommunications contracts also provided a protected refuge (e.g. for GEC and Plessey of Britain, and until recently SGS of Italy). However, even in the latter market, technological superiority and European locations gave American firms limited entry into these markets too. In the end, Philips and Siemens were the only European firms large enough to approach the US firms' R & D investment expenditure and hence retain a competitive toehold in the markets for standardized i.c.'s.

Technological complementarities (or their absence) also affected the changing relative strengths of American and European capital. There is a 'virtuous circle' between electronic components, especially specialized ones, and military equipment, though not between these and consumer electronics; indeed it is difficult for firms to change from defense to consumer work (Maddock 1983). There is a complementarity between mass-produced components and consumer electronics and between the former and computers. In Europe both the military and computer markets were much smaller than the American markets. This illustrates how technological inter-dependencies lend their own influence to the spatial and temporal dimensions of uneven development. These interdependencies mean that any country which lacks the right capability in semiconductors is at a disadvantage as regards the future development of its electronics industry as a whole. Buying in chips from merchant producers is very much a second best to making advanced products in order to monopolize the advantages of using them in their own products. Bought-in chips are liable to be technically less compat-ible with the purchaser's own products than in-house products, and therefore resort to outside sourcing often implies technological dependence, high software costs, vulnerability and reactive rather than pro-active competitive strategies. As we have seen, in the case of i.c.'s, the effects of being distant from the 'technological frontier' (Dosi 1981) are dramatic, for the process of integration actually swallows up markets for older products. Not sur-prisingly, the semiconductor sector is now accorded a strategic role in national economies similar to that of steel 50 years ago.

The Japanese firms lacked the stimulus of military spending but more than made up for this by a vigorous process of imitation and improvement behind national barriers to inward investment and licensing (and, until 1974, to imports). After an initial success with transistors in the 1960s, considerable long-term R & D effort was devoted to catching up with the USA in a very particular and well-chosen range of chips – 16K and 64K Random Access Memories. For these products,

> stringent quality control in the production process was relatively more critical than such factors as innovative design in ensuring product competitiveness. Circuit design is a less formidable task in the case of memory chips than in the case of microprocessors. Moreover, the former devices involve no software development and service as do the latter. To a far greater extent [than in the case of microprocessors] successful competition [in memories] depends on the refinement of mass production techniques and process know-how. In memories high yields [i.e. low rejects] – hence tight process control – are the crucial variable since they make possible the dramatic price reductions which have come to characterize competition in this segment of the i.c. market. (UNCTC 1983: 275)

In other words, the Japanese played to their comparative advantage in exploiting their expertise in quality mass production, and they avoided products where they were at a disadvantage *vis-à-vis* the Americans. By such means they were able to take over two-thirds of the world market for 64K memories. American competitors began to complain of 'dumping' and several of them began to join forces in R & D in order to combat the new Japanese challenge and also that of similar European collaborative efforts. Recently, too, American firms such as Motorola, Fairchild, IBM and Texas Instruments have penetrated Japan, usually via joint ventures, and one of their aims in doing this is to try to obtain the same productivity and quality advantages of using a Japanese labor force. In fact, of course, it is not Japanese labor as such which is the attraction but the particular types of work practices developed in Japan.

The Japanese firms also benefited from their unique form of collaboration with the government (via the Ministry for Technology, Trade and Industry, MITI) and unions which forged a coherent long-term strategy, targeting particular products and developing new complementarities between components, consumer electronics and computers. This arrangement also provided security and allowed banks to offer lower interest on loans than is available outside Japan, and this in turn allowed aggressive pricing (UNCTC 1983: 286). In addition the highly vertically integrated character of firms such as Hitachi also allowed them to exploit the complementarities between chip design and system design. In these ways, the social or institutional form of Japanese capital has had a significant effect upon its performance. As Dosi (1981) comments, where other countries took their place in the international division of labor as given and hence took licensing (i.e. the institutional-ization of technological dependency) and inward investment as parameters, Japan treated them as variables and strove successfully to change them.

At several points, we have alluded to the use of the Third World countries for cheap labor by the multinationals. After Fairchild established a labor-intensive assembly plant in Hong Kong in 1962, a procession of firms set up in the Far East, locating first in the newly industrialized countries (NICs) and later diffusing out to countries with still cheaper labor, such as the Philippines (Chang 1971, Ernst 1981, Rada 1982). A smaller number of plants was set up in Latin America, particularly Mexico (Table 6.2). In fact, the attractiveness of such locations to capital lay not just in their low wages but in their 'green' labor forces, their longer working hours, scope for multiple shifts, replace-ability of labor, state repression of labor organization and tax holidays and other benefits provided by the host government. Understandably, given these conditions, the Third World plants have been the subject of consider-able attention on the left (e.g. Grossman 1980, *Global Electronics Information Newsletter* various dates, Elson & Pearson 1981, Fröbel *et al.* 1980). But while it is important that these conditions be exposed, there is a widespread tendency on the left to exaggerate their relative quantitative significance, mainly as a consequence of ignoring the much larger volumes of foreign direct investment going into the developed countries (see e.g. especially Fröbel *et al.* 1980).

In the case of semiconductors, supposedly a 'good example' of the 'runaway industry phenomenon' (e.g. see Fröbel *et al.* 1980: 331–8), several qualifi-cations to the dominant view are needed. First the Third World locations are most favored not by all but by a *subset* of semiconductor firms – *US merchant* producers of *standardized* chips. The main reason for the prominence of this group is their use of manual, rather than automated, assembly which as already noted contrasts with the captive producers using automated assembly.

A. Sayer

Table 6.2 Principal developing country locations of semiconductor assembly

	Value of OECD imports of semiconductors from each country (million dollars)
Malaysia	1066.4
Singapore	820.6
Philippines	482.1
Republic of Korea	385.1
Taiwan Province	359.4
Hong Kong	202.7
Mexico	145.2
Thailand	85.5
Indonesia	62.5
El Salvador	49.3
Brazil	30.7
Barbados	14.0
Total	3703.5

Source: UNCTC 1983: 35.

The group's predominance of American firms does not just reflect their dominance of the industry: it also reflects the fact that the American tariff structure is much more favorable to the (re) importation of semiconductors from offshore plants than is the European one. While the latter has a 17% tariff, American importers only pay duty on value added abroad. However, this does of course give American firms a motive for obtaining access to the European market from European rather than Third World subsidiaries.

Also, as chip integration becomes greater, the relative amount of assembly work to be done becomes smaller. At the same time, increasing levels of integration push up the capital costs of wafer fabrication much faster than assembly costs, which become relatively less critical, thereby reducing the need for cheap labor locations. In any case, in recent years, the merchant producers have also been turning to automated assembly. Rada (1982) reports that, with automation, one worker with two weeks' training can replace 30 manual assemblers with three months' training each. These changes reduce the significance of labor costs and hence the attractiveness of Third World locations relative to the economies of co-locating automated assembly with wafer fabrication in developed countries. Although the Third World plants do not seem to be being abandoned, it does appear that advanced country locations are now more favored for new assembly plants. All of these factors are summed up in the case of Motorola, who recently claimed that increased freight charges, assembly automation and tariff barriers are driving them to shift assembly to advanced countries. Consequently they have now set up two new assembly plants, one at Phoenix, Arizona, the other at East Kilbride, Scotland. An executive of the firm said that 'we have to put as much added value inside the [European 17%] tariff barrier as we can' (*Electronics Weekly* December 7, 1983).

115

Two further influences are also contributing to an increased relative attractiveness of advanced country locations for assembly. First, there is a growing threat of disruption from political instability in the Far East, particularly the Philippines. Second, co-locating assembly and wafer fabrication has the advantage of reducing the large in-process inventories which are needed to maintain continuity of production where the two stages are separated by thousands of miles. This is important because while most faults in chip manufacture are introduced at the wafer-fabrication stage, many of them are not detectable until the final post-assembly test. Reducing the in-process inventories therefore allows more rapid feedback to wafer fabrication so that the production of further faulty chips can be prevented more quickly. Given that 'yield' (the inverse of the reject rate) is probably *the* key variable as regards cost competitiveness in integrated circuit production, co-location may be worthwhile even though labor costs are higher. It is also worth noting that this second factor works on the same principle as that underlying the 'just-in-time' production system pioneered in Japan in the auto industry, but now diffusing to other sectors and countries (cf. Schonberger 1982).

For producers of custom or semi-custom chips, production runs are much shorter, and again this means that the attractiveness of offshore assembly is smaller. This would help to explain why it is that in Silicon Valley's semiconductor plants, with their reputation for 'front-end' R & D and managerial 'high-tech' activities, the largest single group of workers are semi-skilled operatives (Bernstein *et al.*).

Some of the above reasons also help to explain why European firms made less use of Third World assembly locations. While Philips, Siemens, SGS-Ates and AEG-Telefunken have offshore plants in Southeast Asia (UNCTC 1983), their product ranges do not lend themselves to this option as much as those of the US firms. In one case (Siemens), trade-union pressure helped to bring the assembly back to Europe. Other inhibiting factors were their semi-captive nature, their lower involvement in standardized products and the European tariff barrier.

In keeping with their reputation as 'reluctant multinationals,' the Japanese firms also made less use than the Americans of cheap labor countries for assembly, even though they concentrated on mass produced standardized chips: offshore locations have usually had inferior productivity and quality to domestic locations. Also, 'From the start [they] relied to a greater extent than their United States counterparts on the introduction of labor-saving [and yield improving] automated assembly equipment in their domestic facilities' (UNCTC 1983: xvii). As a result they have made much less use of Far East cheap labor locations than the Americans, and where they have had to use them for cost reasons they have also used more automation. It is also partly because of Japanese competition, as well as wage rises in the NICs, that the Americans have recently had to turn more to automated assembly.

In recent years, some Japanese producers have established production bases in other *developed* countries. Virtually their only reason for investing in Europe and making deals with European firms is to pre-empt protectionism, though access to relatively cheap software skills may also be a reason. Within Europe, language and relatively low wages appear to be the chief reasons for

116

A. Sayer

their choice of Ireland and Britain as their main bases. Their investments in fabrication and (automated) assembly plants in the USA (by NEC, Hitachi, Oki, Toshiba and Fujitsu) are also to gain greater market penetration and domestic producer status, and for faster monitoring of US technology.

The need to catch up with American technology has also been the prime motive behind European producers' investments in the USA. Several have made deals with American firms, and as has happened within the American industry itself large diversified electronics firms from Europe have taken over small innovative US firms, exchanging cash for technology and know-how (e.g. Philips-Signetics, Lucas-Siliconix). Most of the American firms also have R & D centers in Europe, which tend to be used for tapping local software skills and for adapting existing products to local markets. In other words, the location of investment by semiconductor multinationals is heavily influenced by the distribution of scarce, relatively immobile technical skills as well as by the localization of and need for access to advanced markets, though over-emphasis of the runaway Third World plants, which deal with just one (often dispensable) type of activity, has led many radicals to miss this point.

The British firm, INMOS, provides an interesting illustration. This was launched in 1978 with government sponsorship in order to try to ensure that Britain had a domestic capability in advanced mass-market chips. Besides raising cash, the main problem it faced was access to technology – for to compete at all in this market it had to be producing 'state-of-the-art' devices. Given its small size it has tended to subcontract assembly to plants in South Korea and the Philippines, in the 'traditional' manner of merchant chip producers. But in order to catch up with technological development, most of the investment to date has been in its *US* plant, and in 1983 employment there stood at 750 as compared to 650 in the UK! Similarly, other firms in microelectronics, like Rodime in Scotland, have felt obliged to invest outside Britain (again in the USA in this case) soon after birth.

If we move down to the level of some of the individual European countries, we can see how the international competitive state of play has been influenced by national governments. EEC-wide initiatives to revive the industry and unite Europe's 'hostile brothers' have been relatively limited and insecure. An initial EEC proposal for a five- to six-year program of R & D collaboration was dropped in 1977 because of disagreements among the participating firms over sensitive product design areas. Later the ESPRIT (European Strategic Programme of Research in Technology) program was set up, beginning with funding not for product development research but for production technology. But then this tended to compete and conflict with national initiatives. Also, while each country is not big enough to support a full range of semiconductor devices, each country tends to be pursuing this goal, even though their home firms tend to be specializing (UNCTC 1983: 232–3).

Divergences in the interests of firms plus the problem of non-European producers within the EEC have weakened such alliances, especially as the largest firms are tempted to go it alone, and most have tie-ups with America. Another factor tending to undermine EEC initiatives is rivalry between the

117

member states and divergences in policies toward inward investment and microelectronics. As might be expected, the national governments' policies tend to vary not only with their political character but with the place of their domestic capital in the international market. For example, at one extreme France has a strongly interventionist policy. This involves heavy investment in partly state-owned firms like Thomson-CSF and CII-Honeywell Bull, the promotion of mergers, discrimination against American producers in state purchasing and R & D subsidies, and encouragement of joint ventures with inward investors conditional upon some degree of technology transfer (e.g. Thomson-CSF and Motorola). These policies have not been sufficient to allow the French firms to break into mass markets and escape their dependence on the military markets. In other words, the attempt to set up new complementarities between semiconductors and civilian users such as the French computer industry have yet to succeed.

In characteristically piecemeal fashion, British policy also included investment grants (regional or industry-specific), small selective industry programs like the Microprocessor Applications Project, plus the National Enterprise Board's highly risky attempt to break into the mass market for chips through INMOS. After hesitantly and reluctantly supporting the latter, the Conservative government has allowed it to be sold off to a British diversified electronics firm, Thorn-EMI, after resisting bids from some American firms which were short of production capacity. Generally, the Conservative government has held back from a more directive role in restructuring the electronics industry to exploit the Information Technology market. The foreign firms have produced a few spin-offs, particularly in Scotland which now has the biggest concentration of semiconductor producers (over 90% US-owned) in Europe. Here the foreign firms in semiconductors and other electronic sectors have produced the beginnings of a pool of skilled labor and a number of new small firms related to them through personnel, products or services. However, at the moment it appears that the foreign firms form an enclave and have not really joined or invigorated the British indigenous electronics industry.

Similarly in Ireland, with its generous incentives for foreign firms, and even cheaper labor than Britain, the open-door policy has only been successful in terms of numbers of entries and not in terms of 'quality,' that is, they have mainly been in low-level assembly functions with few spin-offs into the indigenous economy either technologically or in narrow financial terms (*Irish Business* August 1981). In other words, Ireland's position in the international division of labor has remained a lowly one.

The characteristics of nation states and the actions of government therefore contribute to the complexity and contradictory nature of competition. While it is both a highly competitive and internationalized sector, most firms still have an identifiable national character which affects their behavior. State intervention is considerable, and when threatened, firms will appeal to their home governments for protection and will enter into agreements with other home firms. But they also simultaneously attempt to steal a march on other domestic firms and collaborate with firms of other domiciles to catch up or gain an advantage over rivals. As always capitals exploit this situation thoroughly opportunistically and it is only in Japan that collaboration and competition are regulated and combined in a fairly stable manner, so that it has been possible to change rather than accept their initial position in the international division of labor.

For labor, the implications of the above changes in the nature and geography of the industry are diverse. Employment in the semiconductor industry is small and increasingly polarized between a group of very highly skilled occupations which is increasing both relatively and absolutely, and a group of semi-skilled operatives which is declining relatively, if not absolutely. Given the restriction of women to the operator grade and their absence in the highly skilled grades, the changing skill structure and the relative decline in the firms' needs for cheap assembly labor imply a decreasing rather than an increasing proportion of women. Contrary to the glamorous images of 'high-tech,' the pay and working conditions of the latter group vary from poor to appalling in the Third World plants, although despite state and company repression in the latter, many work-forces have rebelled, sometimes successfully. By American standards, pay and conditions – including work hazards – for operators in Silicon Valley are also poor, again contrary to popular images (Siegel 1980). Finally, the sector is probably one of the least unionised of all manufacturing industries, and in this respect, not to mention the lack of worker control and defense-orientation of products, the sector represents a challenge to organized labor and the left in devising strategies.

Conclusions

It should now be clear that many features of the geography of semiconductor production do not fit the popular radical stereotypes of locational strategies of multinationals and the changing international divison of labor. The most obvious clashes were the dispensability of labor-intensive procedures as automation proceeds and hence the existence of alternatives to cheap labor locations; related to this, the possibility of *rising* levels of average skill requirements as process and product technology change (cf. Sayer 1985); the continued importance of geographical proximity in terms of access to markets, especially to specialist users and related industries (e.g. to computer systems manufacturers in the case of custom and semi-custom products), and access to localized pools of labor for R & D and process engineering; the difficulty of reproducing Japanese levels of productivity and quality overseas, which tends to conflict with the idea that standardized, 'overspill' branch plants can be set up anywhere; and finally the influence of tariffs and other barriers and incentives placed by nation-states on geographical patterns of internationalization.

The contrasts with the radical 'orthodoxy' can best be demonstrated by reference to the influential 'new international division of labor thesis.' Fröbel *et al.* (1980) isolate three sets of conditions influencing the reorganization of the international division of labor:

(a) *The development of a world wide reservoir of potential labour power* . . . [which]

displays the following characteristics which indicate its potential use in the valorization and accumulation process of capital. [low wages, long hours, opportunities for higher rates of exploitation, etc.] (p 34).

(b) *The development and refinement of technology and job organisation makes it possible to decompose complex production processes into elementary units such that even unskilled labour can easily be trained in quite a short period of time to carry out these rudimentary operations* (p 35).

(c) *The development of a technology which renders industrial location and the management of production itself largely independent of geographical distance* (p 36).

We accept that all three are *possibilities* which may be open to some industries for certain periods of time. But *equally* we could argue the following points. First, the developing worldwide reservoir of potential labor power may fail to be exploited more than marginally, precisely because the recession is heightening the pressure on firms to automate, and microelectronics itself offers possibilities of a cheapening of some key production technology, often in ways which favor developed country locations (e.g. see Kaplinksy 1984).

Secondly, the development of technology and job organization makes it possible to eliminate highly specialized but low-skilled labor and to recombine activities that had formerly been separated. And finally, some technological developments make proximity *more* important, and particularly for custom products (by no means insignificant) seller–user proximity is critical. But in any case, the 'effects of space' are always double-edged, contrary to crude notions of the 'annihilation of space by time.' Reduction of the 'friction of distance' can enable *greater* proximity between activities, and the effect of capitalist competition may be to drive firms to treat this possibility as a necessity – as in the case of the flood of European investments in electronics into California. Even the runaway industry phenomenon itself proves the point: it was only when transport costs were lowered that access to (i.e. proximity to) cheap labor in the Third World become more than an academic possibility. And once a few leading firms took advantage of it, others had to too, unless other possibilities for competing were found: as we have seen, they are being found.

Although we have only provided evidence from one industry, and a small one at that, its geographical tendencies are by no means unique. The consumer electronics industry also combines a runaway industry element with (subsequent) renewed investment in the advanced countries (Morgan & Sayer 1983). Where British and American producers tended to treat products such as television sets as mature products, whose costs of manufacture could only be lowered by producing from cheap labor countries, Japanese producers pursued what proved to be the superior strategy of introducing significant process and product innovations which nearly decimated the European and American television industries. Automation and changes in product design shifted cost advantages back toward production in the major markets, symbolized by Matsushita's takeover of an ailing television plant in Chicago and the procession of Japanese television firms into Europe, particu-

A. Sayer

larly Britain. Again, tariff barriers were an additional factor. Even in the clothing industry (the main example examined by Fröbel *et al.* 1980), where the nature of the material makes assembly (i.e. sewing) particularly difficult to automate, automated pre-assembly (i.e. cutting, dyeing, etc.) is diffusing and leading manufacturers, especially the Japanese, are researching automated assembly methods. Rapid access to the market has also remained important in clothing. In the computer industry, access to buyers of systems, not just for sales themselves but for lucrative after-sales service contracts, requires location in developed countries and the industry's rising relative costs of software also encourage market location. In Europe, part of the reason for the success of the American firms lies in the ability to finance a denser network of centers from which they can 'service' the market in each country.

Many of these other industries are relatively 'mature' compared to semiconductors, and less dramatically subject to continual technical change. As Abernathy *et al.* argue, until recently management in many of the leading American firms in these industries had come to assume that they *were* 'mature' and therefore that they could only continue to make economies by increasing their scale of operations and/or finding cheaper labor (Abernathy *et al.* 1983). However, as has been shown particularly by Japanese firms, these industries can 'de-mature,' through the introduction of different ways of organizing production (in particular the just-in-time system; cf. Schonberger 1982) and through the use of new kinds of automation which give the possibility of more flexible manufacturing systems and which, as Kaplinsky (1984) argues, tend to favor agglomerated rather than dispersed production locations. At any rate, decentralization of production to cheap labor locations (through the 'annihilation of space by time') is by no means the only 'way out' for capital in the recession.

Note that I am not suggesting that these centripetal tendencies will either lead to a slump in the fortunes of the main Third World producers or a reversal of manufacturing employment decline in the metropolitan countries. In the first case, the diversity of cost structures for different types of firms means that the automation and use of cheaper labor will have different advantages and disadvantages for each one. In the second place, the effect of further investment in the developed countries may be to displace more jobs than are being added. So 'deindustrialization,' in the sense of job loss in manufacturing, may paradoxically be as much if not more a result of a certain kind of reindustrialization (in investment rather than employment terms) than a result of a dispersal of manufacturing to the Third World.

Neither the patterns identified by the radical stereotypes nor the different patterns identified in this chapter are incompatible with the marxian abstract theory of capital. On the contrary, the latter is vital for understanding the dynamics which make the various contingent factors or mediations which affect concrete situations relevant to capital. For example, the employment effects of new technologies are not simply functions of the latter but of using new technologies under capitalist 'rules.' But this of course does not mean that the particular nature of the technology makes no difference. In other words, this is to re-state the importance of distinguishing between concrete

121

and abstract research and of taking seriously the influence of mediations.

Finally, there is perhaps another source of distortion in the popular radical views of the internationalization of production which gives rise to the neglect of *particular kinds* of mediations and not just random omissions. *Assembly* activities – particularly in mass production – tend to be treated as the only significant part of industrial capital, at the expense of pre-assembly fabrication work, small batch, custom and semi-custom work, R & D, management and administration and marketing and service functions, often performed by the same firms. I have suggested elsewhere (Sayer 1985) that this arises from a combination of theoretical reasons (the easier applicability of ideas about de-skilling and 'Taylorism' and 'Fordism' to mass assembly work) and political priorities (favoring the study of blue collar workers). Some of the latter are understandable in left research (e.g. the priority given to workers over managers and administrators) but others are more arbitrary, arising from dated ideas about who are 'typical' members of the working class, a preoccupation with the 'mass collective worker' (a declining species), and a blindness towards both working-class occupations which do not fit the stereotype and more 'middle-class' occupations. Yet even in the case of the more reasonable political priorities, it must be remembered that the fortunes of the favored groups are tied up inextricably with those of the higher-status groups involved in the 'front-end' activities of industry such as management, R & D workers and graduate engineers. Political priorities should not be rigidly pre-set and then allowed to determine the visibility of important concrete developments; rather they should be continually reassessed in the light of more open and wide-ranging empirical investigations. As I hope this chapter has shown, we should always be alive to the diversity and changeability of capital's forms of development and resist the temptation to treat particular forms as the only possible outcomes of capital accumulation.

Note

This paper arises from research undertaken with Kevin Morgan and funded by the Economic and Social Research Council.

References

Abernathy, W. J., K. B. Clark and A. M. Kantrow 1983. *Industrial renaissance: producing a competitive future for America.* New York: Basic Books.

Bernstein, B., B. DeGrasse, R. Grossman, C. Paine and L. Siegel 1977. *Silicon Valley: paradise or paradox?* Mountain View, Calif.: Pacific Studies Center.

Chang, Y. S. 1971. *The transfer of technology: the economics of offshore assembly: the case of semiconductor industry.* New York: United Nations Institute for Training and Research.

Dosi, G. 1981. Technical change and survival: Europe's semiconductor industry. *Industrial adjustment and policy*, II. Sussex European Research Centre, Paper 9, University of Sussex.

Duncan, M. 1981. The information technology industry in 1981. *Capital and Class* **17**, 79–113.

Dunford, M. and D. Perrons 1983. *The arena of capital*. London: Macmillan.

Dunford, M. and D. Perrons 1984. *Integration and unequal development: towards an understanding of the impact of economic integration on Ireland and Southern Italy*. University of Sussex Urban and Regional Studies Working Paper 36.

Elson, D. and R. Pearson 1981. Nimble fingers make cheap workers. *Feminist Review* **7**, 87–107.

Ernst, D. 1981. *Restructuring world industry in a period of crisis: the role of innovation*. New York: UNIDO.

Fröbel, F., J. Heinrichs and O. Kreye 1980. *The new international division of labour*. Cambridge: Cambridge University Press.

Global Electronics Information Newsletter (various dates). San Francisco: Pacific Studies Center.

Grossman, R. 1980. Bitter wages: women in East Asia's semiconductor plants. *Multinational Monitor* **1**(2), 8–11.

Kaplinsky, R. 1984. *Automation: the technology and society*. London: Longman.

Lipietz, A. 1982. Towards global Fordism? *New Left Review* March–April.

Lipietz, A. 1984. Imperialism or the beast of the apocalypse. *Capital and Class* **22**, 81–109.

Maddock, I. 1983. *Civil exploitation of defence technology*. London: National Economic Development Council.

Mandel, E. 1975. *Late capitalism*. London: New Left Books.

Morgan, K. and A. Sayer 1983. *The international electronics industry and regional development in Britain*. University of Sussex Urban and Regional Studies Working Paper 34.

Palloix, C. 1975. The internationalisation of capital and the circuit of social capital. In Radice 1975.

Rada, J. 1982. *Structure and behaviour of the semiconductor industry*. New York: United Nations Center on Transnational Corporations.

Radice, H. (ed.) 1975. *International firms and modern imperialism*. Harmondsworth: Penguin.

Sayer, A. 1985. Industry and space: a sympathetic critique of radical research. *Society and Space* **3**(1), 3–29.

Schonberger, R. J. 1982. *Japanese management techniques*. New York: Free Press.

Sciberras, E. 1977. *Multinational electronics companies and national economic policies*. Greenwich, Conn.: JAI Press.

Siegel, L. 1980. Delicate bonds: the global semiconductor industry. *Pacific Research*, special issue, **9**(1), 1–26.

Teulings, A. W. M. 1984. The internationalization squeeze: double capital movement and job transfer within Philips worldwide. *Environ. Plann. A* **16**, 597–614.

UNCTC 1983. *Transnational corporations in the international semiconductor industry*. New York: United Nations Center on Transnational Corporations.

PART III

Work and labor markets

7

The crisis of
the midwest
auto industry

GORDON L. CLARK

The word 'crisis' is probably overused and abused. Too often contemporary observers of the economic scene label as crisis even the most temporary of economic turning points and the shallowest of economic downturns. And too often the vicissitudes of capitalist life are taken as signs of an impending disaster, one so catastrophic that it will remake the whole mode of production. O'Connor's (1984) latest book on the crisis of the American economy is filled with such warnings. However, the trouble with these warnings is that it is difficult for the reader to identify what is so unique about present crisis conditions, given that past crises passed without the promised collapse.

Whether or not the economy is posed at the precipice of a millennial turning-point is the heart of current marxist writing, even journalistic newspaper commentaries on Third World indebtedness and the banking industry[1]. Cassandras abound on the left, and Dr. Pangloss is represented politically by none other than the President of the United States. Somewhere in between, residents of midwest industrial communities live 'lives of quiet desperation' – mass unemployment is too close for comfort, the welfare state cannot be relied upon to bolster local welfare, and solutions to the crisis of local industry are not obvious. In this context, a more than trivial understanding of the notion of crisis is vital for those involved in, and for those who write theory.

However, it is with some trepidation that I embark upon an essay on the crisis of the midwest auto industry. We must thread a story that does not reduce to yet another apocalyptic vision of local collapse. On the other hand, we must be wary of those who claim there is a much brighter future just around the corner, if only the local economy is allowed to respond. This is surely the message of the Reagan Administration. For instance, the 1982 urban policy report (US Department of Housing and Urban Development 1982) proclaimed the virtues of rapid adjustment to changing economic fortunes while ridiculing the capacity of government to improve local conditions. There is no urban policy, rather national economic development policy (Hanson 1983). Nevertheless, midwest auto communities face a crisis of depression proportions. There is a very real danger that these communities of industry and commerce will be destroyed over the next decade. Even in the oldest of these communities, like Flint, Michigan, the home of the original consortium which put General Motors together in the early years of this century, communities are fundamentally at risk.

This chapter is an exercise in interpretation. I do not propose to 'prove' my case so much as indicate the logic of an alternative conception of regional growth and decline. The next section deals in detail with aspects of this crisis, especially as relating to the labor market. Two arguments are then advanced. First, it is suggested that contemporary regional crisis theories are overly mechanical. Indeed, a very real problem with such theories, whether radical or orthodox, is their use of logical devices to drive historical events. In such theories, crisis is inevitable and unavoidable. The problem, though, is that these theories remove all prospects for human agency, especially changing local circumstances.

Secondly, it is also suggested that regional crises are inherently political in that adjustment to changing economic fortunes requires reconfiguration of class bargains. Where bargains are ossified by the past, even the most minor of economic events can become a crisis. Generally, I suggest in this chapter that class relations make and restructure crises. By this perspective, local crises are points of tension located in space and time by a conjunction of past class relations and unintegrated events. As such, crises are more like transition points than cliff edges over which whole communities must inevitably tumble. In this context, the central issue facing workers in the midwest region is the fashioning of a new class bargain which can both overcome the past and garner enough support from labor and capital to be relevant for current conditions. While class tensions and class conflict are exacerbated by current conditions affecting the relations between workers and between workers and management, only a restructured class bargain will save the midwest auto industry.

The dimensions of local crisis

There are any number of ways of describing the crisis of the midwest auto industry. For example, we could focus upon social indicators like local mental health-care admissions, crime, or even divorce rates. So, for instance, any analysis of local crime rates in midwest auto cities over the past few years would lead one to conclude that they have been nothing short of astronomical[2]. All these indicators of local social stress have close connections with local economic wellbeing (see for example, the study by Dear, Clark & Clark 1979 on community mental health and the economy). Attempts have been made by other scholars to give full weight to these dimensions of local crisis (see, for example, the study by Hill 1984 on the racial and welfare consequences of crisis in Detroit).

Here, I wish to concentrate on the crudest of measures of economic crisis: unemployment, employment, wages, and hours of work. It has been argued elsewhere (Medoff 1979, Clark 1983), that the latter three variables are the basic instruments of firms' control over labor in the production process. On the labor input side of firms' adjustment strategies, these three levers control the volume of labor power. As such, these variables reflect the conditions of firms as well as workers. Note, however, that local contracts may have quite specific effects on these strategies whatever the level of overall aggregate demand (Clark 1983). Measured unemployment rates hide a good deal, especially as economic conditions worsen. Clark and Summers (1979) showed that as unemployment increases, more and more people leave the labor market at such rapid rates that measured unemployment rates are systematically distorted and underestimated. There are also quite particular regional effects to be considered, although little work has been done on this phenomenon in the USA, compared to Britain (see Cheshire 1973). Even so, unemployment rates can be used to trace the path of local economic changes, if not their absolute dimensions.

The time frame of the current crisis in the midwest auto industry can be dated from about the mid 1970s. After the brief, but sharp, recession of 1974, employment in the industry and region expanded until 1978 – the peak year of output and employment for the whole decade. Nationally, all durable goods industries prospered through these years, and 1978 was a peak year in national economic activity compared even to the mid 1960s[3]. However, by 1982 the economy was in the worst slump since the end of World War II. The automobile industry was particularly affected, as the midwest economy plummeted into a depression. The General Accounting Office (1982: 11) noted, 'given the industry's geographic concentration, its plight has been felt disproportionately in the midwest, especially in Michigan and Ohio.' These two states, and other midwestern states like Minnesota and Wisconsin, came close to default on their budget debts; states' revenues were severely cut as welfare demands rose remarkably quickly. Even in late 1984, midwest unemployment rates were the highest in the nation, despite a recovery in the durable goods industries.

Beginning with Table 7.1, is it apparent that the 1982 recession caused tremendous hardship in Michigan auto-based cities. The city of Flint went from an unemployment rate of 8.8% in 1978 to 27.1% in 1982, before returning to an unemployment rate in the teens in 1984 (13.4%). While Flint recorded the highest official unemployment rate during this period, it was not unusual. Two other cities had unemployment rates over 20%, and many Michigan cities had rates of at least 15% or more. Compared to 1978, unemployment in these cities in 1984 was still very high. Compared to the national average unemployment rate of around 7.2% in 1984 (close to what some economists term as the 'natural' unemployment rate), the midwest remained in the grip of its most severe recession since the great depression of the 1930s[4]. Given the severity of the 1982 recession, the subsequent economic recovery has not returned these cities to their late 1970s heights of prosperity. And, given the patterns of local unemployment, one can only guess how massive unemployment has affected local labor force participation rates. Going on the national evidence of Clark and Summers (1979), it is quite possible that local unemployment rates are underestimated by between 7.0% and 14.0%.

By necessity, local unemployment rates are only crude indicators of local joblessness. Moreover, these figures do not directly address the patterns of job

Table 7.1 Percent unemployment in Michigan cities, 1978–84.

City	1978	1980	1982	1984
Ann Arbor	3.6	4.1	6.1	7.2
Battle Creek	8.0	11.4	18.5	12.7
Bay City	7.8	15.4	16.0	14.3
Detroit	8.3	18.5	20.3	12.2
Flint	8.8	18.2	27.1	13.4
Grand Rapids	5.5	8.5	14.9	9.9
Jackson	6.4	11.4	17.8	13.4
Kalamazoo	6.8	7.9	12.3	9.8
Lansing	6.5	9.2	14.2	8.7
Saginaw	7.2	19.0	23.5	11.6
Michigan	6.9	11.0	15.5	12.4

Sources: Data for 1978 were made available by the Michigan Employment Security Commission (MESC). Data for 1980 and 1982 were derived from the *County and City Data Book*, with additions from the MESC. Estimates for 1984 were derived from the June 1984 *Area Trends in Employment and Unemployment*, and news releases from the US Department of Labor. Note that for 1978, 1980, and 1982 the data are yearly averages.

loss in the local auto industry. In Table 7.2, detailed figures are given for local job loss in the industry. Here, the dimensions of change from 1978 to 1982 are also of crisis proportions. Overall, Michigan lost some 120 000 jobs during this period, a decrease of about 28%. While all cities lost a large number of jobs over this period, some cities were more affected than others. For instance, Bay City lost over 40% of its auto jobs, Jackson lost over 46% of its auto jobs, and Detroit lost about 32% of its auto jobs. Only Battle Creek was

Table 7.2 Job loss in the transportation equipment industry: Michigan auto cities, 1978 and 1982.

City	1978	1982	% change
Ann Arbor	21 800	16 100	−26.1
Battle Creek	2 400	2 200	−8.3
Bay City	4 400	2 600	−40.9
Detroit	260 400	175 400	−32.6
Flint	62 200	45 700	−26.5
Grand Rapids	4 800	3 500	−27.1
Jackson	4 900	2 600	−46.9
Kalamazoo	3 600	2 800	−22.2
Lansing	27 400	24 400	−10.9
Saginaw	15 600	10 700	−31.4
Michigan	432 700	303 200	−29.9

Sources: Employment, Hours and Earnings, States and Areas, 1939–82, Bureau of Labor Statistics, US Department of Labor. Bulletin 1370–17.
Note: This date refers to SIC 37. The more specific SIC category would be SIC 371; however, this was not available for all the cities listed above.

relatively slightly affected, losing just over 8% of its auto jobs. Even Ann Arbor, which had about the average national unemployment rate in 1984 (7.2%, see Table 7.1), lost over 26% of its auto jobs from 1978 to 1982.

It would be tempting to believe that the economic recovery of the past few years will absorb those workers who lost their jobs during the 1982 recession. However, all the evidence suggests that many of these workers will not be re-employed. In 1978, General Motors (GM) produced about 6.9 million cars and trucks with about 500000 hourly workers. By late 1984, GM was producing about 5.1 million units with 380000 hourly workers. Moreover, GM has announced plans to further reduce its work-force by at least 120000 through to the end of 1986. If its plans are realized, GM will have reduced its work-force by about 50% over the course of six years. The number of workers involved in this manpower shedding are large, even overwhelming compared to the base levels of employment of 1978. While the 1982 recession made massive inroads on the levels of employment in Michigan cities, economic restructuring is a continuing process. This will be likely to impoverish Michigan auto cities for the immediate future.

More detailed evidence of this recent crisis of the midwest auto industry is presented in Table 7.3 for Detroit. In the period 1978 to 1982, employment shrank considerably in the local machinery (SIC 35) and electrical and electronic equipment (SIC 36) industries (−17.7% and −10.5% respectively). In the fabricated metals (SIC 34) and motor vehicle (SIC 371) industries, employment shrank dramatically (−38.0% and −33.8%). Similarly, average weekly hours also declined dramatically, as the local economy went from relative boom to recession.

Table 7.3 Employment and compensation in Detroit auto-related industries, 1978 and 1982.

Industry	Employment (000s)		(% change)	Average weekly hours		Average weekly earnings ($)		Average hourly earnings ($)	
	1978	1982		1978	1982	1978	1982	1978	1982
fabricated metals	83.3	51.6	(−38.0)	42.4	39.5	347	425	8.20	10.76
machinery	89.1	73.3	(−17.7)	45.5	40.7	400	508	8.81	12.49
electrical and electronics equipment	7.6	6.8	(−10.5)	38.7	35.7	223	292	5.78	8.19
motor vehicles and equipment	252.8	167.4	(−33.8)	44.6	42.7	413	545	9.27	12.78

Sources: Employment, Hours, and Earnings, States and Areas, 1939–82, Bureau of Labor Statistics, US Department of Labor. Bulletin 1370–17.

Note: Fabricated metals is SIC 34; machinery is SIC 35; electrical and electronic equipment is SIC 36; and motor vehicles and equipment is SIC 371.

In terms of wages, however, average earnings continued to increase, reflecting the patterns of national and local consumer prices. The typical auto contract, like that signed by GM and the UAW in late 1984, protects real wages by factoring cost-of-living changes into money wage increases. Complete wage indexation is characteristic of this region[5]. The most recent round of negotiations in the industry between auto firms and the UAW resulted in a further extention of this agreement. The typical auto assembler will make about $12.78 per hour under this contract, not including overtime and other benefits which are partly included in the data for Detroit (Table 7.3). Recent evidence does suggest, however, that the rate of increase in local wages has slowed dramatically. The US Department of Labor reported in late 1984 that the Detroit area ranked only 181st out of 314 cities in terms of wage rate increases. This was despite the city's very high rank (9th) in the overall level of its wages relative to all other US cities.

It is generally assumed that Japanese auto makers have a manufacturing cost advantage of about $1500 per car over domestic auto makers[6]. Despite this advantage (or perhaps because of it) voluntary import quotas have remained stable and in force over much of the last six years (see Crandall 1984). Overall, domestic auto producers account for nearly 77% of the domestic American market. While this share has certainly declined since the early 1970s (from around 85%), shares have remained relatively stable in recent years. The threat of foreign competition is ever present, but still of limited importance. There is another more important threat: the power of GM. In 1984 this firm accounted for just over 40% of the US market, and over 65% of the US market served by domestic producers. Ford, its nearest competitor, had less than half the market share of GM, while Toyota and Nissan had just 4.7% and 4.6% of the domestic market respectively. Even though Ford and Chrysler have marginally improved their market shares at the expense of GM, GM remains firmly in control of the market.

There is a crisis in the midwest auto industry, but its effects are unevenly distributed. Just as auto firms have announced plans to shed more labor, these same firms have announced significantly higher profits. Crandall (1984) estimated that auto industry profits have returned to their late 1970s level. In 1982, the trough of the recession, average profit per auto was about $27; in 1983 profits per auto were about $353 (discounted by 1972 dollars). Most recent estimates of industry profits suppose that American auto firms have tripled their returns over the past year. This crisis seems to be less one of firms' integrity and more one of workers and their communities. Job loss has been dramatic and will continue. While real wages continue to increase, the base of employment shrinks. There is no evidence to suggest that midwest auto cities will regain employment levels of past years. Indeed, all the evidence seems to suggest just the reverse.

Regional crisis theory

In the regional economic literature there is a tendency to believe that crises are catastrophic – implying the existence of inevitable and fundamental turning-points in economic activity. For example, Casetti's (1981) attempt to formulate a model of regional economic reversal posits the existence of a unique inflexion point on a region's cost curve which switches growth from one region to another. This switching mechanism is introduced by Casetti through the medium of catastrophe theory. At one level, his model is really a physical analogy. It is an intuitive device which is used to explicate, in theoretical terms, a supposed reversal of the fortunes of US regions[7]. At a deeper level, his model is purely mechanical. It depends on a logical shift in the parameters of the regional system to drive actual change in the various regions of the economy. At this level, structural change is inevitable.

Casetti's model is incoherent for a number of reasons. While it depends upon neo-classical theory for the logic of reversal, it denies the central thesis of neo-classical economics: the efficiency of the market mechanism. Casetti begins with the conventional assumption of increasing and then decreasing returns to scale. He applies this assumption to the regional growth process, arguing that local scale diseconomies (like pollution, congestion, etc.) set in at the regional level after a period of economic growth and prosperity. His analysis is marginally based in the sense that he assumes that firms decide their location in accordance with locationally relative marginal costs. And his analysis is price-oriented in that it is the marginal differences in local prices which switch firms between regions. The inflexion point on the regional production frontier is the point where, according to Casetti, the whole regional economic system is transformed[8].

As a neo-classical theory, it is strangely less than neo-classical. By that I mean that Casetti assumes the regional switch-point to be unknown and unanticipated. Otherwise, if economic agents knew of its existence (which they would given Casetti's full information assumption), it would be integrated into the market prices for different locations much before it was actually reached (Fisher 1983). This suggests that there would be no sudden switch in the competitive position of one region versus another. In fact, fully anticipated switches imply regular and smooth regional transformation, not discontinuous crises. To make Casetti's model work as a neo-classical model we must either assume that the switch he has in mind is unique or, if anticipated, it cannot be avoided. Casetti appeals to qualitative evidence regarding the existence of increasing and then decreasing returns to scale, but constrains his agents from using this information in their relative pricing decisions. Thus his model is both neo-classical and anti-neoclassical. Of course, he needs this kind of reasoning to generate catastrophic switches in regional structure. However, there does not seem to be any reason why we should accept this kind of logic.

Casetti's model has also been criticized from a different vantage point. Gertler (1986) suggested that the problem with Casetti's model is that it is not dynamic, despite appearances. Time is treated by Casetti as a logical sequence of actions, given an imagined context. No 'real-time' dynamics are involved. Rather an assumption (or set of assumptions as we saw above) is invoked to shift the parameters of the regional economic system. Events, circumstances, even the behavior of rational market-oriented agents are irrelevant in this kind of world. The switch is mechanically pulled by the author at some point on the regional cost curve. Nothing is said about the adjustment behavior of economic agents, and nothing is said about the time horizon over which the switching process is supposed to proceed[9]. It is little wonder that Gertler was unable to find any real-time evidence of catastrophic parameter shifts – Casetti's model is not about real circumstances.

Elsewhere, there have been a few attempts to develop a more context-specific theory of regional crisis. A crucial point of emphasis in the radical literature on regional crisis has been the behavior of multilocational firms. English writers like Massey and Meegan (1980) and Lloyd (1984), and US writers like Bluestone and Harrison (1982) and Markusen (1984), have developed closely detailed studies of firms and industries and their regional forms of organization. In this literature, regional crises are the result of firms' decisions regarding production, employment, and technological change. Whereas Casetti's model depended upon the existence of a unique switching-point on a region's aggregate cost curve, industry-related regional crisis theories depend upon firms to restructure local conditions. Decisions regarding the organization of production are then the switch-points in the regional economic system.

This type of model of regional crisis is actually a regional relative-advantage model. That is, firms decide on their spatial configuration of production with reference to various regions' attributes. It may be the case that some firms have limited discretion in locating their production units. Whether because of fixed technical coefficients between labor and capital (Oi 1962) or task complementarities, decisions of what to produce, how to produce, and where to produce are inseparable (Clark 1981). As a consequence, some regions may be more useful than others, depending upon the functional characteristics of firms' production plans (Walker & Storper 1981).

In this kind of world, regional switching occurs as firms restructure their production systems, from one form of production and its associated region, to other forms of production and their best-use regions. Thus, for example, as firms shift from high-skill component forms of production to more routine production technologies employing less skilled labor, it is presumed that these firms will shift regions so as to take advantage of different regional labor markets more appropriate to their needs[10]. The only constraints on interregional switching is the need to maintain control of remote production facilities while ensuring an adequate return on capital. Even here, though, recent tax policies introduced by the Reagan Administration seem to have accelerated the process of regional switching[11]. Such switching is then the immediate source of regional crisis. To the extent a region is dominated by one or more such industries, any switch in the regional location of production will have catastrophic effects on the local region. And if some regions are more hospitable homes for firms which continue to switch their production plans, then these regions will exist on a roller-coaster of alternate economic growth and economic collapse.

What kind of assumptions are implied by the radical model of regional crisis? What is the 'engine' of local transformation of firms' and regions' production profiles? Answers to these two questions raise serious doubts of the veracity of the radical theory of regional crisis. Why should firms alter their production profiles in accordance with the economic landscape? An immediate answer might be that they have little choice, given the environment within which they operate. Implied is a competitive market environment; if not perfect competition, then at least a form of market competition more consistent with neo-classical price competition than Kaleckian price-setting theory[12]. A more subtle answer might be that firms continually fight with labor over the distribution of the surplus. Thus decisions to relocate may be defensive and offensive.

If we assume for the moment that these assumptions are plausible, how is regional switching represented in these theories as a temporal process? (Remember Casetti used a logical device to generate a one-time switch between regions.) Unfortunately, I believe that the radical literature has less to say about the timing issue than one might initially suppose. There appears to be nothing in these models to indicate whether or not regional switching is a slow or fast process or a continuous or discontinuous process. Obviously we would be uncomfortable with any logic which would replicate Casetti's. But if it is assumed that there is a point at which local capital accumulation is threatened by labor resistance to further exploitation, then I suspect the points raised in criticism of Casetti's model also apply here. That is, we must either assume that this point is unknown (but fundamentally dangerous once encountered) and/or that the market system is not adequately integrated to plan for its eventuality.

Of course, radical theorists need not be embarrassed for failing to follow the logic of neo-classical theory. Yet there is a disturbing issue here, just below the surface of radical regional crisis theory. Why should regional crises occur *if* firms know about the dangers of over-accumulation and over-exploitation? Why don't firms plan to avoid these crises by adjusting their production plans well before the crisis point? If they did plan in this way, then there would be no regional crises, but rather smooth paths of transition evidenced by continuous temporal profiles of investment and disinvestment. After all, these latter kinds of path are the time profiles of actual regional capital investment in the USA, as shown by Gertler (1984). As was noted above when discussing Casetti's conception of regional capital dynamics, there does not seem to be any evidence of massive parameter shifts in regional capital series since World War II.

How could this kind of crisis theory be justified, given what we know about real-time adjustment profiles? To assume that firms know about the dangers of over-concentration but are unable to do anything about it presumes that these firms operate in a highly competitive price environment. Thus, in this instance, it is the assumption of competition rather than any internal behavioral component which drives regional switches in this kind of model. Essentially, firms are captured at locations and have to wait for a regional crisis before being able to switch location. While it may be accurate to describe local employment restructuring in this manner, this is not the same as explaining the origins of employment crises. Indeed, the historicity of local crises imply a good deal of planning, particularly when it comes to switching production facilities between regions[13]. The problem with many radical regional crisis theories is that they depend upon quite particular assumptions of a neo-classical type regarding the limited capacity of firms to adjust to changing circumstances.

One way of avoiding this theoretical stance would be to add on another 'engine' of transformation. For some writers (Lloyd 1984), this engine is the Kondratieff cycle, a supposedly regular 40-year cycle of innovation, maturity, and stagnation. According to the logic of this model, waves of innovation pass through the economy on a regular basis, transforming and destroying past forms of production and firm organization. Regional crises are crises because these waves suddenly transform the existing spatial configuration of production. Whole spatial regimes of production are thrown into disarray as the relative advantages of regions are suddenly turned upside down. Though these cycles are supposed to be regular in timing and pattern (this is taken as evidence of their existence; see Mandel 1979), their effects are supposed to be irregular and discontinuous[14].

Again, like Casetti's model, whole regional systems are at the mercy of autonomous parameter shifts; no human agency is involved. Like Casetti's model, the modified radical-Kondratieff regional crisis model never specifies the process whereby a regular cycle becomes a real-time economic event. And like Casetti's model, it depends upon ignorance of the theory by economic agents (firms, labor, government, etc.) to generate regional switching, but then asks the reader to recognize its existence in the patterns of history. Why readers should have such a privileged position while ordinary economic agents do not remains a mystery. The logic of both types of models, conventional and radical, is that regional crises are unanticipated and unavoidable. All agents can do is respond; they cannot anticipate the process itself.

There appears to be no satisfactory theory of regional crisis. Yet, at the same time, there are important clues in our previous review of the regional crisis literature which can help us analyze the current crisis of the midwest auto industry. If any progress is to be made in interpreting recent events in the midwest region, we must acknowledge the reality of the following conditions. First, employment shifts, even though sudden and severe, should be acknowledged as having a recognizable origin. Local investment profiles should also be so interpreted, although their profiles appear more regular and planned. Secondly, it should be recognized that the current crisis has been coming for quite some time. It was not wholly unanticipated but neither was it wholly avoided. Thirdly, whether or not this crisis could have been averted must be evaluated in terms of the capacity of local economic agents to respond to the exigencies of circumstances. The fact that the crisis did occur must imply something about the nature of local class relations.

Essentially, I would argue that the theory of regional crisis must allow for knowledge of the economic system, continuous change, and discontinuous economic transformation. It should also allow for local control of events; classes must be able to grasp their history. Instead of assuming regional crisis to be the inevitable march of structure, history must be open to re-structuring (Pred 1984). The following section aims at interpreting the crisis of the midwest auto industry in the light of these conclusions regarding the proper logic of regional crisis theory.

G. L. Clark

A crisis of local class relations

The midwest auto industry has been more than aware of external competition for at least the past two decades. Just the development of the industry's 'southern strategy' indicates the planned nature of recent declines in the local industry. The extended multiplant production system, so typical of GM and Ford, has reached into all corners of the USA and Canada. Signing the Auto Pact with Canada in the mid 1960s prompted both the unions and the auto companies to restructure their modes of institutional organization; the UAW became an international union, and the auto companies committed a significant level of capital to their new territory[15]. While no one would suggest that the UAW is that well integrated spatially, trends in firm and union organization over the past 20 years have broadened the spatial scale of the industry considerably. The latest round of competition, this time from overseas, is then not so different in type as previous changes in the competitive environment. However, while local companies are involved with foreign companies in joint production ventures, here and abroad, the UAW has not been as successful in integrating foreign firms within the network of existing American labor relations.

Since the devastating conflicts between labor and capital in the midwest auto industry during the 1930s, labor and management have developed an intricate class bargain. This bargain allowed both sides to prosper, especially from the 1950s throughout the 1960s and most years of the 1970s. Of course, both sides have experienced ups and downs in their material fortunes. Recessions have always cost labor income and even jobs; temporary lay-offs have always been part of the bargain. But so too has re-hiring been part of the deal when the economy recovers. Similarly, management have had to accept lower profits during recessions and booms as part of the price of industrial harmony. As well, there have been considerable constraints placed on managements' shop floor discretion, especially with respect to the pace, organization, and pattern of production. Nonetheless, what has been so impressive about this bargain has been its resilience over the past 30 years.

But, I would contend, it is precisely this resilience which has made the changing international competitive environment a regional economic crisis of unparalleled proportions. Whereas the class bargain of the post-World War II era accommodated changing economic circumstances through to the mid 1970s, it now stands in the way of adjustment and adaption. This class bargain has ossified adjustment capacities at two levels. Between labor and management (what will be termed here as 'internal relations'), the previous pattern of labor agreements have paralyzed firms' capacities to adjust production strategies in the midwest region. As a result, regional switching has taken the place of *in situ* adjustment. One consequence has been the massive dislocation of local employment. I don't mean to 'blame' labor for this situation. The previous regime of labor relations was highly beneficial to both parties. And it is because of the past that local adjustment is now so tortuous. Moreover, managements, unlike labor, have an extraordinary advantage in this situation: they can walk away from old agreements without appearing liable for the situation they helped to create. The idea that labor is

137

to blame for current conditions has been fostered by the media and federal government.

This class bargain also ossified adjustment capacities in another way. Externally (between the industry and the rest of the US economy), this bargain made both labor and capital politically vulnerable to attack from other elites situated elsewhere in government and industry. According to some elites, the midwest auto industry has been unnecessarily protected. It is supposed by some that labor in particular prospered more than it deserved to through less than competitive market pricing practices. High wages have been paid for by consumers in the form of excessive auto prices given the relative quality of the product (relative, that is, to foreign competitors). The fact that the auto industry has allied itself to the conservative wing of the Democratic Party has not helped workers in their attempts to build a multi-union coalition to help protect midwest workers. Indeed, the very fact that these workers have been so privileged, and have resisted previous attempts by other unions and workers' groups to open up the industry to less privileged groups, has essentially isolated (spatially and functionally) the midwest region.

As a result of these two factors, labor is more vulnerable politically than capital in the process of regional restructuring. To understand why labor is apparently so locked in to past labor practices, and why firms have chosen to invest elsewhere, we need to consider in more depth the actual class relations of midwest auto cities. Generally, I would contend that these cities explicitly represent the class hierarchy embedded in the relations between labor and management in this region. There are two basic aspects to these local class relations.

First, there are the class relations of community. Plants, assembly lines, and product divisions have been traditionally organized by firms within communities. For instance, Flint, Michigan, has been the home of the Chevrolet division of GM. The Fisher Body firm (now part of GM) has been traditionally located in a neighborhood of Detroit. And the names of other Michigan communities, like Pontiac, are immediately associated with the functional structure of firms within the local economy. The growth of divisions, the success of product lines, are all replicated on the landscape by towns and cities. Unions have a close connection with these communities. Like the auto firms, the unions have been highly decentralized, depending upon their close family-like connections within these places for their power and stability. While both the unions and the firms have higher-level corporate entities, the midwest auto industry has been an industry of places.

This social cum spatial organization of production was consciously fostered by firms and unions. For firms, community association with particular product divisions fostered worker loyalty. Just like the much vaunted 'Japanese model of labor relations,' these communities offered workers employment from cradle to grave[16]. But, as well, this decentralized mode of organization allowed firms to restructure whole product lines without placing their other plants at risk in terms of labor unrest. As long as the industry itself remained viable, any local restructuring could be accommodated within the class bargain. Even now, a strong image held to by older workers in the

138

industry is of this 'family' association between plants and communities. And who can blame them for holding on to this image? Since the 1920s, whole generations of families have lived with these local plants, despite periodic bouts of unemployment.

The structure of decentralized class relations embodied in the spatial configuration of production also fits neatly with the dominant ideological framework of postwar American labor law. Stone (1981) described this framework as one of *industrial pluralism*; where collective bargaining takes place in a decentralized setting according to local contingencies. Cox (1947) described this model as replicating the republican ideal of local self-rule. And, more recently, Stone (1981) indicated how this version is still a dominant force in the interpretation of local labor relations. This model has maintained decentralized class relations just as firms have organized production on a local basis. While contract bargaining has often proceeded at the level of the firm and union (just as the recent accord was reached between the UAW and GM) through what have been called 'master contracts,' the local level has remained as the ultimate point at which such contracts are ratified, rejected, and complied with. Moreover, there are many instances where local negotiations have set the specific standards by which master contracts are to be evaluated.

Unlike so many other American communities, class position structures the everyday lives of residents. From the plant shop floor through to the local shopping mall, from residential location through to community organizations, management and workers are intimately related by relative status, power and position. In these ways, midwest auto communities are class communities. They were structured, economically and socially, by the organization of production. The reverse is just as true; the organization of production has been structured by the spatial configuration of the midwest economy.

The second dimension of local class relations is closely related to the first. As local class relations are the relations of community, so too are they the relations of authority. Theoretically, management has a great deal of authority in deciding upon, and running, the local configuration of production. As representatives of owners, management 'owns' the plant, machinery, materials used in production, and even the output produced by labor. Essentially, these are 'first-order' legal structures; fundamental property rights, codified in American constitutional law (see Calabresi & Melamed 1972 on the constitutional logic of such structures). These rights are protected by the state, and form the very basis of class relations in American capitalist society (Clark & Dear 1984). While all citizens have the right to own the means of production, actual patterns of ownership depend upon initial patterns of wealth. There is no substantive right, implied or expressed, of all citizens to an equal share of society's resources. Simply, property rights in a capitalist society reinforce and legitimize inequality (Clark 1982).

By virtue of these rights, managements have the *unilateral* power to hire and fire workers at will, and control the process of production as they see fit. However, in reality, particularly in the midwest auto industry, the possibility of firms' exercising their unilateral powers has been systematically eroded over the past three decades. As each new contract has been signed with labor, workers have further constrained managements' exercise of their unilateral powers. The doctrine of employment-at-will, for so long a basic right of capital (Atiyah 1979), has ceased to be relevant in these circumstances. All manner of contract clauses have narrowed the exercise of this right (including grievance clauses, peer review, seniority, and long-term employment contracts), so much so that management is very restrained in how it can discipline labor. Moreover, it has become very difficult for management unilaterally to fire labor as economic conditions have worsened. Temporary lay-offs are, of course, built into labor contracts; however, reconfiguration of the production process itself has required long and often painful negotiations, which have not always favored management.

These ossified class relations did not happen overnight. Contracts have cascaded over time, collecting past agreements and concessions, and adding new conditions to past conditions. By virtue of the many years of prosperity of the industry, the unions have developed extraordinary bilateral power. And it is an historical legacy which is not easily forgotten. The effects of this contract cascading process are all too obvious in the patterns of local auto industry wages. As Table 7.3 demonstrated, hourly wages in the industry are very high, especially if we compare auto industry wages to other local sectors (see the differences between auto wages and electrical and electronics wages in Table 7.3). Further, the most recently signed contract reinforces the advantages of local auto workers in terms of their wages and benefits.

I believe, though, that too much can be made of the high wages of auto workers. After all, price competition between auto firms was not encouraged by the industry or government over the past decade. Voluntary quotas have ensured a limited supply of foreign cars, stimulating quite high prices for imported automobiles. More important than wages has been the effects of cascading contracts on managements' authority in the design and running of the actual production process. Up until very recently, unions were able to block managements' attempts at changing the pace of production, the introduction of new production techniques, reducing manning levels, even redefining skill definitions and job descriptions. While these issues may appear relatively innocuous, these points of discretion are important for any firm wishing to adjust its organization of production to changing circumstances[17]. While no one would suggest that the unions have had it all their own way, the pattern of authority on the local shop floor has become quite ambiguous.

How did this come about, given the unilateral powers of American society? There are two principal answers to this question. Most obviously, the industry was very prosperous for many years. Whatever the costs of these cascading contracts, an ever-expanding market, relatively stable demand, and nationally increasing real incomes absorbed the effects of these contracts. Even though the industry went through a series of economic ups and downs over the postwar period, customary work practices were not major barriers to local adjustment. Indeed, as each shift in economic activity was integrated into the contract structure, work rules became more complex and more ambiguous. It has been mentioned in conversation more than once by union activists that the success of the postwar regime of local class relations in incorporating shifts in the economic system is evidence for assigning culpability to management for the current crisis of the midwest auto industry.

A more subtle answer to the question requires a further appreciation of the spatial structure of local class relations of the industry. Being so geographically concentrated and so integrated with respect to class position and status, the community character of the industry sustained union drives for greater and greater control over the production process. Class power was the ultimate point of contention. Workers sought not only a significant role in the organization of production, they also sought to assert their power through the local community. In an economy where class and community are inextricably linked, negotiations over shop floor power were also negotiations over community social status. Both labor and management participated in this class conflict; in terms of organizing power, the unions won. As a result workplace authority relations were diffused throughout the local community.

Yet another dimension of this issue requires recognition. Both the unions and the firms have long acknowledged the need to respond to shifts in the economic environment. Recent challenges from overseas are just one example of a stream of events which the industry has had to respond to over the past 50 years. While we recognize the ossified nature of local class relations, not as often acknowledged is the contingent nature of union power with respect to union locals. Due to the decentralized nature of production, the logic of American labor laws, and the importance of the union locals in contract ratification, the major unions have not had complete authority in negotiating with management on behalf of the union membership at large. Just as an example, the recent vote by UAW workers ratifying the UAW–GM contract was a close victory for the union leadership. Of those GM workers who were eligible to vote only two-thirds did so, and only 57% of these voted in favor of the contract agreement. That is, 138 000 workers voted in favor, 103 000 voted against. Large union locals in Michigan were especially critical of the agreement, but so too were locals in California and Georgia.

Authority relations within union organizations are just as vulnerable to the geographically fragmented nature of the industry as are firms. While it appears at the level of contract negotiation that the unions and the firms are operating as the decision agents, in reality the local level retains an incredible amount of power. Since most negotiations over work rules, technology, the pace of production and so on take place at the local level, the union leadership and the auto firms have very little unilateral power at the national level. They must persuade rather than decide, and campaign for contract ratification rather than unilaterally accept a national agreement. For both the union leadership and the auto firms the institutional structure of class relations is an important limit on their abilities to adjust to new challenges.

To summarize, the crisis of the midwest auto industry was the result of the following conditions. First, an outmoded regime of local class relations, reflecting past economic conditions and class advantage. Secondly, an institutional arrangement of class relations which has had the effect of diffusing firms' and unions' authority. Thirdly, a cascade of contract negotiations and renegotiations which have narrowed the scope of firms in designing and controlling production. Fourthly, a decentralized spatial configuration of production which has the simultaneous effect of objectifying local class interests *and* isolating classes from one another in terms of their collective interests. Fifthly, a changing competitive environment which has not been integrated within the regime of class relations.

The future of the midwest auto industry

In late 1984, the UAW and American auto companies signed a series of contracts for the next few years. For the industry as a whole, these contracts have been hailed as a major step forward in resolving the crisis conditions which have haunted the industry since the mid 1970s. *The Wall Street Journal* reported on September 24, 1984 that industry analysts believed that the contract between the UAW and GM would both help the economy by moderating wage demands 'and should help in the long run to make the US auto industry more internationally competitive' (p. 1). Both the unions and the auto firms have claimed that the new contracts are blueprints for the future; marking what Quinn Mills termed 'a landmark pact that shows labor and management in a new cooperative relationship' (*The New York Times* October 7, 1984). In this final section I wish to consider the implications of these new contracts for midwest communities and the spatial configuration of production. In closing some brief remarks are also made concerning other possible futures for the midwest auto industry.

The UAW signed first with GM, the 'target company' in their negotiations with the auto industry at large. As was noted above, the master contract was not well received by the union membership. Only a bare majority of workers voted in favor of the contract, and just over a third of those eligible to vote abstained from voting. Furthermore, contract negotiations between GM and the UAW in Canada collapsed when their contract was rejected by Canadian auto workers. A short strike ensued, and many American GM workers were affected because of the multiplant parts transfer system which links GM plants in the USA and Canada. After having signed with GM, the UAW quickly signed with Ford and other much smaller companies. Many of the clauses of these contracts are similar, although in the case of Ford the company agreed to a ban on plant closings to have effect for three years. Industry commentators noted that Ford already out-sources a large portion of its parts production, thus implying that internal rationalization through Ford's production network is not a major goal in the next few years.

Realistically speaking, the contract between GM and the UAW was a compromise; 'neither a victory for one side nor a defeat for the other' (*The New York Times* October 7, 1984). A middle course was chosen by the union between outright class warfare, on the one hand, and total capitulation to GM, on the other. The essentials of the contract were fourfold. First, union workers received significant real wage gains while maintaining previous cost-of-living allowances (COLA). Wage gains were of the order of 2.25% with the COLA calculated on a base year of 1967[18]. Secondly, retirees were granted increases in their pensions, as new retirees were made eligible for up to a $50 000 lump sum payment upon retirement. Thirdly, GM won substantial concessions from the UAW on matters like shop floor control and management discretion over the pace and technology of production. Fourthly, GM made a pact with the union to provide displaced workers with retraining schemes, training allowances, and maintenance of benefits.

Both the union and the firm expect large numbers of workers to be affected by plant 'modernization.' As was indicated above, GM has already shed over 120 000 workers in the past five years and has announced plans to shed another 120 000 over the next two years. The UAW–GM agreement essentially legitimated planned reconfiguration of production by protecting the wages of those still working and those who will be laid off in the future. It also encourages early retirement of older workers and lays the conditions for wholesale retrenchment of younger workers with limited seniority. The wage bargain is consistent with past agreements and maintains auto workers' privileged positions in the midwest region. Notice, however, that it has been explicitly recognized by both the union and the firm that these real wage gains are to be paid out of higher labor productivity. Essentially, GM has claimed back a significant degree of shop floor control under an agreement with the union that, in doing so, the incomes of those who continue to work in the industry will be protected.

While at first sight this bargain appears to be of national character, the reality of the contract will be most immediately felt at the local level. Even though wage maintenance appears as a national bargain, implementation of labor productivity programs to pay for these contract provisions will be a subject of intense local negotiation. As is often the case, the speed of assembly lines, the organization of production, and the pattern of technological transfer are matters of local discretion; negotiated at the local level within the framework of the master contract. How well communities respond to this imperative will decide their fate: whether they are to share in reduced employment at higher wages or lose their whole industrial base. The effect of negotiating productivity agreements at the local level, in a climate of retrenchment, will be to pit auto communities against one another in a struggle for scarce jobs and company investment.

One way or another, all midwest auto communities are going to lose jobs. Retrenchment will be through retirement of older workers and laying off of younger workers. But also, retrenchment will take the form of plant closings, as some plants and communities fall behind in the race to improve local labor productivity. Even in those communities which respond most successfully to the imperative of higher labor productivity, their integrity, their very existence, is under fundamental threat. Simply by reducing manning levels, opportunities for younger workers will be dramatically curtailed. And given that these same workers were most affected by the 1982 recession, an essential ingredient of these communities is at risk: the idea that local auto plants are an integral part of family and community. Instead of younger members of the community following their fathers into the local plants, they will be denied entry. The effect will be a gradual erosion of the social fabric of these communities. In other communities left behind in the race for higher productivity, the effects will be more devastating: all workers face the prospect of losing their jobs.

Going on the pattern of support for the new contract with GM, many communities will be reluctant participants in this program of local trans-formation. Whether or not this reluctance will translate into a coordinated cross-local non-compliance with GM's policies will depend on two things: the role of the national union leadership, and the solidarity between union locals. In the first instance it is clear that the national leadership has staked its future on the success of the contract. It believes that the future of the union as a whole depends on the competitive stance of GM *vis-à-vis* the international auto industry. If this requires the sacrifice of midwest auto communities, then I believe that they are willing to go that far in their attempts to save the industry in general. Even though total union membership is bound to shrink, the loyalty of those who continue to work will be maintained by higher and higher wages. One way to interpret the union leadership position is to understand its role as one side of a corporatist pact with the industry in general.

Cross-local solidarity will be difficult to achieve. The whole industry was built on a logic of decentralization. To expect the various communities to combine around an alternative logic, thereby resolving past adjustment problems, seems difficult to imagine. The history of past actions is ever present in the social relations of production. What makes the present bargain so plausible is that it is based on the past: decentralized production and differential local investment. But what makes it so different is the likelihood that the whole midwest auto industry will shrink, something which has not happened for nearly 50 years. The question remains whether or not the auto communities have the capacity to organize against the interests of the national leadership and the auto companies. Only if this occurs will the community fabric of the midwest auto industry have any hope of surviving.

Notes

Thanks to Alec Murphy, James Bater, and the editors of this book for comments on a previous draft. Research for this chapter began while the author was a National Research Council Fellow at the National Academy of Sciences. It is based on a series of interviews with local officials, union members, and management in a set of midwestern auto cities during 1981/2, funded by the National Academy of Sciences. I am indebted to Royce Hanson for making my fellowship possible. More recently, research reported in this chapter was supported by the National Science Foundation. Of course, all opinions remain the responsibility of the author.

1 For example, see the October 12, 1984 edition of *The Wall Street Journal* for a series of interviews with prominent economists on the capacity of the government to avoid a 'great depression' type of collapse. The context for the article was obviously current concerns over the ability of Latin American countries to repay their debts.

2 In cities like Detroit and Battle Creek, 1981 estimates of local crime rates were 11 987 and 10 586 per 100 000 people respectively. These rates were far above the

average for Michigan (6820) and the lowest estimate, found in Allen Park (4917). See the *County and City Data Book, 1983* for more details.

3 A study of recent macroeconomic trends and policies by the General Accounting Office (1982) noted that in 1978 the auto industry sold nearly 9.3 million units, an extraordinary level of sales compared to most postwar years.

4 The natural unemployment rate is thought to be that minimum rate consistent with stable prices. Despite its image of being 'natural', it is in fact historically derived. Recent government estimates, using as the base period 1977–9, put this rate at between 6.1% and 7.0% (Gordon 1981).

5 Note, however, that there are significant differences between US regions and industries in the extent of wage indexation. Clark and Tabuchi (1984) demonstrated that wage indexation is more prevalent in the northeast and traditional manufacturing industries than in the south. In fact the regional pattern of real wages over the 1970s is closely tied to institutional factors rather than local labor demand conditions.

6 Abernathy, Clark & Kantrow (1983) estimate that some $700 of the difference is in the wage differentials between Japanese and American auto workers. They also estimate that there is a further $500 to $700 difference in labor productivity, and perhaps another $600 to $800 difference in the cost of input materials. Thus a conservative estimate of the difference in production costs between the two countries would be $1600. A more extensive estimate would put the difference at around $2200. See also Lawrence (1984) on cost differentials between US and other countries' auto firms.

7 Casetti attempted to explain what he and others believe to have been a fundamental shift in regional economic growth patterns: away from large cities to non-metropolitan regions. However, it should also be recognized that recent empirical evidence suggests that this reversal was short lived at best. Garnick (1983) indicated that non-metropolitan areas are again lagging behind larger urbanized areas in terms of their rates of growth.

8 In this manner, Casetti departs from the logic of regional growth theorists such as Kaldor (1970). It should be remembered that Kaldor supposed that the inflexion point is never reached because of more than compensating productivity effects in the dominant region.

9 But, of course, no neo-classical theory is capable of describing the path of adjustment. The theory is designed to compare end-states, assuming the economy has fully adjusted according to a known equilibrium target (Fisher 1983).

10 This may mean switching from large urban areas to ex-urban areas, even to Third World regions. There are many examples of this kind of behavior, ranging from conventional industrial firms, like GM, through to service firms, like the First National Bank of Chicago which switched its clerical VISA services from downtown Chicago to a peripheral ex-urban location.

11 For further information see the study by Mary Briggs (1983) on the regional investment effects of the Economic Recovery Tax Act of 1981. She argued that the Act effectively accelerated depreciation of existing assets, making it easier for firms to leave behind older production facilities, especially in the northeast USA.

12 Kalecki (1971) argued that most capitalist firms set prices in accordance with the costs of production *plus* an increment for profit. In contrast, neoclassical theory supposes that prices are set in accordance with supply and demand.

13 For instance, the recent shift of Clark Equipment out of its traditional home in Jackson, Michigan, was made possible by a series of investments in southern towns over the course of a decade. Although the local community was quite surprised by the move, any reading of the company's annual reports for the 1970s would have quickly alerted the community about what was being planned.

14 What is surprising in this literature is that so few people have bothered to question the process whereby these cycles are identified. Slutsky (1937) long ago demonstrated that cycles can be found even in random time-series data, if these series are smoothed enough.

15 The Auto Pact enabled auto firms to treat Canadian plants as part of their extended multiplant network. In effect tariffs were abolished between the two countries on parts and equipment which circulated within the firms' networks. Recently, GM has announced plans to step up investment in Canada, especially in Ontario, to take advantage of the vast differences in value of the American and Canadian dollars.

16 There is a good deal of irony in recent calls by labor 'experts' for revising American labor relations along the lines of the Japanese model (see, for example, Hayes 1981). After all, the kind of loyalty pointed to in Japanese workers with regard to their firms is precisely what was so characteristic of the American auto industry for so many years.

17 For a theoretical discussion of this issue relevant to the US context, see the study by Edwards (1979). Recently, Bowles, Gordon, and Weisskopf (1983) have argued that, in response to workers' gains on the shop floor, management has added more supervisors and managers in an attempt to regain control of labor productivity. They argued that this is reflected in the increasing significance of so-called 'non-production' workers in the total composition of American employment. For a related study at the regional level, see Clark (1984).

18 GM had bargained for a new base year for COLA adjustments in an effort to reduce the cost of the provision. The union did agree, however, on a one and two cent return to the firm on COLA allowances, as well as a smaller portion of the accumulated COLA adjustments since 1979.

References

Abernathy, W., K. B. Clark, and A. Kantrow 1983. *Industrial renaissance*. New York: Basic Books.

Atiyah, P. 1979. *The rise and fall of freedom of contract*. Oxford: Oxford University Press.

Bluestone, B. and B. Harrison 1982. *The deindustrialization of America*. New York: Basic Books.

Bowles, S., D. M. Gordon, and T. Weisskopf 1983. *Beyond the waste land: a democratic alternative to economic decline*. New York: Doubleday.

Briggs, M. 1983. *The Economic Recovery Act of 1981: investment distortions of public policy*. Manuscript on file at the Kennedy School of Government, Harvard University, Cambridge, Mass.

Calabresi, G. and A. D. Melamed 1972. Property rules, liability rules, and inalienability: one view of the cathedral. *Harvard Law Rev.* **85**, 1089–128.

Casetti, E. 1981. A catastrophe model of regional dynamics. *Ann. Assoc. Am. Geog.* **71**, 572–9.

Cheshire, P. C. 1973. *Regional unemployment differences in Great Britain*. Regional Papers II. Cambridge: Cambridge University Press.

Clark, G. L. 1981. The employment relation and spatial division of employment. *Ann. Assoc. Am. Geog.* **71**, 412–24.

Clark, G. L. 1982. Rights, property, and community. *Econ. Geog.* **57**, 120–38.

Clark, G. L. 1983. Fluctuations and rigidities in local labor markets part 1: theory and evidence. *Environ. Plann. A* **15**, 165–85.

Clark, G. L. 1984. The changing composition of regional employment. *Econ. Geog.* **60**, 175–93.

Clark, G. L. and M. Dear 1984. *State apparatus: structures and language of legitimacy.* London: Allen & Unwin.

Clark, G. L. and T. Tabuchi 1984. Regional wage and price dynamics. *Geog. Anal.* **16**, 223–43.

Clark, K. B. and L. Summers 1979. Labor market dynamics and unemployment: a reconsideration. *Brookings Pap. Econ. Activity* **1**, 13–72.

Cox, A. 1947. Some aspects of the Labor Relations Management Act. *Harvard Law Rev.* **61**, 1.

Crandall, R. W. 1984. Import quotas and the automobile industry: the costs of protection. *Brookings Rev.* (summer), 8–16.

Dear, M., G. L. Clark, and S. Clark 1979. Economic cycles and mental health care policy. *Soc. Sci. Med.* **13**, 45–53.

Edwards, R. 1979. *Contested terrain.* New York: Basic Books.

Fisher, F. 1983. *Disequilibrium foundations of equilibrium economics.* Cambridge: Cambridge University Press.

Garnick, D. 1983. *Shifting balances in metropolitan and non-metropolitan area growth.* Washington, DC: US Department of Commerce.

General Accounting Office 1982. *An analysis of fiscal and monetary policies.* Washington DC: Comptroller General.

Gertler, M. 1984. Dynamics of regional capital accumulation. *Econ. Geog.* **60**, 155–74.

Gertler, M. 1986. Discontinuities in regional development. *Environ. Plann. D: Society and Space* **4** (forthcoming).

Gordon, R. J. 1981. *Macroeconomics.* Boston: Little, Brown.

Hanson, R. (ed.) 1983. *Rethinking urban policy.* Washington, DC: National Academy Press.

Hayes, R. 1981. Why Japanese factories work. *Harvard Business Rev.* (July–August), 57–66.

Hill, R. C. 1984. Economic crisis and the political response in the motor city. In *Sunbelt/snowbelt*, L. Sawers and W. Tabb (eds.). New York: Oxford University Press.

Kaldor, N. 1970. The case for regional policy. *Scottish J. Polit. Econ.* **17**, 337–48.

Kalecki, M. 1971. *Essays on the dynamics of capitalist economies.* Cambridge: Cambridge University Press.

Lawrence, R. Z. 1984. *Can America compete?* Washington, DC: The Brookings Institution.

Lloyd, P. 1984. *Recession, local restructuring, and technical change.* Seminar presentation. The University of Chicago, Chicago.

Mandel, E. 1979. *Long waves of capitalist development.* Cambridge: Cambridge University Press.

Markusen, A. 1984. *Profit cycles, oligopoly, and regional development.* Cambridge Mass.: MIT Press.

Massey, D. and R. Meegan 1980. *The anatomy of job loss.* London: Methuen.

Medoff, J. 1979. Layoffs and alternatives under trade unions in U.S. manufacturing. *Am. Econ. Rev.* **69**, 380–90.

O'Connor, J. 1984. *Accumulation crisis.* New York: Blackwell.

Oi, W. 1962. Labor as a quasi-fixed factor. *J. Polit. Econ.* **70**, 538–55.

Pred, A. 1984. Place as historically contingent process: structuration and the time-geography of becoming places. *Ann. Assoc. Am. Geog.* **74**, 279–98.

Slutsky, E. 1937. The summation of random causes as the source of cyclic processes. *Econometrica* **5**, 107–52.

Stone, K. 1981. The post war paradigm in American labor law. *Yale Law J.* **90**, 1509–80.

Thompson, W. 1965. *A preface to urban economics*. Baltimore: Johns Hopkins University Press.

US Department of Housing and Urban Development 1982. *The Presidents' urban policy report*. Washington, DC: USGPO.

Walker, R. and M. Storper 1981. Capital and industrial location. *Prog. Human Geog.* **5**, 473–509.

8

Labor demand, labor supply and the suburbanization of low-wage office work

K. NELSON

The suburbanization of offices is a well-established trend in the metropolitan areas of the USA and other advanced capitalist nations[1]. Since much of the office work which is being relocated consists of low-wage clerical jobs that do not support long journeys to work, the trend signifies a redistribution of job opportunities from central city workers, many of whom are low-income minority women, to suburban workers, who tend to be white and middle class. Office suburbanization has serious consequences for central city low-wage work-forces, not only because of the number of entry-level jobs lost[2], but because these jobs often provide workers with the possibility of entering an internal labor market with bureaucratically regulated advancement, unlike most other low-wage jobs in the central city's growing 'service economy.' The locational dynamics of routine office work are particularly critical to minority female workers because they are likely to be supporting families on their income alone[3].

To get a better understanding of the movements of this employment sector that so profoundly influences central city female labor markets, I conducted a locational study of 'back offices' in the San Francisco–Oakland Standard Metropolitan Statistical Area (Nelson 1984). The back office was defined as a consolidation of corporate internal services[4] that require little face-to-face contact with either the corporate personnel they support or with the extra-corporate world. Examples of such internal services are computer operations, accounting, payroll, billing, credit card services, centralized word processing, and certain office-based (i.e. non-laboratory) technical or research activities. Back offices tend to be highly automated and employ a high proportion of low-wage clerical (or 'computerized clerical') workers.

Standardized, high-volume office activities such as mass data entry have been consolidated and moved to areas of low factor costs since the first stage of office computer applications in the 1950s (Administrative Management Society 1956, Foley 1957, Hoos 1961). Spatial division of office labor increased greatly in the late 1960s, however, as part of a widespread productive reorganization in response to an accumulation crisis (Massey 1978, Bluestone & Harrison 1982). Adminstrative activities were an important target of rationalization. Costs had risen dramatically as an enormous postwar growth in office functions, due in large part to the necessity of managing more complex and far-flung enterprises, put pressure on increasingly inadequate supplies of land and clerical labor in traditional downtown office districts. Administrative rationalization usually included: (a) reorganization of office work, resulting in a new division of office labor; (b) electronic automation of office work; and (c) relocation of the newly divided offices to escape high factor costs.

Advances in microprocessor and telecommunications technology facilitated the proliferation and differentiation of back offices. Whereas back office work had previously been limited to one-time 'batch' operations, whose product then had to be physically transported to other offices, the linking of dispersed electronic terminals now allowed work to progress interactively over space. Office work that required review by 'front office' personnel but not 'face-to-face' meetings (document preparation or computer programming, for example) could now be consolidated and relocated in back offices. Metropolitan integration through the Interstate system and other high-speed highway networks also facilitated the back office form of business rationalization, by improving access to both other office units and to labor.

In the past ten years the San Francisco Bay Area has seen an acceleration of this corporate rationalization whereby back office functions are separated from headquarters, divisional offices and other 'front office' activities and moved out of traditional downtown office districts. One particular outer suburban region bordering a circumferential Interstate highway (which is referred to as the 'I-680 corridor' see Fig. 8.1) has attracted more of these relocating back offices than any other region in the Standard Metropolitan Statistical Area (SMSA). The purpose of the locational study referred to above was to explain the particular attraction of this one Bay Area subregion to back offices.

It must be stressed that technical considerations cannot explain the destination of these relocating offices: supplies of such factors as land or highway access do not distinguish the I-680 corridor from areas that have been notably unpopular for back office development. The high-minority cities of Oakland and Richmond, for example, are well-supplied with all important back office technical requirements[5]: low land and rental values; good highway access; land parcels of an adequate size (given local height allowances) to allow very large blocks of office space to be housed, while leaving adequate clear grounds for employee parking and future office expansion; and 'pro-business' local governments that will allow relatively free development of this land.

To explain why the I-680 corridor has attracted disproportionate numbers of relocating back offices we must turn to the remaining back office locational requirement, labor.

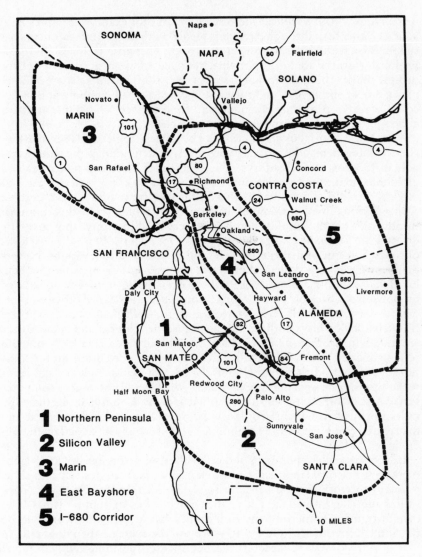

Figure 8.1 San Francisco Bay Area suburban office subregions.

Back office labor demand

Contact needs in administrative work are normally highly correlated with salary rank (Tornqvist 1970, Goddard 1975). Therefore, back offices, since they are by definition a consolidation of activities with low contact needs, will tend to employ a high proportion of low-wage office workers, compared to other office types[6]. Yet not every back office work-force is 'clerk-intensive;'

certain highly paid technical and research work, for example, requires little contact (other than through electronic media) with the corporate functions it supports or with the extra-corporate world. Therefore technical and professional workers are an important employee component in certain back offices.[7] Back offices also include a supervisory staff, including some middle-management employees, and may also include a small component of blue-collar workers providing maintenance, food service, and transportation, although this work is commonly subcontracted.

Thus back office labor demand cannot be reduced to clerical labor demand. Clerical labor demand is primary, however, in determining the *intrametro-politan* location of back offices. The blue-collar labor component can be discounted in the location decision, not only because of its small size (averaging less than 4% of total work-force in the case study offices), but because such positions involve minimal investment in training and thus minimal turnover cost to the employer, and can be easily filled in any labor market – i.e. they are 'secondary labor market jobs' (Doeringer & Piore 1971). This is of course not true of managerial, technical or professional positions. Nevertheless, such highly skilled labor is not as important an intrametropolitan locational determinant as clerical labor, even when it makes up a large proportion of a back office labor force, simple because salaried office workers tend to have substantially longer journeys to work than clerical workers (Daniels 1980). This is both because their income is higher and because they are usually male, and therefore less geographically restricted by household responsibilities. Thus, while office managers interviewed during the locational study stated they would consider the supply of higher-wage labor when choosing *between* metropolitan areas (they would not locate a computer services back office, for example, in Mendocino County, more than 100 miles north of San Francisco), they assumed that qualified technical and managerial employees would commute to an office anywhere *within* the San Francisco SMSA.

In contrast, all respondents indicated they were limited to local labor markets for clerical labor, since most clerical workers are restricted to short journeys to work. Like other industries dependent on female labor[8], back offices must be located very near their intended labor supply: it has been demonstrated in numerous empirical studies that women who work outside the home have shorter journeys to work, on the average, than do men[9].

If clerical jobs were 'secondary labor market' positions with minimal training and turnover costs, the relative immobility of clerical labor would be no more location-determining than is that of other low-wage workers, since the appropriate labor supply would be nearly ubiquitous. But, since the mechanization and feminization of office work in the late 19th century, clerical labor demand has become *contradictory*[10]: rather high skills, both technical and social, pose significant productivity and turnover costs to the firm, while job rewards (wages, benefits, working conditions and the nature of the actual tasks) are often no higher than those of secondary labor market positions. Far from being ubiquitous in the metropolitan area, a labor supply that satisfies this specialized labor demand is quite localized, as we shall see.

152

Automation and modern clerical labor demand

It might be supposed that automation would decrease the contradictory nature of clerical labor demand by lowering skills to the point where they were more commensurate with job rewards. Yet although computer mechanization has lowered the skill requirements of many office jobs by such means as removing decisions from operators to the software, or increasing hardware sophistication (as in optical character readers), it has not resulted in a simple, across-the-board 'de-skilling' of clerical work. Indeed, automation may actually *increase* the importance of high worker performance:

> Sophisticated, automated technical processes may be particularly vulnerable to worker error, noncooperation, or sabotage because they require more expensive capital equipment and may require greater interconnection of procedures and continuity of production. (Walker & Storper 1980: 48)

At the same time, computer mechanization may erode the traditional white-collar working conditions (such as personal mobility and self-pacing of work) and working environment (personal desks, proximity to prestige management offices) that formerly served as clerical job benefits. As conditions grow similar to those in factory production the threat of organization among clerical workers increases (Harvard Business School 1974).

Thus electronic mechanization, rather than lessening the contradictions of the traditional clerical labor demand, may actually exacerbate them. Under these conditions, the modern, computerized office will be at least as dependent as the 19th-century mechanized office on an educated but tractable labor supply: one that will remain not only productive but resistant to militance, at the usual low job rewards.

The hypothesis that electronic automation of clerical work results in an increased demand for a 'high-quality' yet docile female labor supply was investigated in the back office locational study by means of an analysis of nine computerized clerical jobs comprising six separate occupations[11]. All but one of these jobs exhibited what was defined above as a contradictory labor demand: they either demanded high performance (errors and turnover posed significant cost to the firm) or docility (i.e. high resistance to militance) on the part of workers (or both), but did not reward workers well enough, in either working conditions or the nature of the work itself, to ensure such qualities.

For example, a customer assistance operator in the Credit Card Customer Assistance department at a multinational oil company's back office requires two to four months of formal training and another nine months of on-the-job experience in order to reach the department's minimum performance standards. Employees must have a grasp of the entire credit card billing process as well as the computer's 'system logic' in order to perform their jobs well, since they are responsible for altering customers' credit histories and billing cycles. Errors on the computer can cause system malfunctions that affect other workers' output; impolite or inept responses to customers can damage the firm's public image. The firm needs workers who will not only obey rules, but to some extent internalize the company's goals (Storper 1982).

Thus customer service operators who perform badly, or leave the job soon after training, pose significant costs for this firm. In addition, the work unit is quite large (48) and occupationally homogeneous, with moderate worker interaction allowed; and there is a strong union presence among the firm's production workers in the county. Therefore, worker organization is also a significant threat (in the absence of the office's current, anti-union supply, of course).

The occupational analysis attempted to abstract the production relation[12] in any job, as far as that is possible, from the firm's current labor supply conditions, and pose the question: does the firm successfully control poor performance, turnover, and worker organization through its job rewards, or does it rely on an 'external' solution – a labor force that carries its own internal controls?

For customer assistance operators in this oil firm, wages slightly above the occupational median in this SMSA, benefits at the median level, and a moderately pleasant working environment are reduced to a low level of job rewards by slightly longer hours than the metropolitan median for clericals, mandatory overtime, the onerous nature of the work itself, and the technical control methods. The pace is strenuous (an average of 160 calls per day) and automatically set by the computer's automatic call distributor, tasks are repetitive, and workers are isolated in carrels on duty, while their movement is restricted by their headsets and the necessary concentration on the VDT screen. Machine-measured performance statistics are the basis for promotion: for each operator the computer measures the number of calls taken, the length of each call, the number of callers who 'abandoned' before being answered, and the amount of time spent off the telephone or away from the work station. In order to monitor performance, supervisors listen in on 10% of each operator's daily call volume (approximately 16 calls) each month, using a telephone pickup that cannot be heard by the operator. More than three errors places the operator below the shop standard for 'accuracy.' One supervisor and former operator observed, 'You can tell when they've been working the phones too long; their voices on the phone get louder and louder without their noticing it.'

In sum, customer assistance operator job rewards in this firm seem insufficient to ensure the degree of reliability and stability required from workers, and remove the threat of worker organization, in the absence of the surrounding female labor supply. This supply was praised by one male manager:

> We get a lot of women who get married, and then work here because of the opportunity to work close to home. Most of them have worked before, and most have some college experience. They have families and own homes, so they tend to be more stable workers, with a stronger work ethic. . . When we moved out here, we tapped the beautiful source of suburban womanhood!

Without this suburban female labor force that is *internally* controlled, both through its class position and its lack of power in the market and the domestic economies, this firm stood to lose money through high turnover, poor performance, or worker organization in its Credit Card

Customer Assistance Department. The occupational analysis determined this to be true for eight of the nine jobs examined, indicating that electronic automation of clerical work has not yet lessened the pressure to seek out a highly productive, yet docile female labor supply.

While clerical labor demand has thus remained quite stable over the last century, the *supply* of labor with such qualities has changed, particularly in the last 20 years.

Spatial changes in female labor supply

From the last decades of the 19th century until World War II, employers could rely on attracting the preferred clerical labor supply – young, white, native-born, relatively well-educated women working just until marriage – to downtown offices (Davies 1975, Smuts 1976, Kocka 1980). Financial districts were at the hub of public transit systems, a particularly important locational asset before the widespread use of automobiles. The preferred clerical labor supply was also attracted to downtown offices by the nearby opportunities for shopping and after-hours recreation, important for young women in a time when the predominant social conception of women's work was as an avenue to their real career, marriage (Hoover & Vernon 1959).

After World War II, this traditional clerical labor supply began to shrink. The number of young, single women over 16 actually declined by 46% between 1940 and 1960 (due to low birth rates during the Depression years), while more of these young women continued their education rather than seeking work (Oppenheimer 1970: 170, 180). The postwar rise in household formation and fertility also produced a shortage of young women in the labor market, since at this time it was still the rule for women to withdraw completely from the wage economy at marriage (Easterlin 1968). As a result, rising demand for female labor could only be met by the increased employment of older married women. During the 1940s and 1950s, women past their child-bearing years were the major new source of female labor, while increases in women's labor force participation rates during the next two decades were mainly due to the growing numbers of women with young children joining the paid work-force.[13].

During the 1960s and particularly the 1970s, both the traditional (young, single white women) and the 'expanded' (older, married white women) preferred clerical labor supply became increasingly scarce in central cities (Gordon & Thal-Larsen 1969, *Dun's Review* 1978). Well-educated, young, single women became more likely to plan careers rather than stopgap jobs between school and marriage. 'White flight' from the central cities decreased the average income level and increased the proportion of minorities in central city labor forces nationally[14]. In the past two decades central city female labor forces have become increasingly characterized by two different classes of primary-earner women: low-income women, many of them minority group members or (in certain cities) recent immigrants; and higher-income, career-oriented women.

The 1960s and 1970s saw an increasing breakdown of the traditional (male breadwinner) domestic economy, manifested in a rapid rise in divorce rates and an increase in births to single women and in the proportion of women keeping their children rather than giving them up for adoption, as well as in the number of never-married women adopting babies (Johnson 1978). For these reasons the number of households with young children headed by women increased dramatically, from 7.4% of all households with young children in 1960 to 18% in 1981. This phenomenon affected poor and minority women disproportionately. As lower-income groups are more heavily represented in households headed by women than in the female population in general, so are lower levels of education: in 1977, for example, 39% of working women who headed families had not finished high school and only 9% had completed college (Johnson 1978: 37, 35).

Poor female heads of household are concentrated in central cities through necessity, since they are dependent on low housing costs and public transportation, which are rarely found in suburban areas (Freeman 1981). Women in this group do not satisfy employers' demands for 'high quality' clerical labor, because they tend to have low levels of education. Neither do they satisfy the demand for docility, because being heads of families gives them a much more powerful incentive to demand higher wages and benefits and greater job mobility than women who view their work as supplementing a husband's income.

Middle-class primary-earner women (either single or part of a dual primary-earner household) are also increasing as a proportion of central city work-forces. Most of these women live in central cities through choice rather than necessity, in order to take advantage of its growing white-collar social and cultural ambiance, and, in the case of many 'two-career' households, in order to maximize access to two workplaces (Markusen 1981). Women in this group fulfill the demand for 'high-quality' clerical labor, of course, since they constitute a highly educated group that is close to management in culture and socialization, but they fail the second criterion of docility. Their high career goals make them unlikely to remain at dead-end jobs for long: as one San Francisco employer stated, 'The typical secretary you get here is some gal who has gone to college, takes the job while waiting for something better, and is unhappy from the day she takes it.'

The 'secretarial shortage' decried by managers from the 1960s onward (Hoos 1961, *Datamation* 1978, *Dun's Review* 1978) is thus in reality a shortage of the 'preferred' clerical worker that central city firms formerly recruited easily. Clerical workers in general have *not* been in short supply. Between 1965 and 1977, for example, real wages for clerical workers rose by only 4.9%, compared to an average of 25.4% rise for all other female full-time workers, while clerical unemployment rates rose from 11% to 15%, according to an Urban Institute report. The report concluded, 'These figures suggest that the demand for clerical workers since 1968 simply has not kept up with the supply of women seeking clerical work' (Barrett 1979: 50). Yet corporations moving offices from San Francisco to the suburbs reported annual turnover rates of up to 30% among clerical workers, and stated that 'the cost of retraining was threatening their profit line' (Del Beccaro 1982: 6). What *has* become scarce in US central cities is the relatively well-educated female worker who is content to stay with low-paid dead-end clerical work.

Suburban areas of new single-family housing are now the best source of such female labor, due to their class structure and related household structure. First of all, suburban women are more likely to be relatively well educated and similar in race and class to employers, compared to women living in central cities. For example, in 1977, 72% of suburban females over 18 were high school graduates, compared to 61% of central city females nationwide; and 93% of suburban women between 18 and 64 were white, compared to 76% of the same age group in the central cities (US Bureau of the Census 1978: 20). As a manager of one San Francisco back office (72% of whose workers are minorities) stated: 'There is a very serious concern about the ethnic mix [in San Francisco]. In a lot of our large, low-level clerical departments, you'll see minorities wall-to-wall. A lot of them don't speak English well – and there is great value in communication on the job.'

Demand for language skills and middle-class socialization can disguise racist employment criteria: the supervisor of a customer service department (8% minority) in a suburban back office said she warns her two black and two Hispanic operators not to use ethnic speech mannerisms on the telephone to customers, because 'there are a lot of prejudiced people out there,' some of whom have called her with racially based complaints. White, suburban women are preferred because they are closer to the 19th-century feminine clerical ideal: their 'relative good manners and educational distribution make them desirable workers from an employer's point of view, compared to the employer's image of unskilled, unruly minority workers in the city' (Saegert 1980: 111).

The individualistic consumerist ideology prevalent in middle-income suburbs is also attractive to employers. One suburban back office manager (of a data entry department) commented: 'It is very important to people here to maintain the lifestyle they have chosen.' He felt that the family and homeownership responsibilities characterizing his work-force (88% female) made for more stable and productive workers. And since many middle-income suburban women have 'biographical ties with entrepreneurial elements,' they are more likely to identify with the managerial ethos and turn away from collective organization (Mills 1951: 317).

Areas of new single-family housing are also attractive sources of clerical labor because couples with young children are more prevalent in such areas than in other metropolitan regions, particularly central cities (Freeman 1981). The subsidy which employers have historically gained from the patriarchal structure of social reproduction[15] – qualified women available at cheap prices because they have limited their career demands in response to domestic duties – has become more rare in advanced industrial countries as more middle-class women plan careers before child-rearing. Whereas in the 19th century US business could count on such a subsidy from nearly all young, unmarried middle-class women, in the past 20 years it has become increasingly available only from married women with children.

Relatively educated women who have deferred career plans for domestic responsibilities are now most commonly found in 'starter home' suburbs, because families with young children and headed by husbands are prevalent, while social mechanisms for sharing child-rearing are uncommon. Neither extended families nor full-time servants are available to most middle-income suburban women; employer-provided day care is still extremely rare in the USA[16], and mechanisms to release the husband's labor (paternity leave, part-time work in high-wage, responsible jobs) are non-existent. Many low-income mothers in central cities face these same constraints, of course, but do not have the alternative of performing domestic labor in return for a husband's support. Suburban communities aimed at young, growing families are thus the best place for employers to find women whose primary responsibilities lie in the household, but who are eager for alternative employment that can be fit around domestic duties. The personnel manager of another case study office in the I-680 corridor characterized his labor supply thus: 'We draw people from out here – it's a bedroom community. There are a lot of people working here for second incomes . . . they want something where they can get home quickly, in time to get dinner on the table before their husband gets home.'

The advantage of these secondary-earner women to employers lies not only in their objective lack of power in the household, but in a (related) internal sense that wage work occupies a secondary place in their lives: research has shown that 'many women, even when they work, think of themselves first as homemakers' (Saegert 1980: 111). As Piore (1979) points out, workers who define themselves in terms of activities outside of the workplace – students, migrant workers from different cultures, or house-wives – are valuable to employers because they do not view the job as a central and permanent part of their life, and will thus put up with worse wages and working conditions, and little or no guarantees of job stability[17]. Indeed, as in the case of students, they may not *want* job stability. They will be much less likely to organize or demand upward mobility than workers whose self-conception and social network coincides more closely to their market job.

A shift to a demand for these married, secondary-earner women ('homemakers') further increases the importance of proximity to the desired labor supply, since it has been demonstrated that married women, particu-larly with small children, have a much shorter journey to work on average than single women (Andrews 1978, Howe & O'Connor 1982). The elasticity of supply of homemakers depends not only on the earnings they are offered but on their real earnings, equal to gross wages and benefits less all the expenses incurred in taking a job, including:

> transportation, taxes, clothing, purchase of lunches, substitution of more expensive prepared foods for foods made in the home, purchase of other time-saving equipment and paid household help. By some esti-mates, the net benefit of the wife's income to the family may be reduced by as much as one-third to one-half, depending on the need for paying for child care. (Sweet 1973: 140)

Transportation is one of the largest discretionary items on this list. Lowering transportation costs is thereby one major method by which a homemaker can justify taking an outside job. Andrews' study of married women in five Canadian urban areas in 1968 found that the sensitivity of labor force partici- pation to travel costs was highest among 'current non-workers for jobs paying the lowest of the three earnings levels:' a precise description of the female labor a back office wishes to attract (Andrews 1978: 18). Thus sites within easy highway access of single-family residential neighborhoods characterized by young families are the best source of this new 'preferred' labor supply.

Corporations often claim they choose sites for relocating back offices in order to move the workplace closer to the communities where their 'key people' (professional and technical employees) already live (*San Francisco Chronicle* 1982). The preceding discussion showed that in one sense this is true. A corporation can look to the residential areas preferred by their professional and technical employees when seeking a concentration of the 'preferred' clerical labor. Firms may be able to raise the productivity, lower turnover, or ease recruitment of salaried employees by shortening their commuting time, but it is the contention of this chapter that they do not move to 'family-oriented' suburbs primarily for this reason. Clearly there is no shortage of qualified salaried employees willing to commute to central city financial districts, while there *is* a shortage of the desired type of clerical labor there. Potential savings on salaried employees are a secondary benefit received by back offices following the class and family values that the residences of these employees represent.

Supply of the 'preferred clerical labor' in the San Francisco– Oakland SMSA

A demographic analysis carried out in the back office locational study (Nel- son 1984) showed female labor supplies to be highly differentiated in the San Francisco–Oakland SMSA. In order to contrast the clerical labor available to employers at different sites in the SMSA, demographic profiles of the residents within approximately half an hour commuting distance (a 10-mile radius) of six potential back office sites were constructed. Two of these potential sites were in the I-680 corridor, near current centers of back office development – Walnut Creek/Concord and the San Ramon Valley; two in older central cities – San Francisco and Oakland; and two in older, inner suburban areas – Marin and San Mateo counties (see Fig. 8.2). Although these 10-mile 'laborsheds' are simplified models of the actual half hour commuting fields for the potential office sites, they are fairly representative of the actual choice of labor supply confronting back office employers. For instance, the two case study back offices located in San Francisco received 60% and 78% of their clerical employees from the 'San Francisco' laborshed, and the back office located in Concord received nearly 80% of its clerical workers from within the 'Central Contra Costa' catchment area (Fig. 8.2).

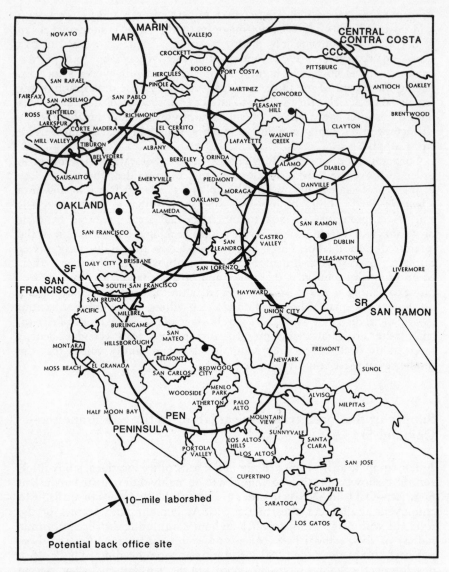

Figure 8.2 Ten-mile laborsheds of six model San Francisco Bay Area office sites.

The laborshed profiles consist of social and economic statistics selected from the 1980 census as indicators of the 'preferred clerical labor supply' discussed above. Chosen as positive indicators were: percentage of white, non-Hispanic people in the population, percentage of native English speakers in the population, mean family income, owner-occupied housing as a percentage of all housing, growth in owner-occupied housing between 1970 and 1980, percentage of women over 15 who are married, and who are living in husband–wife families with children, and the percentage of high school graduates among women over 16 (see Figs 8.3–8.9). Negative indicators of the preferred labor supply include: percentage of families with incomes under the poverty level, number of divorced women (compared to married women), and the percentage of families (with young children) headed by women (see Fig. 8.10–8.12).

When the demographic profiles of the six laborsheds are compared (Fig. 8.3–8.12), the outer suburban area that has attracted the most back office development to date (the 'Central Contra Costa' laborshed) stands out because of its complete consistency: it ranks high on every indicator of the desired clerical labor supply, and low on every negative indicator. The commuting field centered on the newest outer suburban back office growth area (the 'San Ramon' laborshed) ranks very close to the Central Contra Costa level on most indicators of the preferred clerical labor supply. This is because these two laborsheds, comprising between them most of the I-680 corridor, are characterized both by rapid growth and by a low percentage of low-income, high-minority communities[18]. Such communities make up only 20% of the Central Contra Costa and 26% of the San Ramon laborshed population, compared to 79% of the Oakland and 85% of the San Francisco laborshed population, for example.

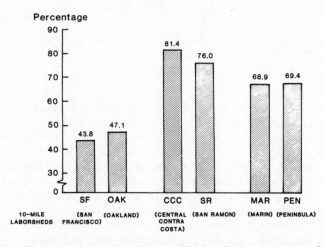

Figure 8.3   Six San Francisco Bay Area model laborsheds: percentage of white and non-Hispanic population, 1980.

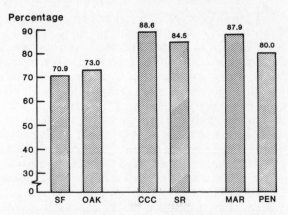

Figure 8.4 Six San Francisco Bay Area model laborsheds: percentage of native English speakers in the population, 1980.

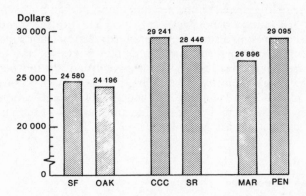

Figure 8.5 Six San Francisco Bay Area model laborsheds: mean family income (dollars), 1979.

The population within 10 miles of the central city potential office sites, in sharp contrast to that in the I-680 laborsheds, ranks consistently low on indicators of the 'preferred' clerical labor force (see 'San Francisco' and 'Oakland' laborsheds, Figs. 8.3–8.12). The combination of low levels of housing growth, home-ownership, income, white non-Hispanic people, native English speakers, and female education, with high levels of families living in poverty and headed by women, paints a picture to employers of a labor supply that can significantly raise clerical labor costs – not only through increased training or lower production standards and higher absenteeism and turnover, but also in increased potential for worker militance.

The older, inner suburban laborsheds ('Marin' and 'Peninsula') include the most affluent towns, and some of the highest female educational levels, in the

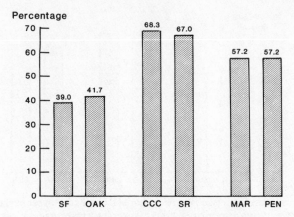

Figure 8.6 Six San Francisco Bay Area model laborsheds: owner–occupied housing as a percentage of all occupied housing, 1980.

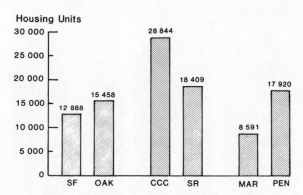

Figure 8.7 Six San Francisco Bay Area model laborsheds: increase in owner-occupied housing units between 1970 and 1980.

metropolitan area. These high-income communities have been slow growing in the 1970s, however, and are not areas where young families can typically afford to buy their 'starter' home. This is shown by relatively low fertility rates: for example, in both the 'Marin' and the 'Peninsula' laborsheds, less than one-quarter of married women (husband present) have young children (see Fig. 8.8). The Marin and Peninsula laborsheds also include fairly high proportions of low-income communities (Richmond, with one of the lowest per-capita incomes in the SMSA and a population that was 48% black in 1980, is within the Marin laborshed; see Fig. 8.2) with many of the same socioeconomic characteristics which employers see as undesirable in the central city laborsheds. Only in the two newer, outer suburban laborsheds around the I-680 corridor can employers wishing to lower clerical labor costs

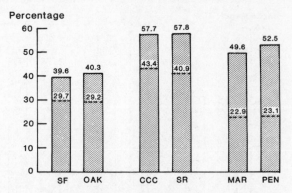

Figure 8.8 Six San Francisco Bay Area model laborsheds: (*upper line*) percentage of all women over 15 who are married, and (*lower line*) percentage of women over 15 living with husband and children under 18, 1980.

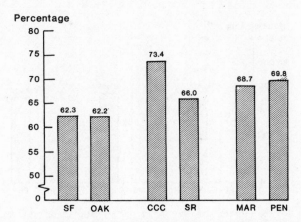

Figure 8.9 Six San Francisco Bay Area model laborsheds: high school graduates as a percentage of all females over 25, 1970.

count on acquiring a local female labor supply with the minimum of these characteristics.

Thus, the back office locational study concludes that the I-680 corridor has attracted more back offices than other areas within the San Francisco metropolitan region because it alone has excellent supplies of the preferred clerical labor, as well as all other necessary back office factors of production. As the personnel manager of one (80% clerical) back office succinctly stated when comparing his present office site in the I-680 corridor to the previous site in Oakland: 'The great advantage here is good people and plenty of them.'

164

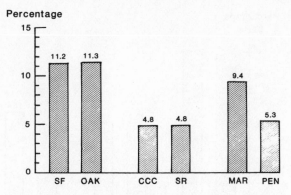

Figure 8.10   Six San Francisco Bay Area model laborsheds: percentage of families with incomes below poverty level, 1979.

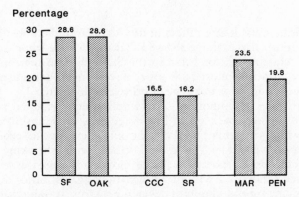

Figure 8.11   Six San Francisco Bay Area model laborsheds: divorced women per 100 married women over 15, 1980.

Conclusion

As female-dominated industrial and occupational sectors continue to grow in the advanced capitalist economies, the conjunction of the household and the wage economies in the local labor market becomes increasingly important to industrial location analysis. The location of back offices in the San Francisco Bay Area is a case in point. To the managers of offices employing large numbers of low-wage clerical workers, a female labor supply associated with areas of growing single-family housing represents a significant lowering of labor costs through reduced turnover, lowered training time, increased productivity, a longer working day, and a reduced chance of unionization. And two important elements of this cost-saving labor supply, its cheapness and attachment to home responsibilities, forfend long commuting distances;

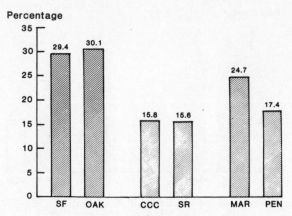

Figure 8.12 Six San Francisco Bay Area model laborsheds: percentage of families with children under 18 headed by women, 1980.

therefore firms must locate offices nearby to achieve the potential savings. The study summarized above showed that this female labor supply is the major differentiating factor between the San Francisco metropolitan sub-region now attracting most back office development and other areas that have not been sought for this type of office development.

This conclusion has important social implications. As noted at the beginning of the chapter, back office low-wage jobs offer unskilled workers, particularly minority female workers, the only alternative to secondary labor market service positions in central cities with shrinking industrial employment bases. Corporations and developers often use this social welfare value of back offices as a weapon in their fight against office development restrictions such as height limits or development fees, arguing that these costs and restrictions are driving back offices to the suburbs. This is, in effect, an argument that municipalities can retain back offices, or attract new ones, if they satisfy the demand for land as defined in this study, particularly the requirement that land be easily developed.

Yet the locational study demonstrated that back office development has avoided areas that satisfy land and linkage requirements if they do not also satisfy the traditional clerical labor demand for educated and docile female workers. The transfer of jobs from central city low-income, predominantly minority female work-forces to higher-income, predominantly white suburban female work-forces is not an unfortunate side effect of back office relocation necessitated by land cost considerations – it is one of the major reasons for back office relocation. Municipalities hoping to provide desperately needed employment for their low-income population by relinquishing planning controls and assuming the costs of all office development externalities are likely to find themselves paying for yet more headquarters, branch, or business service offices providing a small complement of clerical jobs in comparison to managerial or technical positions.

166

K. Nelson

Notes

1 See Tumminia 1953, Foley 1957, Goodwin 1965, Cowan 1969, Armstrong 1972, Jones & Hall 1972, Davis & Hartshorn 1973, Goddard 1973, 1975, Manners 1974, Daniels 1974, 1975, 1977, 1979, 1980.
2 A 1981 survey estimated that 9000 jobs in 22 firms would be transferred from San Francisco to suburban areas between 1981 and 1983 (in addition to 10265 jobs transferred between 1977 and 1981), and that 41% of these jobs were low-wage clerical and data processing positions (*San Francisco Business* 1981).
3 For example, in 1981, 47.1% of black families with one or more children under 18 were headed by women, compared to 13.9% of white families with children under 18 (US Bureau of the Census 1982a: 51).
4 These are services that the firms could purchase on the external market but does not, presumably because they have been deemed more profitable to 'make' than to 'buy' (Chandler 1977).
5 Interviews on the subject of back office locational demands were conducted during the winter of 1982–3 with managerial staff at six private firms representing the oil, banking, insurance, trucking, and mass retailing industry sectors. Four case study sites were suburban back offices; two were central city offices planning to move back office functions to suburban locations in the ensuing year.
6 This is why many back offices are referred to as 'routine,' 'bulk clerical' or 'factory-type' offices. Three case study back offices devoted to administrative and accounting services exemplified this type: clerical employees made up from 79% to 83% of the total work-force.
7 For example, in the two case study back offices devoted to computer services, technical workers made up 41% and 60% of the total work-force.
8 Clerical workers as a whole are 80.5% female, and some of the most common office clerical jobs are nearly totally female, e.g. secretary 99.1%, receptionist 97%, typist 96% (US Census 1982a: 389).
9 For historical studies of the female journey to work see Pratt 1911, London Transport Executive 1950, Taafe *et al.* 1963; examples of current studies are Andrews 1978, Daniels 1972, 1975, 1979, 1980, Fagnani 1977, Hanson & Hanson 1980, Madden 1980, Madden & White 1980, Howe & O'Connor 1982.
10 This term, as well as the structure of labor demand analysis used in the back office locational study, is derived from Storper (1982). He uses the term to describe a similar demand for high-quality labor at low job rewards in the semiconductor industry.
11 The analysis was based on the US Department of Labor's *Handbook for analyzing jobs* as adapted by Storper (1982) for the study of labor demand. Occupations were: key entry operator, word processing operator, in-file (customer service) operator, computer operator, authorization clerk, and collections clerk.
12 The balance of power between employers and workers in a given production process, firm and industry (Storper 1982).
13 In 1960, labor force participation rates were highest in women aged 45 to 54 (40%), while women in the traditional childbearing and child-rearing years, 25–34, had the lowest participation rates of any group under 65 (36%). By 1979 overall participation rates had not only risen dramatically but had become much more even over the female life cycle, and women in the 25–34 cohort actually had the *highest* participation rate (64%) (US Bureau of the Census 1981: 394).
14 Whites made up 82% of the US central city population in 1960 and 75% in 1977 (US Bureau of the Census 1971a, 1978).
15 Heidi Hartmann's term for the social structure in which 'women are employed

partially or wholly in the service of men in the household and where the returns to both women's and men's labor are contained in the family wage, which the man controls' (in Markusen 1981: 27).

16 No case study office had, or was considering, day care facilities.

17 A study of temporary workers found that some were willing to work for years at a firm while remaining on the temporary service's payroll, receiving no fringe benefits, because they were covered by their husbands' benefit plans (Mayall & Nelson 1982).

18 'Low-income, high-minority' towns are defined as having *either* less than 60% white, non-Hispanic populations, or per capita incomes of less than $8000 in 1979.

References

Administrative Management Society 1956. *Administrative automation through IDP and EDP*. New York: Administrative Management Society.

Andrews, H. F. 1978. Journey to work considerations in the labour force participation of married women. *Regional Studies* 12, 11–20.

Armstrong, R. B. 1972. *The office industry: patterns of growth and location*. Cambridge, Mass.: MIT Press.

Barrett, N. S. 1979. Women in the job market: occupations, earnings, and career opportunities. In *The subtle revolution: women at work*, E. Smith (ed.), pp. 31–61. Washington, DC: Urban Institute.

Bluestone, B., and B. Harrison 1982. *The deindustrialization of America*. New York: Basic Books.

Chandler, A. D. 1962. *Strategy and structure*. Cambridge. Mass.: MIT Press.

Chandler, A. D. 1977. *The visible hand: the managerial revolution in American business*. Cambridge, Mass.: Harvard University Press.

Cowan, P. 1969. *The office: a facet of urban growth*. New York: American Elsevier.

Daniels, P. W. 1972. Transport changes generated by decentralized offices. *Regional Studies* 6, 273–89.

Daniels, P. W. 1974. New offices in the suburbs. In *Suburban growth: geographical processes at the edge of the Western city*, J. E. Johnson (ed.), Chichester: Wiley.

Daniels, P. W. 1975. *Office location: an urban and regional study*. London: G. Bell.

Daniels, P. W. 1977. Office location in the British conurbations: trends and strategies. *Urban Studies* 14, 261–74.

Daniels, P. W. 1979. Perspectives on office location research. In P. W. Daniels (ed.), *Spatial patterns of office growth and location*, pp. 1–27. New York: Wiley.

Daniels, P. W. 1980. *Office location and the journey to work: a comparative study of five urban areas*. Corbridge, Northumberland: Retailing and Planning Associates.

Datamation 1978. Consider the Bank of America. Sept., 153–5.

Davies, M. 1975. Woman's place is at the typewriter: the feminization of the clerical labor force. In *Labor market segmentation*, R. Edwards, M. Reich, and D. Gordon (eds.), pp. 279–96. Lexington, Mass.: D. C. Heath.

Davis, S. and T. A. Hartshorn 1973. How does your city grow? The changing pattern of activity location in the Atlanta metropolitan area. *Atlanta Econ. Rev.* July–August, 4–13.

Del Beccaro, E. 1982. *Office development in the San Ramon Valley*. Speech delivered at the Conference on Economic Development in the San Ramon Valley, May 17. Printed by Grubb and Ellis Real Estate Brokerage.

Doeringer, P. and M. Piore 1971. *Internal labor markets and manpower analysis*. Lexington, Mass.: D. C. Heath.

Dun's Review 1978. The big hunt for secretaries. May, 89–90.

Easterlin, R. 1968. *Population, labor force, and long swings in economic growth*. New York: National Bureau of Economic Research.

Fagnani, J. 1977. Activités feminines et transports urbains. *Annales de Geographie* **477**, 542–61.

Foley, D. 1957. *The suburbanization of administrative offices in the San Francisco Bay Area*. Berkeley, Calif.: Real Estate Research Program, Research Report No. 10.

Freeman, J. 1981. Women and urban policy. In *Women and the American city*, C. Stimpson *et al.* (eds). Chicago: University of Chicago Press.

Goddard, J. B. 1973. *Offices linkages and location*. Oxford: Pergamon Press.

Goddard, J. B. 1975. *Office location in urban and regional development*. London: Oxford University Press.

Goodwin, W. 1965. The management center in the United States. *Geogr. Rev.* **55**, 1–16.

Gordon, M. S. and M. Thal-Larsen 1969. *Employer policies in a changing labor market*. Report of the San Francisco Bay Area Employee Survey, 1967. Berkeley, Calif.: Institute of Industrial Relations, University of California.

Hanson, S. and P. Hanson 1980. Gender and urban activity patterns in Uppsala, Sweden. *Geogr. Rev.* **70**, 291–9.

Harvard Business School 1974. *First National City Bank Operating Group*. Case study prepared by John Seeger for Prof. Jay Lorsch. Part B.

Hoos, I. 1961. *Automation in the office*. Washington, DC: Public Affairs Press.

Hoover, E. and R. Vernon 1959. *The anatomy of a metropolis*. New York: Doubleday.

Howe, A. and K. O'Connor 1982. Travel to work and labor force participation of men and women in an Australian metropolitan area. *Prof. Geog.* **34**, 50–64.

Johnson, B. L. 1978. Women who head families, 1970–1977. *Monthly Labor Rev.* **101**, 32–7.

Jones, D. and R. Hall 1972. Office suburbanization in the United States. *Town and Country Planning* 470–3.

Kocka, J. 1980. *White collar workers in America 1890–1940*. London: Sage.

London Transport Executive 1950. *London travel survey 1949*. Plaistow: The Curwen Press.

Madden, J. F. 1980. Urban land use and the growth in two-earner households. *Am. Econ. Rev.* **70**, 191–7.

Madden, J. F. and M. J. White 1980. Spatial implications of increases in the female labor force: a theoretical and empirical synthesis. *Land Economics* **56**, 432–6.

Manners, G. 1974. The office in metropolis: an opportunity for shaping metropolitan America. *Econ. Geog.* **50**, 93–110.

Markusen, A. 1981. City spatial structure, women's household work, and national urban policy. In *Women and the American city*, C. Stimpson *et al.* (eds.). Chicago: University of Chicago Press.

Massey, D. 1978. Capital and locational change: the U.K. electrical engineering and electronics industries. *Rev. Radical Polit. Econ.* **10**, 39–54.

Mayall, D. and K. Nelson 1982. *The temporary help supply service and the temporary labor market*. Report prepared for the US Dept. of Labor Employment and Training Administration. Salt Lake City: Olympus Publishing.

Mills, C. W. 1951. *White-collar: the American middle classes*. New York: Columbia University Press.

Nelson, K. 1984. *Back offices and female labor markets: office suburbanization in the San Francisco–Oakland SMSA*. Unpublished PhD dissertation. University of California, Berkeley.

Oppenheimer, V. 1970. *The female labor force in the United States*. Berkeley, Calif.: Institute of International Studies.

Piore, M. 1979. *Birds of passage*. Cambridge: Cambridge University Press.

Pratt, E. E. 1911. *Industrial causes of congestion of population in New York City*. New York: AMS Press.

Saegert, S. 1980. Masculine cities and feminine suburbs: polarized ideas, contradictory realities. *Signs*, Spring Supplement, 96–111.

San Francisco Business 1981. No room to grow. **16**(5),6–10.

San Francisco Chronicle 1982. 3 firms that went over the hills. June 1, p. 52.

Smuts, R. 1976. *Women and work in America*. New York: Schocken.

Storper, M. 1982. *Technology, the labor process, and the location of industries*. Unpublished PhD dissertation. University of California, Berkeley.

Sweet, J. 1973. *Women in the labor force*. New York: Seminar Press.

Taafe, E. J. *et al.* 1963. *The peripheral journey-to-work – a geographic consideration*. Evanston, Ill.: Northwestern University Press.

Tornqvist, S. 1970. *Contact systems and regional development*. Lund Studies in Geography, Series B:35. Lund, Sweden: C. W. K. Gleerup.

Tumminia, A. E. 1953. *Locational factors for the office function of industry*. Unpubl. MA thesis, Columbia University.

US Bureau of the Census 1971a. *Social and economic characteristics of the population in metropolitan and nonmetropolitan areas: 1970 and 1960*. Series P-23, No. 37. Washington, DC.: US Government Printing Office.

US Bureau of the Census 1971b. *1970 census of housing*. Vol. I, Chap. A, Part 6: *General housing characteristics, California*. Washington, DC: US Government Printing Office.

US Bureau of the Census 1972. *1970 census of population*. Vol. I, Chap. B, Part 6: *General population characteristics, California*. Section 1. Washington, DC: US Government Printing Office.

US Bureau of the Census 1978. *Social and economic characteristics of the metropolitan and nonmetropolitan population: 1977 and 1970*. Series P-23, No. 75. Washington, DC: US Government Printing Office.

US Bureau of the Census 1981. *Statistical abstract of the United States, 1981*. Washington, DC: US Government Printing Office.

US Bureau of the Census 1982a. *Statistical abstract of the United States, 1982–3*. Washington, DC: US Government Printing Office.

US Bureau of the Census 1982b. *1980 census of population*. Vol. 1, Chap. B, Part 6: *General population characteristics, California*. Washington, DC: US Government Printing Office.

US Bureau of the Census 1982c. *1980 census of housing*. Vol. I, Chap. A, Part 6: *General housing characteristics, California*. Washington, DC: US Government Printing Office.

US Bureau of the Census 1983. *1980 census of population and housing, supplementary report: Provisional estimates of social, economic and housing characteristics.* Washington, DC: US Government Printing Office.

Walker, R. and M. Storper 1981. Capital and industrial location. *Prog. Hum. Geog.* **5**, 473–509.

9

Contesting works closures
in Western Europe's
old industrial regions:
defending place
or betraying class?

RAY HUDSON and DAVID SADLER

In the 1950s and 1960s, major plant closures in northeast England in most 'traditional' industries, but above all coal mining, were largely uncontested by those who were directly or indirectly affected by the accompanying loss of jobs (Hudson 1983, 1984a, 1984b). By contrast, the latter years of the 1970s and the initial ones of the 1980s in the same area saw a series of campaigns to contest decisions concerning works closures or major employment losses. By no means all such decisions were challenged, but those that were were concentrated in places where the region's 'traditional' (and by then often nationalized) industries such as coal mining, iron and steel making, shipbuilding and heavy engineering were the major, even sole, source of industrial employment. These anti-closure campaigns were characteristically organized around the threatened works and the community (village or town) reliant upon it for employment and wage income (for example, North Tyneside Trades Council 1979, Save Scotswood Campaign Committee 1979, Borough of South Tyneside 1982, Cleveland County Council 1983, Durham County Council and Sedgefield District Council 1983a, 1983b, Easington District Council 1983, Tyne & Wear County Council 1983, Evenwood Labour Party 1983). Furthermore, it was clear that such campaigns were by no means confined to this particular region, as similar ones developed or revived in other 'old' industrial regions elsewhere in Great Britain (Scotland, Wales) and in continental Western Europe (Lorraine and the Nord in France, the Ruhr in West Germany, Wallonia in Belgium). In contrast to northeast England, where anti-closure campaigns tended to remain confined to the particular groups of workers, works, villages or towns directly affected, in several of these other cases protests became generalized within an industry at regional – even national – level, and throughout particular regions across a wide spectrum of social groups. Several of these campaigns, then, were characterized by attachments to place and class becoming contingently conjoined in a variety of often-complex ways, so that these became complementary rather than competitive bases for social

organization in defense of place. What was emerging was a series of territorially based campaigns, the aims of which may be summarized in a phrase
borrowed from one of the campaign slogans in Longwy (France) in the late
1970s: to defend the right to 'live, learn and work' in particular places, though
the ways in which these objectives were pursued and the degree to which they
were successfully attained were highly varied. These campaigns were not
simply evidence of a deeply felt, and to varying degrees collectively shared,
attachment to place that was grounded in the spatially defined routine of
everyday life, but also of the active involvement of working people, their
families, friends and neighbors in the restructuring of capital and the
changing geography of industrial production as *their* particular places were
deemed no longer to be (sufficiently) profitable locations in the context of an
increasingly internationalized system of production and trade.

How, then, is the emergence of such territorially based protests, at these
particular times and in these particular places to be understood? Finding
satisfactory answers to this theoretical question took on pressing practical
significance as we became actively involved in some of these campaigns in
northeast England (for example, Hudson & Sadler 1984, Hudson, Peck &
Sadler 1984) and sought a better understanding of past practices with a view
to informing existing struggles against further closures.

Some preliminary clues were provided by the historical geographic development of this particular set of 'traditional' industries. Frequently they were
(a) associated with 'one-industry' towns so that the effects of major closure
were heavily spatially concentrated (unlike, say, textiles, where aggregate
job losses had been very extensive but spatially more diffused); (b) characterized by either public ownership or a high degree of state involvement at
national and/or supranational European Community level, so that closure
decisions were often transparently 'political', while (c) in contrast to the
1960s, by the late 1970s the promises of 'alternative jobs' via reindustrialization programs had worn distinctly thin. These provided no more than
some general indications, however, and certainly offered no explanation of
the rise and variety of territorially based campaigns in defense of place.

Much of the existing literature dealing with attachment to place and
capitalism's uneven development provided at best partial insights. For
example, much of the debate on nationalism and attachment to the 'imagined
communities' (Anderson 1983) of national states is of limited relevance,
focusing on issues (such as linguistic distinctiveness) that were of little
importance for the defense of particular villages or towns against catastrophic
industrial decline. This conclusion holds *a fortiori* for those analyses which
pose the issue in terms of territory (nation) versus class (for example, Hobsbawm 1977), for the precise characteristic of several of the campaigns considered here was their fusion of place and class (at least for a while). While the
writings of humanistic geographers (such as Pocock 1981, Relph 1976, Tuan
1977) on attachment to place and related issues focus more on the spatial
scales of village or town, they tend only to describe individuals' experience of
place. They do not relate this to the context and structures of the societies in
which such people live; to their membership of social groups and classes
through which they learn shared meanings, including those relating to the

173

places in which they live and with which they identify. Conversely, the varied contributions within the marxist tradition on the spatial uneven development of capitalism address themselves to the causally determining powers of unobservable structures (for example, Keat & Urry 1975, Sayer 1982), but tend to neglect the role of people as rational agents affecting change within the limits that these structures impose and reproducing them via their actions. The more sophisticated of these analyses (for example, Harvey 1982) halt at the point of specifying the structural boundaries to a capitalist society and possible tendencies toward spatial uneven development within them. The cruder versions of such analyses (for example, Carney 1980) go so far as rather mechanistically to deduce forms of political organization in defense of place from the inner logic of the capitalist mode of production – explicitly rather than implicitly reducing people to their ascribed roles of bearers of structures (for an extended critique of this position, see Thompson 1978), to the status of 'cultural dupes' (Giddens 1981; 71–2).

The conclusion to be drawn from these brief comments[1], is that a more sophisticated theoretical approach is required in order to begin to grasp the bases for, and character and political potential of, the various campaigns in defense of the right to 'live, learn and work' in particular places. This sophisticated approach is required in order to comprehend more satisfactorily the links between peoples' knowledge of and feelings about space, their patterns of behavior and social practices, and the spatially uneven development of capitalist societies, and so reveal rather more about the processes of uneven development themselves. This approach views people as active, conscious agents, who are rational in that what they do makes sense to them in terms of their own understanding of their individual and collective interests, while recognizing that the way in which they perceive these interests, and the possibilities that at any time are objectively open to them, will be conditioned by (though not determined by) those deep structural forces that shape the societies in which they live. Seeking to integrate the way in which places and the spatial patterning of (capitalist) societies come to have socially endowed meanings for people pre-supposes the creation of some significant theoretical space for conscious and meaningful human behavior in the reproduction of uneven development. In so far as it creates this theoretical space it also potentially creates political space within which people can begin to change the societies within which they live.

As it happened, at about the same time as a concern with place – with the specificity of *their place* – was increasingly coming to the forefront of peoples' consciousness in the villages and towns of Western Europe's old industrial regions threatened by precipitate economic and employment decline, such theoretical perspectives were beginning to be developed. They may be characterized as 'structurationist' approaches (Thrift 1983) and their development can be traced to a generally long-overdue convergence of interests between some social theorists and geographers, centered on the importance of the spatial patterning of society and the meanings of places to people as an integral part of social reproduction and a growing recognition that space is not simply a neutral container into which social processes are poured (for example, Gregory 1978, 1981, 1982, Giddens 1979, 1981, Soja 1980, 1983,

Urry 1981, Weaver 1982). The patterning of capitalist societies in space is both actively produced in social practice as a moment in social reproduction and forms the setting in which social processes are concretely located and those practices take place. As a corollary, there has been an increasing concern with the meaning of place and space, with the reciprocal relations between the processes through which localities and places acquire socially endowed meanings, with how these meanings influence what people do and with how what they do influences how they interpret the space around them in terms of meaningful places. In turn, this has raised issues to do with relationships between agency and structure in social reproduction. It is to this set of issues that the remainder of this chapter is addressed, attempting to use these theoretical developments in interpreting campaigns to defend place and the evidence of these campaigns as a basis for elaborating such theory.

The reproduction of societies as capitalist

Agency, structure

While in many respects provocative to certain strands of both bourgeois and marxist thought, Giddens' 'theory of structuration' (1979, 1981) forms a useful starting point for discussion and is one which accepts the kernel of Marx's arguments about the essential character of capitalist societies. A recognition of the decisive importance of the class structural relation between capital and labor does not imply that the actual development of capitalist societies revolves only around this axis, however. In brief, we must not only recognize the fundamental contradictory relation between capital and labor. We must also recognize the existence of competition between capitals in search of surplus profits. Further, we must acknowledge competition between groups within the (structurally defined) working class, for example on the basis of differences in sector, industry or occupation.

We must also take account of the possibility of conflict between capital(s) and/or groups within the working class and social groups either located outside of capitalist social relations or located within them, but organized on issues and dimensions other than those of production: gender (Rose & Mackenzie 1983), race (Doherty 1983) or an ecological concern for the natural environment, for example. Although the proximate basis of social organization may not be a class issue (in the sense of directly deriving from capital–labor relations of production), it has nevertheless been argued that the capacity of such groups to realize their aims is conditional upon their class location (Olin Wright 1978). What this suggests is that the relationships between social practice and the reproduction of the class structural relation between capital and labor are complicated and contingent ones.

Central to Giddens' analysis of the links between agency and structure are two related notions: the distinction between system and structure and the duality of structure. He summarizes these points as follows (1981: 26–7; for a fuller statement, see 1979):

175

A distinction is made between *structure* and *system*. Social systems are composed of patterns of relationships between actors or collectivities reproduced across time and space. Social systems are hence constituted of *situated practices*. Structures exist in time–space only as moments recursively involved in the production and reproduction of social systems. Structures have only a 'virtual' existence. A fundamental postulate of the theory of structuration is the notion of *duality of structure*, which refers to the essentially recursive nature of social practices. Structure is both the medium and outcome of the practices which constitute social systems. The concept of duality of structure connects the *production* of social interaction, as always and everywhere a contingent accomplishment of knowledgeable social actors, to the *reproduction* of social systems across time–space. (emphases in original)

In this way, Giddens stresses the relations between temporally and spatially situated social interaction and societal reproduction, and emphasizes that the actions of individual agents, pursuing their individually or collectively defined interests, are at once shaped by and reproduce the 'basic principles of organization' of societies, above all in capitalist societies that of the fundamental class relationship between capital and labor; and that they do this as a routine, taken-for-granted element in their behavior as rational agents (in the sense defined above). Whether we are conscious of them or not, and contrary to appearances, structural relationships are not immutably given to us in a manner that renders them unchangeable (or changeable only over time, when the continuing development of the forces of production within the social relations of capitalism attains a critical pitch, after which capitalism somehow mysteriously changes itself into something new and better). The point is that structural relations are routinely socially produced and reproduced in the course of 'everyday life' (on this notion, see also Lefebvre 1971). This being so, a central task of a critical social theory is to uncover that which is unquestioningly taken for granted, discursively to reveal the real basis of '*practical consciousness* . . . "knowing how to go on" in a whole diversity of contexts of social life' (Giddens 1981: 27; emphasis in original). For it is in the unquestioning, perhaps even unconscious, acceptance of the legitimacy of the rules governing everyday life that the structural reproduction of capitalist societies is grounded. Of particular importance is the routine acceptance of the legitimacy of wage labor and of going to work in a particular place as a normal feature of such societies, for in this is grounded the reproduction of the class structural capital–labor relationship (a point developed further below). Attachment to place is grounded in the routine not only of working in particular places, but of learning and living there.

Another important point in Giddens' analysis of the relationships between agency and structure for our purposes is that, while social agents act in a rational manner, it is vital to acknowledge that as a matter of routine they engage in social interaction in circumstances that in part are unknown to them and that, partly because of this, their actions can have outcomes in addition to or other than those that they intended. Furthermore, in pointing out that 'the knowledgeability of actors is always *bounded*, by *unacknowledged conditions* and *unintended consequences* of action' (Giddens 1981: 28), Giddens' conclusions converge with those of Habermas (1975) with respect to the more limited issue of the chronic gap between the intentions and outcomes of the policies of capitalist states, a convergence that is of some importance here in so far as state policies are integrally involved in the spatially uneven development of capitalist societies (a point that is central to later arguments in this chapter).

Place, class

Especially in his latest (1981) work, and in contrast to many other social theorists, Giddens has come to emphasize not only the role of time but also that of space and place (in his terms, locale) as central to the reproduction of capitalist societies. He shows that the time–space constitution of societies is an integral element of the processes of structuration linking agency to structure that are involved in their reproduction. This view can be contrasted with that of certain geographers who wish to cling to the notion of 'spatial forms of human social organisation' (Dunford & Perrons 1983: 78) as the distinctive and specific object of analysis of human geography – thus, maybe inadvertently, reproducing rather than transcending a particular conception of the intellectual division of labor. This focus upon the role of place provides a basis from which to begin to analyze relationships between attachment to and the defense of place and class structure in the historical processes of social class formation.[2]

In the previous section we represented capitalist societies as simultaneously riven with conflict and dissension on several planes. Yet as societies they do hold together with sufficient cohesion and in such ways that capitalist social relations *are* reproduced; precisely how and on what bases such social class groupings form, how the balance of class and other social forces fluctuates, and how capitalist societies are contingently reproduced can only be resolved via theoretically informed empirical investigations. Nevertheless, what can be safely stated, is that in so far as such societies *are* reproduced as capitalist, with the social relations of capital continuing to hold hegemonic sway and to be generally accepted as legitimate (or, if not accepted as legitimate, accepted nonetheless, albeit unwillingly), it is clear that capitalist states, which in practice largely means capitalist national states, play a decisive role in mediating between the claims of competing classes and interest groups (for a review of theories of the capitalist state, see Jessop 1982).

Virtually from the outset, capitalist societies have been constituted in the form of competitive *national* states (Anderson 1983). For it suggests that from the genesis of the capitalist mode of production, there has been a territorial element in the definition of actual class interests. More generally, it suggests that an important dimension to the historical processes of social class formation in capitalist societies, to divisions between and within the (structurally defined) classes of capital and labor, is the influence of place. This may form a basis for the formation of groups which specify their unifying interests in terms of shared location, either within or cutting across structurally defined class boundaries. Thus space, place and the organization of social groups, united by a concern with or attachment to a particular locality (be it a factory, neighborhood or national state), can and in practice persistently and almost without exception do play a key role in the historical processes of social class formation and organization.

Differentiation on the basis of location in space thereby ceases to be something to be appended following the completion of a class analysis, and comes to be regarded as a potentially decisive element in the indentification of class interests. It is the recognition of the potentially central role of territorial attachments in actual class formation in Giddens' 1981 work, building upon earlier comments (Giddens 1973: 199–202, 1979, especially 206–7 and 226–8), that makes it of interest here. While stressing the necessity to ground analysis of capitalist societies in their time–space constitution, Giddens does not focus upon the relationships between spatial uneven development within (as opposed to between) national states, attachment to localities and the processes of capital accumulation in the way that we seek to do here, however. Location in space must cease to be one way of differentiating between groups within a class once the latter has been formed; rather, the point of departure is a recognition that class interests, organizations and practices actually (and usually) within capitalism are formulated at least in part with respect to particular localities. This is especially so at a time when capitals' strategies for internationalizing production are accelerating further so that the options available to them in fragmenting opposition by playing off workers in an increasing number of areas are growing rapidly.

From this perspective, an important dimension of differentiation (and so a possible basis for competition) between capital and labor, between capitals, or between groups of wage laborers and those linked to them, is location in and attachment to place. Similarly, identification with national territories or supra- or subnational territorial units can form the basis or bases for a cross-class identification of interests. It is important to acknowledge, however, that the mechanisms involved in the development of attachment to and identification with territorial units will vary with scale and that even if these all constitute 'imagined communities' what is crucial is 'the style in which they are imagined' (Anderson 1983: 15).

This is particularly so in the way in which people living and working in those one-industry villages and towns where campaigns to defend the right to 'live, learn and work' there take place 'imagine' them to be 'communities,' for this is grounded in the daily routine of life tied to *those* places, in the almost sole availability there of waged work in those industries (for example, Dennis *et al.* 1956, Bulmer 1978, Williamson 1982, Douglass & Krieger 1983). It is perhaps not surprising, therefore, in the context of defending the right to 'live, learn and work' in such places, that territorially defined competition within the (structurally defined) class of labor can be particularly acute. What is surprising is that much marxist writing upon issues such as the uneven development of capitalism, while accepting a differentiated view of capital as many competitive capitals, tends to cling (even if only implicitly) to a utopian view of a working class as unified across territorial boundaries by a recognition of its real class interests. Thus, for example, while Dunford and Perrons (1983: 246) recognize that 'The process of accumulation and the laws of this process are . . . the result of a constant struggle between capital and labor and competing capitals and capital groups,' no consideration is given to competition between groups of workers in the unfolding of this process. While at a deep structural level, this unity of class interests undoubtedly does exist within and across capitalist societies, the real point at issue is to explain why it is not seen in these terms by the relevant agents who perceive their interests in different ways, which then become the basis for particular forms of social organization and practice that become a central element in the uneven development of capitalism. Not least, a correct theoretical specification of this issue is vital in terms of formulating progressive political practices.

Defending places: the strategies of capital, labor and the state

The necessity for an appropriate theoretical specification of the links between agency, structure, and attachment to place and class is sharply revealed when capitals restructure their activities so as to combat their own crises or to further their own self-expansion. For as Harvey (1982 especially 425–31) has put it, devalorization is and must be place-specific. The validity of this proposition has been sharply brought home to groups of workers throughout the history of capitalism, but it has been particularly accentuated since the transition from a long-period phase of expansion to one of recession in the capitalist world economy in the last decade or so (for example, Mandel 1975, 1978, 1980, Frank 1980). It is this transition, and with it the growing recognition that the option of reindustrialization via state regional policies, which could be presented as having some credibility in the 1960s but is widely seen as having no possibility of success in the 'old' industrial regions in the 1980s, has been important in triggering anti-closure campaigns. Seen from the point of view of workers, their families and dependents in such places, the only feasible solution often appears to be to fight to preserve *their* factory, *their* mine, for their community or region, in the sure knowledge that should their struggle be an unsuccessful one then the jobs lost will not be replaced, while the price of success will be the closure of some other factory or mine, a threat to some other group of workers and *their* community, *their* place. Accepting the competitive ethic of capitalism in this way as a legitimate terrain, and fighting on a territorially defined basis within it, rather than posing broader questions as to why restructuring is regarded as either necessary or justified given its extensive social costs, has the precise (albeit unintended) effect of reproducing the basic structural relations of capitalism. Groups of workers consequently compete with one another, sometimes on the basis of cross-class territorial alliances, for the privilege of being able successfully to sell their labor-power in the marketplace and their places on the place market (Robinson & Sadler 1985). Put another way, a concern with more general class solidarity, even if this is recognized, is subordinated to a more immediate concern with living and working in a localized, spatially delimited community, in a particular place.

The place-specific campaigns to contest steel closures in the European

Community (EC) in recent years illustrate the variety of ways in which this defense of place has been contested, in the course of which identification with place and class have been contingently combined in different times and places, and in which capitals and states have sought to secure their interests in closing steel capacity and restructuring production (Hudson & Sadler, 1983a, 1983b, Morgan 1983). For in relation to changes in the global pattern of accumulation and the international division of labor in bulk steel production, Western European steel producers have attempted to restore competitiveness and profits, or at least stem haemorrhaging losses, by closing capacity and/or drastically cutting employment in localities which, because of the historical development of the steel industry, depended very heavily upon steel production as a source of wages and employment. The high level of state involvement in the EC – both at the level of national states and the embryonic supranational EC itself – has meant that the locationally concentrated collapse of employment has frequently been perceived, correctly, as a transparently 'political' decision rather than simply as the outcome of the logic of 'economic' processes and the forces of the market. This deep attachment to such places, built up through generations living, learning and working in them, was largely taken for granted until such times as the threat of major employment loss with the prospect of no comparable replacement became apparent. For this (and other) reasons such job losses have generally been contested in a variety of ways. These protests have themselves become an active moment in the restructuring process, in shaping *which* steelworks will close as steelworkers have been divided, or more accurately, have divided themselves, on a plant or regional or national basis to fight for the survival of their works at the expense of others.

A particularly stark example of this process was the unsuccessful campaign mounted in 1979 and 1980 to save Consett steelworks in northeast England. This was confined solely to the town of Consett itself and saw steelworkers there isolated both from a wider basis of support within the region and from other steelworks in the northeast and elsewhere, as the 'Save Consett' campaign was contested solely on the grounds that it was a profitable steelworks, that its closure was 'a grave commercial error' (J. Carney, cited in Hudson & Sadler 1983a) and, by implication, that it should remain open and some other steelworks within the British Steel Corporation (BSC) should close. At no stage in the campaign was the decisive reason for its proposed closure, BSC's plans to cut overall capacity, and their relation to the political strategies of the UK central government raised or contested (for a fuller analysis, see Hudson & Sadler 1983a). Moreover, even in those cases where there was initially a more marked degree of unity between steelworkers at national level, as in France in the late 1970s where protests against plant closures in Lorraine and the Nord were supported by national strike action, this subsequently crumbled to leave individual plants at best fighting in isolation, at worst competing with one another for survival. In this case, the policies of the French state in terms of differential redundancy payments, differential allocations of resources supposedly to attract new industries and alternative employment in areas affected by steel closures, and so on played an important role in fragmenting steelworkers on a plant and regional basis (for a fuller analysis, see Hudson & Sadler 1983b). In general, the ways in which steel-workers in these localities identified their interests as place specific and organized to protect them ultimately involved setting themselves in competition with other groups of steelworkers in an attempt to secure some employment. The particular ways in which these campaigns evolved cannot be divorced from the history of trades union organization in the steel industry in France and the UK, with the latter case in particular being characterized by strong tendencies to inter-plant competition and regional chauvinism. Nevertheless, despite the rather specific combination of contemporary and historical circumstances surrounding the steel industry in these two nations in the late 1970s, it would be extremely misleading to leave the impression that territorially based competition between groups of workers is an atypical form of contesting proposed plant closures. Quite the reverse, in fact; it has become increasingly the norm as plant competes with plant, increasingly across not just regional but national boundaries and within a particular transnational corporation (for example, Hudson 1983, Lloyd & Shutt 1983).

Furthermore, as the recent history of the steel industry within the EC makes clear, competition between groups of workers in different localities is by no means the only approach to contesting closures. For such closure proposals can also come to form the basis of territorially based alliances, formed for the specific purpose of opposing closures, embracing a broader spectrum of social groups and interests and cutting across (structurally defined) class boundaries. Such alliances can be constructed, for example, because locally based and tied small capitals in retailing and various private service sector activities become aware of the threat to their existence as capitals in those particular places, one that is posed by the imminent precipitous decline of purchasing power that accompanies mass job loss. Once formed, their subsequent development or dissolution becomes integrally involved in the competitive struggles to preserve particular plants as the defense of place, of common territorially defined interests, transcends, at least for a time, (structurally defined) antagonistic class relations. Three examples will be given of this.

The first concerns opposition to steel closures in Lorraine, in France. Partly reflecting a strong sense of regional identity – of being Lorrainese – a result of the region's history of being alternately transferred between France and Germany, the regionally based bourgeoisie recognized the threat to their interests posed by steel closures and began to organize against them before the steelworkers and unions did. An organization, the *Avenir du Pays Haut* (APH), was formed with the specific intention of protecting the Lorrainese economy. It played an important role in broadening the social basis of protests against steel closures, at least until February 1979, after which time the onset of violent protests by autonomous groups of steelworkers operating outside the structure and authority of the steel unions challenged the legitimacy of the French state's monopoly of the means of violence. From this point, the APH increasingly distanced itself from the anti-closure protests (Hudson & Sadler 1983b).

The second example relates to the defense of Ravenscraig steelworks in Scotland. Speculation as to the future of the works grew in the autumn of

1982, against a background of debate about whether BSC could continue to operate its five major integrated production complexes. A broadly based campaign to oppose the threat of closure rapidly developed, embracing not only steelworkers but also groups of workers from other industries in other parts of Scotland. Moreover, drawing on a history of nationalist sentiment in Scotland and an attachment to Scotland as a place with shared, socially endowed meanings that cut across class and other social divisions (for example, Harvie 1977, Nairn 1977, Smith & Brown 1983), the campaign developed to involve a much broader spectrum of class interests and to encompass a wide social basis within Scotland. One important element in it was a powerful cross-party Scottish parliamentary lobby, presented with ammunition by a report of the Parliamentary Committee for Scottish Affairs (1982) on the significance of the Ravenscraig plant to the Scottish economy. Such was the breadth and strength of the campaign to preserve Ravenscraig that, despite the admission in a report of the House of Commons Industry and Trade Committee (1983: paras. 219 and 225) that it was costing BSC £100 million per annum to keep Ravenscraig open, its future was guaranteed as a steel-making plant until 1985. Whether it will be further guaranteed remains to be seen, but even if it turns out to be only temporary, what the success of the 1982–3 campaign demonstrates is that, in certain conditions, territorially based alliances can force a recognition of the fact that ultimately decisions such as those concerning closures are political rather than merely narrowly economic ones; that the right to live, learn and work in a particular place can successfully be defended against the logic of capitalist production (for fuller details, see Sadler 1984).

The third example is more complicated, also involving individual plant, regionalist and nationalist dimensions. It relates to Hoesch's decision to end steel making at Dortmund, in the eastern part of the Ruhr in West Germany (for the historical background to this, see Jablonowski & Offermans 1974, Schröter & Zierold 1977). The course of this (unsuccessful) campaign was strongly conditioned by the merger in the 1960s of Hoesch with the Dutch steel company, Hooghoven, and the subsequent break up of the union of the two companies in the early 1980s. Fears about the ending of steel making in Dortmund in 1980 led to the formation of a broad cross-class alliance, the *Burgerinitiative Stahlwerk*, in an attempt to guarantee the continuation of steel production in Dortmund rather than its further concentration at Hooghoven's coastal Ijmuiden works, with Dortmund reduced simply to a steel rolling plant. The broad social base of the protest movement soon dissipated in 1981, however, partly because it had led to the focus of attention being switched to the provision of alternative employment rather than the preservation of steel making, with the movement to contest the closure proposals becoming much more centered on the Dortmund works and steelworkers. The separation of Hoesch and Hooghoven led to both a revival and a redirection of protest, amid an atmosphere of considerable uncertainty about the proposed restructuring of steel production in West Germany involving the major steel groups (Krupp and Thyssen). Having got rid of the Dutch connection, the way was open to the Dortmund branch of the IG Metall Union to propose, in December 1982, a complete nationalization of West

Germany's steel industry as a means of securing Dortmund's future. (Even though the union at national level was opposed to nationalization, a compromise between local and national levels was agreed whereby proposed government financial aid would take the form of it acquiring share capital in the steel companies.) Thus the definition of place altered as the campaign evolved, changing from one that began as a regionally based cross-class protest movement to one with a narrower basis centered on steelworkers in Dortmund itself, and eventually ending up by proposing a national solution as the route to preserving steelmaking at Dortmund and, by implication, unity of interests between steelworkers in different plants in West Germany (for further analyses, see Sadler 1983, 1985).

There is, then, considerable evidence simply from this review of campaigns against steel closures in the EC of groups within the (structurally defined) working class becoming involved in territorially based cross-class alliances in attempts to pursue what they perceive to be their interests. These are defined with respect to specific places but the effect of people rationally pursuing their interests defined in this way is both conditioned by and helps reproduce the basic structural parameters of society as capitalist. In fact, there is much more evidence which suggests that historically this process of the formation of such territorially based groupings trying to further the interests of their place has become a persistent one within capitalist societies, a central feature of the reproduction of spatial uneven development within and between them that is deeply embedded in the social practices that are central to their reproduction. Thus groups within the working class become actively involved in the forging of territorially defined alliances, at a variety of spatial scales, unified by their organization around or mediated in a variety of ways through capitalist states (a point returned to below). Three examples, at differing spatial scales, will suffice to illustrate the point. At national scale, the formation of cross-class agreements around proposals to nationalize particular branches of industry hinges on a perception of shared interests by some capitals, some elements of labor and the state: for example, in the UK case, the nationalizations of coal, railways and steel were all seen as satisfying these varying (and ultimately contradicting) interests (Hudson 1981, 1984a, 1984b). It is, as we have pointed out, significant that subsequent decisions to close plants in such nationalized industries have been among the most strongly contested. At a regional scale, the formation of cross-class alliances around a shared perception of the need to modernize old industrial regions by public sector investment programs – to build new industrial estates, factories, roads, commercial centers, houses and so on, providing both fresh opportunities for capitals to reap profits and new employment and better living conditions for some members of the working class – became a recurrent feature of contemporary capitalism, especially in the 1960s. It was a crucial reason why works closures then were generally not contested in the way that they were in the late 1970s and early 1980s. For example, such agreements are discernible in Scotland, Wales and the peripheral regions of England from the late 1950s (for example, Hudson 1982a, 1983, 1984b, Morgan 1982, Cooke 1983) and more generally in Western Europe (Hudson & Lewis 1982) and the USA (Clavel 1982), though their roots are often traceable to the interwar years (Carney & Hudson 1978).

At the same time, in so far as such policies are tied to intraregional settlement policies, as is commonly the case, concentrating new public sector investment in terms of general conditions of production and collective consumption within regions (into selected 'growth points,' 'growth zones' etc.), then their effect is to encourage intraregional divisions on a territorial basis. This arises both because of competition to achieve growth-center designation and because of the divisions engendered between those localities which achieve this and those which do not. Thus the promulgation and implementation of state policies, the formally proclaimed aims of which are to reduce *inter*regional inequalities in employment opportunities and living conditions, presuppose increasing *intra*regional fragmentation as alliances of interests tied to particular localities form to promote the interests of their particular place. Perhaps the most extreme example of such intraregional growth point policies is that of the UK New Towns (see Hudson 1976), though similar spatial developmental policies have been developed within other states (for example, Rubinstein 1978). New Town developments in the UK involve the establishment of non-elected development corporations, with a considerable degree of autonomy, cutting across the networks of local political power and control exercised via democratically elected local authorities. In some circumstances, this itself can become a focus for uniting opposition to them within areas (for example, see the case of Peterlee: Hudson 1976, Robinson, 1983); in others it has served more or less to unite local authorities and local political opinion around coalitions to strive for a New Town in or near their area so as to secure new jobs, better living conditions and so on. (For example, in Washington, having previously opposed its designation, local authorities in the area switched to supporting it as fears of rising unemployment in northeast England grew in the early 1960s; Hudson 1979, 1982a, Regional Policy Research Unit 1979: Part 8.)

The final example, to a degree already presaged in the inter- and intraregional competition outlined above, refers to the UK in the 1970s. Central government's macro-economic policies have increasingly been to rely on the market as a steering mechanism, and cut back the scope of its own regional and urban policy initiatives as part of a more general drive to cut public expenditure and roll back the boundaries of the state itself. As this occurs, cross-class alliances have increasingly formed around the structures of local government (metropolitan, county and district councils) in defense of the local economy (see above; also Cochrane 1983). One particularly revealing symptom of competition for jobs between local areas has been the intense lobbying to achieve Enterprise Zone status and so, supposedly, a competitive edge over one's rival areas within the national territory (Anderson 1983), although not necessarily those located in other national territories (Fröbel *et al.* 1980, Hudson & Lewis 1984a, 1984b). Furthermore, as *ad hoc* employment creation agencies such as British Steel (Industry) have proliferated as part of a cosmetic response by national states to place-specific industrial decline, a similar pattern of competition has been set in motion as places strive for the attention of these new organizations.

In summary, then, the 'normal' pattern of social organization within capitalist societies is one that chronically involves competition between territorially defined groups attempting to promote the interests of 'their place.' It is *not* the case that territory replaces class as a basis of social organization and practice but rather that identification with and attachment to place itself becomes integrally involved in the process of class formation. Place and class become contingently related in a complex manner as bases for social organization and thus pivotally involved in the reproduction of spatial uneven development within capitalist societies. Thus the defense of place becomes central to the reproduction of those societies *as* capitalist as an unintended consequence of campaigns to defend or promote the interests of specific places (whether village, town, region or national state) in competition with other places.

Routinization, deroutinization and the reproduction of capitalist societies

A central element in Giddens' theory of structuration is that of the routine, taken-for-granted character of much social interaction within capitalist societies. In this sense, they are routinely, though contingently, reproduced (Giddens 1979: 97–130 especially; 1981: 37–8, 64–5). What is central to the reproduction of capitalist societies as capitalist, then, is the normal routine of 'going to work,' presupposing as it usually (though by no means always) does the separation of home and workplace in time–space. Put slightly differently, what is central is the normative acceptance by people working for a wage within them of their class position as wage labor (of whatever level of qualification), thereby simultaneously accepting, affirming and reproducing the decisive central axis of the contradictory structural relationship between capital and labor.

A corollary of this, however, is that when such people are unable successfully to sell their labor power on the market and become unemployed – when what has been accepted as the normal routine becomes 'deroutinized' – then this *might* lead them to question the legitimacy of their class position, particularly given the close links within capitalist societies between being able to earn a wage, and life-style and living conditions. To borrow Habermas' (1975) terminology, this deroutinization via the ending of the normal routine of successfully selling one's labor power on the market *could* trigger either a legitimation or a motivation crisis, throwing into question the consensual acceptance, if not approval, of the dominant social relations of production. Clearly what requires specification is the precise circumstances under which this process of questioning might arise in particular situations (Giddens 1981: 66, 220–3).

The effects of such deroutinization are obviously severe at the individual level (for example, Hudson 1982b), but when they affect comparatively few individuals in a period of full employment it is usually possible for bourgeois accounts to prevail, generally pointing the finger at individual failings or weakness as the cause of unemployment. Where such deroutinization creates mass unemployment in whole localities, with thousands of people losing their jobs as a result of a single and necessarily place-specific devalorization decision by a capital or a national state, then one might reasonably anticipate a challenge to such accounts and a rather different reaction from those adversely affected. One might reasonably expect that the challenge posed by this collectively experienced and simultaneously imposed deroutinization would lead those made redundant to raise questions about the legitimacy of their class position which left them vulnerable, exposed to bearing the costs of decisions over which they could exercise no effective control; or if not to raise this question, then at least to fight for the right to work, albeit as wage labor. Furthermore, one might expect the strength of protests against such imposed deroutinization to be strongest in those communities that substantially depend upon one industry (such as coal or steel) as their source of employment for wage labor, *a fortiori* when the relevant industries are nationalized, formally subject to a logic of politics rather than of the market, so that the normal separation of the economic and political spheres in capitalist societies is broken and these are *seen* to be re-connected.

Giddens (1981: 123) has pointed out that we can learn a good deal about day-to-day life in routine settings from analyzing circumstances in which it is radically disturbed. His point is neatly illustrated by the various examples referred to above of how threats to the everyday lives of members of the working class have frequently been contested, though not necessarily in ways that have raised questions as to the legitimacy of their class position. Quite the contrary; as Giddens (1979: 112) stresses, all social reproduction occurs in the context of 'mixes' of intended and unintended consequences of action. Thus it is usual for social practices to have effects other than those intended by the agents involved, so that attempts by groups of workers to compete for jobs actually reinforce the acceptance as legitimate of their class position as labor power. Rather than question the legitimacy of the class structural relation between capital and labor, and in particular the class position of working people as wage laborers, the struggles by territorially defined groups of workers to fight for *their* jobs transform the contest into one between such groups for a share of those jobs that are offered on the labor market. So, for example, there is conflict between different groups of workers within a factory or mine over differential levels of redundancy payments and therefore over whether to accept or contest proposals for closure. Or there is conflict between plants in different places (regions within a nation-state or different nation-states) for such wage labor employment as capital offers on the market. Furthermore, as we have demonstrated above, in particular circumstances this competition for jobs can develop on a broader social basis, from simply the groups of workers directly affected into one based on cross-class alliances. While in general we would accept Giddens' critique of functionalist social theories which presuppose a normative consensus among social agents, in so far as members of the working class fight in various ways to preserve their status as wage labor there is little evidence to support his claim that 'those in subordinate positions in a society, particularly those in large-scale societies, may frequently be much less closely caught within the embrace of consensual ideologies than many writers . . . assume' (1981: 67). Whether their position as wage labor is willingly accepted is another matter, but in so far as it is accepted, it is central to the reproduction of capitalist societies as capitalist.

Moreover, this territorially defined struggle for employment between groups of workers (and maybe their allies) in particular localities often takes on an additional dimension. Characteristically it can encompass competition for a greater share of state resources for the acquisition of new jobs as well as the defense of 'old' ones. Indeed, this has become a persistent feature of contemporary capitalist societies and integrally involves capitalist states in a variety of ways: one diagnostic symptom is the identification of a variety of spatially defined problems (for example, inner city or regional problems, or problems of national economic or industrial development) as various groups press their cases for special treatment for their areas. Thus the variety of state spatial policies is to be interpreted not simply in terms of some mechanistic response to the need(s) of capital(s), or as symptomatic of a bad case of false consciousness on the part of members of the (structurally defined) working class, but rather as something fought for by the labor movement, by groups within the working class in such areas, as they rationally (in the sense defined above) engage in forms of social practice intended to further their own interests. Moreover, this is not simply a struggle conducted by such groups within the state as an immutable object, but rather an attempt by them to re-define what are seen as the justified boundaries to the activities of the state in such a way as to protect or further their (territorially specified) interests. It is correct, however, to point out that these spatial policies tend to take their most potent form within capitalist societies when the perception of working-class groups of *their* interests is coincident with the perception of some capitals or the relevant national state of *their* interests. The regional modernization programs in the 1960s in parts of the UK (the northeast of England, Scotland and Wales, for example), together with what is generally regarded as the strengthening of regional policy by the Labour central government in the UK in the same period and its subsequent dismantling after 1979 by the Conservative government, exemplify this point well.

Nevertheless, the actual outcome of these heightened processes of state involvement has been to reinforce tendencies toward competition for 'new' jobs between territorially defined groups within the working class and their party political representatives, sometimes in the context of cross-class alliances. More and more, this competition has been intensified and conducted within the corporate structures of transnational capitals on an increasingly global market for labor power and production sites as part of a new and evolving international division of labor (for example, see Fröbel *et al.* 1980). Its effects on deepening the reproduction of the territorial fragmentation of groups of workers and on their political representatives, on their consciousness of their class position and the possibilities of altering this, can be exemplified by one of many recent examples, taken from the northeast of England. In contrast to the general tendency for capital to abandon the region (Hudson 1984b), a frozen food firm, Findus, announced that it intended to close a factory at Cleethorpes in Lincolnshire while expanding one at Newcastle. Responding to comments by trades union representatives of the Cleethorpes' work-force, Mr. Garrett, Labour Member of Parliament for Wallsend, where the Newcastle plant is located, suggested that 'Newcastle's good news and Humberside's gloom is a fact of life in this harsh commercial world. *Every company has to make the most of all the opportunities that are available.* Findus is established in my constituency and it has established a good reputation with union agreements and wage rates that compare with anywhere else. *The company obviously saw better prospects, better industrial relations and better commercial possibilities.* That is what influenced them' (*Newcastle Journal* June 23, 1983; emphases added). Garrett's reaction neatly encapsulates the sense in which there is a general acceptance of the appropriateness and inevitability of capital's rationality in determining investment and disinvestment decisions. At the same time it captures the way in which particular localities must engage in a bitter and divisive struggle to sell themselves to capitals as the most desirable location for their activities in an attempt to defend the right to live, learn and work in their place. This is especially true at a time of deep recession and little new 'mobile' employment, and in this struggle, albeit unintentionally, the localities help reproduce the class structural relations of capitalism that were responsible for the emergence of economic and employment problems there to begin with.

Moreover, it also indicates the way in which the accumulated failures of state regional policies to achieve their proclaimed intended effects have also come to be seen as an inevitable feature of contemporary capitalist societies. No longer is the notion of a return to 'full employment' on the agenda: all that particular groups of people in defined areas can do is to strive for and hope to obtain a share of available employment. There is no sanction on the state if one group in one area fail, because it simply means that some other group in another place has succeeded in the competitive struggle.

Some concluding comments

We have argued that the deep attachment to living, learning and working in particular places in Western Europe's 'old' industrial regions (and elsewhere) is grounded in the routine of everyday life there. The emergence from the late 1970s onward of campaigns to defend the right to live, learn and work in them reflects their heavy reliance on a single industry as a source of jobs and wages, coupled with a perception of the minimal opportunities for the introduction of new sources of employment should the 'traditional' industries disappear. Characteristically, these campaigns have conjoined attachment to place and class in complex and shifting ways, and have been conducted on the basis of attempts to promote the interests of one ('our') place at the expense of other ('their') places. Nevertheless, it is important to remember that these sorts of contingent class–place relations as a basis for the defense of the place-defined interests of particular social groups are clearly ones that are associated with the legacy of a territorial division of labor associated with much earlier rounds of capitalist accumulation. It is precisely this material basis for the cultural tradition associated with successive generations living, learning and working in the one-industry places, thrown up by the historical geography of capitalist development in old industrial regions, that has been and is being removed by the changing intranational and international divisions of labor and the hyper-mobile switching of investment between locations which to their inhabitants are deeply meaningful places but to capitals are merely another piece of space offering possibilities for profitable production. How then are working-class people to organize successfully to defend their interests in these cases? In what ways can these interests, defined on a place specific basis, be defended? This remains an open question.

What is clear is that the net unintended result to date of these various forms of competition to defend particular places between territorially defined groups is doubly to reinforce the hegemonic position of capital as the dominant and decisive social relation. Not only is wage labor legitimated by working-class people competing for the chance to be able to sell their labor power, but to be without the possibility to sell one's labor power (with all that this entails in capitalist societies) is equally recognized as legitimate. To this extent, spatial uneven development is not only an integral part of the development of capitalism, but one that involves working-class people as rational agents rather than passive cultural dupes – even if the unintended effects of how they engage in social practice in pursuit of their own interests are to reproduce their class position as labor power.

This conclusion raises important questions about the trend toward decentralization of political power or responsibility (to local government, to regional government and so on), which may be emerging as a new spatial planning orthodoxy in major sections of the capitalist world in the 1980s (Hudson & Lewis 1982), in so far as this is explicitly built around the notion of progressive class alliances (Weaver 1982). Such a position clearly requires delicate handling. While not wishing to deny that there are circumstances in which such alliances can be progressive, the danger exists of making interterritorial competition the main axis of actual social conflict and of this becoming a cloak behind which the class-based exploitation of labor as labor power can be intensified, this being justified via an appeal to a territorial unity of interests. It also raises some quite fundamental questions about the control of information relating to acceptance of spatial uneven development as a normal aspect of social development. The deliberate encouragement and fostering of attachment to place and of territorial chauvinism (at various spatial scales) offer a potentially great source of power to capitalist states, first in managing these changes presupposed by and contingent upon the changing locational requirements of accumulation, and thereby in social control.

Notes

The authors wish to acknowledge financial support from the European Economic Community, the Nuffield Foundation and the Social Science Research Council in carrying out the research on which this chapter is based.

It was written while Ray Hudson was Visiting Professor at the Institute for Transport, Tourism and Regional Economics, Copenhagen, and a version was presented by him in a seminar at the Geography Department, Oslo University in October 1983. As well as the editors, John Allen, Ron Johnston and John Urry kindly and constructively commented on a previous draft; the usual disclaimers apply.

1 These brief comments are heavily condensed from the first draft of this paper in response to a request from the editors to avoid repetition of material between chapters. For those who may be interested, the original draft expanding them is available from the authors.

2 While using Giddens' work as a point of departure for such analyses, we would emphasize that we are not concerned here systematically to explore the range of theoretical propositions that it contains (for reviews of his approach, see Dallmayr 1982, Olin Wright 1982), still less to test them empirically in some sort of positivistic sense to assess their validity, a procedure based upon a conception of knowledge that both he and we would reject as an inappropriate one for a critical social theory. Rather than such a systematic exploration of Giddens' propositions, our approach here is to use some of his ideas selectively in order to illuminate a few aspects of the relationships between attachment to and defense of place, social class formation and the spatially uneven reproduction of capitalist societies.

References

Anderson, B. 1983. *Imagined communities*. London: Verso.

Anderson, J. 1983. Geography as ideology and the politics of crisis: the Enterprise Zones experiment. In *Redundant spaces in cities and regions?*, J. Anderson, S. Duncan and R. Hudson (eds.), pp. 313–50. London: Academic Press.

Borough of South Tyneside 1982 (July). *Tyne shiprepair and South Tyneside*. South Shields: Town Hall.

Bulmer, M. (ed.) 1978. *Mining and social change*. London: Croom Helm.

Carney, J. 1980. Regions in crisis: accumulation, regional problems and crisis formation. In *Regions in crisis*, J. Carney, R. Hudson, and J. R. Lewis (eds.), pp. 28–59. London: Croom Helm.

Carney, J. and R. Hudson 1978. Capital, politics and ideology: the North East of England, 1870–1946. *Antipode* **10**, 64–78.

Carney, J., R. Hudson and J. Lewis (eds.) 1980. *Regions in crisis: New perspectives in European theory*. London: Croom Helm.

Clavel, P. 1982. *Opposition planning in Wales and Appalachia*. Philadelphia: Temple University Press.

Cleveland County Council 1983 (January). *The economic and social importance of the British Steel Corporation to Cleveland*. Middlesbrough.

Cochrane, A. 1983. Local economic policies: trying to drain an ocean with a teaspoon. In *Redundant spaces in cities and regions?* J. Anderson, S. Duncan and R. Hudson (eds.). pp. 285–312. London: Academic Press.

Cooke, P. 1983. *The spatial dimension of urban politics – local opposition to a regional coalition*. Paper read to the Seminar on Local State Research, Anglo-Danish Comparisons, Copenhagen (September).

Dallmayr, F. 1982. Agency and structure. *Phil. Soc. Sci.* **12**, 427–38.

Dennis, N., F. Henriques and C. Slaughter 1956. *Coal is our life*. London: Eyre and Spottiswood.

Doherty, J. 1983. Racial conflict, industrial change and social control in post-war Britain. In *Redundant spaces in cities and regions?* J. Anderson, S. Duncan and R. Hudson (eds.). pp. 201–40. London: Academic Press.

Douglass, D. and J. Krieger 1983. *A miner's life*. Henley: Routledge & Kegan Paul.

Dunford, M. and D. Perrons 1983. *The arena of capital*. London: Macmillan.

Durham County Council and Sedgefield District Council 1983a (April). *The case against closure: Shildon Wagon Works*. Durham: County Hall.

Durham County Council and Sedgefield District Council 1983b (May). *Save Fishburn Cokeworks*. Durham: County Hall.

Easington District Council 1983. *Campaign for coal and employment*. Easington: Council Offices.

Evenwood Labour Party 1983. *Randolph Cokeworks, Evenwood: the effects of its closure on the village*. Evenwood.

Frank, A. G. 1980. *Crisis: In the world economy*. London: Heinemann.

Fröbel, F., J. Heinrichs, and O. Kreye 1980. *The new international division of labour*. Cambridge: Cambridge University Press.

Giddens, A. 1973. *The class structure of advanced societies*. London: Hutchinson.

Giddens, A. 1979. *Central problems in sociological theory*. London: Macmillan.

Giddens, A. 1981. *A contemporary critique of historical materialism*. London: Macmillan.

Gregory, D. 1978. *Science, ideology and human geography*. London: Hutchinson.

Gregory, D. 1981. Human agency and human geography. *Trans. Inst. Br. Geog.* n.s. **6**, 1–18.

Gregory, D. 1982. *Regional transformation and industrial revolution*. London: Macmillan.

Habermas, J. 1975. *Legitimation crisis*. London: Heinemann.

Harvey, D. 1982. *The limits to capital*. Oxford: Blackwell.

Harvie, C. 1977. *Scotland and nationalism*. London: Allen & Unwin.

Hobsbawm, E. 1977. Some reflections on 'the break-up of Britain.' *New Left Review* **105**, 3–24.

House of Commons Committee on Scottish Affairs 1982. The steel industry in Scotland. *House of Commons Paper No. 22, Session 1982/3*. London: HMSO.

House of Commons Industry and Trade Committee 1983. The British Steel Corporation's prospects. *House of Commons Paper No. 212, Session 1982/3*. London: HMSO.

Hudson, R. 1976. *New towns in northeast England*. Final Report HR 1734 to the Social Science Research Council. London.

Hudson, R. 1979. New Towns and spatial policy: the case of Washington New Town. In *The production of the built environment: proceedings of the Bartlett Summer School*, pp. 142–61. London: University College.

Hudson, R. 1981. State policies and changing transport networks: the case of post-war Britain. In *Political studies from spatial perspectives*, A. D. Burnett and P. J. Taylor (eds.), pp. 467–88. Chichester: Wiley.

Hudson, R. 1982a. Accumulation, spatial policies and the production of regional labour reserves: a study of Washington New Town. *Environ. Plann. A* **14**, 655–80.

Hudson, R. 1982b. Unemployment in the north. *Town and Country Planning* **51**(1), 8–10.

Hudson, R. 1983. Capital accumulation and regional problems: a study of North East England, 1945–80. In *Regional economies and industrial systems*, F. E. I. Hamilton and G. Linge (eds.), pp. 75–101. Chichester: Wiley.

Hudson, R. 1984a. The paradoxes of state intervention: the impact of nationalized industry policies and regional policies in the Northern Region in the post-war period. In *Public policy studies: North East England*, R. Chapman (ed.). Edinburgh: Edinburgh University Press.

Hudson, R. 1984b. Producing an industrial wasteland: capital, labour and the state in North East England. In *Deindustrialization and the British Space Economy*. R. L. Martin and B. Rowthorne (eds.). London: Macmillan.

Hudson, R. and J. Lewis (eds.) 1982. *Regional planning in Europe*. London: Pion.

Hudson, R. and J. Lewis 1984a. Capital accumulation: the industrialisation of Southern Europe? In *Southern Europe transformed?* A. Williams (ed.) London: Harper and Row.

Hudson, R. and J. Lewis (eds.) 1984b. *Accumulation class and the state in Southern Europe*. London: Methuen.

Hudson, R., F. Peck and D. Sadler 1984. *Undermining Easington: who'll pay the price of pit closures?* Report to Easington District Council.

Hudson, R. and D. Sadler 1983a. The closure of Consett steelworks: anatomy of a disaster. *Northern Econ. Rev.* **6**, 2–17.

Hudson, R. and D. Sadler 1983b. Region, class and the politics of steel closures in the European Community. *Society and Space* **1**, 405–28.

Hudson, R. and D. Sadler 1984. *The impacts of BSC's policies in Cleveland County*. Report to Cleveland County Council.

Jablonowski, H. and J. Offermans 1974. *Teilkrise ohne Ende*. Goiganz.

Jessop, B. 1982. *The capitalist state*. Oxford: Martin Robertson.

Keat, R. and J. Urry 1975. *Social theory and science*. London: Routledge & Kegan Paul.

Lefebvre, H. 1971. *Everyday life in the modern capitalist world*. London: Allen Lane.

Lipietz, A. 1980. The structuration of space, the problem of land and spatial policy. In *Regions in crisis*. J. Carney, R. Hudson and J. R. Lewis (eds.), pp. 60–75. London: Croom Helm.

Lloyd, P. and J. Shutt 1983. *Recession and restructuring in the North West Region: the policy implications of recent events*. Working Paper Series No. 13, North West Industry, Research Unit, School of Geography, University of Manchester.

Mandel, E. 1963. The dialectic of class and region in Belgium. *New Left Review* **20**, 5–31.

Mandel, E. 1975. *Late capitalism*. London: New Left Books.

Mandel, E. 1978. *The second slump*. London: New Left Books.

Mandel, E. 1980. *Long waves of capitalist development: the marxist interpretation*. Cambridge: Cambridge University Press.

Morgan, K. 1982. *State policy and regional development in Britain: the case of Wales*. Unpublished D. Phil. thesis, University of Sussex.

Morgan, K. 1983. Restructuring steel: the crises of labour and locality in Britain. *Int. J. urban Regional Stud.* **7**, 175–201.

Nairn, T. 1977. *The break-up of Britain: crisis and neo-nationalism*. London: New Left Books.

Newcastle Journal 23 June 1983.

North Tyneside Trades Council 1979. *Shipbuilding – the cost of redundancy*. Newcastle.

Olin Wright, E. 1978. *Class, crisis and the state*. London: New Left Books.

Olin Wright, E. 1982. Giddens's critique of Marxism. *New Left Review* **138**, 11–35.

Peet, R. 1983. Relations of production and the relocation of United States manufacturing industry since 1960. *Econ. Geog.* April, 112–43.

Pocock, D. (ed.) 1981. *Humanistic geography and literature*. London: Croom Helm.

Regional Policy Research Unit 1979. *State regional policies and uneven development: the case of North East England*. Final Report RP 270 to the Centre for Environmental Studies, London.

Relph, E. 1976. *Place and placelessness*. London: Pion.

Robinson, J. F. F. 1978. *Peterlee: a study of New Town development*. Unpublished PhD thesis. Univeristy of Durham.

Robinson, J. F. F. 1983. State planning of spatial change: compromise and contradiction in Peterlee New Town. In *Redundant spaces in cities and regions?* J. Anderson, S. Duncan and R. Hudson (eds.), pp. 263–84. London: Academic Press.

Robinson, J. F. F. and D. Sadler 1985. Routine action, reproduction of social relations and the place market: Consett after the closure. *Society and Space* **3**, 109–20.

Rose, D. and S. Mackenzie 1983. Industrial change, the domestic economy and home life. In *Redundant spaces in cities and regions?* J. Anderson, S. Duncan and R. Hudson (eds.), pp. 155–200. London: Academic Press.

Rubinstein, J. 1978. *The French New Towns.* Baltimore: Johns Hopkins University Press.

Sadler, D. 1983. *The steel crisis and the Ruhrgebiet in West Germany: problem, perspective and position.* Paper read to the seminar on 'New Tendencies in Regional Development,' Copenhagen, November 28 – December 2.

Sadler, D. 1984. Works closure at British Steel and the nature of the State. *Polit. Geog. Q.* **3**, 297–311.

Sadler, D. 1985. *Region, class and the restructuring of the EEC steel industry during the recession.* PhD thesis. Durham University. (Forthcoming).

Save Scotswood Campaign Committee 1979. *Economic audit.* Newcastle.

Sayer, A. 1982. Explanation in economic geography. *Prog. Human Geog.* **6**(1), 68–88.

Schröter, L. and H. Zierold 1977. Economic development in the Ruhr: genesis of a crisis. *Abteilung Raumplanung* **7**, 5–16.

Smith, P. and P. Brown 1983. Industrial change and Scottish nationalism since 1945. In *Redundant spaces in cities and regions?*, J. Anderson, S. Duncan and R. Hudson (eds.). London: Academic Press.

Soja, E. 1980. The socio-spatial dialectic. *Ann. Assoc. Am. Geog.* **70**, 207–25.

Soja, E. 1983. *The spatiality of social life: towards a transformative retheorization.* Mimeo, UCLA.

Thompson, E. P. 1978. *The poverty of theory.* London: Merlin Press.

Thrift, N. 1983. On the determination of social action in space and time. *Society and Space* **1**, 23–57.

Tuan, Y.-F. 1977. *Space and place: the perspective of experience.* London: Edward Arnold.

Tyne & Wear County Council 1983. *Save our shipyards.* Newcastle: County Hall.

Urry, J. 1981. Localities, region and social class. *Int. J. Urban Regional Res.* **5**, 455–73.

Weaver, C. 1982. The limits to economism: towards a political approach to regional development and planning. In *Regional planning in Europe*, R. Hudson and J. Lewis (eds.), pp. 182–202. London: Pion.

Williamson, B. 1982. *Class, culture and community.* Henley: Routledge & Kegan Paul.

PART IV

Territorial organization and regional development

10

Regional production
and the production of regions:
the case of steeltown

M. J. WEBBER

Hamilton is Steeltown, Canada. Located on the western end of Lake Ontario (see Fig. 10.1), Hamilton served during the early and mid 19th century as a commercial center and port for the agricultural region of southwestern Ontario (Wells 1973). It became for a few years the center of an extensive rail network serving the southwest of the province, but as rail and finance capitals became more centralized after 1860, the city gradually lost its commercial and financial functions to Toronto (McCalla 1973). The railroads had, however, stimulated the development of steel and metal-working shops using pig iron imported from Britain and, after the Welland Canal was deepened in 1887, from US iron and steel plants on the south shore of Lake Erie (Nader 1976: 250). Both Gilmour (1972) and Wells (1973) describe Hamilton's economy in this period. Pig iron production began in 1895, using – then, as now – Pennsylvania coal. Initially, ore was brought from northwestern Ontario, but this was soon replaced by ore from Minnesota and (more recently) Labrador and Quebec (Kerr 1967). During the 20th century, Hamilton's natural harbor, its access to coal and ore via the Great Lakes, its local limestone, and its location in the heart of the Canadian manufacturing belt have combined to ensure the city's continued dominance of Canada's iron and steel industry. With a population of half a million, Hamilton ranks fourth in manufacturing employment (after Toronto, Montreal and slightly behind Vancouver) among Canada's metropolitan areas (Webber 1983b) and now accounts for over half the total Canadian steel output (Nader 1976: 251).

But the city's economy is in trouble. During the 1970s Hamilton's population has grown at only two-thirds of the Ontario rate and at half the Canadian rate, and its labor force has grown at less than half the provincial rate (Thomson 1983). During the period from May 1981 to January 1983, Hamilton lost a quarter of its manufacturing jobs. In January and February 1983, Hamilton's official unemployment rate had risen to 16.7% (compared to the provincial average of 12.6%) while in August that rate was still 11.1% (9.3% in Ontario). Only 54.4% of Hamilton's working-age population was employed in January (57.4% in Ontario), though this had risen to 58.5% in August 1983 (63.3% in Ontario).

197

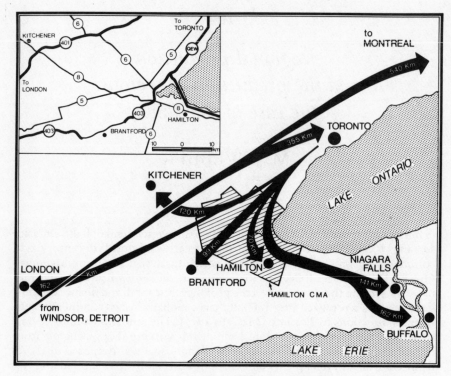

Figure 10.1 Location of Hamilton, Ontario.

Hamilton's recent industrial history and present depression was comparable to the fortunes of many old established industrial regions in Europe and North America. Sternlieb and Hughes (1977) and Perry and Watkins (1977) both discuss the reasons for the relative (and in some places, absolute) decline of the northeastern US. Dunford *et al.* (1981), Fothergill and Gudgin (1982), Keeble (1980) and Massey (1981) all show how during the 1970s British manufacturing employment shifted away from the major industrial centers. Jensen–Butler (1982) does the same for Denmark.

This chapter is concerned with the way in which regional industrial growth becomes regional decline, using Hamilton as an example. The first section briefly analyzes the notions of region and uneven development. Next, a theory of regional development is advancecd, which claims that in capitalism regional decline is implicit in agglomeration and regional growth. The third section of the chapter illustrates the main theses of this argument with some aspects of the recent history of Hamilton. The chapter's conclusion draws some strategic implications from the argument.

Regions

The regional question concerns the spatially uneven development of branches of production within a social formation (Massey 1978). So regional distinctions reflect spatially uneven rates of capital accumulation, possibly in different branches: regional inequality means that the power to command labor is unevenly developed over space and that this generalized wealth is expanding unevenly (Dunford 1977).

Regions are created as social divisions of a territory, by the process of capital accumulation (Massey 1978). In order to analyze capitalist production characteristics, a region must be cognized as an area in which there is established a particular form of the relations of production and a particular constellation of forces of production. The productive forces are the objects used to produce things: first, labor power; and secondly, such means of production as space, raw materials and instruments of production (tools, machines, premises and fuels). Production relations exist between a person (or group) and another person (or group), or between a person (or group) and a productive force (or group of forces); they comprise relations of ownership (i.e. effective control) and relations presupposing relations of ownership (Cohen 1978: 31–5). Productive forces are material but productive relations are social. For example, the proletariat consists of those who own their labor power but not their means of production (Cohen 1978: 65); since this statement concerns the extent of ownership of productive forces (labor power and means of production), it defines the proletariat in terms of production relations. Lipietz (1980) and Massey (1981) both provide examples of regional taxonomies that are derived from their theory of capital accumulation.

Now regionalism means that some regions specialize in labor-intensive activities, others in machine-intensive activities and others in independent commodity production: in short, the forces and relations of production are unevenly developed. But this means that workers and factories and regions have become specialized in particular tasks and in the production of particular commodities. In turn this requires both a division of labor between tasks and the existence of trade and exchange which allow people to specialize in different branches of production. So regionalism requires not simply capitalist relations of production but rather the development of a particular type of production – the division of labor. (The division of labor does not cause uneven development; still, uneven development cannot occur without the division of labor.) However, as capitalism developed, laborers were gathered into factories and paid in wages rather than in kind and commodities were produced for sale rather than for personal consumption, so the extension of the market and the generalization of trade became inevitable (Marx 1967: 322–507). Therefore regional differentiation and capitalism evolved at the same time.

An approach to regional development

A central aspect of regional development concerns the logical relations between regional growth and decline and the requirements of capital accumulation. Just as accumulation proceeds in phases separated by periodic depressions (Aglietta 1979), each phase is characterized by quite distinct forces and relations of production. In each phase the basis for accumulation is laid in high profits from new processes or new production relations, established in new regions, so each phase establishes its own distinct geography of production. Historically, the phases of accumulation have been ended by a decade or more of economic depression. The logic of regional development turns on these issues of growth, falling rates of profit and the geography of new processes.

There are two distinct types of accumulation (accumulation being defined as the expansion of capital's power to command labor). In the first type, surplus value is invested in establishing a logic for development. This involves some types of research and development expenditures (such as those which led to the invention of the assembly line and numerically controlled processes) and expenditures to establish new social relations of production and consumption (such as collective bargaining, wage contracts, unemployment insurance and credit facilities, all of which are required to promote working-class consumption). The second type of accumulation is the process of generalizing this logic (Harvey 1981). On the one hand, some research and development expenditures are needed to apply (known) assembly line techniques to the production of (say) washing machines. On the other hand, the means of production and the labor power must be expanded as the aggregate scale of production is enlarged. Although circulating capital must expand, the characteristics of the growing stock of fixed goods are particularly important. Items of fixed capital are commodities which are used up over several production periods and which therefore give up their value to output only gradually; in the 19th century, they included factories, machinery and railroads, to which roads, banks and commercial facilities have since been added. Particularly in the latest phase of accumulation, fixed goods have begun to include aids to consumption, such as hospitals, schools and shopping centers (as well as roads). These goods are durable (long-lived and difficult to alter), large in scale and difficult to price. (Although fixed capital is not necessarily immobile – e.g. ships, aircraft – the capital items important to this theory are immobile.)

During each phase, accumulation is directed mainly at a few regions, so these regions develop not only unique complexes of industrial production facilities, but also particular bundles of fixed capital and aids to consumption as well as a characteristic structure of class relations and means of reproducing the labor force. In other words, each region's endowment of the forces and relations of production is determined by the logic of development of the phase in which that region's production expanded, and by the nature of its decline since then. Massey's (1981) regionalization of Britain exemplifies this fact. On a different scale, Gordon (1978) divided turn-of-the-century American cities into two main regions, distinguished by reference to their class relations. (Similar contrasts are made between northeastern and southern US towns since World War II.)

The agglomeration of capitalist production is induced by the need to socialize production. Although capitalist production is mostly carried out by private firms, it is nevertheless a social process: the necessity for production is determined socially; and many of the direct and indirect means of production are established socially – capitals share fixed capital goods and cooperate in establishing the requisite relations of production while laborers share some items in the consumption fund and their reproduction is partly collective. It is expensive to provide the material aids and social relations required by capitalist production; costs are therefore minimized if they are produced in as few places as is consistent with the technical and natural requirements of production. Thus, agglomeration is a matter of using and developing forms of cooperation between capitals and between laborers (Lapple & van Hoogstraten 1980).

The degree of development of agglomerated rather than dispersed patterns of capitalist industry depends on the relative balance of several forces. Spatial concentration is enhanced by the need to share material aids and social relations and by the fact that such aids and relations cheapen production. The dispersal of capitalist relations of production is restrained if capital is unavailable to invest in the fixed facilities of new regions while increasing returns can still be reaped in established regions (Mandel 1978: 47). A second obstacle to the spread of capitalist production is the inadequacy of the means of transport (Mandel 1978: 50–1). As transport rates fall and facilities become more general, so capitalist production can disperse – or at least a wider set of regions can be incorporated into a single production system.

Each phase of accumulation thus establishes its own geography, manifest in direct production facilities, fixed capital, aids to consumption and the structure of class relations. Because of the need to socialize production, this capital is accumulated in only a few regions. Once that geography is laid down in the early years of a phase of accumulation, it is fixed by the long life and immobility of the investment in forces and relations of production. The historical geography of the expansionary period of a phase of accumulation is thus a matter of realizing the outcome implied by that logic of development.

A phase of accumulation comprises an early period of rapid growth, as the logic of development is exploited, and a later period of slow growth when the contradictions in the regime of accumulation come to the fore. Using the newest technology, fixed capital and labor relations, the capitals which locate in the new regions have a competitive edge over rivals in other regions. Accumulation can therefore proceed more rapidly in the new than in the old regions. Consequently capital gradually loses power to labor, for the ratio of the rate of capital accumulation to the rate of growth of the labor force is relatively high. Labor thus gains power – and gains more in the agglomeration than elsewhere (Damette 1980) – a power that has several elements: ability to negotiate higher real wages than were paid before or are paid in other places; power to command progressive welfare policies; strength to organize high levels of unionization and to extract good conditions of work; and ability to demand environmental policies which contribute to a better life. One effect of trapping accumulation is thus to raise the real social wage, most particularly in the agglomeration.

Inter-capitalist competition ensures that technical and social changes occur throughout the phase of accumulation. To remain competitive, capitals in the new region must adopt these new means of raising the rate of surplus value;

but the relative power of labor there ensures that capital can only raise the rate of surplus value by increasing productivity (using machinery to replace labor) rather than by reducing wages or increasing the quantity of work per pay period: the second effect of trapping the high rate of accumulation is to promote mechanization to offset the power of labor, particularly in the agglomeration where that power is greatest. During a phase of accumulation, this process is one of gradual and small-scale technical changes within the limits established by the terms of the regime. Thus the shared aids and relations which fix the geography of accumulation not only offer a competitive benefit, but also foster a contradiction as the balance of class strengths swings against capital during the years and in the regions of fast accumulation.

There is a third aspect of the geography of accumulation. The shared aids to production and consumption and the established relations of production are the consequences of expenses that must be written off over a long time and whose renewal must be agreed by most of the shared users. The anarchic way in which external facilities and relations are renewed and the difficulties of replacing some facilities without disturbing others lead to the situation in which regional aids and relations gradually become obsolete: are overtaken by new forms of external economy and new relations of production established elsewhere in the social formation. The region becomes obsolete as a production unit (Walker 1978).

Profit rates therefore fall as a phase of accumulation progresses. Because the phase has a particular logic and is expressed geographically through a particular historical form of fixed capital and production relations, capitals face problems of replacing obsolete social fixed capital and become constrained by a falling rate of profit (because the real wage rises and production becomes more mechanized; see Webber 1983a). These problems appear most acutely among those capitals which produce in the region of agglomeration, where labor has the greatest strength. During the later period of the phase of accumulation, then, capital must try to re-establish the basis for accumulation by raising the rate of profit.

This can be accomplished by replacing obsolete fixed capital, devaluing constant capital and reducing real wages (or at least the value of the real wage). Devalorization is the process whereby capital loses part of its value (Mandel 1978). If the value of commodities is reduced by technical change, the value of fixed capital in place is reduced; and if firms go bankrupt the exchange value of their fixed capital falls. Real wages can be reduced only if capital gains power relative to labor. In postwar France and Italy, the value of labor power was reduced by destroying pre-capitalist agriculture and replacing it with 'industrial agriculture' that freed labor and reduced the value of food (Carney 1980). In postwar Britain, immigration depressed the real wage. Furthermore, if accumulation ceases in an industrial region or if technology allows labor to be replaced by machinery, then the natural increase of population beyond the demand for labor causes the local reserve army of labor to grow and so the real wage falls.

Thus the rate of profit can be raised if obsolete aids are replaced, constant capital devalorized or the wage rate reduced. Although these changes to the balance of the class strengths are required by the logic of conflict between the classes, they are in large measure effected by competition between capitals. For the value of constant capital can be reduced by the method used to reduce the power of labor: halt accumulation in the industrial region and focus investment in other regions, where capitals have acquired a competitive advantage over capitals in the industrial region. As accumulation ceases, the value of fixed capital, of the aids to consumption and of labor power all begin to fall in the industrial region, for their supply exceeds their socially necessary level. At the same time accumulation can begin in a new region, where there is no obsolete fixed capital to fetter production, where the shared forces of production can be built up using modern methods and where labor is weak (where the relations of production are favorable to capital). Thus the old geography, based on an earlier logic of development, has become a fetter upon accumulation. The new phase has a new logic which dictates a new geography, one that must be uncorrelated with the old in order to avoid the contradictions that earlier led to falling profit rates.

The logic of regionalization is the logic of accumulation. Regions contain capitals which share accumulated forces of production and established social relations. These advantages promote rapid accumulation which eventually causes the contradictions (to high profits) of rising real wages, increasing mechanization and obsolete aids to production. In turn the rate of profit falls, which prompts capital to change location in order to devalue constant capital, diminish the power of labor and replace obsolete fixed capital. Hence, capital mobility is the obverse of regional uneven development.

The case of Hamilton

Figure 10.1 shows the location of Hamilton in relation to major routes and markets in southern Ontario. Figure 10.2 provides a guide to the administrative structure of the area. Throughout this section, 'Hamilton' is used to refer to the Census Metropolitan Area of Hamilton, an area which includes the Regional Municipality of Hamilton–Wentworth, Burlington and Grimsby. Smaller still is the City of Hamilton, which contains some 60% of the half million people who live in the metropolitan area.

The occupational structure of Hamilton is compared to that of other metropolitan areas and of Ontario as a whole in Table 10.1. The table reveals the main distinctive points of the Hamilton economy. Managerial, professional and artistic or sporting occupations are underrepresented in Hamilton compared to Ontario (the 1.65% difference represents nearly 3500 jobs in Hamilton). Presumably related to this fact, clerical jobs are also underrepresented in Hamilton (nearly 5000 jobs). By contrast, the blue–collar manufacturing, transport and construction occupations are overrepresented – most particularly, the processing and machining occupations (nearly 8000 jobs). These data confirm the stereotypical image of this area, as one in which manufacturing is overrepresented and managerial and professional occupations are underrepresented. The regional municipality exhibits these characteristics to an even greater degree than does the metropolitan area.

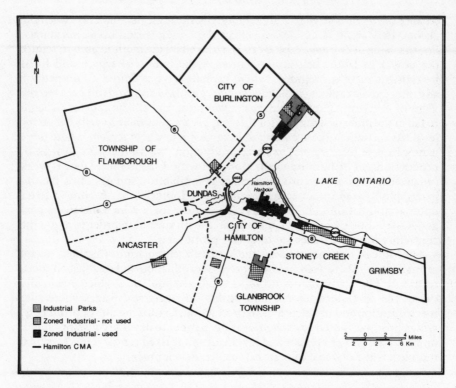

Figure 10.2   Administrative structure and industrial land in Hamilton, Ontario.

One context for these data is the occupational structure of two other medium-sized metropolitan areas in southern Ontario. Although Hamilton is well known for its reliance upon manufacturing jobs, in fact Kitchener is even more markedly a blue-collar city (nearly 45% of its employment is blue collar, compared to nearly 42% of Hamilton's). By contrast, London is revealed to be a managerial/professional city which also performs regional service functions (22% of London's jobs are managerial/professional, compared to 18% of Hamilton's and 17% of Kitchener's; 45% of London's jobs, compared to 40% of Hamilton's and 38% of Kitchener's, are in clerical, sales and service occupations). These data confirm Hamilton's minor role as a regional service center.

Equally, the data in Table 10.2 confirm the stereotype of the structure of Hamilton's manufacturing industries. Over 40% of the employment and nearly one half of the value of shipments and value added are accounted for by one major industry group: the primary metal industries, which include iron and steel mills, steel pipe and tube mills, iron foundries, smelting and refining and other similar industries. (Confidentiality prevents the publication of data for the individual industries in this group.) Another fifth of the manufacturing activity of the city is in the metal fabricating and machinery groups. By

Table 10.1 Occupational characteristics of Hamilton (Ontario), 1971.

	Percentage of employment in occupation				
Occupation	Hamilton	Hamilton–Wentworth	Kitchener	London	Ontario
managerial, administrative	4.35	2.90	4.60	5.00	5.37
natural sciences, engineering and mathematics	3.39	2.70	2.80	2.80	3.59
social sciences	0.85	0.78	0.79	1.30	1.13
religion	0.22	0.22	0.24	0.31	0.25
teaching	4.43	3.70	4.70	5.20	4.40
medicine and health	4.38	4.70	3.10	6.40	4.26
artistic, literary and professional	0.80	0.70	0.82	1.10	1.17
subtotal	18.42	15.70	17.05	22.11	20.17
clerical	17.88	18.00	17.60	20.20	20.21
sales	11.14	9.40	10.70	12.30	10.97
service	10.82	12.10	10.10	13.00	12.17
subtotal	39.84	39.50	38.40	45.50	43.35
processing	6.37	7.40	6.70	2.30	4.21
machining	6.05	6.60	7.40	3.70	4.36
fabricating, assembling and repairing	9.55	9.80	14.30	9.30	9.53
subtotal	21.97	23.80	28.40	15.30	18.10
construction trades	6.99	7.20	6.10	6.40	7.14
transport equipment operating	4.03	4.10	2.90	3.90	4.13
materials handling	4.15	4.60	3.30	2.80	2.88
other crafts and equipment operating	1.29	1.20	1.10	1.50	1.58
other occupation	3.32	3.70	2.80	2.50	2.61
subtotal	19.78	20.80	16.20	17.10	18.34
total	100.00	100.00	100.00	100.00	100.00

Note: Employment in each occupation is expressed as a percentage of all employment, excluding farming, forestry, fishing and mining occupations and those for whom occupations were not stated. 'Hamilton', 'Kitchener' and 'London' refer to Census Metropolitan Areas; 'Hamilton–Wentworth' to the Regional Municipality (i.e. excluding Burlington and Grimsby).
Source: Statistics Canada, *Census of Canada, 1971. Occupations,* Catalogue 94–715 to 94–727, Ottawa.

contrast, these three groups together account for only a quarter of Ontario's employment and a fifth of its value of shipments. All other manufacturing industries are underrepresented in Hamilton. By contrast, both Kitchener and London have a more diversified structure of manufacturing.

Table 10.3 contains additional data on the nature of the manufacturing industries in the three metropolitan areas. Several features of this table are significant.

First, a far smaller proportion of manufacturing employees are female in Hamilton than in Ontario as a whole: only 14.6% of the production workers and 25.1% of the administrative workers, compared to 23.3% and 29.9% for the province. By contrast both Kitchener and London employ more female production workers than does the province as a whole. In Hamilton's two major industries, primary metals and metal fabricating, the proportion of

Table 10.2 Structure of manufacturing in Hamilton, Ontario, Kitchener and London, 1979.

Industry	Percentage of Hamilton's			Percentage of Ontario's			Percentage of Kitchener's			Percentage of London's		
	Employ-ment	Value of shipment	Value added	Employ-ment	Value of shipment	Value added	Employ-ment	Value of shipment	Value added	Employ-ment	Value of shipment	Value added
food and beverage	5.9	8.8	4.5	9.5	12.2	10.6	11.9	22.5	17.3	16.7	18.2	19.7
tobacco products	—	—	—	0.4	0.7	0.6	—	—	—	—	—	—
rubber and plastic	1.6	0.7	0.8	4.4	3.1	3.8	—	—	—	7.5	9.8	12.3
leather	3.0	1.4	1.7	1.5	0.7	0.8	4.4	2.6	2.8	—	—	—
textiles	—	—	—	3.4	2.2	2.6	6.1	4.0	3.8	—	—	—
knitting mills	—	—	—	0.8	0.3	2.4	1.7	1.7	—	—	—	—
clothing	2.4	1.3	1.7	2.7	1.1	1.6	2.8	1.8	2.5	2.8	1.1	1.5
wood	0.5	0.2	0.3	2.5	1.5	1.9	1.5	1.2	1.3	1.0	0.5	0.4
furniture and fixtures	0.5	0.2	0.3	2.7	1.2	1.7	4.2	2.6	3.5	—	—	—
paper and allied products	—	1.5	1.5	5.1	4.4	5.1	—	—	—	—	—	—
printing, publishing	2.2	1.0	1.6	5.6	2.7	4.8	2.1	1.2	1.8	8.1	3.6	5.1
primary metals	41.6	47.9	47.5	8.3	8.0	9.1	—	—	—	3.9	3.9	2.8
metal fabricating	12.4	12.3	11.2	10.2	6.9	8.9	15.1	12.6	13.8	7.6	4.9	5.3
machinery	6.5	4.7	6.3	6.6	5.7	7.1	9.5	10.2	11.4	7.7	7.0	6.9
transport equipment	—	—	—	13.5	25.4	16.3	9.6	9.6	11.4	—	—	—
electrical products	—	—	—	8.7	6.1	8.0	9.8	8.1	7.5	16.3	11.1	16.7
non-metallic mineral products	3.3	2.3	2.7	3.0	2.2	3.2	—	—	—	1.4	1.3	1.4
petroleum and coal products	—	—	—	1.2	4.7	1.3	—	—	—	—	—	—
chemicals	2.8	7.1	7.7	5.5	7.5	8.5	1.6	4.3	3.1	—	—	—
miscellaneous	1.2	0.5	0.7	4.5	3.3	3.8	—	—	—	1.9	0.9	1.1
total	100.0	100.0	100.0	100.0	100.0	100.0	100.0	100.0	100.0	100.0	100.0	100.0

Source: Statistics Canada, *Manufacturing industries of Canada, 1979; Sub-provincial areas*, Catalogue 31–209, Ottawa.
Note: Industry percentages do not add to 100 because missing data are suppressed for confidentiality.

Table 10.3 Characteristics of manufacturing in Hamilton, Ontario, Kitchener and London, 1979.

Industry	Production workers			Administrative workers	Share of value of shipments		
	Female (%)	Wages ($/hr)	As percentage of all workers	Female (%)	Materials (%)	Wages (%)	Profit and depreciation
Hamilton							
food and beverage	39.6	6.54	70.2	31.2	79.1	9.9	11.0
tobacco	–	–	–	–	–	–	–
rubber and plastics	–	–	–	–	–	–	–
leather	73.5	4.62	88.5	43.5	49.3	25.0	22.0
textiles	63.0	5.72	85.6	30.1	51.7	26.1	21.6
knitting mills	–	–	–	–	–	–	–
clothing	87.9	4.50	91.2	44.7	48.1	20.1	34.8
wood	17.1	5.50	81.4	28.3	52.9	26.2	19.5
furniture and fixtures	9.0	6.40	72.4	30.3	39.6	34.1	21.7
paper and allied products	27.9	7.30	79.7	29.4	60.4	25.0	15.1
printing, publishing	29.0	8.10	55.9	34.5	33.3	36.3	29.8
primary metals	2.1	9.21	86.1	17.2	57.3	18.0	22.8
metal fabricating	7.7	7.90	76.8	26.3	62.1	18.1	19.5
machinery	21.4	7.40	92.0	28.2	47.6	24.0	31.0
transport equipment	–	–	–	–	–	–	–
electrical products	–	–	–	–	–	–	–
non-metallic mineral products	15.7	7.30	76.9	28.0	43.0	24.4	25.6
petroleum and coal products	–	–	–	–	–	–	–
chemicals	16.2	8.90	76.2	31.5	55.7	7.6	37.0
miscellaneous	33.4	5.40	80.2	38.4	47.5	26.9	25.5
total	14.6	8.12	80.2	25.1	58.5	18.3	22.9

Table 10.3 (continued)

Industry	Production workers			Administrative workers	Share of value of shipments		
	Female (%)	Wages ($/hr)	As percentage of all workers	Female (%)	Materials (%)	Wages (%)	Profit and depreciation
Ontario							
food and beverage	29.1	6.94	65.1	29.0	68.8	12.2	18.7
tobacco	36.5	8.22	64.4	28.2	70.9	9.5	18.0
rubber and plastics	32.0	6.43	95.1	27.8	57.4	20.6	18.0
leather	62.6	4.86	85.4	43.6	60.3	22.8	16.7
textiles	49.3	6.16	81.3	34.5	56.1	25.8	18.2
knitting mills	71.9	4.56	86.6	45.8	51.6	30.2	19.1
clothing	80.1	4.67	87.1	51.3	51.0	22.1	24.7
wood	12.2	6.18	84.2	25.7	53.9	23.1	22.3
furniture and fixtures	23.7	5.60	84.3	38.2	49.9	28.4	21.7
paper and allied products	14.7	8.06	77.6	29.0	53.2	20.6	20.7
printing, publishing	28.1	7.63	55.9	44.3	37.8	32.8	29.3
primary metals	3.7	8.70	79.7	20.0	57.2	19.7	20.8
metal fabricating	13.0	7.20	77.8	28.6	54.5	23.6	21.3
machinery	8.1	7.62	70.1	25.4	58.5	19.5	21.1
transport equipment	10.5	8.51	78.8	21.2	77.3	10.0	11.8
electrical products	38.1	6.92	65.6	28.6	55.3	23.1	20.8
non-metallic mineral products	9.9	7.75	74.0	26.9	43.0	22.9	27.1
petroleum and coal products	2.3	10.10	29.6	34.6	90.0	6.1	3.7
chemicals	20.6	7.71	52.2	29.1	56.2	13.4	26.8
miscellaneous	44.1	5.77	68.6	37.8	60.2	18.9	20.6
total	23.3	7.27	72.3	29.9	63.9	16.4	19.1

Table 10.3 (continued)

Industry	Production workers			Administrative workers	Share of value of shipments		
	Female (%)	Wages ($/hr)	As percentage of all workers	Female (%)	Materials (%)	Wages (%)	Profit and depreciation
Kitchener							
food and beverage	28.0	7.54	80.6	30.0	66.3	12.4	20.5
tobacco	—	—	—	—	—	—	—
rubber and plastics	—	—	—	—	—	—	—
leather	68.7	4.81	83.4	55.2	54.1	23.5	22.8
textiles	45.5	5.40	86.0	44.0	59.8	26.1	14.0
knitting mills	62.7	5.03	84.7	31.4	55.0	24.4	18.1
clothing	86.7	4.69	89.1	53.9	44.9	23.5	37.6
wood	13.1	5.63	79.1	23.4	53.3	25.2	21.9
furniture and fixtures	23.6	5.55	81.8	31.1	43.5	29.8	28.3
paper and allied products	—	—	—	—	—	—	—
printing, publishing	28.8	7.40	53.0	39.5	33.6	38.9	26.7
primary metals	—	—	—	—	—	—	—
metal fabricating	16.9	6.73	77.6	25.0	54.8	28.9	18.1
machinery	11.6	6.92	65.7	27.0	53.5	21.1	27.4
transport equipment	15.4	8.12	85.0	24.2	46.3	27.3	24.2
electrical products	47.3	5.79	73.9	29.3	61.7	23.3	16.7
non-metallic mineral products	—	—	—	—	—	—	—
petroleum and coal products	—	—	—	—	—	—	—
chemicals	13.8	6.86	57.5	24.8	68.4	9.6	21.7
miscellaneous	—	—	—	—	—	—	—
total	29.6	6.64	78.2	29.8	57.4	21.6	21.5

Table 10.3 (continued)

Industry	Production workers			Administrative workers	Share of value of shipments		
	Female (%)	Wages ($/hr)	As percentage of all workers	Female (%)	Materials (%)	Wages (%)	Profit and depreciation
London							
food and beverage	31.6	7.57	73.4	31.1	52.0	16.9	30.2
tobacco	—	—	—	—	—	—	—
rubber and plastics	32.9	8.00	44.8	36.3	14.9	46.9	46.0
leather	—	—	—	—	—	—	—
textiles	—	—	—	—	—	—	—
knitting mills	—	—	—	—	—	—	—
clothing	87.2	4.25	89.4	50.7	37.7	29.1	33.9
wood	8.4	5.38	88.4	26.9	58.6	26.4	13.9
furniture and fixtures	—	—	—	—	—	—	—
paper and allied products	—	—	—	—	—	—	—
printing, publishing	26.3	6.78	56.5	37.7	38.2	38.9	23.2
primary metals	30.4	6.70	87.3	32.5	67.2	15.8	15.9
metal fabricating	17.1	6.52	78.1	22.6	55.7	25.7	21.7
machinery	4.1	7.26	71.4	27.3	59.2	20.0	23.4
transport equipment	—	—	—	—	—	—	—
electrical products	48.5	8.85	82.5	26.3	36.0	29.3	36.2
non-metallic mineral products	3.0	7.87	78.4	24.7	50.6	21.1	26.5
petroleum and coal products	—	—	—	—	—	—	—
chemicals	—	—	—	—	—	—	—
miscellaneous	26.5	5.97	79.7	40.7	46.7	30.2	22.0
total	30.1	7.41	72.9	30.3	57.1	18.4	25.3

Notes and sources: see Table 10.2.

female production employees is low provincially and even lower in Hamilton. (This pattern holds among administrative workers, too.) In virtually all its other industries, Hamilton employs a higher percentage of female production workers than does the province.

Overall, production workers in Hamilton earned in 1979 nearly 90¢ per hour more than the average provincial worker. London workers earned slightly more than the provincial average and Kitchener workers 60¢ per hour less. Yet this comparison conceals a peculiar aspect of Hamilton's industrial wage structure. Workers in printing and publishing, primary metals, metal fabricating and chemical industries earn high wages and are generally more likely than their provincial counterparts to be male, whereas food and beverage, leather, textiles, clothing, wood, furniture, paper, machinery and non-metallic mineral workers earn less and are more likely to be female than their provincial counterparts.

Thirdly, the particularity of Hamilton's occupational structure, noted earlier, is evident: 80% of Hamilton's manufacturing industry employees are production workers, compared to only 72% for the province as a whole. Kitchener is like Hamilton in this respect, London like the province. In every industry except the wood and furniture industries and metal fabricating, Hamilton lacks administrative workers.

Table 10.4 shows how Hamilton's manufacturing structure has changed over the last decade. In the years 1971–9, the productive work-force grew by 12.4% compared to a provincial rate of 17.2%. The only industries in which Hamilton's employment grew faster than the provincial employment are textiles and clothing (two fairly small industries) and primary metals. In fact, the primary metals and chemicals industries, both having employment increases of over 20%, were the fastest growing industries in the city. Thus Hamilton's reliance on the primary metals sector for employment has increased over the decade: the city's economy is becoming more, not less, specialized. By contrast, in Kitchener and London, the faster growing industries tended to be the smallest ones.

The table also shows the change in the number of administrative workers during 1971–9. For the province as a whole, there existed no trend toward white-collar working in industry: whereas the productive work-force increased by 17.2%, the administrative work-force grew by only 7.1%. In Hamilton, this difference was even more pronounced: the 12.4% rise in the productive work-force was accompanied by an 8.0% fall in the administrative work-force. Only in textiles and the primary metal industries did Hamilton's administrative work-force grow faster than Ontario's. Since 1970, several of Hamilton's major employers have shifted their head offices out of the city: Stelco (the largest single employer in the city) to Toronto and Laidlaw Transport to Chicago. Again, then, Hamilton's characteristic reliance upon blue-collar employment has increased rather than diminished over the 1970s. In neither Kitchener nor London was there such a difference in rates of change of productive and administrative manufacturing employment. As a result of these various changes, Hamilton's manufacturing labor force grew by 7.6% over the eight years (compared to the provincial 14.2%). Hamilton's relatively slow growth was a result of the

211

Table 10.4 Changes in industrial structure, Hamilton, Kitchener and London, 1971–9.

Industry		No. of production workers, 1971	1971 administrative workers as % total 1971	Value added per $ of salaries and wages, 1971	% increase of production workers, 1971–9	% increase of administration workers, 1971–9	1979 value added per $ of salaries and wages
Hamilton							
food and beverage	1	3201	28.4	1.97	−8.4 (8.5)	−2.2 (−1.8)	no data for Hamilton
tobacco	2	—	—	—	(−11.0)	(45.6)	
rubber and plastics	3	—	—	—	(39.7)	(22.1)	
leather	4	—	—	—	(1.5)	(7.5)	
textiles	5	1599	14.5	1.72	15.2 (9.5)	14.0 (7.9)	
knitting mills	6	—	—	—	(−2.0)	(−9.5)	
clothing	7	1366	11.7	1.41	15.9 (10.1)	−15.3 (17.6)	
wood	8	252	26.3	1.47	4.4 (38.2)	33.3 (25.7)	
furniture and fixtures	9	307	23.8	1.54	−24.1 (30.1)	−7.3 (−3.7)	
paper and allied products	10	1459	23.7	1.66	−8.7 (8.6)	−24.9 (−4.8)	
printing, publishing	11	751	44.0	1.87	15.2 (19.7)	15.4 (20.4)	
primary metals	12	20476	15.8	2.39	23.9 (10.0)	7.1 (−1.6)	
metal fabricating	13	5672	27.1	1.85	18.5 (21.9)	−3.8 (8.4)	
machinery	14	3702	25.9	1.48	−10.4 (29.9)	1.2 (10.0)	
transport equipment	15	1662	17.6	1.95	(29.1)	(8.7)	
electrical products	16	4096	37.1	1.73	(3.3)	(−4.6)	
non-metallic mineral products	17	1933	23.4	1.81	−8.6 (1.4)	−10.0 (5.0)	
petroleum and coal products	18	—	—	—	(59.4)	(16.7)	
chemicals	19	1255	41.8	3.70	20.4 (22.0)	−47.6 (19.0)	
miscellaneous	20	686	34.3	1.86	−3.1 (16.4)	−57.4 (11.3)	
total		50546	23.2	2.12	12.4 (17.2)	−8.0 (7.1)	

Table 10.4 *(continued)*

Industry		No. of production workers, 1971	1971 administrative workers as % total 1971	Value added per $ of salaries and wages, 1971	% increase of production workers, 1971–9	% increase of administration workers, 1971–9	1979 value added per $ of salaries and wages
Kitchener							
food and beverage	1	40141	28.0	2.33	22.7	− 23.9	4.12
tobacco	2	—	—	—	—	—	—
rubber and plastics	3	4209	19.1	2.18	—	—	—
leather	4	1979	11.0	1.57	−5.0	53.1	1.97
textile	5	2759	12.8	1.67	−3.2	7.4	1.53
knitting mills	6	560	19.4	1.54	88.8	41.5	1.74
clothing	7	1378	14.7	1.29	−8.2	−35.0	2.60
wood	8	286	17.6	1.68	108.7	159.0	1.87
furniture and fixtures	9	1561	22.2	1.35	12.3	−12.4	1.95
paper and allied products	10	228	17.4	1.95	—	—	—
printing, publishing	11	451	40.3	1.85	27.7	67.8	1.69
primary metals	12	—	—	—	—	—	—
metal fabricating	13	5662	23.5	1.69	−18.8	.69	1.63
machinery	14	1681	31.8	2.08	—	—	2.30
transport equipment	15	2871	18.1	1.88	46.0	16.5	1.88
electrical products	16	3791	27.2	1.66	−1.5	−6.92	1.72
non-metallic mineral products	17	331	20.4	1.84	—	—	—
petroleum and coal products	18	—	—	—	—	—	—
chemicals	19	124	53.7	2.46	291.1	149.3	3.27
miscellaneous	20	853	27.2	1.88	—	—	—
total		33364	22.5	1.87	20.9	15.6	1.99

Table 10.4 (continued)

Industry		No. of production workers, 1971	1971 administrative workers as % total 1971	Value added per $ of salaries and wages, 1971	% increase of production workers, 1971–9	% increase of administration workers, 1971–9	1979 value added per $ of salaries and wages
London							
food and beverage	1	3409	27.2	2.69	−16.2	−18.5	2.79
tobacco	2	—	—	—	—	—	—
rubber and plastics	3	—	—	—	—	—	3.99
leather	4	393	10.3	1.66	—	—	—
textile	5	49	31.0	1.77	—	—	—
knitting mills	6	202	11.8	1.78	—	—	—
clothing	7	350	17.6	2.00	65.7	−8.0	2.17
wood	8	330	17.3	1.88	−38.5	−62.3	1.53
furniture and fixtures	9	97	10.2	1.75	—	—	—
paper and allied products	10	847	29.8	1.66	—	—	—
printing, publishing	11	1104	40.5	1.51	−2.9	9.6	1.60
primary metals	12	—	—	—	—	—	—
metal fabricating	13	1440	26.5	1.49	−3.3	−24.9	1.84
machinery	14	1440	32.1	2.11	−10.5	−24.2	2.17
transport equipment	15	4980	20.5	1.29			—
electrical products	16	3056	28.0	2.78	2.4	−44.1	2.23
non-metallic mineral products	17	366	18.1	1.91	−27.6	−9.9	2.26
petroleum and coal products	18	—	—	—	—	—	—
chemicals	19	320	44.7	2.83	—	—	—
miscellaneous	20	237	23.2	1.96	51.1	3.4	1.73
total		19661	28.0	2.07	−13.6	−17.1	2.38

Note: Ontario data are in parenthesis. Sources are as for Table 10.2.

M. J. Webber

relatively poor performance of its non-primary metal industries and of its loss of administrative jobs.

Far fewer data are available with which to describe the period since 1979. Statistics Canada collects monthly labor-force data from larger corporations (those which employed over 20 people in any one month of a calendar year), which, while not comparable to the censuses of populations or of manufacturers which were used to construct Tables 10.1–10.4, can be used to assess recent trends. Manufacturing employment reached a peak in May 1981 in Hamilton. Since then, employment in both the city and the province has fallen precipitously; by January 1983, Hamilton had lost nearly 18000 manufacturing jobs, almost one-quarter of its total (Ontario's manufacturing employment was then 83.7% of its May 1981 level). Hamilton's workers, indeed, were paying the price for the city's increasing specialization in production and primary metal jobs: production jobs had declined to 69.4% but administrative jobs to only 92.5% of their May 1981 levels; and durable manufacturing jobs had declined to 73.1% (contrast non-durable: 84.5%) of the number of May 1981.

Table 10.5 Measures of unemployment, Hamilton, Toronto, London and Kitchener, 1976–83.

	Unemployment rate (%)				Percentage of population employed			
Date	Hamilton	Toronto	London	Kitchener	Hamilton	Toronto	London	Kitchener
Dec. 76	5.8	5.9	7.9	7.6	57.3	61.6	58.7	68.5
Dec. 77	6.3	6.1	5.7	7.4	58.7	63.0	62.9	63.6
Dec. 78	7.1	5.5	5.3	7.2	60.3	65.4	63.4	63.2
Dec. 79	6.2	5.0	6.5	7.5	61.7	66.5	64.3	64.9
Jun. 80	7.4	5.9	7.2	9.1	61.8	67.0	67.7	66.4
Dec. 80	4.3	3.8	9.6	9.5	63.4	66.8	60.0	64.1
Jun. 81	5.9	5.1	5.0	8.4	63.5	70.2	66.2	66.2
Dec. 81	8.7	5.1	6.8	8.7	59.7	66.6	61.0	66.6
Mar. 82	9.6	7.3	8.8	8.1	58.1	65.0	61.6	66.9
Jun. 82	12.5	8.7	8.9	8.9	58.4	66.7	62.6	69.3
Sep. 82	13.2	9.1	11.8	11.4	58.3	63.4	58.6	63.5
Dec. 82	15.1	9.1	11.8	10.8	55.7	64.1	59.0	63.9
Mar. 83	15.7	10.8	11.6	11.0	56.2	63.1	61.7	63.5
Jun. 83	11.2	9.7	9.8	8.0	58.9	64.6	64.6	67.4

Note: Unemployment rate is expressed as a percentage of the officially defined labor force. Rates are estimated by sampling. For Toronto, the 95% confidence interval on unemployment rates is an interval of 10.2–20.0% of the quoted rate on either side of that rate; thus the June 83 confidence interval lies between the limits (8.7, 10.7) and (7.8, 11.6). For Hamilton, the interval extends 20.2–33.0% of the quoted rate on either side. For London and Kitchener, it extends for 33.2–50.0% of the quoted rate on either side.

Source: Statistics Canada, *The labour force*, Catalogue 71–001, Ottawa.

The performance of Hamilton's economy over the last seven years can be summarized by its ability to provide jobs for its inhabitants. Table 10.5 compares Hamilton's performance on this criterion to the performance of other southern Ontario cities. One indicator is the official unemployment rate. Whereas Hamilton's unemployment rate was at or below the rates for

215

other cities until the end of 1980, it then began to grow rapidly to reach a rate nearly 50% higher than the other three cities by the end of 1982. Given the doubts that exist about official unemployment statistics, the employment to population ratios are more revealing. Throughout the period, a smaller proportion of Hamilton's population has been employed than of any of the other three cities and by 1982, Hamilton's ratio was only 90% of that of the others. Despite a slowly growing population, Hamilton's economy has proved unable to provide sufficient jobs.

Hamilton's problem, then, has two facets. The very high unemployment rates of the last few years reflect the particular response of the city's durable goods manufacturers to the lack of investment in the Canadian economy. For example, the primary metal industry in Canada has been working at less than 75% of capacity since 1975 and at less than 60% of capacity in 1982 and 1983. If fixed capital formation rises again in Canada, the demand for Hamilton's products will rise correspondingly. Yet this cyclical component has been superimposed on a longer-term trend: throughout the 1970s, Hamilton has not grown at the provincial rate, for the city lost administrative jobs, failed to expand its service sector at the rate of other cities and failed to attract new firms in rapidly growing industries. The implications of this trend will extend far beyond any immediate effects of cyclical recovery.

The relative decline of Hamilton's economy during the 1970s and its precipitous decline in the past few years can be understood in the light of the theoretical considerations of the previous section. Although the region's manufacturing firms do not exhibit an above average ratio of materials to wages in price terms (see Table 10.3), nevertheless its local class structure and its fixed capital characteristics both draw negative comment from potential locating firms (Currie, Coopers & Lybrand 1978). After discussing these two characteristics in general, lessons will be drawn from the most spectacular capital withdrawal from the region (Stelco's $1.2 billion new steel plant on the shores of Lake Erie, 35 miles south of Hamilton).

Consider first the city's stock of fixed capital. The perceived shortage of industrial land near the main freeways, the lack of business park sites and the lack of land are all cited by business-people (Woods, Gordon 1977: 21). Indeed, as Fig. 10.1 indicates, the region lies 20 miles south of Ontario's major east–west freeway (Highway 401) and its vacant industrial land is largely inaccessible to freeways (Fig. 10.2). Equally, during the 1970s, whereas Hamilton accounted for some 6% of the province's work-force, it claimed only 5.8% of industrial construction, 4.7% of the commercial construction and 4.3% of institutional and government construction (Statistics Canada, *Building permits, annual summary* for the years 1971–82). Thus, the crucial investments in commercial and public facilities needed to modernize the city's fixed capital stock were not being made.

Several aspects of the regions' class structure (or, in business parlance, its 'labor situation') draw comment. Table 10.3 shows that the workers in Hamilton are paid above provincial rates and the correlation between above average wage rates and above (provincial) average male employment suggests that the male work-force is particularly well paid. The apparent militancy of the city's work-force also draws comment: with 6.3% of the

216

province's work-force, Hamilton claims 7.1% of the non-government union members. But more crucial for the city's work-force has been the effect of the reliance upon blue-collar jobs and the primary metal sector: not only a male-dominated work-force, but also a poorly educated one (Table 10.6). In 1976, over 45% of Wentworth County's work-force had only a Grade II education or less, compared to 42.5% in Ontario and only 35.6% in London; conversely, only one-third of its work-force had some post-secondary education (37.3% Ontario, 41.7% in London).

Yet it is the recent history of Stelco that most clearly reveals the connections between technical change, the relations of production and the location of capital. Stelco is Canada's largest steel producer, accounting for over a third of domestic steel production. In its peak year to date, 1980, it produced 6.28 million tons of raw steel, making sales of $2229 million with a work-force of 25000 people (Stelco, *Annual Report, 1982*, p. 27). The company operates a fully integrated steelworks in Hamilton (the Hilton works, with a capacity of nearly 6 million tons), operates electric furnaces in Quebec and Edmonton (each with a capacity of about 250000 tons), and owns finishing plants in Hamilton (four), southern Ontario (five), Quebec (four), Alberta (two) and Regina (one). Stelco either owns outright or owns a large share of coal mines in Pennsylvania, Kentucky, West Virginia and British Columbia, iron ore mines in Minnesota, Michigan, Quebec and Labrador, and a limestone quarry in Beachville, Ontario (Stelco, *Annual Report*, 1982).

The iron and steel industry in Canada has not suffered the decline of its American counterpart. Nevertheless, it has been accumulating less successfully than other sectors in Canada and than iron and steel industries in the Third World, particularly since the early 1970s. Table 10.7 shows some of the indices of this accumulation. The rate of growth of the net stock of fixed capital in the primary metal industries has consistently fallen since the 1950s, and since 1970 has been lower than the net growth of fixed capital in Canadian industry as a whole. Equally, the growth of the labor force has been slow since the spurt of the early 1950s. Data on rates of profit are more limited, but they reveal that the primary metal industry has consistently been less profitable than other manufacturing since 1967; and whereas Hamilton's primary metal industry was more profitable than the Canadian industry until the early 1970s, its relative profitability has fallen since then. The overall impression is of an industry and a city that are less profitable and less able to accumulate than manufacturing activity as a whole. One of the responses of the city's iron and steel industry has been to try to restore profitability by investment in new plant.

During the 1970s, Stelco invested about $1.76 billion (Chesnut 1983), nearly twice its net income for the decade (Stelco, *Annual Report, 1976*, p. 18, and *Annual Report, 1982*, p. 27). While this period saw the opening of the Quebec furnace and a 25% increase in the capacity of the Hilton Works, over two-thirds of this investment was spent on developing a new iron and steel plant on the shore of Lake Erie, 35 miles south of Hamilton (Chesnut 1983: 2). This mill began operation in June 1980; by 1983, it had a raw steel capacity (in slabs) of 1.4 million tons and had just opened a 600000-ton hot strip mill. Stelco's goal is to build a fully integrated plant on Lake Erie, having a capacity

Table 10.6 Education and labour force participation rate, Ontario, 1976.

Place	All levels of education			Grade II or less schooling			Post-secondary education		
	Population over 15 years (000)	Labor force (000)	Partici-pation rate (%)	Proportion of population (%)	Proportion of labor force (%)	Partici-pation rate (%)	Proportion of population (%)	Proportion of labor force (%)	Partici-pation rate (%)
Ontario									
All	6191	3856	62.3	50.6	42.5	52.2	30.7	37.3	75.9
Females	3157	1515	48.0	—	48.9	36.5	—	37.7	62.7
Hamilton									
All	399	242	60.6	50.7	42.1	50.5	30.1	36.8	74.2
Females	204	91	44.5	—	48.5	33.3	—	37.4	60.7
Wentworth									
All	313	187	59.8	54.0	45.4	50.3	27.2	33.6	74.1
Kitchener									
All	201	132	65.7	51.8	45.5	57.7	31.2	36.0	76.0
Females	102	53	51.9	—	45.3	43.6	—	34.0	64.3
London									
All	206	132	64.1	43.7	35.6	52.2	35.9	41.7	74.3
Females	107	55	51.4	—	32.7	38.3	—	43.6	64.9

Source: Statistics Canada, *1976 Census of Canada, Supplementary Bulletins: Economic Characteristics*, Vol. 10, Catalogue 94–831, Ottawa 1978.
Note: 'Hamilton,' 'Kitchener,' 'London' refer to Census Metropolitan Areas; 'Wentworth' to the Regional Municipality of Hamilton–Wentworth (formerly Wentworth County).

Table 10.7 Performance of primary metals industry, Canada, 1950–80.

	1950–56	1956–69	1969–74	1974–80
All manufacturing in Canada				
growth of labor force[1]	1.67	0.95	1.80	0.57
growth of capital stock[2]	5.45	4.38	4.39	3.41
rate of profit[3]	43.50	37.50	34.00	30.40
Primary metals industry in Canada				
growth of labor force[4]	4.69	0.09	1.95	0.09
growth of capital stock[5]	7.64	5.01	4.12	2.55
rate of profit[6]	—	23.00	23.30	21.30
capacity utilization rate[7]	—	88.70	86.50	75.80
Primary metals industry in Hamilton				
growth of labor force[8]	12.54	−0.00		1.90
rate of profit[9]	—	30.60	27.30	18.70

Notes and sources:
(1) Number of production workers employed in the manufacturing activity of manufacturers, expressed as a percentage rate of change per annum. The years that divide the periods are peaks of the level of output in constant dollars; from Webber and Rigby 1985. Data are from Statistics Canada, *Manufacturing industries of Canada*, Catalogue CA1 31–203, Ottawa, annually.
(2) Percentage rate of change per annum of the mid-year net fixed capital stock, in constant 1971 dollars. Data are from Statistics Canada, *Fixed capital flows and stocks*, Catalogue 13–568, Ottawa, occasionally.
(3) Average of the annual rates of profit in Canadian manufacturing. The rate of profit is the total surplus (value of output of manufactured goods less costs of fuel, material, wages and depreciation) divided by the total capital invested (mid-year net capital stock plus mid-year owned inventory). The computations are described more fully and the data are presented in Webber and Rigby 1985.
(4) Same as (1), except that data are recorded for SIC 12, Primary Metals Industries. This Major Group includes Iron and Steel Mills; Steel Pipe and Tube Mills; Iron Foundries; Smelting and Refining; Aluminium Rolling, Casting and Extracting; Copper and Copper Alloy Rolling, Casting and Extracting; and other Metal Rolling, Casting and Extracting. Data are available only for the period since 1967.
(5) As (2), but for SIC 12.
(6) As (3), but for SIC 12. Inventory data are from Statistics Canada, *Inventories, shipments and orders in manufacturing industries*, Catalogue 31–003, Ottawa, monthly.
(7) Averages of the annual average capacity utilization rates, for SIC 12, since 1961, from Statistics Canada, *Capacity utilization rates in Canadian manufacturing*, Catalogue 31–003, Ottawa, monthly.
(8) As (1), except for SIC 12 in Hamilton Census Metropolitan Area.
(9) As (3), except for SIC 12 in Hamilton Census Metropolitan area. The total capital invested is measured as Canadian capital invested in SIC 12 multiplied by Hamilton's share of the SIC 12 labor force.

of 5.4 million tons of steel a year (*Financial Post* October 22, 1981).

It has been claimed that two reasons governed Stelco's decision to build a new integrated steel works outside Hamilton (Chesnut 1983: 3). On the one hand, the Hilton plant, occupying a thousand acres on Hamilton's harbor front, is hemmed in by another steelworks (Dofasco) and by an International Harvester plant, so that expansion on the Hamilton harbor front was impossible. And the capacity that was added there during the 1970s could not be planned as efficiently as an entirely new plant. On the other hand, in the late 1960s when the Lake Erie plant was first seriously planned and in the mid 1970s when its construction began, Stelco is said to have anticipated that Canadian demand for steel would grow at 5% per year. At that rate of expansion, using a 1970 base, Stelco's 1980 sales would have been almost two million tons greater than their actual sales (over the period 1970–80, Stelco's production rose by about 30% rather than by the 63% needed to maintain a 5% average increase).

Whatever the expectation, the reality is this. Stelco's raw steel capacity is now 7.8 million tons per annum. Of this capacity, 0.25 million tons are in each of the two electric furnaces (Contrecoeur and Edmonton), 1.4 million tons are at Lake Erie and 5.9 million tons are at the Hilton Works. But production in both 1981 and 1982 has been about 4.5 million tons (Stelco, *Annual Report, 1982*, p. 27). The electric furnaces and Lake Erie are operating at capacity, so in 1982, the Hilton Works produced just over 2.5 million tons: in the last quarter of 1982, the Hilton Works were operating at less than 40% of capacity (Stelco, *Annual Report, 1982*, p. 7). Although formally the Lake Erie works represents an addition to capacity, in practice it represents a transfer of production from Hamilton to Lake Erie. A consideration of the production advantages gained by this transfer illuminates the problems of old industrial regions such as Hamilton.

The first advantage is simply that of being able to plan the Lake Erie works from scratch on a greenfield site, using the latest technology available. The Lake Erie site occupies over 6000 acres of land (Allan 1979), has a new, privately owned docking facility and was planned to optimize the flow of materials through the works (Stelco, *Lake Erie Works*, undated). Extensive use was made of numerical control of processes (Stelco, *Annual Report, 1982*, p. 11), giving a plant which has the lowest operating costs of any in North America (Chesnut 1983: 4) and which can produce steel of a quality to match imports from Japan and South Korea (Chesnut 1983: 4). Thus, whereas the Hilton Works' output of 5.5 million tons of raw steel in 1980 needed a work-force of 12500 people (440 tons per worker), Lake Erie's 1.4 million ton capacity needs only 1700 people (823 tons per worker) and the planned ('Stage Three') expansion to 5.4 million tons is expected to employ no more than 3000 people (1833 tons per worker) (Allan 1979). If the Lake Erie works is expanded to 5.4 million tons capacity by the year 2000 as planned, that may mean the end of raw steel production in Hamilton, for Stelco's capacity would then be twelve million tons, equal to two-thirds of the peak total Canadian consumption (in 1980). The Hamilton plants would then be reduced merely to finishing Lake Erie steel.

The sheer technical advantages of starting anew rather than altering or rebuilding the old are clear. Yet the choice of a greenfield site away from existing steel-making capacity offered other advantages to Stelco; these involve starting anew in the sense of industrial relations. There are two such advantages in particular. In the first place, Stelco had, as part of its collective agreement with the Hamilton Local (1005) of the United Steelworkers of America, agreed that technical change which caused redundancies in Hilton would be compensated. To update the Hilton plant to shed labor would therefore be costly. But this agreement does not cover the Lake Erie case: the new plant (with a new local) is technically more advanced and displaces Hilton workers because the economy is not sufficiently buoyant to support capacity working at both Hilton and Lake Erie. Thus, the unemployment at Hilton is said to be due to marketing problems, not technical change. (This information was provided in conversation with 1005 members and officers.) Secondly, by starting anew, Stelco has been able to redefine job classifications so as to amalgamate the duties, to merge the jobs and to require additional maintenance duties of plant tradesmen (Taylor 1980): for example, the category 'industrial mechanic' at Lake Erie replaces the Hilton categories 'millwright' and 'electrician.' This reclassification reduces the total need for such tradesmen at the same time as it eliminates a source of disputes over duties between skilled workers.

The third type of advantage derived by Stelco from its greenfield site revolves around the lower degree of worker militancy at the Lake Erie works than at the Hilton plant. Of the 1700 people who now work at Lake Erie, about 700 were drawn from the Hilton Works (Pagden 1980); these were mainly younger workers who had been in junior positions at Hilton and wanted promotion (Heneault 1980). The remaining workers came from the Lake Erie region – which until the 1970s had been a depressed agricultural region with few small towns and little industry. Thus these workers often lived 15 or 20 miles from the plant and were not familiar with organizing and using unions (MacDonald 1980). The result of these hiring practices is a less militant work-force at Lake Erie than at Hilton: in the latest strike against Stelco, for example, the Hilton workers were on strike for 125 days but the Lake Erie workers for less than four weeks (Stelco, *Annual Report, 1981*, pp. 8, 12). The militancy of the work-force is important to Stelco for two reasons. First, Stelco feels that it loses markets to competitors, especially the non-union plant of Dofasco, when it cannot guarantee delivery during a year in which the contract must be renegotiated (Freeman 1982: 188). Secondly, the militancy translates into wage differences: whereas the 1981 agreement (the first since production began at Lake Erie) at the Hilton Works allowed for base-rate wage increases of $1.15 per hour in the first year, $0.25 in the second and $0.30 in the third, the Lake Erie local accepted increases of $1.00, $0.15 and $0.15.

Conclusions

Regions grow and their characteristics are produced during particular periods of capitalist expansion. Yet these produced characteristics, once an advantage to capital, became a fetter on expansion as profit rates fall, local real wages rise and fixed capital becomes increasingly obsolete. The case of Hamilton illustrates the difficulties of replacing fixed capital *in situ* and reveals the advantages to be drawn from locational changes – the physical characteristics of new sites and their class structure are thus turned to the advantage of capital.

The advantages of relocation out of established industrial regions develop as a logical consequence of the earlier growth of those regions. Fixed capital must become obsolete. The demand for labor in relation to its supply must be greater in growing regions than in depressed ones. And falling profit rates at the end of expansionary periods must flush out less profitable firms. Capital must, then, seek new sites at which to establish a new basis for accumulation. This process is not peculiar to certain regions – though its effects will differ, depending on location, industrial mix and access to political power – but is a logical consequence of the way in which regions are produced.

It is clear, too, that the process of regional decline can be offset only when the then-existing conditions are altered. This implies that the region's fixed capital must be renewed – for example, by state promotion of renewal of the built environment and by state subsidies for industrial investment; this process has begun in Hamilton as the downtown core is rebuilt and plans for new industrial parks and expressways are being developed. Barnard (1981) is an example of the planning for this renewal. The second requirement is that the city's class structure be altered to the advantage of capital or, at least, circumvented. Unemployment has already begun to reduce worker militancy, as has competition for markets from plants outside the region. Thus by mid 1984, Stelco felt powerful enough to announce plans for a new, less labor-intensive hot rolling mill at Hilton which will throw 2000 employees out of work. And the existing working-class power, for example in the Steelworkers, can be circumvented by introducing new manufacturing and business services industries that use a different segment of the labor force, such as the female work-force, or the youths who have yet to hold a job (see the recommendations in Woods, Gordon 1977: 9, 33). These, then, are the policies which the city's workers can anticipate: state spending on the fixed capital of the city; redundancy and capital flight; and employment of non-traditional workers.

References

Aglietta, M. 1979. *A theory of capitalist regulation*. London: New Left Books.

Allan, J. 1979. It *looks* like a park but it *is* a steel mill. *Water and Pollution Control* **117**(10), 10–12.

Barnard, P. 1981. *An industrial land development strategy for Hamilton–Wentworth*. Report to Planning and Development Department, Regional Municipality of Hamilton–Wentworth, Barnard and Associates.

Carney, J. 1980. Regions in crisis: accumulation, regional problems and crisis formation. In Carney *et al.* (1980), 28–59.

Carney, J., R. Hudson and J. Lewis (eds.) 1980. *Regions in crisis*. London: Croom Helm.

Chesnut, B. R. 1983. *Canadian Research Report: Stelco Inc*. Richardson, Greenshields of Canada Ltd. Toronto, April 29, 1983.

Cohen, G. A. (1978). *Karl Marx's theory of history*. Oxford: Clarendon.

Currie, Coopers and Lybrand Ltd. 1978. *The regional municipality of Hamilton–Wentworth: an action plan for economic growth*. Unpublished report to the Regional Municipality.

Damette, F. 1980. The regional framework of monopoly exploitation: New problems and trends. In Carney *et al.* (1980), 76–92.

Dear, M. J. and A. J. Scott (eds.) 1981. *Urbanization and urban planning in capitalist society*. New York: Methuen.

Dunford, M. 1977. *Regional policy and the restructuring of capital*. Working Paper 4, University of Sussex, Urban and Regional Studies, Brighton.

Dunford, M., M. Geddes and D. Perrons 1981. Regional policy and the crisis in the UK: a long-run perspective. *Int. J. Urban Regional Res.* **5**, 377–410.

The Financial Post 1981. Stelco Inc. (article). October 22.

Fothergill, S. and G. Gudgin 1982. *Unequal growth*. London: Heinemann.

Freeman, B. 1982. *1005: political life in a union local*. Toronto: Lorimer.

Gentilcore, R. L. 1967. *Canada's changing geography*. Toronto: Prentice-Hall.

Gilmour, J. M. 1972. *Spatial evolution of manufacturing, southern Ontario, 1851–1891*. Toronto: University of Toronto Press.

Gordon, D. M. 1978. Capitalist development and the history of American cities. In Tabb and Sawers (1978), 25–63.

Harvey, D. 1981. The urban process under capitalism: A framework for analysis. In Dear and Scott (1981), 91–121.

Heneault, R. 1980. Interview. *The Spectator* September 16, p. 14b.

Jensen-Butler, C. 1982. Capital accumulation and regional development: The case of Denmark. *Environ. Plann. A* **14**, 1307–40.

Keeble, D. 1980. Industrial decline, regional policy and the urban–rural manufacturing shift in the United Kingdom. *Environ. Plann. A* **12**, 945–61.

Kerr, D. 1967. The spatial organization of the iron and steel industry in Canada. In Gentilcore (1967), 139–48.

Läpple, D. and P. von Hoogstraten 1980. Remarks on the spatial structure of capitalist development: The case of the Netherlands. In Carney *et al.* (1980), 117–66.

Lipietz, A. 1980. The structuration of space, the problem of land, and spatial policy. In Carney *et al.* (1980), 60–75.

McCalla, D. 1973. The decline of Hamilton as a wholesale centre. *Ontario Hist.* **65**, 247–54.

MacDonald, B. 1980. Interview. *The Spectator* September 16, p. 14b.

Mandel, E. 1968. *Marxist economic theory*, 2 vols. New York: Monthly Review Press.

Mandel, E. 1978. *Late capitalism*. London: Verso.

Marx, K. 1967. *Capital*, Vol. 1. New York: International.

Massey, D. 1978. Regionalism: some current issues. *Capital and Class* **6**, 106–25.

Massey, D. 1981. The UK electrical engineering and electronics industries: the implications of the crisis for the restructuring of capital and locational change. In Dear and Scott (1981), 199–230.

Nader, G. A. 1976. *Cities of Canada, II: Profiles of fifteen metropolitan cities*. Toronto: Macmillan.

Pagden, R. 1980. The greening of Nanticoke. *Indust. Management* **4**(3), 32–4, 76.

Perry, D. C. and A. J. Watkins (eds.) 1977. *The rise of the Sunbelt cities*. Beverly Hills: Sage.

Sternlieb, G. and J. W. Hughes (eds.) 1977. *Post-industrial America: metropolitan decline and inter-regional job shifts*. New Brunswick, N. J. Rutgers.

Tabb, W. K. and L. Sawers (eds.) 1978. *Marxism and the metropolis*. New York: Oxford University Press.

Taylor, C. 1980. Interview. *The Spectator* September 16, pp. 12b–13b.

Thomson, R. W. 1983. *The economy of Metropolitan Hamilton – some basic facts and recent trends*. Unpublished paper. Department of Economics, McMaster University.

Walker, R. A. 1978. Two sources of uneven development under advanced capitalism: spatial differentiation and capital mobility. *Rev. Radical Polit. Econ.* **10**, 28–37.

Webber, M. J. 1983a. *Technical change and the rate of profit*. Paper presented at 79th Annual Meeting, AAG Denver.

Webber, M. J. 1983b *Theory of industrial location*. Santa Monica, Calif.: Sage.

Webber, M. J. and D. L. Rigby 1985. *The rate of profit in Canadian manufacturing*,

1950–1981. Paper presented at the 81st Annual Meeting, AAG, Detroit.

Wells, D. 1973. *The Hamilton Region – 1880–1882: The inter-relationships between transportation and industrial development.* MA Thesis. Department of Geography, University of Waterloo, Waterloo.

Woods, Gordon and Co. 1977. *Hamilton–Wentworth steel and related industries substudy.* Toronto: Woods, Gordon and Co.

11

Integration and unequal development: the case of southern Italy, 1951–73

M. DUNFORD

In this chapter attention will be paid to the impact of the closer integration of the Italian South or Mezzogiorno into the national and international economy. (The main territorial divisions of Italy are shown in Fig. 11.1.) After World War II the Mezzogiorno was integrated as an essentially open economy into the national economy at the same time as the Italian economy experienced (a) a process of reconstruction and rapid export-led growth, followed by (b) a series of recurrent crises, which gave way in the 1970s to (c) a vicious circle of decline characterized by a falling exchange rate and runaway inflation. Throughout the period preceding the first oil crisis, on which we shall focus, southern development policy was to be consistent economically and politically with overall national development, but not without generating sharp inter-class tensions and conflicts, and major disequilibria which acted as a constraint on modernization. As a result of the economic integration of the South with the North and the industrialization of the region, the structure of the Mezzogiorno was transformed. But the gap between the two main parts of Italy was not narrowed: inequality was reproduced, new forms of dependency appeared, and at the end of the 1970s a radically transformed southern Italy was still among the poorest parts of the nine countries of the EEC (see Fig. 11.2).

The transformation of the Mezzogiorno: development without employment and financial dependency

In the period 1951–73 the South was transformed from a predominantly agricultural and rural to a predominantly urban society with a significant level of industrial activity. Undoubtedly the wave of industrialization of the late 1960s and early 1970s, in particular, played an important part in creating employment and in securing the development of a modern industrial working class in the region. Yet at an aggregate level the increase in industrial investment was associated with an extremely limited expansion of

Figure 11.1 The regions and main territorial divisions of Italy.

employment in industry (excluding construction). Whereas the share of the South in national industrial investment increased from 15.7% in 1951 to 43.9% in 1973, its share of industrial employment decreased from 19.6% to 17.7% over the same period. As Graziani (1978: 359 and 1979: 17) has pointed out, the process that many have described as one of industrialization without development could perhaps be more adequately described as one of development without employment.

One reason for the modest contribution of investment to manufacturing

226

M. Dunford

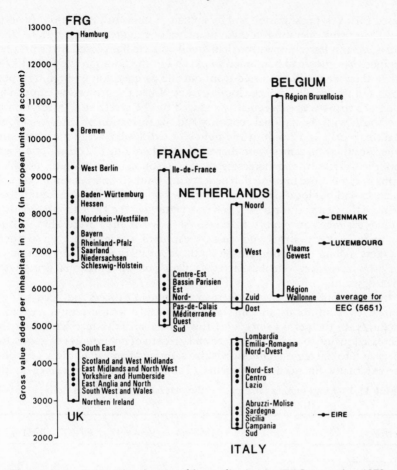

Figure 11.2 Regional and national inequality in nine EEC countries, 1978.

employment growth lay in the concentration of southern investment on increasingly large projects in sectors and branches with high and rapidly increasing capital intensities, while investments in the modern engineering industries with medium capital intensities were located overwhelmingly in the Center-North. The investment undertaken in the South accordingly led to an increase in output and employment that was low compared with the outcome that would have ensued from a more diversified set of investments. On the other hand employment did increase, especially with the decentralization of a number of investments in engineering and electronics in the early 1970s.

The limited growth of industrial employment in the Mezzogiorno, on the other hand, stemmed from the decline of independent and dependent employment in traditional consumption good industries (Tables 11.1 & 2). These industries were characterized by a predominance of artisan and family-

227

based forms of organization and by archaic systems of production. In addition, the firms operating in these branches of production were more labor intensive and less competitive than small and medium-sized firms in other regions. Yet they had continued to expand in the South in the early 1950s, when they were still protected from outside competition by high transport costs and the small size of the local market. When the protection enjoyed by southern firms was subsequently reduced by the accelerated integration of the South with the national economy and the formation of a single national market, partly as a result of the policy of extraordinary intervention, and when southern incomes were increased and the mode of consumption was modified partly by the increasing flow of resources to the South, northern firms became more interested in penetrating southern markets and were able to do so without locating themselves in the region. Small and medium-sized firms in the Center-North had been restructured in the 1950s to increase their competitiveness on export markets. As a result they were able to outcompete southern firms and quickly captured a large share of southern markets. Along with competition on the labor market, this competition on the product market contributed to the collapse of many marginal firms in the Mezzogiorno.

In the second place the southern development process has been accompanied by continuous and increasing imbalance in the region's external accounts. In the period since 1951 this particular imbalance has arisen and increased mainly because of the size and growth of net imports of goods and services into the region, although it also stemmed from an outflow of profits on externally financed investments (Table 11.3). The imbalance in the

Table 11.1 Employment change in the Mezzogiorno and in Italy, 1951–72 (thousands).

Sector	1951–58	1958–64	1964–69	1969–72	1951–72
Mezzogiorno					
agriculture	−725.6	−693.4	−293.7	−208.3	−1,921.0
industry	386.7	169.6	6.9	4.3	567.5
manufacturing	157.3	−36.0	16.7	33.6	171.6
construction	226.4	203.3	−11.3	−28.5	389.9
services	279.8	46.2	109.9	16.8	452.7
public administration	50.3	94.4	77.1	33.0	254.8
total	−8.8	−383.2	−99.8	−154.2	−646.0
Italy					
agriculture	−1,666.0	−2,007.0	−944.0	−668.0	−5,285.0
industry	1,273.9	919.1	52.0	−31.0	2,214.0
manufacturing	723.7	465.2	157.1	136.0	1,482.0
construction	536.4	444.5	−119.1	−160.5	701.3
services	970.6	222.7	295.7	272.0	1,761.0
public administration	159.5	282.2	180.4	90.0	712.1
total	738.0	−583.0	−415.9	−337.0	−597.9

Source: Based on ISTAT 1973.

Table 11.2 Manufacturing employment change in the Mezzogiorno and in Italy, 1951–72 (thousands)

Sector	Mezzogiorno					Italy				
	1951–58	1958–64	1964–69	1969–72	1951–72	1951–58	1958–64	1964–69	1969–72	1951–72
consumption good industries	113.5	−73.5	−17.0	−33.6	−10.6	352.5	83.0	−22.9	−76.2	170.1
permanent	−13.6	−39.7	1.4	−19.0	8.5	−10.4	290.5	32.8	−32.3	280.6
dependent	12.1	56.8	19.3	−3.4	84.8	−30.9	313.4	70.8	8.2	423.3
independent	−25.7	−17.1	−17.9	−15.6	−76.3	−41.3	−22.9	−38.0	−40.5	−142.7
marginal	127.1	−113.2	−18.4	−14.6	−19.1	362.6	−373.5	−55.7	−43.9	−110.5
dependent	75.4	−71.9	−7.0	−9.6	−13.1	204.8	−205.4	−17.0	−32.5	−50.1
independent	51.7	−41.3	−7.0	−9.6	−6.0	157.8	−168.1	−38.7	−11.4	−60.4
equipment good industries	16.9	3.3	5.9	43.8	69.9	208.9	346.0	140.9	128.6	824.4
permanent	16.0	14.0	20.6	43.6	94.0	186.7	370.9	200.4	126.0	884.0
dependent	15.3	14.6	19.5	41.1	90.5	159.6	357.8	187.2	126.6	831.2
independent	0.7	−0.6	0.9	2.5	3.5	27.1	13.1	13.2	−0.6	52.8
marginal	0.9	−10.7	−14.5	0.2	−24.1	22.2	−24.9	−59.5	2.6	−59.6
dependent	−1.2	−0.3	−12.1	0.0	−13.6	6.7	15.6	−50.6	2.0	−26.3
independent	2.1	−10.4	−2.4	0.2	−10.5	15.5	−40.5	−8.9	0.6	−33.3
intermediate good industries	26.9	34.2	27.8	23.4	112.3	162.6	202.2	39.1	83.6	487.5
permanent	23.4	36.3	29.1	23.6	112.4	158.0	207.2	42.9	83.8	491.9
dependent	24.5	37.2	29.2	23.1	114.0	150.9	204.0	44.2	83.8	482.9
independent	−1.1	−0.0	−0.1	0.5	−1.6	7.1	3.2	−1.3	0.0	9.0
marginal	3.5	−2.1	−1.3	−0.2	−0.1	4.6	−5.0	−3.8	−0.2	−4.4
dependent	3.5	−2.1	−1.3	−0.2	−0.1	4.6	−5.0	−3.8	−0.2	−4.4
independent	0.0	0.0	0.0	0.0	0.0	0.0	0.0	0.0	0.0	0.0

Source: Based on ISTAT 1973.

Notes:

(1) Traditional and current consumption good industries: food, drink and tobacco; textiles, clothing and footwear; leather and leather goods; furniture and wood products; printing and publishing; and other manufacturing industries. Equipment good industries: engineering, and transport equipment. Intermediate good industries: metal manufacturing, non-metallic minerals; chemicals and allied industries; rubber, and paper.

(2) Permanent and marginal employment broadly correspond to full-time and part-time employment, while dependent and independent employment broadly correspond to employees and self-employed persons.

region's accounts has been offset to a decreasing but nevertheless significant extent by a net inflow of capital. But the deteriorating trade balance has been financed largely by an expanding volume of net transfers into the region. The latter were composed in part of emigrants' remittances. But the major part was made up of incomes distributed to southern residents by the public administration in the form of subsidies, pensions, and grants.

Table 11.3 Balance of payments of the Mezzogiorno in relation to gross income, 1951–73 (percentage values).

Year	Net exports	Net exports of goods and services	Net income from abroad	Net current transfers from abroad	Current balance	Gross income	Gross income (milliard lire in current prices)
1951	−18.6	−15.8	−2.8	8.6	−10.0	100.0	2452.3
1952	−24.0	−21.4	−2.6	10.1	−13.9	100.0	2614.2
1953	−19.5	−18.9	−2.6	10.3	−9.2	100.0	3018.6
1954	−20.2	−17.5	−2.7	10.8	−9.4	100.0	3142.9
1955	−23.4	−20.7	−2.7	11.5	−12.0	100.0	3397.0
1956	−20.6	−18.2	−2.4	11.5	−9.1	100.0	3772.9
1957	−17.8	−15.6	−2.2	10.8	−6.9	100.0	4076.7
1958	−18.6	−16.4	−2.1	12.9	−5.7	100.0	4299.4
1959	−18.9	−16.9	−2.0	13.6	−5.3	100.0	4478.0
1960	−24.4	−22.2	−2.2	13.7	−10.6	100.0	4742.9
1961	−21.2	−19.3	−1.9	13.7	−7.5	100.0	5878.2
1962	−24.9	−23.3	−1.6	15.4	−9.5	100.0	5951.9
1963	−25.5	−23.9	−1.6	16.7	−8.8	100.0	7047.7
1964	−25.0	−23.4	−1.6	14.9	−10.1	100.0	7634.6
1965	−17.6	−16.2	−1.3	17.0	−0.6	100.0	8536.2
1966	−18.7	−17.4	−1.3	17.3	−1.4	100.0	9139.5
1967	−18.9	−17.3	−1.6	16.6	−2.3	100.0	10151.8
1968	−18.6	−17.1	−1.5	17.9	−0.7	100.0	10786.9
1969	−19.4	−18.0	−1.4	19.0	−0.3	100.0	11910.4
1970	−23.5	−21.9	−1.6	19.0	−4.5	100.0	13061.4
1971	−22.2	−20.8	−1.4	20.0	−2.2	100.0	14481.8
1972	−24.4	−22.9	−1.5	18.7	−5.7	100.0	15647.5
1973	−26.1	−24.0	−2.1	18.5	−7.7	100.0	18628.7

Source: Based on ISTAT 1974.

Note: The trade balance is equal to net exports of goods and services plus income from abroad and the current balance in the balance of payments is equal to the difference between net exports and net current transfers. The current balance is assumed to be equal to net investment abroad, i.e. the net increase in the value of external assets acquired by southern residents less the net increase in the value of assets in the South acquired by non-residents. Total available resources are equal to gross income plus net imports.

Graziani (1979: 49–65, 1978: 366–71) has pointed out that the mechanism lying behind this phenomenon and behind the development process as a whole was a pattern of infrastructural and industrial investment that increased aggregate demand without promoting a balanced expansion of the productive system: the flow of industrial investment and public expenditure into the Mezzogiorno increased income and demand in the region and led to the establishment of industries producing energy and intermediate goods, but not until the early 1970s to the development of industries producing items of industrial equipment or modern consumption goods.

The expansion of demand for goods and services that could not be imported led to a rapid development of local production. For example, the local construction industry and commercial and distributional services connected both with the maintenance of plant and equipment and with consumption activities expanded rapidly. These industries were almost entirely under southern entrepreneurship. But they tended to provide only relatively precarious employment for comparatively unskilled and low-paid workers.

In the case of manufacturing industry, on the other hand, the increase in demand led in most cases to an increase in imports rather than to an expansion of local production. The growth in imports was most pronounced in the case of producer goods: capital goods industries were not well represented in the southern industrial system, and so most items of capital equipment had to be imported. But the same point applied to consumption goods industries. Not only did the pattern of consumption switch away from traditional consumption goods and toward the modern products of northern-based industries, but also southern enterprises operating in traditional sectors declined in relation to their northern counterparts. These changes were a result of two factors. One was the loss of protection and their exposure to direct competition from more efficient enterprises in other areas. The second was the increase in local wages and production costs that followed the implantation of modern enterprises in the Mezzogiorno.

The expanding flow of public funds to the South did, however, contribute to an enlargement of employment in the public administration and in the service sector. In addition it augmented the power and influence of clientelistic bureaucracies and local officials controlling the allocation of the jobs and resources involved. In this way state spending played an important role in building consensus around Christian Democracy. Yet expanding welfare spending and the propping up of inefficient sectors along with comparatively limited tax receipts are major factors in the fiscal crisis of the Italian state.

The underlying model of southern development

What we have argued in the last section is that the Mezzogiorno has been transformed and has been turned from a region that was poor and marginal to one that is poor and dependent. It is dependent not only in the sense that new production units are dependent on northern parent plants for a series of functions ranging from marketing to research and design engineering (Giannola 1982: 69), but also in the sense that many of the region's inhabitants rely on transfers from abroad or from the North.

Underlying these phenomena is the model of southern development: the rationalization of farming and the final destruction in the land reform of the central role in southern society of the old landed aristocracy and, more importantly, the process of industrialization that followed the redirection of southern policy in the second half of the 1950s. At that time provisions for the establishment of industrial development areas were introduced (see Fig. 11.3), controls were placed on public sector investment, and a system of grants and low-interest loans was introduced. And by the early 1960s the

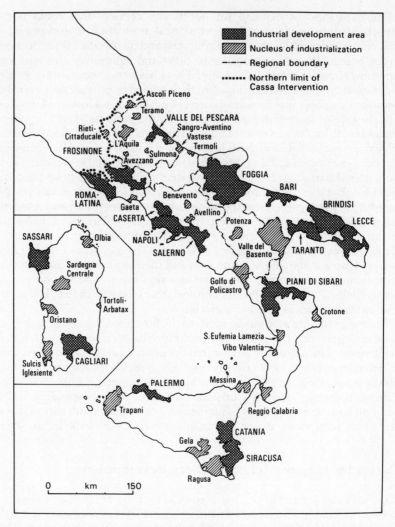

Figure 11.3 Areas and nuclei of industrialization in the Mezzogiorno in the early 1970s.

system of incentives had been amended in order that large capital–intensive projects could be aided.

In 1958–64 a wave of industrial investment occurred in the South at the same time as the wave of growth known as the economic miracle was gripping the country (see Fig. 11.4). The leading role in the investment process was played by the state holding companies. Investment went mainly into a few large projects in the oil, chemicals, and steel sectors including the integrated shore-based iron and steelworks at Taranto. In these sectors, characterized by an integrated production cycle, industrial enter-

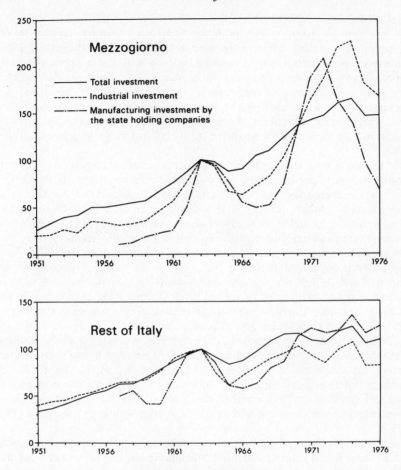

Figure 11.4 Gross fixed investment in the Mezzogiorno and the rest of Italy (index numbers: 1963 = 100).

prises required relatively few links with the local economy in which they were located, and so they could be implanted relatively easily in an area that had not yet been industrialized, as long as certain general types of social overhead capital were supplied.

The South had a number of natural advantages for industrial development of this kind: southern regions were well situated for access to sources of raw materials and to markets in the Mediterranean Basin. Moreover, large areas of land were available for development, and in particular there were possibilities of developing uncongested port facilities with deep water access. Another advantage was that the investment costs of the firms concerned were reduced quite markedly by the receipt of funds for southern development. (Investments of this kind had, however, a more limited impact on long-term employment than equivalent levels of investment in other sectors.)

In addition, decisions to expand in the South were important in augmenting support for the expansion of the state sector. In the 1950s the state holding companies were undoubtedly a modernizing force. But new investment was opposed by various fractions of private capital: the development of integrated production at Taranto was, for example, strongly opposed by private-sector steel interests, led by Falck, which were oriented to the production of steel from scrap in electric furnaces. A choice of southern location was accordingly important in mobilizing the southern lobby behind the project (see Dunford 1986).

At the same time smaller local investments occurred largely as a result of decisions by entrepreneurs who were already operating in the South. Only a small part of these investments were in sectors connected to the activities of large plants or could be seen as being induced by them. Most of them were in construction or related sectors, especially as a result of the surge in residential development in the rapidly expanding large cities of the South.

A second wave of investment in the Mezzogiorno occurred in 1969–74. It was more pronounced than the first, was more strongly dominated by industrial investment, and was also different in that it did not coincide with an expansion of investment at a national level. At this stage investment in the Mezzogiorno had clearly become an alternative to investment in the Northwest for several sections of large capital in Italy.

The most important component of investment was once again investment in capital-intensive branches of production. The state holding companies carried out some major investments in the steel and in the chemicals and synthetic fibers sectors. But at the same time a significant wave of private chemical development occurred in the South. (The location of the major investments in the chemical and synthetic textile sectors are shown in Fig. 11.5.)

In the late 1960s investment in the petrochemicals sector was occurring, in part because of expectations about a continuing increase in demand but also because the four main Italian chemical groups had decided to use aid for southern development to strengthen their market positions *vis-à-vis* those of their rivals in what came to be known as the 'chemical war.' This competitive struggle led, however, to a wasteful duplication of investment and, along with the rise in energy costs and the slackening of demand after the first oil crisis, contributed to the appearance of excess capacity and to the particularly deep crisis of the Italian chemical industry.

In the steel industry the most important investment was the enlargement of the capacity of the Taranto complex to a projected 10.5 million tonnes of crude steel per annum in the second half of the 1970s. On the other hand the plan to build the country's fifth integrated coastal plant at Gioia Tauro in Calabria, chosen in part because of the uprisings in Reggio Calabria and in other large cities in the South in the early 1970s, was dropped after the fall in demand for steel in the mid 1970s.

During the same period the state holding companies, which were progressively transferring their manufacturing base to the Mezzogiorno, started to implement a policy of sectoral diversification, and invested in the

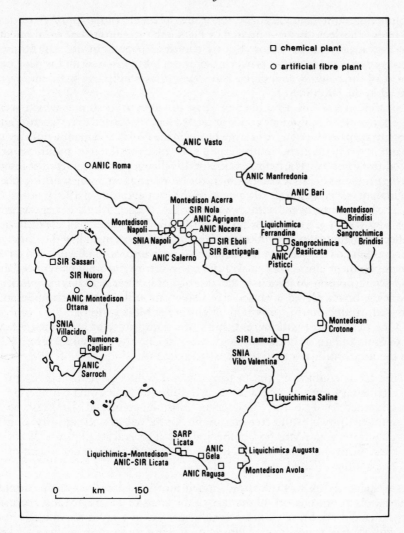

Figure 11.5 The location of chemical and artificial textile plants in the Mezzogiorno in 1974.

engineering and electronics sectors, locating new projects in the South. In other words they were seeking to strengthen their position in the national economy, by diversifying into sectors that were expanding at a national level and in which they were competing with, and not simply complementing, investments by the private sector firms whose growth had led the externally oriented development of the Italian economy. The most striking example was the decision made in the mid 1960s by the Milan-based Alfa Romeo group to start to produce medium-range cars, in which field it would be competing with Fiat, and to locate the new plant at Pomigliano d'Arco near Naples. The decision was opposed by Fiat on the grounds that it would create excess capacity in the sector. But by choosing a southern site Alfa Romeo received backing from the powerful southern lobby. As a result the development of the plant, which embodied standard assembly line methods, went ahead in the late 1960s.

In the early 1970s a number of large private corporations, which were operating in the equipment goods or related sectors, started to restructure and decentralize production from large plants in the North and made a number of major investments in the South. (Equipment goods are durable consumers' and producers' goods). The main reasons for this change in strategy are to be found in the problems of urban congestion in the North and increasing working-class militancy, especially after the events of the 'hot autumn' of 1969.

The hot autumn began with a wave of strikes connected with the negotiations for new wage agreements for the years 1970–2. But subsequent conflicts also reflected discontent with working and living conditions, including the length of the working day, track speeds in assembly line industries, shift work and rising unemployment along with inadequate transport, strained public services and worsening housing conditions in the cities of the Northwest. Immigrant workers from the South played a particularly active part in the ensuing struggles and pressed strongly for the provision of jobs in the Mezzogiorno.

One of the most striking examples of a company which adopted a new economic and geographical strategy was Fiat (see Fig. 11.6 and Amin 1982). In the words of Fiat's head of industrial relations:

> the labor conflicts in the factories have taught Fiat management an elementary truth: large plants like Mirafiori [in Turin] can no longer be governed, and so the Fiat system must be reformed. [It must be reformed] by creating factories in the South, but in a certain way: one does not create a Mirafiori in the South, but several small plants. What these plants have in common is that they are relatively independent of one another. (Cited in Amin 1982: 74)

As is suggested in this quotation, much more was involved than a simple relocation of production. In the face of the crisis of Taylorism and Fordism what Fiat did was break up the assembly line system in favor of a more flexible organization of production, adopt semi-autonomous groups as the principle of organization of assembly work, and introduce some automated and robotized processes of production. And instead of building large integrated plants, it set up a number of smaller and relatively independent factories specializing in a particular phase in the production of a car. The group's new plants were located in small towns and predominantly rural areas where the costs of housing and land were lower and new housing was not always needed, where grants and low interest loans were available for new investment, and where infrastructural items were financially supported by the funds for regional development provided nationally or by the EEC. What was more, great care was exercised in the recruitment of workers with a view to avoiding the problems caused by young immigrants in the North. In moving, Fiat was looking for a less militant and more fragmented working class.

Figure 11.6   The distribution of the Fiat Group's Italian plants (Fiat, Autobianchi, Lancia and Abarth).

The changing role of the South in the national and international economy

So far we have discussed the consequences of southern development and the process of industrial investment which in part underlay it. But what has happened can only be explained by outlining the changing role of the South and Italy as a whole in a changing national and international division of labor respectively. The process of development was not simply a product of investment decisions made by individual firms. The firms themselves were operating in a political and macro-economic environment and were subjected to mediated processes of market validation that also have to be explained.

At the end of World War II the Italian industrial system was dominated by the technologically backward traditional industries such as the food processing, natural textile, and wood processing sectors (Table 11.4). It also included relatively advanced industries in the engineering, vehicle manufacturing, and chemicals sectors, but they were fairly small in size, while other industries that were to become important, like the iron and steel industry, were based to a large extent on traditional techniques of production.

In the postwar period Italy continued to specialize in the export of some of the traditional industrial products of the textiles, clothing, shoes, and leather goods sectors (see Fig. 11.7). Indeed it was the dynamism of these sectors and of the peripheral and parallel economy with which they were associated that was to be highlighted by studies of the Third Italy (Bagnasco 1977, Garofoli 1978). On the other hand the economy lost its export specialization in food processing owing to the relatively slow modernization of Italian agriculture and the expansion of domestic demand.

But the structure of the economy was adjusted through a growing specialization in the production of mass consumption goods such as electrical appliances and motor vehicles for which world demand was expanding rapidly, and through a striking development of industries producing energy

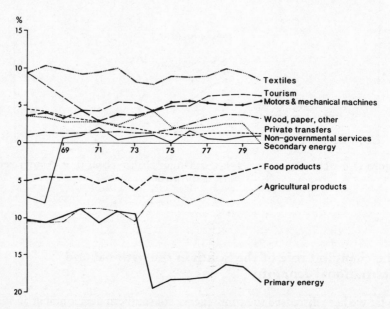

Figure 11.7 The contribution of different sectors to the current balance of trade in Italy, 1967–80.

238

Table 11.4 The sectoral distribution of manufacturing output at factor cost in current market prices and employment in the main territorial division in Italy in 1951 (percentage values).

	Output					Employment				
	North-west	North-east	Center	South	Italy	North-west	North-east	Center	South	Italy
food, drink and tobacco	7.2	19.2	13.3	32.7	13.2	5.4	12.5	10.4	20.7	10.4
textiles	19.3	14.6	11.1	4.4	15.4	25.2	14.2	11.4	3.8	16.9
clothing and footwear	5.9	10.5	13.5	17.1	9.2	10.3	18.5	20.0	30.0	17.1
leather and leather goods	1.3	0.5	1.3	1.2	1.2	1.2	0.7	1.1	0.9	1.0
furniture and wood products	3.2	7.1	6.5	9.4	5.1	5.8	11.4	10.2	16.7	9.6
metal manufacturing	8.1	4.6	7.7	2.9	6.9	4.9	2.0	2.9	1.2	3.4
engineering	24.0	16.3	14.9	10.7	19.7	23.8	19.8	18.1	14.8	20.4
transport equipment	6.9	5.1	2.9	3.6	5.6	6.6	5.0	3.0	2.6	5.0
non-metallic minerals	3.2	7.5	8.7	6.6	5.1	3.7	6.3	8.5	4.7	5.1
chemicals and allied products	10.5	7.7	9.9	7.9	9.6	6.1	4.2	5.4	2.2	4.9
rubber	3.4	0.5	0.8	0.1	2.1	1.6	0.3	0.4	0.1	0.9
paper	3.0	3.6	3.2	1.5	2.9	1.7	1.8	2.1	0.6	1.6
printing, publishing and other	3.9	2.9	6.2	1.9	3.9	3.8	3.4	6.5	1.7	3.7
total	100.0	100.0	100.0	100.0	100.0	100.0	100.0	100.0	100.0	100.0

Source: Based on ISTAT, 1974 and 1973.

and intermediate goods such as chemicals, plastics, and iron and steel that were necessary as inputs for the equipment goods sectors.

These changes in the structure of the industrial system and the development of technologically advanced and internationally competitive industries in these sectors can be attributed to several factors. International agreements and the import of technology and of methods of economic regulation that had been developed in the USA were among them. But also of importance was the impact of a number of national economic policies and the political decisions on which they were based. In this context it has been pointed out by Pizzorno (1981: 110–11) that, in the reconstruction of the Italian economy, several alternative models of development could have been chosen. One could opt for a type of development in which consumption would have been relatively controlled while resources were channelled particularly toward investment goods. But it would have led to an expansion of the working class in the industrial sector and a slower exodus from the countryside, with rural emigrants moving into the industrial rather than the tertiary sector. Or one could choose a type of development in which consumer goods were produced mainly for export, with wages being held down, and internal demand for individual consumption goods coming from a group of middle strata and especially from 'the urban, bureaucratic and professional rentier sector.' In this case the development of working-class categories in the industrial sector would be retarded, while the exodus from the countryside and the development of the tertiary sector would be strong.

The model that was chosen was the second one, in part because of international constraints, but also because of the relative political strength of different groups and the role of the middle strata in the strategy of consensus pursued by Christian Democracy, while the adoption of this strategy was one of the factors which explained why the hopes that Gramsci had entertained about the impact of Fordism were not to be realized (Gramsci 1971).

The decision to retain and extend the system of state shareholding inherited from the fascist decades and to encourage large-scale investments by the state shareholding companies in sectors producing basic intermediate goods and energy was another important factor. On the one hand, it underlay the dynamic growth of the steel and of the oil and chemical industries, and it enabled Italian firms to purchase these products at highly competitive prices on the domestic market. The expansion of these industries was given a major impetus by the provision of capital grants and subsidized loans for investments in these sectors in the Mezzogiorno from the late 1950s onward. The new regional policies introduced with Italian entry into the newly formed EEC in 1957 were accordingly used to promote a form of industrial development that would play an important role in the process of national economic expansion. What was more the managers of state industry were to play a major part in the new social bloc constructed around Christian Democracy (Pinnarò & Pugliese 1979, Pugliese 1979).

The ability of the oligopolistic export and export-related equipment goods sectors to compete successfully on export markets for those manufactured goods experiencing the most rapid rates of growth of demand was also in part due to the existence of widespread marginal employment in backward sectors and regions and to high levels of unemployment. The availability of large pools of labor in the northern and southern countrysides and the elasticity with which it moved to centers of modern industry ensured that wages grew more slowly than labor productivity, and that the share of profits in national income increased until the end of the economic miracle in the early 1960s.

A second element contributing to the low costs of reproduction of labor power was the extremely restricted development and level of satisfaction of human social needs. The domestic market for modern consumer goods was restricted outside the ranks of the middle classes by low wages and a regressive tax system. As a result the home market continued to be supplied to a large extent by traditional consumption good industries. Only in the early 1960s, when wages were pushed upwards, did the situation alter. In addition, the levels of provision of collective goods such as public housing, public transport, health, and educational facilities were extremely inadequate.

The insertion of the South and of Italy in the national and international divisions of labor were based on conditions which could not, however, be maintained indefinitely. Indeed, the pattern of economic expansion and the economic policies pursued by the state resulted in the reproduction and accentuation of economic and social disequilibria that eventually brought the process of export-led growth to an end, and contributed to a protracted economic and social crisis.

Most importantly, the process of externally oriented accumulation depended on working-class weakness. But by the early 1960s the growth process had led to a level, composition, and distribution of the demand for labor that reduced unemployment to very low levels and created labor shortages. As a result the positions of the northern working class and of the trade union movement were strengthened.

The years of crisis can be divided up into various stages. In 1964–9 deflation was the main instrument in a conflict with the trade union movement. At the same time a program of reforms was developed with the intention of rationalizing the economic system and eliminating some of the bottlenecks to growth. In the end these years proved to be ones of class stalemate. The forces pressing for reforms were unable to build a new social bloc and to achieve real political hegemony and yet were capable of disturbing any alternative plan.

With the 'hot autumn' a new phase was ushered in in which the distribution of income moved sharply in favor of employees and dependent workers. The rate of profit fell, and in the state sector and in private firms in the chemical industry large losses were made. In the South, to the problems of a lack of industrialization were added the problems of 'old industrialization,' while at a political level deep conflicts emerged between the state holding companies and semi-public firms in sectors with a high capital intensity and the private firms in the export-oriented engineering sectors.

In 1973 another turning point occurred in Italy and also in the West where the postwar order was finally destroyed. In part because of the rise in oil rents, a balance of payments deficit was recorded in Italy, and the currency was floated along with those of other Western economies. At this stage the economy found itself in a vicious circle of a falling exchange rate and runaway inflation (Aglietta 1982: 24–5).

Conclusion: a regime of intensive accumulation and monopolistic regulation?

In the first section it was shown how industrial development has occurred in southern Italy without a significant growth of industrial employment and how new types of dependency associated with increasing net transfers to the region's inhabitants have emerged. The second problem is related to the structure of the tax system and the Italian state's inability to finance desired levels of spending without recourse to large-scale borrowing. But also involved was the trajectory of the southern economy itself. In the second section I accordingly went on to explain the characteristics of the process of industrial investment, while in the third the composition and timing of investment were related to the model of Italian economic and political development.

The model of Italian development is, of course, specific to Italian society, as are many of its determinations. But through a process of abstraction some elements and some determinations shared with other societies can also be identified. Included are the main elements of a more general regime of accumulation which characterized the development of the national economies of the West after World War II as well as the mechanisms governing the mode of functioning of a capitalist society.

In this concluding section some elements that can be discerned in the first of these steps in the development of a more general analysis of the macro-economics of Italian growth will be identified: a more detailed exposition which moves in the opposite direction from the abstract to the concrete is presented in Dunford (1986), while the interpretation of Italian development presented in this study is, it should be noted, a product of processes of empirical and theoretical work involving movements in both directions.

Underpinning the growth of the Italian economy after 1945 is in fact an unequal diffusion of a regime of intensive accumulation and a system of monopolistic regulation. With the extension and generalization of Taylorism and Fordism and an emphasis on the production of goods capable of being produced in long runs and of yielding considerable scale economies, productivity increased rapidly. Yet the growth of capacity to produce goods and services and the emergence of new sectors producing vehicles and durable household equipment goods came up against limits of demand: in the 1930s consumption of these products was largely confined to the relatively prosperous middle strata. As a result a deep crisis occurred.

After World War II and after a phase of reconstruction, a new wave of very fast growth occurred. On this occasion wages increased along with productivity. The share of household budgets devoted to items other than food and necessary subsistence goods fell. As a result demand increased in line with the expansion of production capacity. Mass consumption emerged as a corollary of mass production. And the conditions of existence of major sections of the skilled and semi-skilled wage-earning class were transformed.

The transformation of the spheres of consumption and reproduction did not merely supply outlets for new types of consumer goods and enable a harmonization of the development of the two departments of production. Workers suited to the new kinds of production and capable of preserving and reproducing the skills and attitudes they required were needed. As Gramsci pointed out, the development of Fordism was associated, first, with attempts to transform the structure of society and to select and develop new types of worker with 'new, more complex and rigid norms or habits of order, exactitude and precision,' and, secondly, with high wages which were necessary to restore the strength and energy worn down by forms of work that were more wearing and exhausting and that demanded new levels of expenditure of muscular and, in particular, of nervous energy (see Gramsci 1971: 294–7, 298–306, 310–13).

The renewal of the opportunities for investment that resulted was eventually to be accompanied by a spectacular development of industries linked to the transformation of the conditions of production (i.e. production of machinery and durable producer goods) and enlargement of the sphere of consumption (i.e. production of housing and of cars and household equipment), and of process industries connected with the supply of energy and intermediate goods. A space for the expansion of those industries on which Italian growth was based was accordingly created at the same time as other related developments occurred in older-established industrial sectors, in services, and in the sphere of domestic life.

After the war, then, the crisis conditions of the 1930s did not recur. Instead a wave of almost unprecedented growth occurred. What was it that differentiated the years after World War II from those that preceded it? What had emerged were new principles of regulation of economic and social life. Out of the conflicts between classes and political groups, the strategies of organized social movements, and political processes unfolding within the state itself, were developed a set of institutional forms within which individual and collective action were to occur. In the West the new social framework was one whose roots lay in the defeat of an old style of conservatism and of fascism and in a more general adoption of some of the social and institutional reforms foreshadowed by the 'New Deal'.

Of these developments one of the most important was a collective contractualization of the direct wage and a linking of wages with productivity and the cost of living (see Aglietta 1979: 66–72, Lipietz 1984: 6–7). The exact situation did, however, differ from one country to another and one industry to another: in Italy the wage relation was generalized, but in comparison with other countries wages were at first held down, and the home market was dominated by middle strata who played an important part in the consensus-forming strategy of the Christian Democrat Party. At the same time the international economic environment was undergoing a transformation with the establishment of a new hierarchy of national economies headed by that of the United States: US technology was exported, as was the US cultural model, while a set of important international institutions were established including the Marshall Fund, the OEEC, GATT, and the IMF.

In these internal and external conditions Italian development was export-led, and with the emergence of relations of complementarity between virtuous circles of growth was rapid until 1964 (see Aglietta 1982). But just as some aspects of Italian growth can be explained by this type of argument, so can some aspects of the crisis that followed. In the industrial sector the crisis is rooted in a crisis of Taylorism and Fordism. Out of that conclusion emerges an interpretation of the changes in the geography of Italian society that have resulted as in part a product of the transformation in the sphere of work and in the wage-relation that a crisis of a preceding regime of accumulation and system of regulation have induced.

References

Aglietta, M. 1979. *A theory of capitalist regulation: the US experience*. London: New Left Books.

Aglietta, M. 1982. World capitalism in the eighties. *New Left Review* **136** (Nov.– Dec.), 5–41.

Aglietta, M. and R. Boyer, 1983. *Poles de competivité, stratégie industrielle et politique macroéconomique*. Paris: Cepremap.

Amin, A. 1982. La ristrutturazione alla Fiat e il decentramento produttivo nel Mezzogiorno. *Archivo di Studi Urbani e Regionali*, ns = new series **13–14**, 47–88.

Bagnasco, A. 1977. *Tre Italie. La problematica territoriale dello sviluppo Italiano*. Bologna: Il Mulino.

Boyer, R. 1978. Les salaires en longue période. *Economie et Statistique* **103** (Sept.), 27–57.

Boyer, R. and J. Mistral 1978. *Accumulation, inflation, crises*. Paris: Presses Universitaires de France.

Del Monte, A. and A. Giannola 1978. *Il Mezzogiorno nell'economia Italiana*. Bologna: Il Mulino.

Dunford, M. 1986. *Social reproduction and spatial inequality* London: Pion, forthcoming.

Dunford, M. and D. Perrons 1983. *The arena of capital*. London: Macmillan.

Garofoli, G. 1978. Decentramento produttivo, mercato del lavoro e localizzazione industriale. In G. Garofoli (ed.), *Ristrutturazione industriale e territorio*. Milan: Franco Angeli.

Giannola, A. 1982. Industrializzazione, dualismo e dependenza economica del Mezzogiorno negli anni '70. *Economia Pubblica* **1**, 65–90.

Gramsci, A. 1971. Americanism and Fordism. In *Selections from the prison notebooks*, 279–318. London: Lawrence Wishart.

Gramsci, A. 1978. Some aspects of the southern question. In *Selections from political writings 1921–26*, 441–62. London: Lawrence & Wishart.

Graziani, A. (ed.) 1972. *L'economia Italiana: 1945–70*. Bologna: Il Mulino.

Graziani, A. 1978. The Mezzogiorno in the Italian economy. *Camb. J. Econ.* **2**(4), 355–72.

Graziani, A. 1979. Il Mezzogiorno nel quadro dell'economia Italiana. In A. Graziani and E. Pugliese (eds.), *Investimenti e disoccupazione nel Mezzogiorno*, Ch. 1. Bologna: Il Mulino.

ISTAT 1973. *Occupati presenti in Italia 1951–72*. Rome: ISTAT.

ISTAT 1974. *Annuario di Contabilità Nazionale 1973*. Rome: ISTAT.

Lipietz, A. 1979. *Inflation et crises: Pourquoi?* Paris: François Maspero.

Lipietz, A. 1982a. Towards global Fordism? *New Left Review* **132** (March–April), 33–47.

Lipietz, A. 1982b. The so-called 'transformation problem' revisited. *J. Econ. Theory* **26**(1), 59–88.

Lipietz, A. 1984. *L'audace ou l'enlisement*. Paris: François Maspero.

Marx, K. 1976. *Capital: a critique of political economy*, vol. 1. Harmondsworth: Penguin.

Mistral, J. 1982. La diffusion internationale de l'accumulation intensive et sa crise. In J. L. Reiffers (ed.), *Economie et finance internationales*, pp. 205–37. Paris: Economica.

O'Connor, J. 1973. *The fiscal crisis of the state*. New York: St. Martin's Press.

Pinnarò, G. and E. Pugliese 1979. Changes in the social structure of southern Italy. *Int. J. Urban Regional Res.* **3**(4), 492–515.

Pizzorno, A. 1981. Middle strata and the mechanisms of consensus. In D. Pinto (ed.), *Contemporary Italian sociology: a reader*. Cambridge: Cambridge University Press, and Paris: Editions de la Maison des Sciences de L'Homme.

Podbielski, A. 1976. *Twenty-five years of special action for the development of southern Italy*. Milan: Giuffre.

Pugliese, E. 1979. Evoluzione della struttura di classe nel Mezzogiorno. In *Investimenti e disoccupazione nel Mezzogiorno*, A. Graziani and E. Pugliese (eds.). Ch. 2. Bologna: Il Mulino.

12

Unequal integration in global fordism: the case of Ireland

DIANE PERRONS

The development and extended reproduction of capitalism is associated with the profound and continuous transformation of cities and regions. But while it is the development of capitalism, its fundamental drives and structure of priorities which are responsible for these changes, there is no simple shaping of the world after its own image. The way in which the regions of the world are penetrated and subsequently incorporated into the world capitalist sphere varies, and these different regions then share very unequally in the gains in wealth and productivity that the progressive nature of capitalist production makes possible. This chapter is concerned with the role played by Ireland in the international division of labor that has been established since 1945. This period was initially characterized by growth based on the development of a regime of intensive accumulation but subsequently by relative stagnation as this regime of growth went into crisis.

Ireland and the old international division of labor

From the 1940s until the early 1960s Ireland was a relatively backward, under-developed economy with limited industrialization and a low rate of economic growth. The population, which was declining, experienced low levels of mass private and collective consumption. These conditions arose from the underdevelopment of Ireland during the period of British colonial rule and from the largely unsuccessful attempt to develop an autonomous growth path from the early 1930s.

For several centuries Ireland was a colony of Britain. Before the industrial revolution legislation was enacted to prevent Irish industries from competing with those in Britain. It was clear that Ireland's role was to be a subordinate one, limited to producing products which required little processing and which would be complementary to those produced in Britain. With the introduction of more sophisticated labor processes such as manufacture and machino-facture in the 19th century, the material competitive superiority of the British products was sufficient to undermine and eliminate many of the industries that had been established in Ireland, and restrictive legislation was no longer necessary. In the agricultural sphere the internal expansion and intensification of arable production especially in eastern and southern England and later on the import of wheat and other arable produce from the Americas meant that Ireland's role became one of supplying labor-extensive primary agricultural commodities such as sheep and cattle to the British market. This led to the transformation of a major part of Irish territory into little more than a sheepwalk and cattle pasture, with the displaced population becoming industrial and military recruits for the expanding British economy and empire (Marx 1976). At various times the indigenous Catholic population was not even guaranteed a marginal existence. The country was consequently characterized by population decline through emigration and starvation, and also by political unrest which took the form of a nationalist movement culminating in a limited victory for the indigenous bourgeoisie. The country was partitioned, and after a decade the bourgeoisie in the independent southern state adopted a strategy of autonomous growth through import-substitution. Although this had been part of the philosophy of one of the nationalist parties, Sinn Fein, it was a strategy followed by many other countries in the 1930s, both developing countries trying to establish some form of independent development and developed countries experiencing industrial crisis. In the case of Ireland, as indeed for many other countries, this strategy failed to produce the basis for the development of a strong internal industrial sector capable of producing goods for both the domestic and foreign markets and for providing the foundations of economic modernization.

In general terms Lipietz argues that these import substitution strategies failed because 'neither in the labour process itself nor in the structure of demand had the social conditions for such a system of accumulation really been achieved.' More specifically, countries pursuing these strategies were affected by a shift in the terms of trade against raw material exports which had been used to finance the import of equipment goods, and by the failure to obtain the same levels of productivity as in the already industrialized countries, partly owing to the lack of industrial experience on the part of the labor force but also as a consequence of the limited size of the internal market, which in its own right also constrained the extent of industrialization (Lipietz 1982: 40–1). This limitation was particularly important in the Irish case.

Many firms, especially British ones, established themselves behind the tariff walls to supply only the Irish market, and consequently they remained small with limited productivity levels. In some instances, expansion beyond this level was prohibited by the licenses under which production took place, thereby negating the logic underlying the protection policy but reflecting the desire of the firms involved not to compete with their other branches elsewhere. Thus the industrial policy led to a superimposition of a highly protected, small-scale industrial sector on to an economy dominated by the primary export sector. Although industrial employment increased this was not sufficient to offset the decline in agricultural employment. Emigration continued and the concentration of Dublin as the main focus of economic activity grew. Irish capital continued to be exported to obtain higher profit levels elsewhere and it was consequently left to the state, which was prepared to accept lower returns, to finance much of the industrial investment that did take place.

World War II did not bring about a significant expansion of economic activity and initially Ireland did not share in the postwar economic boom. Conditions of low growth, poverty and emigration remained and there was considerable political unrest. The Fianna Fáil government was displaced and replaced by a succession of coalition governments, until Fianna Fáil was returned to power in 1957. The coalition governments tried a number of strategies aimed at stimulating growth. Various institutions were established to encourage industrial investment and to arrange finance for industry, and tax concessions were granted to exporting firms. However, the costs of these policies tended to fall on the working classes in the form of lower social and money wages, thereby in some ways recreating the dissatisfaction which initially gave rise to the policies.

In 1958 there was a formal reversal of strategy. Protection was abandoned and the Irish economy was opened to foreign investment and competition. The state began to play a more explicit role in the management of the economy, through the introduction of formal planning and through higher levels of expenditure. State expenditure was increased in order to provide improved industrial infrastructure, incentives for international firms and aid for restructuring within the indigenous industrial sector. The levels of spending on welfare, health, education and housing were also increased. It was recognized that some of the indigenous firms would be unable to survive in international conditions of competition, but thought that the development of a smaller but truly competitive Irish industrial sector, together with the development of a foreign sector and an expanded agricultural sector (which would follow from the existence of wider markets) would provide a more satisfactory platform from which to generate economic growth and to raise living standards such that the continuing loss of population might be halted (Meenan 1970).

Clearly at this time the Irish economy was in severe difficulties and its viability as an economic unit was threatened. However, it is too simplistic to attribute the transformation of the Irish economy and society which undoubtedly took place in the following two decades to this change of strategy alone. On the one hand it was not in reality such a radical departure from existing strategies, and on the other hand such developments were not unique to Ireland. Consequently it is necessary to pay attention to the changing world economic conditions within which the transformation of Ireland has taken place, and especially to the forces which gave rise to the rapid expansion of world economic activity which occurred at this time.

The development of a regime of intensive accumulation or fordism

In the postwar period many Western capitalist economies experienced unprecedented and sustained levels of growth. Underlying this wave of growth were new sources of energy and new methods of production. These methods, which included the introduction of 'scientific management' or 'Taylorism' and the flow-line principle of Henry Ford, were particularly important in the newly developing consumer goods industries, and they raised labor productivity so that real wages and profits could rise simultaneously. These developments enabled a link to be established between the sphere of production and the sphere of consumption so that some of the obstacles to and instabilities within the accumulation process were overcome at least for a while (Aglietta 1979, Dunford & Perrons 1983).

The higher levels of productivity obtained in the new labor processes of fordism and scientific management enabled real incomes to rise without affecting profitability. Consequently, workers found their incomes and jobs were more secure and they were able to purchase the new commodities either directly or through the growing number of lending institutions. Thus the internal markets in these countries were expanded significantly, giving rise to an internal generator of growth. At the same time the higher levels of profitability that were obtained meant that capitalists were keen to invest and financial institutions were prepared to advance money to them. In other words, the linked development of production and reproduction, which was supported by the state through the introduction of keynesian demand management policies and by increased expenditure on general conditions of production, collective consumption and welfare, gave rise to a new stability in the economic system. Thus money was advanced in the production process, the surplus value contained in the commodities produced was realized and the accumulation process continued in an outward spiral of growth. Production and reproduction were linked, a balance between the departments of production was internally secured, and harmonious and rapid growth ensued (Aglietta 1979).

The reproduction sphere in fact played a triple role. First, as stated, the growth of income linked with the productivity increases raised the spending power of the working class. Thus they were increasingly able to purchase cars, consumer goods and housing and by so doing they provided an outlet for the higher levels of production. At the same time many of these purchases were financed through loans and it has been argued that the extension of long-term credit to the working class enhanced their regularity and reliability at work. This in turn was essential for the efficient operation of the larger-scale and higher-cost production processes. Finally, work in these new processes was more intense and less varied. Consequently, there were few opportunities at work for recuperation or self-expression. Thus the sphere of reproduction was important both for reconstituting workers' abilities and energies and for providing an outlet for human creativity.

The reproduction of individuals, however, did not take place purely within the private market place. The state provided increased levels of social security in order to enable workers to maintain some income and therefore expenditure in times of unemployment. The state also provided supportive conditions for the higher levels of private consumption, for example, by housing subsidies and road building. Moreover, it was left to the state to finance part of the reproduction of the working class in the form of collective consumption goods, for example, health and education (O'Connor 1973, Aglietta 1979).

The actual form of state provision in these respects varied from country to country, reflecting different political traditions and different economic structures. Likewise the patterns of national growth diverged. In general the levels of growth were very rapid in Japan, Germany and France while countries such as the UK, the US and Belgium experienced lower levels of growth. In the case of Ireland the late 1940s and 1950s were years of very low growth and of high emigration to the comparatively faster-growing British economy[1]. It was not until the 1960s that growth rates in Ireland reached those of other European countries. Then other firms, initially British, began to set up units in Ireland on an increased scale. This may have reflected an overspill of growth from Britain as in some respects the economies of Britain and Ireland operated as a single entity, that is, with production taking place for a shared market. However, in Ireland the rate of growth continued at a relatively high level into the 1970s (Blackwell 1983: 43–4, Rottman & O'Connell 1982: 65)[2], whereas in many of the other countries declining growth rates were experienced from the mid 1960s when the regime of intensive accumulation on which the postwar growth had been based itself went into crisis.

The reasons for the ending of the wave of growth in Western Europe and America lie mainly in the exhaustion of the possibilities for raising labor productivity and profitability within the fordist labor processes in the production of mass private consumption goods. There were both technical and social problems. With the prevailing production techniques, productive time was wasted owing to the existence of unavoidable gaps between the different partial operations on the production line. Aglietta refers to this as the balance delay time. At the same time attempts to increase productivity by raising the intensity of work met with resistance from the working class, whose strength or bargaining position had been enhanced by the years of growth and full or near full employment. Moreover, this tendency toward declining productivity and profitability occurred simultaneously with an increase in international competition and rivalry occasioned by the successful reconstruction of the West German and Japanese economies in particular, and by the establishment of increasingly open trading conditions. Thus profitability began to decline and the incentives to advance money in the production sphere were weakened (Aglietta 1979).

In the production of mass collective consumption goods, also an integral part of the growth process, fordist labor processes were often not applicable. This meant that the costs of production of these goods had increased relative to those of private consumption. While it was possible to finance these costs in periods of expanding profitability this was no longer possible when profitability began to decline, and thus the production of these goods and services also ceased to expand (see below).

However, the responses made by units of capital to the declining levels of profitability in the central economies were conducive to the location of production units in peripheral economies. On the one hand existing production processes could often be established and operated profitably there, owing to the existence of lower overall wage costs, that is, lower social and money wages and less worker resistance expressed in terms of lower levels of absenteeism and higher quality products. On the other hand, the introduction of the more automated or neo-fordist labor processes, based on electronic information systems with automatic feedback mechanisms to counter the problem of the balance delay time and worker resistance, meant that locations in peripheral areas were technically possible. The new units of production typically had lower degrees of internal interdependence, that is, they carried out a smaller range of more integrated tasks. They required quickly obtained and firm-specific skills rather than general ones and employed a smaller number of workers relative to the level of output produced. Thus it was possible to establish small units of production in geographical isolation from other plants belonging to the same company (Aglietta 1979).

With these changes the material foundations are laid for a new wave of economic growth. Whether this takes place or not clearly depends on a whole range of specific conditions. However, when production is profoundly reorganized in this way then location decisions may arise and the conditions prevailing in peripheral economies proved to be attractive to many companies. Ireland as an internal periphery was particularly attractive. As far as the general conditions of production, legal practices, trade relations and industrial customs and so on are concerned, there were few differences from advanced economies and yet some of the conditions more characteristic of peripheral economies were also found. For example, government incentives were at a high level, wages were comparatively low and large amounts of space could be found for new developments (Perrons 1981, OECD 1982: 22).

From the early 1970s Ireland, which had by this time become a member of the EEC, began to attract an increasing number of branch plants of multinational enterprises. The reason for this lay in the combined effect of the change conditions of accumulation found at the center, together with the specific conditions found in Ireland at this time. However, having attracted some of the most modern firms in the world to Ireland does not mean that Ireland will be able to embark on a harmonious growth path like the one that was experienced in Europe in the 1950s and 1960s. This would depend crucially on the nature of the capitals attracted to Ireland and on their relationships with the domestic sector. Thus it is necessary first of all to examine the nature of the domestic industrial sector and outline its response to the establishment of open trading conditions that were a prerequisite for the attraction of foreign capital.

The industrialization of Ireland

The domestic industrial sector[3]

With the opening of the Irish economy in the 1960s and 1970s it was recognized that many Irish firms would have difficulty in remaining viable. Adaptation councils were established in an attempt to assist the rationalization of these firms such that a domestic presence might be preserved.

However, many firms seemed to be unwilling to participate in such schemes and although many firms survived until the early 1970s, since then there has been import penetration on a massive scale resulting in considerable numbers of job losses, especially in the traditional industrial regions. Even where rationalization did take place it has not guaranteed survival[4].

In the case of the textile and clothing sectors much of the indigenous industry has been replaced on the one hand by foreign plants operating in Ireland, often predominantly for export markets, and on the other hand by imports of foreign goods. In fact the level of import penetration in clothing has increased from 27% of the domestic market in 1973 to 66% in 1980. In the same period more than 10 000 jobs were lost in the textile, clothing and footwear sectors. These industries have been referred to as those subject to 'low wage competition' and Irish production has been undermined by the products of newly industrializing countries whose industries have been able to combine new technology with very low wage costs (NESC 1982: 87–94, 300; see also Table 12.1)[5].

Table 12.1 Import penetration in Irish 'traditional' industries, 1973 and 1978.

| | Imports as a percentage of domestic consumption | |
	1973	1978
clothing	27	61
hosiery	31	61
footwear	37	66
textiles	64	67

Source: NESC 1982: 300.

Nevertheless, the domestic industrial sector as a whole still accounts for two-thirds of manufacturing employment; three-quarters of employment in domestic industry is found in the traditional sectors of food, clothing and footwear, cement and glass, paper and packaging, textiles, wood and furniture, and drink and tobacco, and only one-quarter is found in newer industries such as metals and engineering which have expanded considerably in recent years (NESC 1982: 86).

Both the shake-out of firms within sectors, and the albeit limited sectoral shift from traditional to modern industry, would seem to correspond to the modernization of the Irish industrial system that had been desired from the late 1950s. Indeed, there has been a considerable expansion of some Irish firms. The growth of Jefferson Smurfit in paper and packaging and of Cement Roadstone in construction materials are striking examples. However, it has been argued that at a deeper level of analysis the changes that have taken place are not sufficient to produce an industrial sector capable of leading to rising living standards for an expanding population and of promoting long-term growth (NESC 1982: 87). This view, which has been put forward by many writers, especially those on the left, was supported by the findings of a report produced by the Telesis Consultancy Group and published by the

National Economic and Social Council (NESC). This report (hereafter referred to as the Telesis report) represents one of the most comprehensive studies of the Irish industrial sector carried out in recent years.

In the report a distinction is drawn between traded and non-traded sectors. The former refers to firms producing goods which are typically traded internationally or are at least subject to international competition, and the latter to firms producing goods which for mainly logistical reasons are sold locally. This categorization provides an indication of the growth potential of particular firms or sectors. As far as the Irish economy is concerned, the major expansions of indigenous industry that have taken place have been in the non-traded sector. The long-term growth of these firms will therefore be largely dependent on the growth of firms in the traded sector[6] or on the growth of the domestic consumer market. Thus rather than being initiators of growth impulses these firms are in fact dependent upon growth elsewhere in the economy. Some indigenous firms do in fact produce traded goods, but many of these exports go to Northern Ireland or to the west coast of Britain. In paper and packaging, for example, 85% of exports are for the UK market, and in furniture the figure is 95%; it is possible that these exports owe more to geographical proximity than to competitive advantage (NESC 1982: 87–9).

For long-term industrial growth, however, it has been argued that the development of Irish firms trading outside Ireland in 'complex factor cost' operations (that is operations where competition is dependent on more than labor costs and which are more often found in other developed economies) are essential, but that Ireland's present industrial strategy is not really contributing to this end in either the indigenous or the foreign sector. With reference to the former it has been found that of the Irish exports that are fully subject to international competition 80% come from the top 100 Irish exporting firms, of which 95% were established before 1967 (NESC 1982)[7].

Clearly Irish firms are constrained by the size of the internal market, especially in the case of textiles where competitiveness can only be secured via long production runs. Even in non-basic goods, the introduction of new electronic and automated technology has enabled faster set-up times and greater flexibility, enabling larger-scale capitals to enter niches of production formerly occupied by small-scale firms focusing on quality products. Ireland neither has the advantage of large-scale capitals capable of this kind of investment nor the web of interlinked firms which can together realize economies of scale, as for example Prato in Italy. It has been argued that to generate indigenous firms capable of engaging in complex factor cost businesses and of exporting their products, the blanket subsidies of the Industrial Development Authority should in part be replaced by assistance to those operators attempting to market their produce abroad. But even with some form of assistance in this respect the problems faced by potential Irish exporters such as marketing and distribution would be considerable. Moreover, large amounts of capital would be required for the retooling of production equipment necessary to meet American or European design and measurement standards. These investments would be very risky and it would be difficult for most Irish firms to obtain the necessary finance even if the investments were thought to be viable. There have been a few successes in high quality products, for example, Waterford Crystal, and in some woollen products, but these are exceptions (NESC 1982: 99–101)[8].

The foreign-owned manufacturing sector

While the domestic industrial system has been transformed to some extent over the last two decades, many small firms using outmoded practices remain. It was on this foundation that from the late 1960s and early 1970s US, European and Japanese capitals came to Ireland and established larger plants using taylorist and fordist labor processes giving rise to the super-imposition of a more modern industrial system[9].

The foreign sector has a presence in both the modern and traditional industrial sectors with mechanical engineering, electrical and electronic engineering, food, drink and tobacco and textiles being the most important in terms of their share of employment (NESC 1982: 134; see Table 12.2)[10]. The foreign sector now accounts for one-third of Irish manufacturing employment compared to only one-quarter in 1973. This increased share represents a net increase of over 22000 jobs, while in the domestic sector in the same period there was only an increase of 2000 jobs. While these gains are not unimpressive, given the prolonged world economic crisis, they tend to disguise the potentially unstable nature of employment in the foreign sector. These gains were in fact made up of an addition of 12400 jobs to existing companies and 26500 jobs created by new ones. They were offset by 16800 jobs losses, in other words 29% of jobs in foreign companies existing in 1973 had been lost to the economy by 1981 (NESC 1982: 134).

Overall, then, manufacturing employment has increased in Ireland. In the domestic sectors the gains exceeded the jobs lost but in the foreign sector

Table 12.2 Employment in foreign-owned manufacturing industries in Ireland, 1973 and 1980.

Sector	Employment (thousands of people)		Change (%)
	1973	1980	
food, drink and tobacco	11.1	11.1	0
textiles	5.3	9.3	4.0
clothing	5.3	4.6	−0.7
wood, furniture, paper and printing	2.5	2.5	0
chemicals and pharmaceuticals	5.6	8.6	3.0
glass, clay and cement	0.9	1.5	0.6
mechanical engineering	14.7	18.6	3.9
electrical and electronic engineering	5.1	10.3	5.2
other	8.6	13.7	5.1
total	58.1	80.2	22.1

Source: NESC 1982: 360.

there was a more significant increase in employment. The resulting changes in industrial employment exhibit significant regional variations. Many of the old firms were concentrated in Dublin and the east, and, although this area has received a proportion of all new industry, some of the new plants have been established in the remoter parts of Ireland, such as the south and southwest, and even in the most underdeveloped areas of the west and northwest, such as Mayo and Donegal, where as a consequence overall employment in manufacturing has increased.

In the textile sector and in assembly type operations such as pharmaceutical products, female employment has been particularly important. As Lipietz has argued, women's exploited role in household production has prepared them for the twin requirements of taylorist industry: complete acquiescence in the goals of the labor process, and complete involvement in the job (Lipietz 1982: 42). In the case of Ireland, patriarchy has been given added depth by the practices of the Catholic church, and as a result the ambivalent attitude toward paid work held by many women has been reinforced. Not only does this fact further their acquiescence to the demands of the production line and reinforce the position of male supervisors, but it also accounts for the failure of women workers to press for improvements in working conditions such as crèche provision, maternity leave or even equal pay. The fact that male workers who tend to occupy positions of power in the unions hold similar views about the status and role of women means that these issues rarely become a matter of union concern. Accordingly the subordinate position of women in the work-force is reinforced yet further, and, as the concerns of the union are frequently not those of women workers, in time they come to view the union as part of the company rather than their own worker-based organization. 'Sweetheart agreements' and the way in which union structures and working conditions are established prior to the arrival of the workers tends to reinforce this particular situation (Harris 1983). Nevertheless the presence of these industries has had some progressive effects. In an area such as Donegal or Mayo the future for women in the 1950s and 1960s was marriage, fairly isolated work for a small employer, or emigration. Now it is possible for some women to become involved in relatively highly paid contractual work outside the home but in their local areas.

Access to paid work provides an independent source of money which in capitalism is the means of entry to the social world or to the world of commodities, and this in itself is a source of power. In fact much of the money is spent on items of low-level conspicuous consumption such as clothing and on household adornments which represent a display of the 'good housekeeper' or 'good woman'. The means by which the finance is obtained remains, however, undiscussed or socially hidden: 'the bad woman works.' But even some financial independence represents a move in a progressive direction.

In fact the involvement of women in paid work has given rise to both inter-gender and inter-class tensions. An illustration is provided by the fairly recent protests by workers subject to PAYE (Pay As You Earn, a form of taxation where tax is deducted at source by the employer from the employee's wages) about the unequal incidence of taxation and in particular about the discrepancy between the level of taxation of PAYE contributors and of farmers. In Mayo, where there are several branch plant operations, there was a demonstration in Ballina, a town of 7500, in which 7000 people took part. It is said, however, that many women, some of whom were or would soon be related to farmers, shielded themselves from the cameras (Harris 1983).

Despite the increases in manufacturing output and exports in the past two decades it has been argued that the foreign sector in Ireland does not really provide a satisfactory basis for the long-term industrial growth. Although there have been gains in employment, there has been a large disparity between the number of jobs approved and the numbers actually created (see Table 12.3) and the employment that has been created has in general been of a low quality[11]. Moreover the linkages that have been established between the foreign and domestic sectors have been few and consequently the foreign sector has not acted as a catalyst for the initiation of a virtuous cycle of cumulative growth. For example, only 8% of the components and subassemblies used by the largest foreign sector, engineering, were sourced in Ireland in 1976 (NESC 1982: 114). In general the survey carried out by Telesis found that Irish firms had difficulty in being cost competitive and in meeting the degree of quality and sophistication required by the foreign firms. These difficulties arose primarily from the small-scale nature of many Irish operations, the limited internal division of labor that existed within them[12] and the lack of an industrial tradition in Ireland[13]. In other words it was not purely a question of the foreign branch plants using their pre-existing international supply networks, although there are many instances where firms would probably prefer this option, for even in the case of domestic industry the degree of internal sourcing was only in the order of 18% (NESC 1982: 114–19).

Table 12.3 Sustainable job creations and job approvals for foreign firms in Ireland, 1970–8 and 1981.

Sector	Job approvals 1970–8 (I)	Jobs created and still existing in 1981 (II)	Job creations as a proportion of job approvals (II/I)
mechanical engineering	24665	4127	16.7
electrical engineering	20908	8793	42.1
chemicals	14529	5335	36.7
plastics	5449	1668	30.6
food, drink	4178	1025	24.5
tobacco, fertilizer	15901	6682	42.0
furniture, print and paper	2654	817	30.8
clay, glass, cement	1452	776	53.4
other	6290	1509	24.0
total	96026	28937	30.1

Source: Irish Business 1981.

Nevertheless, branch plants in Ireland do import the majority of their inputs, engage only in fairly routine production or assembly activities and export a major proportion of their output (see Table 12.4)[14]. In fact the foreign branch plants are using Ireland, which offers a shelter from taxation, relatively high capital incentives and relatively low-cost labor, primarily as a 'manufacturing satellite' for sales in the EEC (NESC 1982: 135)[15].

Table 12.4 Contrasting patterns of foreign investment in central and peripheral economies in Ireland.

	Employment in foreign-owned companies as a percentage of total employment	Foreign-owned companies' exports as a percentage of their production
Singapore	52 (1980)	90–95
Puerto Rico	73 (1980)	90–95
Ireland	34 (1980)	90–95
Belgium	33 (1978)	68
Germany	15 (1974)	17
Great Britain (including Scotland)	13 (1975)	38
USA	3 (1977)	7

Source: NESC 1982: 367.

Clearly if the objectives of the state's industrial strategy are simply to provide employment in the short term, then there is no divergence between the interests of the companies and those of the state. However, if the objective is to provide a platform for industrialization and economic development then it is not clear that these objectives will be achieved through the current wave of industrialization. The development of the electrical and electronics sector illustrates some of these more general points about the development of the foreign sector in Ireland. As a modern expanding sector providing considerable employment at different skill levels it was strongly sought after by the Industrial Development Authority, and some 70 branch plants have been established widely throughout Ireland, with clusters around Shannon and the Dublin periphery. In all about 10 000 people are employed (NESC 1982: 137).

In the case of the electrical equipment companies the firms present in Ireland are from the large groups which have manufacturing operations in many different countries and these are primarily engaged in assembly operations. In electronics the companies present are from the middle range of the world league table. Examples are Mostek and Fujitsu, which are ranked 15th and 21st in the world respectively. These firms are fast growing and profitable, but are often faced with cash shortages and for this reason find the government cash incentives particularly attractive. The leading firms tend to be located in the larger European countries (NESC 1982: 138–9).

However, the majority of electronic firms are manufacturing satellites, performing only assembly, testing and packaging functions and as such are vulnerable to competition from low-wage countries. Moreover they do not really provide the necessary basis for the development of a highly skilled work-force or for long-term growth[16]. Of the 60 firms interviewed by Telesis, none had a truly 'stand alone' capacity or autonomous status; they were all firmly integrated into the parent corporation and would have little authority to develop new products or designs which might lead to the generation of new firms in Ireland. In fact only three had operations in Ireland which contained key competitive elements such as product design including hardware and systems software. Most of the engineering functions in these firms were limited to product adaptation and marginal process improvements.

For these reasons, then, 'it is inaccurate to contend that Ireland is really participating in the heart of worldwide computer activities' (NESC 1982: 141). Despite the current levels of growth in the industry and the ensuing expansion of employment the fact that companies have not committed large amounts of fixed capital or located key competitive elements in Ireland, together with the fact that a well integrated sub-supply network has not been established, means that the industry will be very vulnerable to any shake-out that might occur in the future should the present expansionary phase go into decline (Perrons 1981, NESC 1982: 136–41).

Thus the industrialization that has taken place in Ireland is of a limited kind. Effectively Ireland operates as an export platform for those international firms seeking an entry into European markets. In this sense Ireland has advantages over other such export platforms, as for example in Southeast Asia, which to some extent may offset the inability to compete purely in terms of wage costs. In view of the small-scale nature of the internal market and the increasing interpenetration of national economies it is recognized that any form of development will to some extent be externally controlled. Nevertheless the sectoral and occupational structure of those foreign firms presently located in Ireland does not really provide a sound basis for long-term economic or social advance. Moreover the ability of the state to finance the present pattern of development and the rising levels of unemployment is increasingly uncertain.

State finances

In common with many other national and local states, Ireland is experiencing a fiscal crisis or, given its prolonged nature, what should perhaps be called sustained fiscal stress. State spending has been rising both in absolute terms and as a percentage of GNP, and the Irish state has had difficulty in financing these levels of expenditure.

As O'Connor and Aglietta have pointed out, increased levels of state expenditure formed an integral part of the regime of intensive accumulation. For a variety of reasons general conditions of production in an infrastructural sense had to be provided. The health care and education required to produce a healthy, literate, flexible, disciplined and differentiated working population were supplied with state help. Housing, which formed a vital part of the raised levels of consumption linked with the wave of growth, was supplied either directly by the state or with the help of state subsidization. At that same time the state had the task of providing a safety net for the casualties of the growth process as family and community networks broke down in increasingly atomized societies (O'Connor 1973, Aglietta 1979).

In the case of Ireland, state expenditure rose rapidly in the immediate postwar years as an attempt was made to raise the standards of general infrastructural conditions and social welfare to those of the UK. But in the 1950s balance of payments constraints led to the enforcement of high deflationary policies (Gould 1981, O'Malley 1981). From the late 1950s until the present, with Ireland's increased participation in the new regime of accumulation and experience of higher rates of growth, state expenditure rose rapidly (see Table 12.5). Capital expenditure, including infrastructure provision and aid to private industry administered through the IDA, has in fact risen faster than current expenditure. It increased from 25% of government expenditure in 1958 to 35% in 1978 (Gould 1981). In fact Ireland had a very high rate of gross domestic physical capital formation, increasing from 12% of GNP in 1958 to 30% in 1980 (McDowell 1982). But despite these higher levels of investment the rate of growth of productivity seems to have slowed down. Clearly the slackening of productivity growth is partly a consequence of the recession and the under-utilization of capacity. But the nature of the investments made in Ireland should also be considered, especially in view of the problem of finance.

Table 12.5 State expenditure in Ireland, 1958–78.

Year	Gross national product (GNP) at market prices	Public authorities' current spending (Cg)	Public authorities' capital spending (Kg)	G (Cg + Kg)	G/GNP%
1958	600.9	145.4	37.4	182.8	30
1962	783.8	196.2	58.8	255.0	33
1966	1073.9	303.6	83.1	386.7	36
1970	1648.5	546.1	157.7	703.8	43
1974	2968.5	1091.1	411.9	1503.1	51
1978	6403.4	2667.6	943.1	3610.7	56

Source: McDowell 1982: 184.

In Ireland the higher levels of state expenditure have increasingly been financed by incurring debts. As a result an increasing amount of the revenue raised by the government has to be used to pay interest charges and to repay outstanding debts. For example, in 1980 government expenditure exceeded government revenue by an amount equal to 14.5% of GNP. But in the same year the amount of government expenditure required for servicing the debt was equivalent to 80% of the total receipts from income tax (Kennedy 1981: 137). Moreover, as Kennedy has argued, the burden of debt is rising rapidly in relation to taxable capacity. He has pointed out that while in 1975 the service of debt in relation to non-agricultural wages and salaries was 11%, in 1981 it was in the order of 17%. As Kennedy goes on to say, expenditure on the basis of borrowing is not inherently problematical. Nor is the fact that an increasing proportion of exchequer borrowing has been from abroad. But if the resources so used do not yield returns in the form of new goods and services, which is the case at present, then the burden of taxation will increase, and where foreign borrowing is concerned there may also be a balance of payments problem. If the latter leads to a devaluation of the currency, the amount of Ireland's resources that will have to be used to service these debts will rise (Kennedy 1981: 140).

Given the scale of these problems considerable attention is paid in the literature to ways of either reducing state expenditure or of raising revenue. However, it is recognized that in view of the expanding population the state's budget must be balanced without damaging the growth potential of the economy or by increasing unemployment. The ways most commonly identified of reducing state expenditure are cuts in so-called 'unproductive' expenditures, of which particular attention is paid to public sector employees' pay (Kennedy 1981: 145–6). Other suggestions from more liberal writers are for the introduction of a wealth tax, the restoration of domestic rates and motor vehicle tax, a reduction of housing subsidies, which are regressive, and the introduction of charges for some government services, particularly higher education, which is also regressive (Kennedy 1981: 146, Rottman & O'Connell 1982: 82–3). Most suggestions for restoring a balance in the budget involve reduced living standards for working people. The industrial sector pays little or no tax, as minimal taxation is one of the incentives used to attract foreign industry, and for historical and political reasons the farming sector is also largely immune. However, as has already been pointed out, working people have strongly resisted the imposition of extra taxation or reduced living standards.

One of the root causes of fiscal stress at a general level lies in the fact that a considerable socialization of production has been accompanied by a privatization of the gains and a socialization of the costs. The ensuing expenditures incurred by the state are, however, largely unproductive in the sense that they do not themselves yield surplus value and represent a drain on surplus value produced elsewhere in the economy (Aglietta 1979: 247). Basically state expenditure must be financed by increases in the public debt, which as Aglietta has pointed out represents 'an acquisition of rights on future fiscal levies,' by a levy on incomes, or by a levy on consumer spending. These levies on incomes may fall either on wages or on overall profits. In the case of the former such taxation increases the costs of the social reproduction of labor power. If wages are not maintained at the pre-tax level, then effectively the nominal reference wage has been cut, and workers are no longer receiving sufficient income to enable them to purchase the same set of commodities and to enable the accumulation process to be sustained. In other words the balance between capital goods and consumer goods would be destroyed. Yet in the postwar period, where raised internal levels of consumption reduced the need for expanded external markets, an internal balance between the two sectors was an essential condition of growth (Aglietta 1979: 235–7).

If on the other hand the tax represents a levy on overall profits, then the effect will depend on whether its impact is on dividends or industrial profits. If it affects dividends, the only effect will be that luxury consumption is reduced. If, however, the taxation hits industrial profits, the accumulation process will break down as the tax will impede the formation of money capital (Aglietta 1979: 237).

The explanation of the fiscal crisis which follows from this analysis is that many states find themselves in a cleft stick. On the one hand the costs of state activities have continued to rise. On the other hand the growth of the industrial economies has slackened or ended, with the result that the ability of governments to finance this expenditure without affecting real incomes or industrial profits no longer exists. As a result state expenditure is contradictory, in the sense that it is both necessary for and a limit on the accumulation process. In the case of Ireland, which is a peripheral rather than a central economy, where there has been an underdevelopment of capital goods industries and many of the consumer goods industries that are present are not specifically directed to the internal market, the question of internal balance or regulation is not so important. Ireland's economy is not self-centered, and its regulation is to a large extent externally controlled. In this situation it has been possible for firms and the state to try to reduce working-class living standards in order to finance the rising costs of the development process without having such a damaging effect on the development of the industrial sector as in more internally oriented economies. At the same time it has not been possible to raise taxes significantly on industrial profits, since minimal industrial taxation has formed a central part of the industrialization strategy. However, attempts to ease the fiscal stress by cutting state expenditure in the social sphere and raise taxation from working people, both of which imply a reduction in real living standards, may come up against very real limits.

There have already been signs of tension in the form of demonstrations and frequent changes of government, usually in the aftermath of attempts to introduce austerity measures. An austerity policy is clearly a corollary of the unwillingness of international financial institutions to allow countries to maintain living standards by accumulating external debts. But it poses several problems. It can jeopardize the political stability which is a critical factor in attracting foreign capital. If real living standards are depressed the size of the home market will be a constraint on development, not simply because it is small but also because it is poor. Without some development of the internal market and of local industry Ireland will have considerable difficulty in moving away from its status as a relatively low-wage, extroverted economy and in coping with competition from newly industrializing economies.

Conclusion

During the last two decades the Irish economy and Irish society have been transformed, and this transformation has been linked to the arrival of foreign multinationals. The population decline has been reversed and Ireland has experienced fast rates of economic growth. The traditional industrial sector has been modernized, agriculture has become more prosperous though less important in terms of its share of output and employment and the standard of living has increased.

Many writers have referred to Ireland's industrial revolution and to the 'Irish miracle,' and even on the left Ireland has been referred to as an illustration of a capitalist success (Wickham 1980). However, while these developments should not be underplayed, especially in view of their potentially progressive social effects, neither should the limitations of this form of industrialization be overlooked. When analyzed within a framework which recognizes the changing nature of capitalist industrialization and the changing international division of labor, then the limitations inherent in the structure of Irish economic development become more apparent. While a certain level of modernity has been attained in the industrial sphere this has not been accompanied by social conditions and levels of consumption characteristic of core economies. In other words while fordist labor processes have been internationalized, the extension of fordism as a combined system of production and reproduction has been more limited and Ireland's status as a semi-peripheral economy remains.

Ireland continues to be one of the poorest countries in the EEC, and even its relative position has not improved. It is faced with severe problems of indebtedness, and experiences high levels of inflation and unemployment. Within the context of the present strategy of development, it is not clear that these problems can be resolved.

Notes

1 In the 1950s Ireland's viability as an economic unit was in doubt. Unemployment was rising and the economy was relatively stagnant. For example, between 1949 and 1956 GNP increased by 8% compared to increases of 21% and 42% in Britain and the OEEC respectively. Four hundred thousand emigrants left the country during the decade (Rottman & O'Connell 1982: 65).

2 In terms of growth rates the average annual rate of growth between 1947 and 1957 was 2% but in the period 1957–80 it nearly doubled to 3.7%. This latter period can be subdivided. In the period 1957–73 both GNP (4.0% per annum) and output per head rose rapidly. Afterwards output per head declined owing to a slow down in economic growth, with GNP increasing at 3.2% per annum, and a more rapid expansion of population. In the period 1973–80 the growth of output was also more volatile: the growth rate ranged from 1.2% in 1976 to 6.1% in 1977. In fact Ireland differed greatly from the UK in experiencing growth in the manufacturing sector and managed to increase its share of developed countries' manufactured goods exports by two and a half times between 1970 and 1980 (Blackwell 1983: 43–4).

3 Following the Telesis report, this is defined as companies owned in the majority by Irish interests. Official definitions can be confusing. For example, if a foreign manufacturing firm already present in Ireland applies for expansion or the development of a new plant in Ireland it may be classified as domestic or indigenous industry by the Industrial Development Authority (NESC 1982).

4 Telesis reports that 'the largest part of Irish cotton spinning and weaving operations was progressively regrouped by one company in the 1960s. In 1970, this company had seventeen plants in Ireland, was exporting 94 per cent of its production to the UK, and made £2m in profits. Since then it has declined in employment from 2,000 to 160 people and has retreated into two small businesses less exposed

to low wage based competition' (NESC 1982: 92). What seems to have happened in this case is financial restructuring rather than a restructuring of production. But even if the latter had been carried out this industry would still be subject to low wage competition (see note 5 below).

5 For example, in the production of cotton shirts even in the most modern plant labor costs amount to 20% of factory costs, and in some cotton producing countries the cost of labor may be ten times lower than in Ireland leading to an overall production cost advantage of about 18% (not allowing for differences in productivity and capacity utilization (NESC 1982: 92)).

6 Some of the indigenous firms do produce goods and services used by the foreign sector and have undoubtedly benefited from the expansion in consumption and in infrastructural investments generated by the presence of foreign firms. However, few firms are involved in the production of components for the foreign sector. Irish firms had performed best in sectors where few skills were required and in the service sector where there is little competition (NESC 1982: 113–19).

7 The domestic sector only represents 30% of total Irish exports of manufactured goods. They only export about 30% of their production, compared to 75% in the case of foreign firms (NESC 1982: 86).

8 This kind of investment would be beyond the capabilities of many Irish firms. It is very risky and the pay back period is typically a long one. For example, 'One Irish company had to hire an American designer to adapt to the requirements of the US market in "fashion" leather shoes. The total investment for the company was around £240 000 between 1977 and 1980; this resulted in a current sales level of £450 000 in the US after three years' effort' (NESC 1982: 101–2).

9 The relative importance of the US as a source of investment and employment has increased during the 1970s. In 1981 it represented about 42% of total employment and was responsible for 70% of the job approvals in 1979. The relative importance of the UK has declined during these years (NESC 1982: 134).

10 The relative importance of the mechanical and electrical engineering sectors has increased in recent years. Between 1978 and 1980 these sectors accounted for 60% of all job approvals (NESC 1982: 134).

11 For example it has been discovered that only 30% of the jobs approved by the IDA between 1970 and 1978 actually existed on the ground in 1981, and in the case of the mechanical engineering sector the figure is as low as 16.7% (Irish Business 1981).

12 In some cases the owner of a firm would also be the manager, designer and production control engineer, and given the sophisticated nature of contemporary components, many of these individuals did not possess the necessary skills to be competent in all three fields (NESC 1981: 117, 120).

13 For example in Belgium, another small country, the level of internal sourcing is much higher, up to 24%, perhaps because of its greater industrial tradition (NESC 1981: 115–16).

14 In fact between 90% and 95% of the production of foreign-owned companies is exported. Similar figures exist for Puerto Rico. In countries such as Germany where foreign firms are present partly to exploit the larger and more developed domestic market, then this figure is much lower, for Germany 17% and for Great Britain 38% (NESC 1982: 367, and see Table 12.4).

15 Over 80% of the companies surveyed by Telesis came to Ireland primarily because it provided a tax shelter for penetrating the EEC. Ireland has the lowest average tax and wage rates of all the EEC countries (NESC 1982: 135).

16 Only about 1% of the employees are currently engaged in engineering activities, and only about 1% are technicians. The managers are essentially satellite managers and the engineering functions have until now been limited to product adaptation

and marginal process improvements. These developments are not those likely to be crucial to competitive advantage and thus the spin-off effects such as those associated with Silicon Valley are unlikely to occur (NESC 1982: 139–40).

References

Aglietta, M. 1979. *A theory of capitalist regulation: the US experience*. London: New Left Books.

Blackwell, J. 1983. Government economy and society. *Administration* **30**(2–3), 43–4.

Dunford, M. and D. Perrons, 1983. *The arena of capital*. London: Macmillan.

Gould, F. 1981. The growth of public expenditure in Ireland, 1947–77. *Administration* **29**(2), 115–35.

Harris, L. 1983. Industrialisation, women and working class politics in the west of Ireland. *Capital and Class* **19** (Spring), 100–17.

Irish Business 1981. Telesis: an indictment of Irish industrial policy. *Irish Business* (August).

Kennedy, K. A. 1981. The state of public finances. *Administration* **29**(2), 137–52.

Lipietz, A. 1982. Towards global fordism? *New Left Review* **132** (March/April), 33–47.

Lyons, F. S. 1973. *Ireland since the famine*. London: Fontana.

McDowell, M. 1982. A generation of public expenditure growth: Leviathan unchained. *Administration* **30**(2–3), 183–200.

Marx, K. 1976. *Capital: a critique of political economy*, vol. 1. Harmondsworth: Penguin.

Meenan, J. 1970. *The Irish economy since 1922*. Liverpool: Liverpool University Press.

NESC (National Economic and Social Council) 1982. *A review of industrial policy: a report prepared by the Telesis Consultancy Group*. Dublin: NESC.

O'Connor, J. 1973. *The fiscal crisis of the state*. New York: St. Martin's Press.

OECD 1982. *OECD economic surveys: Ireland*. Paris: OECD.

O'Malley, E. J. 1981. Industrial policy and development: a survey of literature from the early 1960s to the present. *National Economic and Social Council Report* **60**. Dublin: NESC.

Perrons, D. C. 1981. The role of Ireland in the new international division of labour: a proposed framework for regional analysis. *Regional Studies* **15**(2), 81–100.

Rottman, D. and P. J. O'Connell, 1982. The changing social structure. *Administration* **30**(2–3), 63–88.

Whelan, N. 1980. Ireland's national and regional development: issues for consideration. *Administration* **28**(4), 371–408.

Wickham, J. 1980. The politics of dependent capitalism: international capital and the nation state. In *Ireland: divided nation divided class*. A. Morgan and B. Purdie (eds.). London: Ink Links.

13

The state, the region,
and the division of labor

R. J. JOHNSTON

. . . regional problems have become a permanent feature of late capitalism. (Carney 1980: 60)

Much academic and political attention has been focused in most industrialized countries during recent years on the 'regional problem', characterized by substantial spatial variability in unemployment rates and prospects for economic development. The spatial concentration of economic problems that this involves has been widely interpreted as a political problem, threatening the economic and social cohesion of the nation-state. Consequently, governments have felt it necessary to intervene, and to manipulate the economic geography of their territories – mainly by manipulating the costs of production – in order to prevent the problem developing and harming the fabric of the local social formation.

Regional policies have taken a great many forms, and their relative success has similarly varied quite substantially. But the problems tackled by such policies are changing, not so much in their empirical appearances – spatially varying unemployment rates, for example – as in their underlying causes. The economic processes governing the creation of regional problems have altered in recent decades, as a consequence of the increased mobility of capital and the closer integration of the capitalist world-economy. As a consequence, it is argued here, regional policies as traditionally conceived are increasingly obsolete.

Regional crises under global capitalism differ from those which emerged during the preceding era of industrial capitalism, and the response of the state has altered accordingly. This is illustrated here with particular reference to the British situation. There, the response of one particular political party – Conservative – to the international and regional crises of global capitalism has been to argue that in such a context regional policy is an irrelevant impossibility: national economic survival within the world-economy requires that the state promote the most efficient use of resources rather than subsidizing uneconomic locations. Against this is the response of other parties – especially Labour – which seeks to solve the national crisis through insulation from global capitalism and the regional crises through the promotion of strong local government. Whereas the former promotes a world-view founded on the neo-classical economic principles of Weber and von Thunen, therefore, the latter promotes an anarchic territorial structure.

265

The present chapter sets this pair of world-views in context. It begins with an outline of the international division of labor and the role of the state in capitalism, and proceeds to a discussion of regional crises and policies under industrial and global capitalism. This provides the structure within which the relevance of the two world-views can be assessed.

The dynamics of capitalism, spatial division of labor, and the state

The goal of a capitalist economy is the accumulation of wealth by the minority of the population who are the owners of capital. This is achieved through the exploitation of labor. Saleable commodities are produced by the application of labor power to materials – with the owners of the labor power being paid less than the price received for the commodity. This appropriation of surplus value is the basis of profitability for a capitalist enterprise. It is based on an antagonism between the employers of labor who wish to extract as much surplus value as possible, and the owners of labor who wish to increase their proportion of the selling price.

Capitalist enterprises are bound, in most situations (the exceptions refer to monopolies, including spatial monopolies), to seek continually to increase their rate of accumulation of surplus value, irrespective of the characteristics of the individuals involved in the operation of the enterprises. This is because they are in competition with others producing similar goods. If they are unable to compete, then their sales will fall, and their extraction of surplus value will decline – leading to the ultimate demise of the enterprise. To be competitive, they must lower prices in real terms, which means increasing their exploitation of labor.

Even if enterprises can remain competitive by continually increasing their extraction of surplus value, this will not guarantee long-term success. There is no long-term, continual linear 'progress' in a capitalist system. Rather, it proceeds by a series of crises, with intervening periods of 'economic boom'. The crises come about because of the inbuilt tendency of the rate of profit to fall, as capital moves between sectors and as the ability to produce out-paces the ability to consume. Such a fall in the profit rate may occur in one industrial sector, causing a 'localized crisis'; it may, however, occur in several simultaneously, stimulating a more general crisis.

As the capitalist system evolves, therefore, it encounters continuing problems of two types. There are those of falling profitability because of inability to extract surplus value, and there are those of falling profitability because of a lack of markets for the system's products. To counter these problems, the system and its parts must be continually restructured. The problems of the first type must be countered by creating more productive arrangements, in which the relative costs of labor decline; greater use of machines and the consequent replacement of skilled by unskilled labor is a common policy here. For the problems of the second type, new and more profitable investments must be sought – with capital being transferred from industrial sectors with stagnant markets to those with better prospects.

Both of these sets of solutions affect the antagonisms between capital and labor. The drives for increased productivity threaten greater exploitation; the deskilling process implies a reduction in real wage levels whereas the replacement of labor by machines implies redundancy. The mobility of capital implies that industrial sectors experiencing disinvestment will suffer major redundancies.

The role of the state

The capitalist economic system is therefore continually restructuring itself, via its component parts, in order to survive. At the level of individual enterprises, particularly in the short term, this involves identifying methods of increasing labor productivity. In the longer term, it involves evaluating the nature of the investment, and determining whether capital should be shifted from one type of activity to another. In both cases, the interrelationships between capital and labor are implicated.

Assistance in these processes has been provided, throughout the history of the capitalist system, by the state. This is not a part of the capitalist organization (the network of economic institutions) itself, because of the nature of the tasks that it undertakes. The state is a definable institution within capitalist society, necessary to the success of capitalism but explicitly separate from it (and giving the appearance of independence too).

The state plays two major, linked roles in a capitalist system (O'Connor 1973). First, it *promotes capitalist accumulation* by providing the environmental context within which surplus value can be extracted. The British state, for example, has guaranteed property rights and the currency, legalized certain types of employer–worker contract, ensured internal law and order, limited worker contestation of capitalist practices, and protected investments overseas (see Strinati 1983). In these ways, using revenue raised from all segments of society, the state supports capitalist operations.

The second role of the state is the *legitimation of capitalism*. The tensions between capital and labor are a constant threat to the viability of both individual enterprises and the system as a whole. Capital thus requires an institution which will legitimize what it does and ensure worker compliance. This the state does in part at an ideological level by promoting capitalist operations as in the interest of all, for example, and by inculcating a view that enterprise is to be encouraged and rewarded. It also legitimizes the system by obtaining concessions for labor (thereby establishing its bona fides as separate from capital). These may be 'real' in that they harm capital slightly – as with the imposition of health and safety regulations at work, minimum holiday entitlements, and so on – but they protect the long-term health of capitalism. (Only the state, or some other external body, could 'wring' such concessions; if individual capitalists were to yield them unilaterally, their competitive position would be undermined.) Thus the development of the British welfare state and the increased involvement of the working class in the running of the state apparatus have been part of the legitimation program.

Promotion of accumulation and legitimation of capitalism are not independent activities of the state, and some state programs involve contributions to both (hence some of the concessions obtained in the legitimation activities are beneficial to capital as well as to labor). A national health service and a compulsory, 'free' education system may both be presented as gains for the working class. In absolute terms they are – although the hidden costs may in fact mean that there is little subsidy from rich to poor (e.g. Kincaid 1973, Westergaard & Resler 1976). But capital benefits too: it has a healthier and better-educated, and thus potentially more productive, labor force. (Note the argument of Clark and Dear (1984) that the accumulation and legitimation tasks can only be pursued if the state has first secured a social consensus for the current arrangements of the social formation. The three tasks thus defined are interdependent, however, because failure at either or both of the accumulation and legitimation tasks is likely to threaten the state's ability to maintain consensus support, as illustrated here.)

As capitalism evolves, so too must state policies. Means of increasing productivity may need support both in the investment programs – hence tax concessions for investment etc. – and in the negotiations with labor; new working arrangements must be legitimized and old ones (such as restrictive practices, job demarcations, and closed shop unions) shown to be 'obsolete.' And the mobility of capital to new, more profitable areas of investment must be encouraged by, for example, state investment in research to encourage invention and then in the development of innovations.

The geography of industrial capitalism

So far, the discussion of the tensions and dynamics of capitalism has totally ignored the spatial element. Yet this is crucial to those basic features of the system, in many ways. Introduction of the spatial element in this section will assume a bounded territory within which capitalism operates, governed by a single state.

All economic activity takes place at a spatial location and much of it – including the great majority of productive activity – takes place at a fixed location: once invested, fixed capital is immobile. A major question to be answered by students of the location of such capital (economic geography) concerns the spatial determinants of investment. The history of location theory during the last two centuries is the history of tentative answers to this question, but that history is of little relevance to the present discussion.

Capital is invested in productive activities at locations where the potential profits are sufficient incentive – or where space can be manipulated to promote profitability (Cromar 1977). For some activities, locational choice is constrained by the availability of, or accessibility to, certain resources. For others, the constraints are much less, and many 'choices' reflect particular local circumstances only. Once selected, and once investments have been made, the locations chosen become part of the environment of the continuing dynamic of capitalism. Industrial growth becomes self-generating and self-sustaining (until a period of crisis sets in). As a result, some parts of a state's territory develop into industrial regions concentrated on certain sectors only; some develop a broader base, and experience very little industrialization at all.

The geography of regional industrial development conditions the geography of capital-labor relationships. In general terms, the greater the level of industrialization, the greater the degree of local organization of labor to counter the demands of capital. And as the industries restructure themselves, with the tendency toward larger production units and enterprises, so the potential for effective labor organization increases, and with it the calls for state legitimation, including the public provision of a range of non-work-related services.

Over the longer term, the intersectoral mobility of capital introduces changes to the geography of economic activity (Harvey 1982). As a sector becomes less attractive, so disinvestment occurs and jobs are lost. New investment, in other sectors, may provide sufficient jobs to absorb those made redundant in the declining industries, but this depends on capitalist choice to re-invest in the same areas. In specialized industrial regions, this is quite unlikely: the resource base for new industries may be absent; the decaying infrastructure may be unattractive for new investment; the labor force may have the wrong skills and be antagonistic to the development of new ones. In seeking profits new, therefore, capital may also seek pastures new (but see Browett 1984).

Over the longer term, the restructuring of capital may produce depressed regions, areas with high levels of relatively permanent, structural unemployment. Similar results may occur from the shorter-term processes of increasing productivity. Massey and Meegan (1979, 1982) have identified several strategies in operation, including (a) rationalization, whereby total productive capacity is reduced, with consequent labor-shedding; (b) standardization of production, leading to deskilling of the labor force, usually following investment in new technology; and (c) intensification, with a reduction of the labor force (the elimination of 'over-manning') relative to production levels, thereby requiring higher levels of labor productivity. These strategies have locational consequences, and may involve locational shifts. For example, both intensification and rationalization will produce employment losses at the current plant location; in addition, the remaining capacity may be concentrated at certain existing locations in multi-plant firms, with others being closed, or all existing plants may be closed, to be replaced by new ones elsewhere. Standardization of production with new investment may also involve the closure of some plants and the opening of others, the latter in places which are perceived to offer the sort of labor force that the firm requires. As a result of these processes, areas may experience substantial decline in certain industries (Massey & Meegan 1978), creating regional unemployment problems.

Regional problems under industrial capitalism and state intervention

Regional problems under industrial capitalism result, according to the above discussion, from one or both of the following: the decline of staple industries in an area; the restructuring of industries, with consequent mobility of employment prospects. Some of these problems may be stimulated by state intervention – as Massey and Meegan (1979) illustrate for the British Industrial Reorganization Corporation. Their existence is then used as the basis for inviting further state intervention, this time for *places* rather than for *industries*.

Places (the general term 'region' will be used here) pass through a 'cycle of crisis', according to Damette and Poncet (1980), whereby industrial decline stimulates outmigration. To prevent such outmigration, and the consequent stagnation of such crisis regions, the state has been called upon to influence the location of employment. Such calls have been answered in many countries for more than half a century, as the geographical consequences of decline in many industrial regions during the 1920s and 1930s impinged on the public consciousness, and led to the adoption of 'full employment' policies.

The spatial shifts producing concentrations of unemployment resulted from capital seeking better returns. As promoter of accumulation, the state generally supported this, since without a prosperous capitalism the legitimacy of the state itself would be called into question; consensus support would be lacking. But labor is less mobile than capital – it finds it difficult to shift from one segment of the labor market to another; more difficult to shift from one spatial labor market (a town or urban region) to another; and even more difficult to shift between *both* labor market segments (industry to industry) *and* spatial labor markets (place to place). As a consequence, despite substantial outmigration from certain regions (see Law 1980: 55ff.), major pockets of long-term unemployment have been created. These contained the potential, only occasionally actualized, for worker unrest, threatening to lead to overall collapse of support for the economic system.

It was in its role as the legitimator of capitalist accumulation that the state became involved not only in economic policies designed to increase employment generally but also in spatial policies designed to ensure the absorption of unemployed labor in the depressed regions. In this way, the threat to legitimation could be averted, and the electoral influences on partisan support maintained. The policies adopted over the decades, and in different countries, have varied substantially. Some have sought to reduce the costs of fixed capital in certain locations, by state investment in infrastructure, subsidies for private investment in plant, and so on. Some have sought to reduce the costs of variable capital by subsidies for labor costs. (Thus in seeking to solve legitimation problems the state was also, by subsidies, promoting accumulation.) And some have sought to make costs higher in the non-depressed regions. The goal has been both to direct employment-generating activities into the depressed regions and to stimulate growth generally. Conventional wisdom suggested that the former should occur in any case, that the geographical disparities in wages should stimulate the migration of workers to the higher-wage areas and the migration of employers to low wage areas. However, the problems of immobility of labor, of abandoning expensive fixed investments, and of inertia prevented a new equilibrium situation occurring 'naturally' – and quickly.

As a sovereign body, the state is able to take upon itself powers to direct locational choices, or at least to influence them, thereby countering the potential regional crises that threaten the legitimacy of capitalism within its territory. Whether its policies to this end have been successful is a cause of much debate, both academic and political, because of difficulties in answering the counter-factual question: 'What would have happened if the policies had not been enacted?' (On the British debate, see Keeble 1976, Moore, Rhodes & Tyler 1977.)

Below the state, most countries have local governments, some of which have the powers to enact policies that might successfully counter regional crises. They may seek to modify the local economic environments in ways that will make them more attractive to investors, thus bringing jobs to their local unemployed, and they may even invest directly themselves in job creation. In the United States, for example, there have been clear inter-State variations in union activity (Bennett 1982, Earle & Bennett 1982), and a number of States have passed right-to-work acts which outlaw trade union closed shops. The results are lower wages in the right-to-work States than elsewhere (Cebula 1983), and a shift of employment toward the States where the class struggle is poorly articulated and the exploitation of labor is consequently greater (Peet 1983).

Under industrial capitalism, therefore, the state has intervened in a variety of ways, and in a number of guises, to influence locational choices of employers and to avoid regional crises. Its twin roles of promoting capitalist accumulation and legitimation have increasingly been interpreted as ensuring full employment (though attitudes to child and female labor have allowed flexibility in the definition of this concept), and it has perceived that inflexibilities in the spatial organization of labor markets require it not only to stimulate employment but also to ensure a particular spatial distribution. (Over the long term, this distribution may slowly change; the state seeks to counter major, rapid shifts.) As far as possible, accumulation is not harmed, and its legitimation is promoted, if not guaranteed.

Global capitalism and regional crisis

As capitalism has evolved during the 20th century, so its restructuring has produced new forms. In particular, the concentration and centralization of industrial capital into a few large corporations which operate virtually independently of any state, and of finance capital into a few major banks has created a new structure known as global capitalism. It is the dynamics of global capital that provide the environment within which states must now act.

Global capitalism

Global capitalism involves the domination of the world-economy by a small number of giant, transnational corporations, with operations in many countries, with loyalty to no one state, and with surplus value channelled (via complex pricing and other arrangements designed to avoid taxes) to whichever location – in many cases a small island state – offers the greatest incentives (see Kidron & Segal 1981). These corporations are involved in research and development investment (identifying and promoting new products) and in strategies (similar to those described by Massey and Meegan) for achieving high levels of labor productivity (i.e. surplus value extraction) from standardized production processes. Such strategies involve shifting capital from sector to sector (both productive and non-productive, Harvey 1978) and from place to place. They are prepared to shift capital spatially, creating what Susman and Schutz (1983) call the 'hypermobility of capital': 'To avoid the adverse consequences of crises, or even the threat of locally reduced profit rates, transnational corporations and internationally operating financial institutions rapidly shift investments to more desirable locations and sectors' (p. 175).

Individual states have not been closed systems within a capitalist world-economy for several centuries, but the transition from industrial to global capitalism has changed the relationship between state and capital. Under industrial capitalism, most firms, even the largest, conducted most of their operations within the territory of their home state. Their need to exploit labor at certain stages of the production process (notably the extraction of raw materials) and to expand markets led to foreign investments, but these repatriated most of the surplus value of the home state; indeed the state, via imperialist and colonial policies, supported such activity. Under global capitalism, however, the situation has been reversed. The transnational corporation is increasingly larger (in terms of resources and financial power) than, and independent of, the state: whereas under industrial capitalism the individual enterprise sought aid from the state, now the reverse is occurring. Accumulation now operates on a global scale; legitimation remains an issue at the state scale (Giddens 1981: 197).

Not all employment by any means is provided by the transnational corporations. There are still many small and medium-sized firms whose operations are confined within the territory of an individual state, perhaps even some part of it only. Their prosperity is increasingly dependent on the activities of the transnationals, both directly – the smaller, local firms are subcontractors to the transnationals – and indirectly – without the income and employment multipliers stimulated by the transnationals, the local economy is not viable.

Rationalization and standardization of production is fundamental to the success of the transnationals, which seek to exploit cheap, unskilled labor to the utmost. This results in the shift of employment from the 'advanced' to the 'underdeveloped' nations, at a scale hitherto unknown. (See the description of developments on the US/Mexican border in House 1982.) Unskilled labor is extremely cheap in the latter countries, and its exploitation in a wide range of industries more than compensates for the transport costs involved in the movement of materials and final products. (See Taylor & Thrift 1982 and Peet 1983 for examples of the labor cost differentials.)

Global capitalism therefore involves a new industrial division of labor, in which the relatively highly paid skilled and semi-skilled workers of Western Europe and North America are replaced by the much cheaper unskilled workers of Asia, Africa, Latin America and parts of Southern and Eastern

272

Europe. This creates economic problems for the former countries, which are losing employment in production while retaining them in research and development. The regional crises in those countries are being accentuated. Research and development activity is concentrated in a few favored areas (such as Britain's 'M4 Corridor': Hall 1981, Johnston 1983), whereas the regions which have long depended for their prosperity on standardized production are in rapid decline: 'Under global capitalism, regions are more dependent on and sensitive to, not only the movement of capital but capital that moves more rapidly' (Susman & Schutz 1983: 173).

In such a situation, the state faces substantial problems in legitimizing capitalism. Traditional regional policies, as Holland (1976) made very clear, are of little value; the rate of subsidy on fixed and variable capital offered is minimal compared to the international labor cost differentials, and offers little real incentive to transnational investors. The hard-won benefits of the labor force are also a bar to attracting investment: wages are relatively high, unions are traditionally strong, and workers are restive and militant in the face of rapid restructuring. A labor force that is not compliant is unattractive to investors, especially when a much more disciplined labor force is available elsewhere. The state in 'developed countries' may seek to discipline local labor, but this is difficult because earlier concessions have given electoral power and political influence to the working class. The result is political instability, as the forces of labor battle electorally with those of capital; the result is termed 'adversary politics' in Britain (Finer 1975), and creates what is widely interpreted as an unstable political–electoral environment, unlikely to attract substantial long-term investment. Authoritarian regimes elsewhere are more acceptable to capital (Johnston 1984), so long as their power is guaranteed; and capital may provide the basis for such guarantees.

Regional crises, regional policies and global capitalism

The evolution of global capitalism creates a new situation for the state in its legitimation role. Traditional policies relating to the solution of regional problems in advanced industrial countries, such as Britain, are increasingly irrelevant, for two main sets of reasons.

The first set of reasons relates to *the changed spatial scale of locational choice*. Traditional regional policies were devised to make the depressed regions slightly cheaper, through spatially selective subsidies to the costs of variable and fixed capital, than the more prosperous, so seducing locational choices in favour of the former. Such policies assumed – rightly, until very recently – that the majority of locational choices involved selection among a group of sites within the one state's territory. Increasingly that assumption is invalid, and a substantial number of locational choices, including many which involve either major potential users of labor or major potential growth stimulators via local multipliers, comprise selection from sites distributed across a (perhaps substantial) number of countries.

The problem for the state today, therefore, is that the spatial scale within which it exercises sovereign power does not conform to the spatial scale of transnational corporation decision making. Faced with a 'regional problem,'

273

it seeks to influence intra-state locational choices. But the key choices with regard to labor-intensive employment are inter-state. If a state is unable to attract sufficient international investment to its territory, it may be unable to approach the full employment goal that it seeks to guarantee. Its regional policies may be relevant to this inter-state contest, but at best only slightly; at worst they may contradict its efforts at the other scale. Thus it may be that the regional incentives offered to attract firms to, say, Scotland are sufficient to win investment from a firm considering alternative locations in Belgium and Ireland. But it may be that the absence of incentives to locate in southeast England (not to mention possible disincentives) remove the United Kingdom as a whole from consideration by the firm.

Under global capitalism, particularly at its present stage of economic crisis, the regional problem and the legitimation issues that it raises occupy an increasingly poor second place to national economic problems and the legitimation issues that they raise. Difficulties of guaranteeing full employment nationally mean that the state has increasingly to focus its attention on the national rather than the regional crisis; regional policy is in large part irrelevant (see also Becker 1983, 1984).

The second set of reasons is linked to the first and suggests that in the face of the national crisis the regional crisis is not only irrelevant but also insoluble. This is because of *the fiscal crisis of the state*. O'Connor's (1973) analysis of this follows his division of state spending into categories reflecting the separation of the accumulation and legitimation roles. As economic crisis deepens, so the demands for expenditure in both areas increase, and the state is called upon to provide more subsidies to ensure successful accumulation; to increase spending on social and other services in order to legitimate a system that is increasingly failing individuals (such services are labor intensive, and so their costs tend to increase disproportionately; Newton 1981); and to spend more on ensuring law and order in the face of increasing challenges to its legitimation. Consensus support is breaking down as the state is increasingly under attack from both capital and labor.

Greater spending involves greater taxation, greater borrowing, and more 'money creation'. All of these, according to many economic analysts and their political associates, are likely to discourage investment, particularly of global capital. High tax rates are disincentives to enterprise, as are the high interest rates consequent upon increased public sector borrowing; the creation of more money fuels inflationary pressures, which again are contrary to the needs of investors. To encourage investment, so the argument goes, taxation must be reduced, borrowing must be reduced, and inflation removed. This means a reduction in the supply of state revenues, with the obvious consequence of a reduction of state spending. The cuts in the latter are in the area of social expenses – the welfare state. Expenditure on the promotion of accumulation is maintained as, necessarily, is expenditure on law and order, and there is a major ideological program aimed at gaining support for this interpretation.

This preferred solution to the fiscal crisis of the state has major implications for the legitimation of both the state itself and the global capitalist system that it promotes. Its justification has become part of the ideology of the modern state in many countries, with an emphasis on the need for worker discipline, on the importance of encouraging incentives, and on the drive for international competitiveness. Regional policy is viewed as an unnecessary luxury; in Britain, the areas eligible for regional aid have been substantially reduced since 1979 (Dicken 1983), and a *laissez-faire* attitude toward locational choice is being promoted. Incentives remain for certain 'employment black spots'. New policies have been introduced too, notably the Enterprise Zones for relatively small inner-city areas, which are unlikely to have any major impact on the creation of jobs, locally or nationally.

Local governments within the state apparatus have traditionally played a role in stimulating employment growth within their territories. With a deepening economic crisis, they have felt the need to increase their efforts to represent local interests. (In Britain, the most active are those with Labour party governments, representing worker interests.) What they are able to do, however, depends on the autonomy allowed to them (Boddy 1983), and high levels of local spending on economic development programs are likely to run counter to central government policies of reduced taxation and borrowing (Young & Mills 1982). Consequently the British central government has introduced substantial curbs on local spending autonomy (Bennett 1983); local governments can act as boosters (Burgess 1982) but not as investors (see also Boddy & Fudge 1984).

Together, the interlocking problems of the national employment crisis, the regional employment crisis, the fiscal crisis of the state, and the Thatcherite interpretations of the solutions to the first and third of these act against the development of regional policies which are likely to succeed. (Thatcherism promotes a view of space akin to the isotropic plain of the neo-classical theorists.) This creates a potential legitimation crisis, but the promotion of a particular ideology of solutions is designed to counter that, and to suggest that the crisis is very much the result of working-class unreasonableness (an alternative ideology suggests that electoral reform will provide the solution, via political stability; Johnston 1984).

Toward alternative regional strategies?

Public policy which serves the interests of workers and older regions must go beyond the current fashion of subsidizing capital in the hope that it will stay in a given place. In the era of global capitalism, the problem for workers is that their employers have a world of choices. (Ross 1983: 158)

As discussed here, traditional regional policies are now obsolete. Can they be replaced by state activities that will protect the interests of workers in particular places? Two possibilities are investigated here.

The first possibility is the *closed economic system* option. According to this – which has several variants – the individual state should isolate itself from global capitalism, and promote its population's interests within its territory. Thus, for example the outflow of capital seeking profitable investments elsewhere would be prohibited, high tariff walls would stem the inflow of cheaper imports, and local employment would then be created; political stability would need to be guaranteed, otherwise investment would not be forthcoming.

Such an economic strategy has its attractions, but its potential for success would depend on the porosity of the national frontiers, particularly to the outflow of capital, and on the amount of productive investment that it stimulated (assuming that private rather than state investment were given priority). If the barriers were effective, and substantial local investment in productive activities generated, then accumulation could once again become an intra-state issue and effective regional policies might be enacted. The likelihood of impervious barriers is remote, however, and only a fully fledged socialist strategy is likely to return the local economy to local control. (As Chase-Dunn (1983) points out, this socialist strategy would need to be worldwide; socialism in one country is not impossible, but is unlikely in the face of a successful global capitalism – with the criteria for success being defined by the global capitalists.)

If the state cannot isolate itself from the world-economy, then perhaps it can negotiate with it. Planning agreements with transnational corporations, for example, may provide both the stability that investors need and guaranteed returns for the local population (e.g. Manley 1982), but they are only in the interests of the transnational corporations if the local resources are very important to them. Alternatively, investment could be attracted by ensuring a disciplined, compliant work-force, probably controlled by an authoritarian regime (as in South Korea and Taiwan); such a solution is an extension of Thatcherism and solves the legitimation problem by repression.

The second set of possibilities relates to the *break-up of the state*, countering the Thatcherite isotropic plain by socialist anarchy. The present system of states would be replaced by a mosaic of many smaller ones, so that regional crises become national crises. Such a solution has been proposed for those 'regions' of Britain with separate nationalist foundations, and indeed a 'break-up of Britain' was predicted (Nairn 1977). Electoral support dwindled, however, and returned to a political party (Labour) which has always championed the depressed regions – the source of most of its votes and even more of its parliamentary seats – but has achieved very little for them (Sharpe 1982).

Moves toward the break-up of the state have been advanced by political parties opposed to Thatcherite economic policies, with proposals for economic decentralization. In its paper *A new deal for Britain: decentralising government* (1982), for example, the Social Democratic party argued that decentralization would 'enable the weaker regions to stand on their own feet,' by making high-level decision makers responsible to regional governments: the party would give such governments 'an adequate range of economic and planning functions.' Similarly, the Labour party document *Alternative regional strategy: a framework for discussion* (1982) proposes regional assemblies with decision-making powers.

Neither of these proposals, if enacted, is likely to have much impact on the regional crisis, for the basic reason that the major fiscal decisions, relating to tax rates and to the value of the currency, will remain with the central government. Thus regions will be competing with each other, offering incentives to influence locational choices, but with the initial inequalities affecting their bargaining positions. Proposals for differential allocations of central grants are insufficient to counter those inequalities – and the regional assemblies will have no control over the absolute size of the central grant. Such a structure, designed to ensure 'Local and democratic representation in the decision-making process' and 'That more decisions about regions are taken within those regions,' would be an ideological device, screening the real legitimation problem but offering no solution to it (see also Clark 1984).

Crises rampant

Habermas (1976) has identified two types of crisis within the political sphere. A *rationality crisis* occurs when the state fails to meet the needs of the economic system, that is, it fails to promote capitalist accumulation successfully. A *legitimation crisis* occurs when it fails to maintain mass loyalty to the economic system. The argument presented in this chapter is that whereas under industrial capitalism the state may expect to solve both crises (to the extent that both can be solved, simultaneously) through policies internal to its own territory, under global capitalism it cannot, since whereas legitimation crises remain intra-state issues, rationality crises increasingly involve inter-state issues.

The British case illustrates this argument. During the economic crisis of the 1930s there was a rationality crisis; there was also a potential legitimation crisis, especially in those regions which suffered greatest from the economic crisis. Solution of both the rationality crisis and the regional legitimation crisis was possible for the British state, which had some autonomy of action within the industrial capitalist system. The early 1980s contain a similar set of crises. This time, however, the regional legitimation crisis is not readily tackled within the attack on the rationality crisis. With global capitalism, the relative positions of the state and the major capitalist actors have been reversed, and in seeking to solve a national legitimation crisis linked to the rationality crisis, the regional legitimation crisis has been subject to ideological arguments that seek to remove it rather than solve it.

This is a new situation for Britain – and for some other 'advanced industrial countries' too – with the rationality crisis developing into a national legitimation crisis subject to dominant forces outside the national borders. In this respect, Britain is being drawn closer to the majority of countries in the world – the so-called 'underdeveloped', 'less developed' and 'developing' where the ability to tackle regional legitimation crises has always been severely constrained by national legitimation crises linked to rationality crises.

Regional problems remain. The traditional solutions – regional policies – were never particularly successful. Now they are obsolete. The state, concerned with an international rationality crisis and a national legitimation crisis, has neither the ability nor the resources to tackle regional problems effectively. It must focus on the national situation and this, it seems, requires it to replace legitimation through consent (democratic participation and a benevolent welfare state) by legitimation through coercion. The latter is not always explicit, and ideological means are used to justify reductions in, for example, welfare state spending and the removal of democratic accountability. But the underlying trend is clear; the state, in the context of global capitalism, is increasingly unable to tackle regional problems and must resort to policies that suppress the promotion of regional demands. While the present system of nation-states remains in place, national economic survival takes precedence over regional difficulties.

References

Becker, B. K. 1983. The political use of territory: a Third World perspective. *IGU Latin American Regional Conference*, Vol. 2, *Symposia and Round Tables*. pp. 233–40. Rio de Janeiro: IGU.

Becker, B. K. 1984. The state crisis and region – a Third World perspective. In *Political geography: recent advances and future directions*. P. J. Taylor and J. W. House (eds.). London: Croom Helm.

Bennett, R. J. 1983. *Central grants to local governments*. Cambridge: Cambridge University Press.

Bennett, S. J. 1982. Labor organizing in the South, 1975–1979: the case of the International Brotherhood of Teamsters. *Geography of American labor and industrialization*. Working Paper 8. University of Maryland, Baltimore County.

Boddy, M. J. 1983. Changing public–private sector relationships in the industrial development process. In *Urban economic development*, K. Young and C. Mason (eds.). pp. 34–52. London: Macmillan.

Boddy, M. J. and C. Fudge 1984. *Local socialism*. London: Macmillan.

Browett, J. G. 1984. On the necessity and inevitability of uneven spatial development under capitalism. *Int. J. Urban and Regional Res.* **8**, 155–76.

Burgess, J. A. 1982. Selling places: environmental images for the executive. *Regional Studies* **16**, 1–17.

Carney, J. 1980. Regions in crisis: accumulation, regional problems and crisis formation. In *Regions in crisis*, J. Carney, R. Hudson and J. Lewis (eds.). pp. 28–59. London: Croom Helm.

Cebula, R. J. 1983. Right-to-work laws and living cost differences. *Am. J. Econ. Sociol.* **42**, 329–40.

Chase-Dunn, C. 1983. Socialist states in the capitalist world-economy. In *Socialist states in the world system*, C. Chase-Dunn (ed.), pp. 21–54. Beverly Hills: Sage.

Clark, G. L. 1984. Labor demand and economic development policy. *Government and Policy: Environment and Planning C* **2**, 45–56.

Clark, G. L. and M. J. Dear 1984. *State apparatus*. Boston: Allen & Unwin.

Cromar, P. 1977. The coal industry on Tyneside 1771–1800: oligopoly and spatial change. *Econ. Geog.* **53**, 79–94.

Damette, F. and E. Poncet 1980. Global crisis and regional crises. In *Regions in crisis*, J. Carney, R. Hudson and J. Lewis (eds.), pp. 93–116. London: Croom Helm.

Dicken, P. 1983. The industrial structure and the geography of manufacturing. In *The changing geography of the United Kingdom*, R. J. Johnston and J. C. Doornkamp, (eds.), pp. 171–202. London: Methuen.

Earle, C. V. and S. J. Bennett 1982. The changing spatial structure of worker protest in the United States. *Geography of American labor and industrialization*, Working Paper 7. University of Maryland, Baltimore County.

Finer, S. E. (ed.), 1975. *Adversary politics and electoral reform*. London: Anthony Wigram.

Giddens, A. 1981. *A contemporary critique of historical materialism*. London: Macmillan.

Habermas, J. 1976. *Legitimation crisis*. London: Heinemann.

Hall, P. 1981. The geography of the fifth Kondratieff cycle. *New Society* March 26, 535–7.

Harvey, D. 1978. The urban process under capitalism. *Int. J. Urban and Regional Res.* **2**, 101–32.

Harvey, D. 1982. *The limits to capital*. Oxford: Basil Blackwell.

Holland, S. 1976. *Capital against the regions*. London: Macmillan.

House, J. W. 1982. *Frontier on the Rio Grande*. Oxford: Oxford University Press.

Johnston, R. J. 1983. And the future? In *The changing geography of the United Kingdom*, R. J. Johnston and J. C. Doornkamp (eds.), pp. 403–20. London: Methuen.

Johnston, R. J. 1984. The political geography of electoral geography. In *Political geography: recent advances and future directions*, P. J. Taylor and J. W. House (eds.), pp. 133–48. London: Croom Helm.

Keeble, D. E. 1976. *Industrial location and planning in the United Kingdom*. London: Methuen.

Kidron, M. and R. Segal 1981. *The state of the world atlas*. London: Pluto Press.

Kincaid, J. F. 1973. *Poverty and inequality in Britain*. Harmondsworth: Penguin.

Law, C. M. 1980. *British regional development since World War I*. Newton Abbott: David & Charles.

Manley, M. 1982. *Struggle on the periphery*. London: New Left Books.

Massey, D. and R. A. Meegan 1978. Industrial restructuring versus the cities. *Urban Studies* **15**, 273–88.

Massey, D. and R. A. Meegan 1979. The geography of industrial reorganisation. *Progress in Planning* **10**, 155–237.

Massey, D. and R. A. Meegan 1982. *The anatomy of job loss*. London: Methuen.

Moore, B. C., J. Rhodes and P. Tyler 1977. The impact of regional policy in the 1970s. *CES Review* **1**, 67–77.

Nairn, T. 1977. *The break-up of Britain*. London: New Left Books.

Newton, K. 1981. *Balancing the books*. London: Sage.

O'Connor, J. 1973. *The fiscal crisis of the state*. New York: St. Martin's Press.

Peet, J. R. 1983. Relations of production and the relocation of United States manufacturing industry since 1960. *Econ. Geog.* **59**, 112–43.

Ross, R. S. J. 1983. Facing Leviathan: public policy and global capitalism. *Econ. Geog.* **59**, 144–60.

Sharpe, L. J. 1982. The Labour Party and the geography of inequality: a puzzle. In *The politics of the Labour Party*, D. Kavanagh (ed.), pp. 135–70. London: Allen & Unwin.

Strinati, D. 1983. State intervention, the economy, and crisis. In *Contemporary Britain*, A. Stewart (ed.), pp. 41–93. London: Routledge & Kegan Paul.

Susman, P. and E. Schutz 1983. Monopoly and competitive firm relations and regional development in global capitalism. *Econ. Geog.* **59**, 164–77.

Taylor, M. J. and N. J. Thrift 1982. Models of corporate development and the multinational corporation. In *The geography of multinationals*, M. J. Taylor and N. J. Thrift (eds.), pp. 117–35. London: Croom Helm.

Westergaard, J. and H. Ressler, 1976. *Class in a capitalist society*. Harmondsworth: Penguin.
Young, K. and L. Mills 1982. The decline of urban economies. In *Fiscal stress in cities*, R. Rose and E. Page (eds.), pp. 77–106. Cambridge: Cambridge University Press.

14

The spatial strategies of the state in the political-economic development of Brazil

PEDRO P. GEIGER and FANY R. DAVIDOVICH

During the past 50 years, the Brazilian state has used spatial strategies, both implicit and explicit, to achieve political and economic goals. In Brazil, the state has been the main actor in the articulation of industrialization with the macro-economy and social formation for this period. State intervention is based on a logic consisting not only of

> the intrinsic needs of the accumulation process imposed by the ruling class . . . but also the political struggle which takes place in the heart of civil society, and which has repercussions in the heart of the State itself . . . with the result that location is no longer merely an economic choice but becomes a political choice as well. The real location of each user of space is the result of the interplay of locational needs and their possibilities in political and economic terms. (Camargo *et al.* 1978)

As economic growth takes place, the spatial requirements of the social formation change. At the same time, the various geographical localities, as 'local social structures' (Urry 1981), become sources of new pressures on the character of the state, affecting the roles it must play.

In the following sections we will deal with urban and regional policies carried out during different historical periods. The period breakdown, which as far as possible will be based on types of spatial strategies adopted, is as follows:

1930–45 A phase dominated by urbanization strategies coupled to the rise of the industrial sector. Political power was greatly centralized, leading to a loss of autonomy for state governments.

1945–55 State governments regained their political autonomy, and took on the role of development agencies for regional industrialization.

1956–63 Manufacturing became dominant in the Brazilian economy resulting in greater spatial concentration in the southeastern region. Paradoxically, this circumstance obliged the *central* government to involve itself in *regional* economic development (Oliveira & Reichstul 1973).

1963–74 After an economic crisis in 1963–4, a military authoritarian regime was established. The regime created a technical–bureaucratic planning apparatus, whose aim was the spatial diffusion of 'modernization.' The urbanization of the countryside was heightened and rural–urban migration was encouraged.

1974–80 In this phase, the consequences of continuous urbanization became apparent. These consequences included the increasing resistance of 'civil society' to excessive centralization and the rise of a stronger business class independent of the state. This last development made room for the state to begin restricting itself to the adoption of policies proposed by the business class. Explicit urban decentralization policies were adopted by the federal government.

1981–   In the context of severe crisis in the urban industrial sector, political autonomy was recaptured at the regional level, increasing the pressures for a reformulation of the role of the central state.

1930–45: the promotion of urbanization

At the beginning of the 20th century, the city of Rio de Janeiro had a population of about 800 000 and the city of São Paulo some 250 000. Situated at the center of a rich agricultural region, São Paulo soon surpassed Rio as the main industrial center of the country. From 1900 to 1919, the number of workers employed in the industrial sector of Brazil rose from 136 400 to 275 000. By 1919, the state of São Paulo already held 33.1% of total industrial production while the city of Rio de Janeiro was left with 22.4% (Villela & Suzigan 1973). The agricultural growth of the 19th century drew a large number of migrants from various European countries, who then contributed to the growth of the main urban centers, the emergence of the urban middle class (in which army officers are included) and the expansion of industrial activities.

In 1920, 5.2% of the total population of Brazil was foreign born, as was as many as 20.0% of the population of the city of Rio de Janeiro and 18.1% of the population of the state of São Paulo. Foreign-born businessmen controlled about 42.0% of Brazil's industrial firms, and foreign-born workers constituted 21.0% of the country's labor force, with 40.0% of the latter in the state of São Paulo (Merrick & Graham 1979). At this point, foreign-born businessmen were not politically active, but European workers took important roles in the development of unions and labor parties in Brazil.

With the world economic crisis of the 1930s, the agrarian economy of Brazil suffered, destabilizing the existing political alliances. A revolution ended the 'Old Republic' and replaced it with a more centralized state. This state was built on the recognition that the agrarian export economy alone could not support the whole of Brazilian society. Thus, both labor and the foreign-dominated urban middle classes became more politically active, advocating further industrialization and internal market growth. Simultaneously, some sectors of the agrarian ruling class insisted on a larger involvement of the central state in sustaining agricultural prices (for example, the stocking and burning of coffee).

Therefore, the year 1930 was a landmark for the relations of capitalist accumulation and the state in Brazil. Governmental power shifted to the hands of a political group capable of simultaneously supporting the expansion of the industrial sector, including channelling of surplus generated by the agricultural sector to this sector, which became the leader in the economic growth of the country; catering to the interest of the exporters and preserving capital accumulation within the agricultural sector; and keeping under control the growing urban masses who were pressing for a greater share of the national income. These diverse interests were brought together under the aegis of an ideology of economic nationalism, which was consistent with conscious intervention of the state in the economy and in territorial organization. Moreover, it appealed to the middle class, and served to legitimize the centralization of power in the face of regional and local oligarchies. The military satisfied all these economic interests by endorsing modernization and centralization of power; but they also took on the role of political guardian, in order to prevent compromises with the masses. Thus, the modernization of the 1930s had a somewhat 'Prussian' character (cf. Moreira 1983).

Table 14.1 shows that from the 1931–40 period, the industrial sector had a higher annual growth rate than agriculture. This rate accelerated from 1931–40 to reach a first peak in the period 1951–60. The transportation and communication sector did not increase at the same speed during the period 1941–50, but improved strongly during the 1951–60 period. The resulting import-substitution industrialization required growth of the main urban centers in order to create social conditions for industrialization and separate them from the countryside. The countryside remained important, however, since non-monetary links between tenants (sharecroppers) and workers on one side and landowners on the other maintained the 'traditional peasant economy' (based on land rent) specifically for production of food for the cities. In the cities, the state set about the task of regulating the capital–labor relation. This was not a directly spatial policy, but it was only possible, in a practical sense, in a concentrated urban environment. It is another example of urban–rural opposition associated with first phases of industrialization (Mingione 1977).

The regulation of the capital–labor relation had important spatial consequences, however. 'Workers' laws' and the welfare system distinguished the 'formal' or 'protected' and 'informal' sectors of work. These laws segment

Table 14.1 Annual growth rates of the Brazilian national product, 1921–72.

	1921–30	1931–40	1941–50	1951–60	1961–70	1971–72
agriculture	3.4	4.3	2.8	4.3	4.3	5.5
industry	3.3	5.2	7.2	8.5	6.7	10.3
transportation and communications	8.1	5.1	4.9	8.2	7.0	9.5
commerce	3.4	4.6	5.2	5.7	5.5	9.3
total GNP	3.7	4.6	4.8	6.6	5.8	8.6

Source: Faria 1976.

the labor market, obliging urban employers to pay a minimum wage, grant paid vacations, limit hours worked, and provide some job stability. Together with governmental involvement in the social security system, these benefits for urban workers created the basis for an enlarged internal market. 'Workers' laws' were also designed to induce rural–urban migration, as evidenced by their provisions for 'family wages,' which were wage increments paid based on the number of children[1]. Moreover, the so-called 'law of two-thirds' forced urban enterprises to employ that ratio of Brazilian to foreign workers, limiting foreign-born entrepreneurs' employment of compatriots brought in from abroad. Thus, either by legislation or by material action, the government set in motion a circular process mutually reinforcing migration and urban population growth.

The capital–labor regulations were only the first step in state involvement in social reproduction in Brazilian cities. To regulate the cost of social reproduction in the larger cities, the government constructed dwellings for the lower and middle classes, financed by public funds through the Federal Saving Bank, and provided housing credit. Urban mass transportation systems were built and fares subsidized. Colonization projects were organized to expand the peasant economy in frontier regions in order to produce food for the cities.

In a few sectors, the state began to take on the role of industrial entrepreneur; it was faced directly with location decisions. From the moment the state took on this role, it became clear that besides rational explanations, there were political motives for locational choices. Indeed, while São Paulo was growing as the base of the private industrial sector, state investments tended to be concentrated in the capital, Rio de Janeiro, which was to become its base of popular support. Headquarters of state enterprises were located in Rio de Janeiro, and factories (whenever possible) in the state of Rio (whose appointed governor was President Vargas' son-in-law). In the city of Rio were located, among others, the headquarters of the National Steel Company (1941); the Vale do Rio Doce Company (mining) (1942); and the São Francisco Hydroelectric Company (1945). With the exception of the Itabira Special Steel Company (1944), all state factories were set up in the state of Rio de Janeiro: Volta Redonda (steel, the National Steel Company); the National Motor Factory (1943); and the National Alkalis Company (1943) (Suzigan 1976). Thus the central state and its professionals increased their power within society after 1930.

Until 1930, the geographical organization of Brazil was described as an 'economic archipelago' of regional economies. Urban-industrial growth, and the accompanying growth of the domestic market, required greater geographical integration of the country as internal flows tended to increase. Thus the state's second important political act was to change the character of the federation. The authoritarian regime of 1937–45 eliminated the autonomy of the states (whose elected heads until then were called presidents) in the name of national integration and against regional oligarchies. Governors were appointed by the federal government and the states lost a number of rights such as levying their own taxes; financial resources were centralized.

It is no accident that at the same time the matter of regional division attracted the interest of the federal technocracy and the Brazilian Institute of Geography and Statistics (IBGE) was established. Statistical, cartographic and geographic activities were part of modernization and the attempt to secure greater control of the territory by the center. Decree 311 of 1938, for instance, required all *municipios* (counties) to draw urban and suburban perimeters around their county seats.

1946–55: states as regional units

From the 19th century on, foreign capital invested in railroads, port facilities, electrical power plants near large cities, and in urban infrastructures. For example, the Light and Power Company had the monopoly on electricity, sewage, trolley and bus transportation in Rio de Janeiro and São Paulo, and in some other cities. Prices of these services were controlled and industry paid lower electricity tariffs than private customers. Hence, the industry that grew there did not provide sufficient incentive for private capital to invest in the provision of additional infrastructure, yet industry did not want to pay market prices for these services. The government therefore began to remove bottlenecks in the industrialization process by providing economic infrastructure. Large government investments were made in electrical power and roads, thus improving general conditions for rapid accumulation. Of about 30 federal companies existing in 1949, 12 were involved in electricity and transportation, 5 were in the financial sector, and 5 were industrial companies. From 1950 to 1960, 15 more federal companies were founded; as it improved infrastructure the state was also increasingly a consumer of goods produced in the private sector. In addition, the goverment began investing in capital goods industries: because of their size, long maturation and long amortization period, these were also neglected by the private sector.

With the end of World War II came the end of the authoritarian *Estado Novo* (new state), and the recovery by the federal states of their political autonomy. The capacity of the states to lobby the central government, either through state governments or entrepreneurs, was an important factor in directing investment of the state entities, especially with respect to resources from the official investment bank, the BNDE. São Paulo state, already the focal point for industrial growth of private capital, received most of the infrastructure and private incentive investments.

1956–63: 'developmentalism' and foreign capital; urbanization and the middle class; the regional issue

During the mid 1950s, about 40% of the Brazilian population, or some 25 million people, lived in urban areas (see Table 14.2). Approximately 6 million of these persons resided in the metropolitan areas of São Paulo and Rio de Janeiro. Consumption habits of the urban population were stimulated when part of the foreign currency reserves, accumulated by Brazil during World War II, were allowed to be spent to import durable goods. But in the second half of the 1950s, imports were limited by an unfavorable balance of payments and the recommendations of the International Monetary Fund, all of which produced a recession. The large foreign corporations, however, developed links with the Brazilian government, and began to produce for the domestic market those goods that could not be imported. Thus it was during the Kubitschek administration (1956–60) that the expression *desenvolvimentismo* (developmentalism) was adopted, indicating an explicit industrialization policy favorable to private monopolistic capital – a 'politically oriented capitalism.' Direct foreign investments rose from $2 million in 1952 to $22 million in 1953, $11 million in 1954, $43 million in 1955, $90 million in 1956, and $144 million in 1957 (Villela & Baer 1980).

Table 14.2   The urban population of Brazil, 1940–80 (percent)

1940	1950	1960	1970	1980
31.2	36.2	41.5	55.9	67.7

Source: IBGE, *Demographic Census*, 1940, 1950, 1960, 1970, 1980.

A large-scale automobile industry crowned the expansion of the durable goods sector. Opportunities in white-collar work strengthened an urban middle class, thereby increasing demand for durable goods. This new phase of capitalism in Brazil further strengthened the role of urbanization as the basis for industrialization. Foreign corporations favored locations within and around the metropolitan area of São Paulo, while a more pronounced relative decline of Rio de Janeiro – locus of the bulk of the state companies – took place. As a whole, the southeastern region of Brazil increased its share of employment and output in the Brazilian economy.

The priority of federal policy was industry and infrastructure, which was effected by channelling resources from agriculture, via a policy of paying exporters a low rate for the foreign currencies obtained through the export of agricultural products from across the country. The difference between the rate paid and the international rate went to finance industrial infrastructure in the urban southeast. This was necessary because no financial market existed to capture private savings commensurable with needs. Thus, the costs of industrialization of one region were spread over the entire country.

Most of the direct investments of the government – in industries, transport routes and the construction of electrical systems – were made in the southeast. The Furnas Company (electricity) and the Federal Railway Network date from 1957; and Electrobras was founded in 1961. The location of the steel industry was due to a compromise between the interests of southeast states and the technical rationale of locating plants at ports. Cosipa (1960) was placed on the coast of Santos (although on a poor site) in consideration of the state of São Paulo; the Vitoria Iron and Steel (1959) was also located on a sea port. Usiminas (1956) was placed near the source of mineral ore in order to satisfy the interests of the state of Minas Gerais.

At the end of the 1950s, the continuous increase in interregional inequalities, mainly between the traditional northeast and the southeast, emerged as a major political issue. This was in part because massive internal migration to the southeastern cities from the northeast transferred the problems of the latter region to the former. As the middle class grew and social inequalities increased, there were greater demands for spatial segmentation of migrants and the poor generally. For instance, in the early 1950s an attempt was made to reduce the influx of northeasterners to Rio de Janeiro by means of a ban on the transportation of passengers in adapted trucks ('paus de arara'). The result was to encourage proliferation of a larger number of interstate bus companies. The creation of the Federal Planning Agency for the Northeast (SUDENE) in 1959 also resulted from this pressure.

At the same time, SUDENE adopted the philosophy of the primacy of the national level, and territorial integration. SUDENE's policies encouraged rapid growth of the northeast's metropolitan areas, which was a part of a general process of metropolitan concentration in Brazil at the expense of the countryside. Thus, a network of metropolitan regions was formed along with the general increase in interregional inequality.

The Kubitschek administration also made use of nationalism to move the national capital from Rio to the new city of Brasilia. The 'interior' was glorified as being more authentically Brazilian than the coast. Both the colonial heritage and modern immigration had concentrated a sizeable portion of the activities of the biggest coastal cities in the hands of foreigners, while in the agrarian interior the ruling class of landowners was made up of natives. Debates held in the Legislature suggest, however, that the relocation of the capital was also motivated by the wish to move the central power away from the direct pressure of urban masses.

1964–73: 'modernization' and 'miracle'

The developmentalism of the 1950s was not capable of launching self-sustained capitalist growth: there remained great income inequalities and the majority of the population was very poor at the end of the decade. Deep political and economic crises occurred at the beginning of the 1960s which culminated in the military takeover of 1964. A strong authoritarian regime was established, capable of impeding social and political unrest while compressing wages, and of modernizing the administrative system in order to sustain both the diffusion of capitalism in the country and the provision of financial resources for development.

The first major step of the economic policy of the new government, which was attuned to the directives of international institutions, was to fight inflation through recession and wage repression. A system of compulsory savings was created by means of changes introduced in workers' laws. These savings were channelled into urban housing construction. The civil construction sector – which absorbs manpower but requires few imports – was to compensate for the recession, a practice frequently employed in developing countries. The National Housing Bank (BNH) was founded, and the ideology of owning one's own home became widespread. The civil construction sector began to undergo a transformation as independent builders were replaced by large firms who vertically integrated housing production, from the purchase of the plot of land to the marketing of housing as a finished product. At the same time, the financial sector increased its involvement in land speculation. Table 14.3 shows that from 1959 to 1967 there was no substantial increase in the share of internal revenue by different sectors except in finance, government and leasings.

Table 14.3   Share of Brazil's internal revenue by different sectors, 1949–78.

| | Internal revenue (%) | | | | | |
	1949	1959	1967	1970	1974	1978
primary activities	*24.9*	19.2	12.9	10.2	11.2	11.4
industry	26.0	32.6	32.5	36.3	*39.8*	37.1
commerce	12.4	14.4	14.8	15.7	*16.3*	15.2
finance	3.8	3.2	5.1	5.8	6.2	*9.3*
transport and communication	7.0	6.2	6.0	5.2	5.1	5.6
government*	6.8	7.1	*9.3*	9.2	7.6	8.0
leasings	6.3	7.0	*9.1*	8.1	6.2	6.2
other services	*12.8*	10.3	10.4	9.5	7.6	7.2
total	100.0	100.0	100.0	100.0	100.0	100.0

Source: Villela & Baer 1980: 16.
*State economic enterprises are computed in the respective economic sectors. The year in which each sector had its greatest share is in italics.

The measures pointed out above, combined with fortuitous circumstances in the world economy, allowed the country to overcome recession and to effect the so-called 'Brazilian miracle' between 1968 and 1972: high rates of growth in GNP and in industrial production. Table 14.3 shows substantial increases for industry and commerce in 1970 and 1974. It should be noted that the events of the late 1960s and early 1970s bear a striking resemblance to those of the early 1950s: production of durable goods and expansion of the middle class aided by the modernization of the tertiary sector. This has become the typical cycle of the development process in Brazil.

During this phase urban space in Brazil was invested with new functions. In the past, the needs of the city had been a motive for the beginning of industrialization by import–substitution, while the growth of the cities provided economies of agglomeration. Now, industrial growth had to be supported by uninterrupted urbanization. Urban space was also the site for the expansion of tertiary activities sponsored by the government and spread across the country (Tables 14.4 and 14.5). This expansion, based on the increase of such sectors as education, health, communication and public administration, involved the enlarging of the urban middle class. The demands for improved urban conditions by this middle class became one of the reasons for expansion of the infrastructure and of the production of collective consumption goods.

The central government created a greater centralization of the decision-making process in the economy. In this regard, for example, a series of companies of mixed control were created both at the federal and state levels.

Table 14.4   Distribution of the economically active population of Brazil according to activity 1950–80 (in percentages).

	1950	1960	1970	1980
primary sector	59.9	54.0	44.2	29.9
secondary sector	9.4	8.5	11.0	15.7
tertiary sector	30.7	37.5	44.8	54.4

Source: IBGE, *Demographic Censuses.*

Table 14.5   Structural changes in Brazil's tertiary sector, 1950 and 1970.

	1950	1970
liberal professions	1.8	2.4
public and private education	4.9	8.1
public and private medical and hospital services	1.6	2.4
social activities	2.2	2.6
financial intermediaries	2.7	3.9
other tertiary activities	86.8	80.6

Source: Almeida 1974: 14.

From 1966 to 1975, of the 231 governmental companies created, 108 belonged to the 'public service' sector (Martins 1978). From 1960 to 1969, 37 new federal and 175 state companies were created (see Table 14.6).

The federal government significantly extended its participation in the industrial sector; in 1969, 14% of industrial income was produced by the state. In the same year, the investments of the federal companies were distributed in the following manner: 37.3% in the industrial sector; 26.7% in the energy sector; 23.7% in the communications sector; 7.9% in transportation, and so on. The state's investments were quite different: 52.6% in energy; 17.1% in public services; 11.3% in transportation; and 7.4% in the financial sector (*Conjuntura Economica* 1973).

The state capitals thus became components of the transmission system of a process of territorial organization originating in the center, thereby establishing a pattern of urban and regional planning. Functional geographical

Table 14.6   Public jobs in Brazil according to level of government, 1950 and 1973 (000s).

	Total	Federal sphere	State sphere	Municipal sphere
1950	1027	506	318	186
1973	3351	1186	1515	650
average annual growth rate (%)	5.3	3.8	7.0	5.6

Source: Rezende & Castelo Branco 1976: 46.

studies of 'homogeneous regions' and 'functional urban regions' assumed special interest in the planning system. Modernization measures similar to those taken by the federal goverment in the administrative apparatus and in the social activities sector of the states contributed to the tertiarization of the economy and the expansion of the middle class. In higher education, for instance, state universities multiplied as they gained federal subsidies.

It is to this process that the considerable population growth of the Brazilian state capitals between 1960 and 1970 was due, even without their being industrialized centers. For instance, Florianopolis, the capital city of Santa Catarina, grew more during this period than did Blumenau or Joinville, industrialized towns in the state. The spatial strategy also encompassed the opening up of spaces in the frontier region, whether to nourish large cattle raising investments or land speculation projects, or to lessen the pressures exerted on rural populations by the great technological modernization of agriculture that began during this phase.

In general, then, the spatial strategy of the authoritarian regime, involving the modernization of tertiary sectors and urban infrastructure, was designed politically to solve both inter-class and intra-class conflicts, by assuming the *representation*[2] of all spatial levels. For example, the regime of 1964 took political autonomy away from the states and counties (*municipios*), and thus directly weakened the class fractions that might have dominated decision making at those levels. But the regime simultaneously penetrated those economies at all those levels much more deeply, and delegated parts of the administration of state enterprises directly to the various levels. This, in turn, reconstituted power relations at each spatial level, but did so in line with the will of the central state.

1974–80: the design of an explicit spatial policy

Brazilian economic growth since the 'miracle' had increased not only foreign and state capital, but the private domestic sector as well, a sector which had grown in consequence of the 'triple alliance' of state, national and multi-national capitals (Evans 1979). However, from the oil crisis of 1973 on, the needs of domestic industrial capital and the terms of the new world economic order began to take different directions. In this phase another split – between the interests of the industrial private domestic sector and the financial sector – dominated by multinational interests, began to open up.

As a remedy to the effects of the oil crisis on the balance of payments, the government turned to a greater domestic provision of capital goods and basic inputs, and looked for alternative sources of energy. This had the aim of decreasing elasticity between imports and economic growth.

New areas were opened to foreign capital (e.g. oil prospecting). However, the government favored the domestic entrepreneurial class by instituting 'market reserves' which encouraged domestic production of machines and equipment and restrained imports (Resolution of December 2, 1974). The Resolution of October 3, 1974 had already favored the use of national equipment by the government; the Resolution of December 4, 1974 outlined the expansion of petrochemicals and the cellulose and paper programs, and so on. In the following years, the Pro-Alcohol Program was established (to replace gasoline with alcohol fuel from sugar beets).

Such measures were linked to a continued expansion of the state sector of the economy and to a planning system increasingly reliant upon research institutions. According to the 1984 annual report of the World Bank, that portion of the current income of the government not coming from taxes or contributions grew from 6.0% in 1972 to 25.8% in 1981. The official *cruzeiro* was overvalued, and interest rates on foreign loans were relatively low. The public sector, like the private, borrowed, thus increasing not only the internal but the external debt.

As the state became progressively more 'autonomous,' it began to reach out again to the civil society. In response to the resistance by entrepreneurs to state intervention, and to the state's own failure in the economy, steps were taken beginning in 1982 to ease authoritarianism. Second, even though economic policy remained oriented to attaining economies of scale and technological modernization, the planning system was increasingly forced to respond to the role that economic policy played in exacerbating social and regional inequalities in the distribution of income. The rise of the big cities also led to the spread of mass media, which in turn highlighted these problems and created public resistance to authoritarianism. Thus, even though the government has become more involved in all geographical scales of planning, from urban and regional to national, it again took steps towards more local and regional autonomy, particularly responding to local demands on issues such as the environment and the greater spatial deconcentration of industry.

Out of these tensions between the economic policy and its outcomes, the expressions 'efficiency' and 'equity,' in which compromise is implicit, emerged full-blown in planning jargon. Efficiency referred to the centralization of decisions, economies of scale, production per employee, and so on. Equity referred to such things as a better distribution of income, to spatial deconcentration of activities. In the name of efficiency and equity, proposals for remodelling the urban configuration were made, favoring greater industrial deconcentration. Support also grew for a rebalancing of investments to favor social reproduction relatively more than industrial production. These investments were urban investments, and so the configuration of the urban system was once more informed by redistributive philosophies. The creation of the National Commission for Urban Policies – which later became the National Council for Urban Development (CNDU) – by Decree 74.154 of July 6, 1974, and the institution of nine metropolitan regions made the urban policy explicit. The state was thus thrust into the role of mediating the contradictions which became apparent in the urban areas as a result of its policies which centralized resources in urban areas in the first place. In so doing, it tried to continue to cater to a wide range of interests in civil society, i.e. both capital and labor, in the improvement of urban mass transportation. The construction of the São Paulo and Rio de Janeiro subways was possible only with the support of the federal government.

Capital used the city more broadly and deeply in this phase, engaging in

291

massive property speculation and attempting to concentrate public and private investments in the most profitable areas. The diffusion of capital from property reached the middle-sized cities of the more developed regions: at Presidente Prudente, São Paulo, the number of property firms grew from 2 in 1972 to 32 in 1984 (Sposito 1984). Increasing participation by oligopolistic capital in property and the oligopoly's lobbying strength also encouraged state intervention in urban planning and infrastructure provision.

A critical element in the spatial strategies designed to mediate conflicts between capital and labor, and to respond to the growing criticism of the interregional inequalities that had been created by the economic policy of the regime, was industrial deconcentration. Deconcentration took its place, along with the improvement of existing urban areas, in the spatial strategies of the state in the late 1970s. In a country the size of Brazil, the term deconcentration has several meanings, and they must be carefully distinguished.

Table 14.7 shows that a spontaneous deconcentration of industrial activity from the great metropolis to peripheral areas was already occurring because of congestion, environmental problems and greater social polarization of the urban population. The data of the Census of 1980 reveal that, while the Metropolitan Region of São Paulo showed an annual geometric growth of 4.4%, the urban agglomeration in its surroundings grew far more: Americana, 7.4%; Campinas, 6.6%; São Jose dos Campos, 6.3%; Jundiai, 5.2%.

In this phase managerial groups and state technocrats strove, with the approval of the federal government, to bring industrial investments (including state investments) to their territories. The state of Minas Gerais increased its participation in the amount of industrial value added in Brazil from 6.4% to 7.0% from 1970 to 1977, and from 8.6% to 10.0% in the intermediate goods sector (Andrade 1982). The FIAT automobile industry was installed in Betim, in the metropolitan area of Belo Horizonte. While the real reasons for favoring the industrial axis of Porto Alegre were political, there was no lack of economic rationales for the choice. The location of the A. Pasqualini refinery or of the Piratini steel mill would permit regionalization; it would offer forward linkages to new small and middle-sized companies.

The state planning systems of the states of São Paulo and Minas Gerais became interested in regional deconcentration. This had political implications, as at that time the country was beginning to open itself up to direct elections for governor. In Minas, the Industrial Districts Company was created. In 1975, in São Paulo, the Secretary for Economy and Planning created the PDUR (Urban and Regional Development Policy), which comprised development programs for middle-sized towns. In the same year, CETESB (Company for Environmental Cleaning and Technology) was founded. It controls the location of new industries and the expansion of old ones (Geiger, Andrade & Baer 1983).

Political interest in interregional deconcentration of industry predates the present tendencies to deconcentration. These latter tendencies may have grown as a result of entrepreneurial reaction to the union movement in the great urban-industrial centers (Storper 1984). However, only toward the end of the Geisel administration (mid 1970s) did organized labor begin to find

Table 14.7 Share in Brazilian value added (percentage) and sectoral specificity (weight of sector in total value added), 1975.

	Metalo-engineering*		Durable goods*		Intermediate goods*		Traditional industries*		Urban industries*		Total	
	Share	Sectoral specificity	Share	Sectoral specificity	Share	Sectoral specificity	Share	Sectoral specificity	Share	Sectoral specificity	Share	Sectoral specificity
metropolitan areas of São Paulo and Rio	53.3	24.5	69.9	16.9	44.5	21.3	29.8	16.2	65.1	19.5	48.8	100.0
other metropolitan areas	11.9	23.0	6.7	6.9	14.4	29.1	11.3	25.8	11.3	14.3	11.6	100.0
southeast–south-center urban agglomeration	15.6	25.4	13.9	12.0	12.6	30.0	11.8	22.7	7.7	8.2	13.7	100.0
cities of south–southeast-center†	5.9	26.8	1.9	4.6	3.4	16.4	6.6	35.8	5.1	15.3	4.9	100.0
north–northeast urban agglomeration	0.4	8.9	0.1	0.8	0.1	19.5	1.7	50.5	1.2	20.0	0.9	100.0
cities of north–northeast†	0.4	7.5	2.6‡	28.5‡	0.8	17.5	1.5	36.6	0.7	9.5	1.1	100.0
rest of Brazil	12.6	22.7	4.9	12.0	19.2	23.7	37.7	26.8	8.9	14.8	19.0	100.0

Source: IBGE, *Industrial Census*, 1975.

*Metalo-engineering comprises metallurgy and engineering; durable goods: transportation materials and electro-electronics; intermediary goods: mining, non-metallics, paper, rubber, chemicals and plastics; traditional industries: timber, leather, textiles, food, beverages and tobacco; urban industries: pharmaceutics, furniture, clothing, printing and sundry.

†Only cities in counties of more than 100000 inhabitants.

‡Owing to industries at Manaus Free-Port Zone.

general political conditions to demand better wages. Since Vargas, government wage policy has invariably attempted to set different minimum wages in each region, aiming to attract investment to less developed areas and to protect local entrepreneurs, however unsuccessfully. Only recently did the regional minimum wages become more uniform, and the number of differentiated regional units decrease. According to the general price index the variation of the minimum wage of 1980 in relation to that of 1970 was 1.14 in Bahia and Pernambuco, 1.11 in Minas Gerais and 1.06 in Rio de Janeiro and São Paulo.

In fact, the entrepreneurial sector resisted deconcentration policies when, partly for political reasons (to decongest the labor force), the government instituted them. For instance, very recently the Michelin Company was reluctant to accept a more distant location and was, finally, permitted to build a plant on the periphery of Rio de Janeiro.

Growth pole strategies were another form of deconcentration. The second national development plan emphasized the comparative advantages of the various regions of the country, and recommended development of regional specializations. In each macro region, with the exception of the southeast, superintendencies were either confirmed or created, and programs were placed under them. The SUDAM area was placed in charge of the agro-mineral or Amazonian growth poles, in conformity with the act of September 18, 1974; SUDENE had Pro-Terra, an agricultural progam with some irrigation projects; SUDECO was the central pole, and had the Cerrado project for improving agriculture in the Savannah (*cerrado*) (act of January 29, 1975). SUDESUL was made responsible for the south of Brazil (Guimaraes & Vianna 1984).

1980– : the crisis in the urban–industrial sector

At the beginning of the 1980s, the oil crisis in Brazil became the debt crisis, and under pressure from the international financial world the goverment ceded some of its nationalism. Since the 1960s, an increasing portion of exports had been manufactured goods, but until the end of the 1970s most economic growth was related to domestic consumption. In the 1980s, as the currency declined sharply and inflation and prices rose, economic policy encouraged the export of manufactured goods, while holding down wages. Also favored were investments in export-oriented agro-mineral projects in the peripheral regions. Imports were sharply cut back. All this set in motion an internal recession which greatly affected the modern industrial urban sector. Some scholars blame the previous government for having supported investments financed by borrowing. However, of the commercial surplus of around $6.0 billion for 1984, $4.5 billion must be credited precisely to these earlier policies designed to increase Brazil's industrial production, as well as to energy programs.

Opposition to the authoritarian regime had been growing since before the debt crisis. The private domestic industrial entrepreneurs who favored a more liberal regime rejected 'capitalism directed by the state,' as 'there is no example of a liberal regime in which free enterprise does not prevail' (Guimaraes 1976). The middle class, the majority of which supported the institutional change (authoritarian military) of 1964, became distant from the urban bourgeoisie. Even though this class had benefited from the growth of corporations and state enterprises, its relative wages collapsed in the economic crisis. The industrial workers of the great cities, now distant from their rural roots and from state paternalism, gradually formed a new union movement with the metropolitan area of São Paulo as its focal point. Spokesmen for 'global capital' also appeared, who were interested in reducing the power of the national state.

All of these forces, located mainly in the metropolitan areas, began to form movements in favor of a new institutional arrangement of the state. They demanded greater local and regional autonomy, and greater participation by civilian society in the formation of the state. The government responded with the policy of *abertura* (opening).

One of the spatial strategies of this policy was to return autonomy, once more, to the states. By holding gubernatorial elections in 1982, the federal government delegated major responsibilities for administration. The federal government maintained power with regard to the overall direction of economic policies, which became concentrated to the administration of the debt. Owing to this, long and medium-range planning and explicit spatial policy were made a lesser priority.

Conclusions

This chapter showed that, in a developing country, when maintenance of the accumulation process can no longer be based only on land rent or commercial capital, new state policies are necessary to provide the continuity of industrialization. Consequently, new social sectors involved in the process of industrialization increase their participation in state power. But it was also shown that as the process requires the state to expand its services, technocracy, and bureaucracy as well as the size of its enterprises, it also acquires a more autonomous character, as during the 1973–1978/9 period, before the current phase of crisis.

The chapter showed how the state was called to act either implicitly or explicitly on various aspects of the accumulation–space relationship, in order to allow a given spatial order to achieve its potential. As the state became more autonomous, its spatial strategies have not always coincided precisely with the interests of the private industrial sector.

During the third decade of the century, when the Brazilian state was dominated by an alliance of the urban bourgeoisie with part of the land-owning class, it decided to transfer resources from agriculture to industrialization. The state thus became more involved in territorial organization. For instance, it promoted concentrated urbanization. This was not only for the economic purpose of lowering the costs of labor by attracting migrants, by subsidizing housing and transportation, and so on. It was also for political reasons: to establish concentrated masses of political supporters. This explains in part state location practices favoring the state and city of Rio de Janeiro until the mid 1950s.

Brazilian growth was never independent of the general process of capital accumulation. Actually, even during the 1940s and early 1950s, a number of missions from US and international institutions advised the Brazilian government in economic planning. But it was during the second half of the 1950s that the Brazilian economy was internationalized by heavy foreign industrial investments. The market grew further as this modern sector provided new and better paid jobs, especially for white-collar workers. But such a process, especially as strong inequalities of income increased, reached a limit. A first strong signal appeared when the continuous concentration of growth in some areas of the southeast and the increase of regional inequalities turned the regional issue into a major political question. Government was obliged to establish the first large federal agency for regional planning (SUDENE).

The rise of a new authoritarian regime in 1964 meant that, as the economic process reached various bottlenecks, the ruling socioeconomic sectors tried to find new means of accumulation, without breaking with the capitalist system or making basic changes in the social structure. This was achieved by maintaining the prior model of growth based on durable goods and on upper and middle class consumption, along with strong social and geographical fragmentation. To make this model viable, higher productivity was necessary, based on economies of scale and lower proportions of production costs paid as wages.

Thus the first deconcentration policies were diffusion oriented and affected the tertiary sector more than the private industrial sector, as the latter did not wish to give up the advantages of agglomeration. As the state enlarged its institutional dimensions and tended to greater autonomy, it could diverge more often from some private interests of the ruling class.

From 1973, the government was forced to be more involved in compromise policies, 'efficiency with equity,' trying to favor capital and labor simultaneously, as in the planning of inter- and intra-urban space. Not only did a spatial strategy related to territorial organization and deconcentration appear explicitly in the official planning records, but there was also discussion of spatial theoretical models. Explicit deconcentration plans were also related to the desire of the different states and regions, with their own improved technocracies, to have a larger portion of the national product.

However, as the world economy shifted to 'global capitalism,' the interests of national and foreign capital diverged. During the period 1973–9, the government followed a nationalistic line under which the industrial sectors linked to capital goods and basic inputs grew, in a second industrialization by import substitution. A large part of this development was made by state and domestic private enterprise. There was also a spontaneous process of geographical deconcentration of industries.

As the state became increasingly autonomous, divergences with private capital also grew. Pressures from all of civil society for political democracy were increasing, and a first step by government was to give back the states' and counties' autonomy. However, as has been shown, this whole process was disturbed by the debt crisis which brought with it a recession. A major current trend seems to be the deepening of the division between the interests of sectors of national industrial capital, which cannot gain much more from exports, and those of international financial capital. An effort is made by these sectors to attract Brazilian mercantile capital and labor into new alliances.

The Brazilian example has shown how political needs have great influence on the location of activities owing to the weight of the state in the direction of the economy and to its centralizing action. Phases of lesser authoritarianism were accompanied by a greater geographic concentration of the economy, while phases of greater authoritarianism involved explicit deconcentration strategies.

Notes

We are very grateful to the editors, Allen J. Scott and Michael Storper, for comments and suggestions which went into the final version of this chapter; we are also grateful to Mary Beckner and Liv Sovik, graduate students at the University of Texas at Austin, who helped with the English version.

1 These articles are still in effect, but the relative size of the premiums has declined sharply during the last decades.
2 The term *representation* is employed here according to the meaning ascribed to it by Lefevbre (1970). For this author, *will* and *representation* are different faces of the power realized in this state. *Will* implies a project developed historically by the leading sectors of the society, involving temporal relations; *representation* is the furnishing of a political and ideological basis for power, related to a spatial projection of the society.

References

Almeida, Jose 1974. *Industrializacão e emprego no Brasil*. Rio de Janeiro: IPEA/INPES (Instituto de Planejamento Economico e Social Instituto de Pesquisas).
Amin, Samir and Kostas Vergopoulos 1977. *A questão agraria e o capitalismo*. Rio de Janeiro: Ed. Paz e Terra.
Camargo, Azael Rangel *et al* 1978. *Nota introductoria sobre a construcão de um estudo: o urbano*. São Paulo: FUNDEP, mimeo.
Conjuntura Economica June 1973. Rio de Janeiro: Fundacão Getulio Vargas.
Davidovich, Fany R. 1978. Escalas de urbanizacão. Uma perspectiva geografica da sistema urbano Brasileiro. *Rev. Bras. Geog.* **40**(1), 51–82.
Evans, P. 1979. *Dependent development: the alliance of multinational, state and local capital in Brazil*. Princeton, NJ: Princeton University Press.
Faria, V. E. 1976. *Occupational marginality, employment and poverty in Brazil*. PhD Thesis. Harvard University.
Geiger, Pedro P., Andrade, Thompson and Werner Baer 1983. Regional differences in Brazil's industrial system. *Luso Brazilian Rev.* **20**(1), 13–43.
Guimaraes, Caesar 1976. *Empresariado, tipos de capitalismo e ordem politica*. Paper presented at the Congress of the International Association of Political Science, Edinburgh, August.

Guimaraes, Caesar and Maria Lucia Teixeira Vianna 1984. *Autoritarismo, planejamento a formas de centralizacão decisoria: os casos do Conselho Monetario Nacional e do Conselho de Desenvolvimento Economico.* Encontro Anual da APDCS, IUPERJ.

IBGE. *Demographic and Industrial Censuses* Rio de Janeiro: Instituto Brasileiro de Geografia e Estatistica.

Lefevbre, Henry 1970. *La révolution urbaine.* Paris: Editions Gallimard.

Merrick, Thomas and Douglas H. Graham 1979. *Population and economic development in Brazil 1800 to the present.* Baltimore: Johns Hopkins University Press.

Mingione, Enzo 1977. Theoretical elements for a marxist analysis of urban development. In *Captive cities*, Michael Harloe (ed.), pp. 89–109. Chichester: Wiley.

Moreira, Ruy 1983. *Contradicões fabris, espaco e ordenacão de classes (a questao cidade/campo no Brasil).* Master's Dissertation, Universidade Federal do Rio de Janeiro, Instituto de Geo-Ciencias.

Oliveira, Francisco and H. P. Reichstul 1973. Mudanças na divisão interregional do trabalho no Brasil. *Estudos CEBRAP* 4 (April–June), 151–68.

Rezende, Fernando and Flavio P. Castelo Branco. O emprego publico como instrumento de politica economica. In *Aspectos da Participacão do Governo na Economia*, Serie Monografica **26**, pp. 35–76. Rio de Janeiro: IPEA/INPES.

Sposito, Maria B. 1984. *Os agentes produtores do espaco urbano em Presidente Prudente.* Paper presented at the Congres of the Association of Brazilian Geographers, São Paulo, July.

Storper, Michael 1984. Who benefits from industrial descentralization? Social power in the labour market, income distribution and spatial policy in Brazil. *Regional Studies* **18**(2), 143–164.

Suzigan, Wilson 1976. As empresas do governo e o papel do estado na economia. In *Aspectos da Participacão do Governo na Economia*, Serie Monografica **26**, pp. 77–134. Rio de Janeiro: IPEA/INPES.

Urry, John 1981. Localities, regions and social class. *Int. J. Urban Regional Res.* **5**(4), 455–74.

Villela, Annibal and Werner Baer 1980. O setor privado nacional: problemas e politicas para o seu fortalecimento. In *Colecão Relatorios de Pesquisas* 46. Rio de Janeiro, IPEA/INPES.

Villela, Annibal and Wilson Suzigan 1973. *Politica de Governo e Crescimento da Economia Brasileira 1889–1945.* Serie Monografica 10. Rio de Janeiro: IPEA.

PART V

The geographical anatomy of industrial capitalism

15

Industrial change and territorial organization: a summing up

A. J. SCOTT and M. STORPER

In this concluding chapter, we seek to sum up and reconstruct the preceding discussion by focusing on the central question of industrial change and territorial development. As the argument proceeds we show how the rather narrow idea of *location* can be assimilated into the much richer conception of *territory*. We also indicate the relevance of our notion of territorial development to a prospective theoretical human geography. Our statement is intended as a preliminary sketch of a theory of the origins, reproduction, and transformation of territorial complexes of human activity in capitalism.

The foundations of territorial development: some preliminary propositions

It is our contention that the most viable point of departure for an analysis of territorial development in modern capitalism is an investigation of the production system as an articulation of technical, social and political relationships (see Chapters 2 & 13 above). In other words, territory (i.e. humanly differentiated geographical space) is a creature of those forces that underlie the material reproduction of social life and that find their immediate expression in various forms of production and work. Let us at once allay any budding anxieties that these remarks may provoke. We are in no sense about to advocate a deterministic base-superstructure model in which human actions are consistently overridden by mechanical causalities. Nor do we wish to deny the significance of culture and consciousness in the formation of territorial outcomes. Nevertheless, and in line with all of the theoretical work adumbrated above, we do want to insist that any discourse about the modern space-economy is most effective when rooted in the problem of the expressive effects of the commodity production system as it is organized in space. Let us now elaborate on the implications of this claim.

The term 'commodity production' signifies a system of social arrangements in which labor is combined with capital in order to bring forth outputs that can be sold at a profit. The logic of this productive activity gives rise at once to a process of capital accumulation which establishes the broad structure of the temporality in which social and geographical reality unfolds. This logic is primary in the sense that it constitutes the driving dynamic of social existence in capitalism, though it does not, of course, fix patterns of life in any simple one-to-one manner. Even so, and important as these remarks may be as a prelude to any understanding of territoriality, they still do not give us any immediate clues about the ways in which geographical processes function. For this, we must turn to some secondary forms of knowledge about spatial organization as such. Here, we invoke the same meso-level analytics to which we alluded in the introductory chapter; these analytics help us mediate between the macro-economic processes of capitalism and concrete micro-geographical instances.

Why, we may ask, is the landscape of capitalism characterized not so much by a pattern of widely dispersed production sites and equal levels of income, as it is by a tremendously uneven distribution of economic activity and marked disparities of income and social welfare? As we see in Chapters 6, 9, 10, 11 & 14, some regions are richly endowed with dense agglomerations of capital and labor whereas others are only thinly developed. An obvious but only partially correct response to the question is to suggest that geographical unevenness is induced by the patently irregular distribution of basic resources and transport opportunities. Even if we put aside the effects of given underlying physical irregularities, however, it is apparent that the landscape of capitalism is pre-ordained to developmental disparities. Geographical unevenness is socially and historically produced out of the basic dynamics of commodity production as such. In capitalism, the organization of labor processes, the transactional structure of production, the peculiarities of local labor markets, and the many different external economies that arise out of dense localized forms of development all create pressures that lead to high levels of development in some areas, and relative backwardness and stagnation in others (Chs. 5, 6, 7 & 10).

The spatial variability and discontinuities of capitalism are thus endemic. Capital and labor concentrate together at privileged sites where significant increasing returns to scale (through external economies) are available. Subsequent to this concentration, many potent territorial effects emerge. Geographically specific forms of technical change in the production system are set in motion; a localized division of labor appears; affective and political expressions of communal life are engendered; urbanization processes get under way; and so on. At the same time, as the level of spatial concentration increases, diseconomies of agglomeration increase. These diseconomies help to intensify the geographically specific forms of technical change alluded to above, with the typical result that more and more units of capitalist production are steadily shifted out to various decentralized locations. In all these ways, a restless system of territorial processes creates and recreates the geographical anatomy of industrial capitalism. It is in this sense that we may think of the logic of the production system as being analytically prior to everything else in human geography. Production and work constitute the fundamental reference points of the entire human landscape. However, as we shall see below, these reference points are by no means to be interpreted as simple 'exogenous variables.' In the complex world of historical and geo-

302

graphical reality, the locational structures of production and work and the contingent social and political activity that flows around them shape each other (Ch. 6).

With these broad remarks in mind, our task is now to examine in more detail the conditions under which territorial agglomeration of economic production occur, and how they operate within generalized patterns of uneven regional development.

Growth centers in the landscape of capitalism

The major foci of territorial development in capitalism coincide with intensely concentrated centers of growth. A skeletal – and ultimately incomplete – story about the emergence of these growth centers can be outlined as follows. First, a propulsive industry with many backward linkages may be assumed to locate itself at some site, for whatever reason. Second, firms in upstream sectors of production move into the vicinity of the propulsive industry in a process of import-substitution. Third, much additional (tertiary) economic activity is generated by various multiplier effects. Fourth, the entire economic base of the system is sustained by a proliferation of transport connections. Fifth, the growth center is then consolidated by economies of scale in the provision of major infrastructural artifacts and by urbanization economies generally.

Now, as useful as this story undoubtedly is (when appropriately filled in with the necessary details and subtleties), it nonetheless overlooks what is perhaps the most fundamental process of development, growth, and internal differentiation in any spatially concentrated center of industrial production. It is silent, in short, on the central and critical issues of the division of labor, the vertical disintegration of production, and the structure of inter-establishment transactional activity (Ch. 5). These are all different aspects of a single process of development. With increases in the market for final outputs from any growth center, the division of labor will tend to increase. The point is admirably summed up in Adam Smith's dictum to the effect that 'the division of labor is limited by the extent of the market.' As the market grows, there is a tendency for labor processes to begin to fragment into innumerable specialized components. This is manifested in both an increasing technical division of labor within the individual firm, and an increasing social division of labor *among* firms. The precise conditions under which an increasing social division of labor among firms (i.e. vertical disintegration) occurs remain something of an unresolved question, and it is evident that much more research in this area will have to be done before a really systematic account of the process can be finally sketched out. It does seem, however, that labor processes are especially susceptible to vertical disintegration where (a) production methods physically resist capital-deepening and resynthesis, (b) output markets are unstable and unpredictable, with the consequence that producers will disintegrate in order to avoid the backward transmission of uncertainty through the vertical structure of the firm, and (c) the labor force is segmentable so that work can be readily subcontracted out to low wage plants in secondary labor markets.

As a direct outcome of vertical disintegration the inter-plant transactional structure of production becomes increasingly labyrinthine. This transactional structure is composed from many different specific kinds of linkages: materials flows through spot markets, subcontracting relations, long-term contracts, face-to-face exchanges of information, and so on. Many of these linkages are quite costly in unit terms, particularly when activity levels are small in magnitude so that economies of scale are not available to transactors. Within any given structure of linkages, there is a strong proclivity for those producers who are most tightly linked together to coalesce out as a functional entity in geographical space. Where spatially determinate transactions costs are especially high (i.e. where linkages are small scale, irregular, ephemeral), this tendency to coalescence will be all the more exaggerated. In this way, the production system is reconstituted in large degree as a constellation of interacting geographically convergent industrial plants. Such complexes are often fertile centers of invention, innovation, and horizontal disintegration. They contain rich organizational possibilities which help to sustain new entrepreneurial activity; and they are a reservoir of experienced individuals who are structurally positioned to take advantage of new technical and business opportunities as they present themselves. The histories of development in the Lancashire cotton textile complex in the 19th century, or of the semiconductor industry in Silicon Valley in the 1960s and 1970s, are exemplary in this regard.

From all of this, we see that the growth and expansion of industrial complexes proceeds on two separate fronts. On the one hand, the development of any complex is driven forward by increases in demand. On the other hand, these same increases also often (though not necessarily always) encourage fragmentation of production processes, so that the complex becomes internally and dynamically differentiated (in other words, the 'roundaboutness' of production increases). These processes operate, moreover, no matter whether the complex is founded upon a major central pole of economic activity (such as the car industry of Detroit) or upon an amorphous sector of production in which no one particular segment stands out as the driving pole (such as clothing manufacture in almost any large metropolitan area). The more they expand (up to a certain point, at least), the more such complexes become attractive as centers of profitable commodity production by reason of their increasing external economies.

With the growth of these complexes of productive activity, a larger and larger labor force is drawn into the local area. Complicated labor market mechanisms then come into play, and these also have many different implications for external economies in the adjacent region. Among these mechanisms we may point to such things as intra-regional wage-setting processes, turnover activity, job search behavior, occupational reproduction, and all the rest. Chapters 7, 8 & 10 above contain many important insights into these matters. But in spite of our rapidly augmenting stock of knowledge about local labor markets we are still far from any generally agreed upon systematization of their basic operation. Certainly, the massing together in one place of large populations which collectively embody many different skills and attributes is an important agglomeration economy. However, such massing can also be a double-edged sword, for dense communities of workers have traditionally formed the basis of labor movements (unionization in particular) in industrial America and Europe. These varying social and political attributes of large agglomerations create a constant stream of reactions and counter-reactions with many implications for the further development of the space-economy. We investigate some of these implications in more detail below. First, however, we must look carefully at the related problem of territorial reorganization and the spatial division of labor.

Territorial reorganization and the spatial division of labor

In spite of the potent tendencies to industrial complex formation and growth center development as described above, various counter-tendencies are also an important element of the formation of the economic landscape. Above all, some kinds of production processes are amenable to organizational and geographical disarticulation from the rest of the production system, and are hence able to avail themselves of locational niches in various hinterland areas. The forms of production that seem most susceptible to this sort of disarticulation are in those segments of the economy where the 'roundaboutness' of production is decreasing or where the scale and standardization of production units are increasing dramatically. They tend to have simplified input–output structures so that they face minimal transactions costs per unit of output. Large branch plants are a familiar expression of this phenomenon. Plants like this tend to avoid dense territorial complexes with their typically high wages, their high land prices, and their politically sophisticated labor forces. Moreover, such plants in general make use of unskilled labor. Thus, they have many positive inducements to locate themselves in peripheral areas where their production costs are likely to be low, and where they can find abundant resources of unskilled and inexperienced labor. Increasingly today, these peripheral areas include not just stagnant regions of the national territory, but also any and all (politically reliable) Third World countries (Chs. 2, 6, 11 and 12).

Thus some forms of technical and organizational change in capitalist production systems bring about reversal of the social division of labor and concomitant polarization tendencies. Localized territorial complexes of productive activity can be in part or whole dissolved away by the resynthesis (i.e. vertical integration) of labor processes, and by the concomitant emergence of large capital-intensive standardized units of production with streamlined external transactions. As this happens, affected growth centers enter into periods of crisis, and decentralized branch plants start to spring up at widely dispersed locations. These kinds of outcomes have been characteristically associated with periodic rounds of financial and institutional restructuring in industry, particularly when foreign competition starts to become intense.

The dissolution of territorial production complexes through the resynthesis of labor processes is reinforced by the secular improvements in transport and communications technologies that have taken place with the development of the forces of production generally in capitalism. In the 19th century, some enterprising capitalists had already made attempts to break away from the major centers of industrial production by setting up independent mill towns. However, this process of dispersal could not become a more generalized means of organizing the spatial basis of capitalist production until sectoral conditions of resynthesis and various transport improvements had made their historical appearance. It is also important to note here that as industries have steadily decentralized to the periphery over the course of the last several decades they have sometimes – but by no means always – sparked off rounds of growth in the surrounding area. We shall deal with this issue in more detail below.

We have now identified three important moments in the process of territorial development: the emergence of growth centers, the tendency of those growth centers to decay under specifiable circumstances, and the pushing out of the extensive margin of industrial space into new hinterlands. Each of these processes occurs simultaneously. In general, in the highly developed economies, new industries seem to be associated with concentrated growth centers, and old mature industries with decentralization. In the Third World, however, mature forms of industry may be converging on major growth centers even as they vacate traditional centers in the developed nations.

Added to the temporal development of the forces of capitalist production and the locational dynamics of specific sectors is the development over the course of the 20th century of the multi-divisional, multi-establishment firm. Such firms have grown steadily in size as the upper limits on managerial economies of scale and scope have been continually raised. Increasing firm size and complexity have in turn enabled managements to split up the internal functions of the firm and to assign them to widely scattered locations. This increasing geographical specialization of the internal units of the firm vastly increases corporate flexibility. Such strategies as global scanning, multiple sourcing, and the running of parallel production facilities now become viable corporate possibilities. These developments allow firms to deal effectively with localized obstructions in the production system as and when they occur. They give firms leverage with respect to local governments and enable them to bargain effectively for various concessions in matters of land-use regulations, infrastructural services, taxes, and so on. Above all, they permit large multi-establishment enterprises to bypass stubborn labor difficulties at particular sites, for problem plants can simply be run at low capacity or even idled for extended periods. With its wide array of locational choices, but with often very little dependence on any particular locality, the multi-establishment firm is able to make widely separated hinterlands compete with each other for development; in recent years an interregional and international bidding war for plant locations has been effectively ignited. This is part and parcel of the system of pressures currently at work on the European social democracies as noted in our introductory chapter.

All of the tendencies we describe here have ushered in a new spatial and international division of labor, with many localized effects and manifestations. For the most part, white collar management and control functions have been assigned to large metropolitan regions where they interact with constellations of (vertically disintegrated) business, commercial and financial service functions. Concomitantly, much blue-collar manual production (what Perrons alludes to as fordist branch plants, Ch. 12) has been shifted out to diverse peripheral territories. Much of the time, this reindustrialization of peripheral areas produces little in the way of developmental side-effects. This is demonstrated with some force by Dunford in his study of industrial decentralization to southern Italy (Ch. 11). In fact, many of the branch plants that are shifted out to the periphery have remarkably restricted local multiplier effects, for they comprise in general mature mass-production units with extremely narrow ranges of external transactional activity. Even so, it is just occasionally the case that decentralized production units will begin to stimulate developmental impacts in the surrounding region. At the very least, decentralization increases the movement of goods and capital to the periphery and so encourages further transport improvements. If the demand for transport and communications grows to the point where significant economies of scale come into play, additional industries that might not have viewed that part of the periphery as a potential location may begin to regard it more favorably. In this way, the extensive margin of industry is expanded as more hinterland areas are incorporated into the set of potential locational choices for those industries undergoing resynthesis and geographical specialization of their own internal functions. Furthermore, a few selected areas in the United States and Western Europe (e.g. some of the new high technology industrial centers of the Sunbelt, like Dallas, Texas, or Orange County, California) have recently begun to evince a marked tendency to local complex formation and fragmentation of labor processes. We can thus now observe, along with the passive industrialization of the periphery, the rise of new industrial complexes at privileged locations where intense manufacturing activity was formerly largely absent. It must be added at once that in these booming new industrial centers a deeply segmented occupational and wage structure is apparent, with blue-collar wages actually declining in some areas. Even *within* these complexes, then, the process of development remains quite uneven.

Similarly, many of the old large metropolitan centers of North America and Western Europe are experiencing increasing segmentation of their occupational structure. At one end of the scale, as we have shown, these centers are increasingly becoming foci of management and control of the corporate economy of capitalism. At the other end of the scale, there is a simultaneous growth of large immigrant lumpenproletariats engaged in low-paying manufacturing, service and office work. Between these two extremes lies a middle range of high-wage skilled craft labor (often unionized) which is steadily disappearing as its employment base is restructured and decentralized. Thus, even though these metropolitan centers (among which the most prominent in the United States are New York, Los Angeles, San Francisco, and Chicago) have currently extremely active economies, the internal manifestations of this are (again) quite uneven. Along with massive office and apartment construction and redevelopment (including gentrification) in the portions of these centers reserved for white-collar production and social reproduction, we also observe vast areas given over to slum and *barrio* dwellers who work in local sweatshops and low-grade service industries.

None of these outcomes conforms to the predictions of the hierarchical diffusionist theories that continue to dominate much discussion of the process of regional economic development. Most especially, convergence of interregional systems has signally failed to occur. Instead, we observe a series of complex mechanisms that reproduce in historically evolving ways a changing geographical mosaic of unevenness and disparity. These processes of territorial development and transformation are inscribed everywhere on the landscape of capitalism. Their specific character at any time, of course, is very much a function of the currently operative regime of accumulation, as Lipietz has it (Ch. 2). Their immediate manifestation is the extraordinarily varied places and local histories that go to make up the totality of the geographical and historical circumstances of capitalism. The latest round in this continuing process of geographical evolution is marked by the new spatial division of labor. However, it is important not to lose sight of the point made earlier by Sayer to the effect that the new spatial division of labor by no means exhausts the totality of the modern space-economy (Ch. 6). On the contrary, it is superimposed upon and articulates with a pre-existing and enduring pattern of regional production and specialization.

Class and community

In any given community of workers, the class bargain, as Clark calls it (Ch. 7), involves a common structural condition, namely, the capital–labor relation. The class bargain in any community is also characterized by local variations whose origins reside in the peculiarities of place and locale. These peculiarities grow out of the particular kinds of industries and jobs that are found in any region, out of the levels of political consciousness that exist there, out of the uniqueness of the region's past, and so on. At this point, precisely, the social theorist is face to face with an intricate intersection between the demands of theoretical generality on the one hand, and the integrity of historical experience on the other hand. Thus workers *qua* members of the working class accumulate generalized political responses to the predicaments of working and living in capitalism. But the specific regional forms that these responses may take are often extremely varied. This variety means that political attempts to aggregate the responses into transcommunity movements are often doomed to failure. It also means that the theorist must tread cautiously in any attempt simply and unproblematically to assimilate these responses into the general category of class struggle.

Despite these cautionary remarks, it does seem to be the case that the formation of localized communities of workers is one of the necessary preconditions for the building of class consciousness, no matter how mediated it may be in any given case. Communal organization is one of the conditions of informal association just as it is of political mobilization. Moreover, purely local political issues will often combine with other more general political questions, and may contribute to the class capacity (i.e. the power to act collectively) of workers. On occasions, indeed, communities may be mobilized to the point where direct clashes between workers and management become part of the common experience of daily life. This will be especially the case where workers are also strongly organized into unions. These clashes may be over wages, conditions of work, the direction of technical change, and so on. As Clark points out (Ch. 7 above), the communal responses of workers to management can sometimes force ossification of the employment relation, thereby making it difficult for management to introduce new technologies, or reorganize production, or exploit the external labor market. Whatever their precise substance in any given case, these kinds of collisions between workers and management invariably represent heavy costs to the latter. Sooner or later, management may be expected to take evasive action.

This evasive action is part of the normal process of territorial evolution in capitalism. A wide variety of managerial tactics is typically brought to bear upon the problem depending on local circumstances: technical change, financial restructuring, increased subcontracting beyond the local area, *in situ* substitution of immigrant labor for local labor, plant closure, decentralization, and all the rest. Hitherto, plant closure and decentralization have probably been the most pervasive means of dealing with rising worker mobilization and high labor costs (see Chapter 9), though we must not overlook Sayer's warning that these kinds of processes are heavily overlain by contingencies of one sort or another, and what may have seemed to managements to have been a ready solution to the predicaments of agglomeration at one moment may well no longer appear so at another (Ch. 6). In any case, capital has hitherto shown a marked proclivity eventually to abandon that which it has engendered in the first instance, namely, dense communities of workers together with their various social appendages. By the same token, commodity production is re-energized, so to speak, where the capital–labor relation can be re-established anew. Where this can be achieved, the slate of local history is wiped clean and communities of workers reconstructed on fresh terrain. This latter process seems currently to be occurring in several of the more important growth complexes of the American Sunbelt.

The locational switches we have described here allow management to escape from any position of entrapment within a particular community of workers. This, of course is what in part accounts for the new spatial division of labor; if spatial mobility were not a managerial option we would undoubtedly be observing today a vastly different pattern of urban and regional development from the one that currently exists. At the same time, the work rules, technologies, labor market practices, and so on established in the new growth centers provide examples to and pressures on those capitalists who remain within the older-established manufacturing communities. Thus, the various practices that develop within these growth centers (especially their more conservative employment relations) may well be diffused backwards to older regions. In this way, interregional spatial relations come to be further important factors in the reproduction of class relations in national economies, and hence in the evolution of national income distributions and social inequality generally.

Conclusion: the agenda of theoretical human geography

The salient feature of the geographical landscape under capitalism is its status as an assemblage of territorial complexes of human labor and emergent social activity. The configuration of this landscape can be understood at three specific levels of analysis. First, it is constituted out of an overarching system of rules of order rooted in the basic relationships of capitalist society (Chs 2, 3, 4 & 13). Secondly, it is the direct manifestation of a set of intricate locational *cum* spatial processes (Chs 5, 6, 8, 11, 12 & 14). Thirdly, its immediate phenomenal form consists in a congeries of human communities in which the bases of social reproduction and social action are secured (Chs 7, 9 & 10). All of these analytical levels are, to be sure, intimately interconnected. They constitute a basic framework of meaning around any investigation into the logic and dynamics of territorial organization in modern capitalist societies. This framework raises many analytical questions of rather forbidding proportions. As difficult as they may be, these questions are starting to appear with increasing frequency on the agenda of theoretical human geography. Concomitantly, human geography seems to be poised on the threshold of a new kind of conceptual synthesis whose objective is to grasp the dynamics of the creation, reproduction, and transformation of territorial complexes of human labor and social activity in capitalism.

These central questions of theoretical human geography are capable of illuminating issues of major political significance in the modern world, and this in itself implies that we have little option but to take these questions very seriously indeed. The dynamics of territorial complexes are part of a new economic order whose geographical extent is now nothing less than the world itself. Territorial production complexes form the material bases of the relative positions of nations within the world economy, and so they are integral to the evolution of world political relations. They are also the framework within which specific urbanization and regional development processes unfold. Further, it is in these complexes that social reproduction occurs, and thus the creation of or resistance to new forms of domination that appear on the historical scene can be discerned through the window of territorial dynamics.

More importantly, perhaps, this suggested framework for understanding territorial complexes raises the possibility of new theoretical syntheses in all the social sciences. We have suggested that territoriality is important not only to urban and regional development as such, but also to the unfolding of the forces of production and the evolution of class relations and thus, to the macro-economic trajectories of capitalist economies. A major puzzle for all the social sciences is therefore how historical eventuation – that is, the historical development of capitalism as a whole – is played out through the intervening effects of locale. We suggest that the analysis of modern capitalism in terms something like these would significantly augment the whole corpus of contemporary social theory. A more forceful way of making the same point is to suggest that the largely spaceless social theories that currently dominate our intellectual culture stand in urgent need of retotalization via the dimensionality of geographical space and the particularities of place.

In light of these comments, we want to advance the proposition that the geographical analysis of modern capitalism can no longer be considered simply as the rather esoteric project of a coterie of professional geographers. As is evident from the chapters laid out above, such analysis calls on all the different social sciences, and, in turn, it offers them significant enrichment. We are indeed inclined to go so far as to claim that the question of the geographical anatomy of industrial capitalism is likely to become rapidly of major theoretical significance throughout the social sciences at large. This book, we hope, is an important prelude to the full fruition of this project.

Contributors

Gordon L. Clark is Professor of Labor Studies and Urban Policy at Carnegie–Mellon University in Pittsburgh, Pennsylvania. He has taught at the University of Chicago and the Kennedy School of Government at Harvard University, and has been a Fellow at the National Academy of Sciences in Washington DC. His principal research interests are in urban political economy, especially urban labor markets and judicial decision making. Recent publications include *Regional dynamics: studies in adjustment theory*, co-authored with Meric Gertler and John Whiteman (Boston: Allen & Unwin, 1986); *Judges and the cities* (Chicago: University of Chicago Press 1985); *State apparatus: structures and language of legitimacy*, co-authored with Michael Dear (Boston: Allen & Unwin 1984); and *Interregional migration, national policy and social justice* (Totowa, N. J. Rowman & Allanheld 1983). He is also Associate Editor of *Regional Studies*. Currently, he is engaged in a study of the determinants of union certification election results since 1970.

Michael Dunford is a lecturer in Human Geography in the School of European Studies at the University of Sussex. His major research interests are political economy and economic geography; and current aspects of British, French and Italian urban and regional development with reference at present to the relation between state regional policy and developments in telecommunications and electronics. With Diane Perrons he is the author of *The arena of capital* (London: Macmillan 1983). He has also just completed a book on French and Italian regional development, *Social reproduction and spatial inequality* (London: Pion 1985).

Fany Rachel Davidovich has been since 1960 a senior geographer at the Instituto Brasileiro de Geografia e Estatistica (Rio de Janeiro). She is currently a member for Latin America of the IGU Commission on 'Urban Systems in Transition.' Her main research interests are in urban and industrial geography. She has published many papers in Portuguese.

Pedro P. Geiger was one of the first geographers to graduate (in 1943) from the Universidade Federal do Rio de Janeiro. He has worked at the Instituto Brasileiro de Geografia e Estatistica since 1942. He is the author of *Evolução da rede urbana do Brasil* (Rio de Janeiro: CPE, Ministério de Educação e Cultura 1964), co-author of *Estudos rurais na Baixada Fluminense* (Rio de Janeiro: IBGE 1956) and co-editor of *Dimensões do desenvolvimento Brasileiro* (Rio de Janeiro: Editora Campus 1978). Most of his articles are published in the *Revista Brasileira de Geografia*.

John Holmes is Associate Professor of Geography at Queen's University, Kingston, Ontario, Canada. He received his first two degrees from the University of Sheffield and his doctorate from the Ohio State University in 1974. His research interests are in the current restructuring of the Canadian economy, and in the changing organization and locational structure of the automotive products industry. He has published on various aspects of the political economy of urban and regional issues in advanced capitalist societies.

Contributors

Ray Hudson is senior lecturer in Geography in the University of Durham. His research interests focus on spatial uneven development in southern and western Europe. Recent publications include *Regions in crisis*, co-edited with J. Carney and J. R. Lewis (London and New York: Croom Helm and St. Martins' Press 1980); *Regional planning in Europe*, co-edited with J. R. Lewis (London: Pion 1982); *Redundant spaces in cities and regions?* co-edited with J. Anderson and S. Duncan (New York: Academic Press 1983); *Uneven development in Southern Europe*, co-edited with J. R. Lewis (London: Methuen 1985). His current research includes work on the industrialization of rural areas in southern Europe and reasons for and impacts of restructuring on the coal, chemicals, steel and textile industries in western Europe's old industrial regions.

R. J. Johnston is Professor of Geography at the University of Sheffield, having worked previously in Australia and New Zealand. His main research interests are in urban and political geography, and his recent publications include *City and society* (London: Hutchinson 1984) and *Residential segregation, the state and constitutional conflict in the USA* (New York: Academic Press 1984).

Alain Lipietz is an engineer-economist and a member of the French Centre National de la Recherche Scientifique. He currently works at CEPREMAP, Paris. His major research interests are the marxist theory of capitalist development and crisis, value and prices, urban and regional economics, leftist economic policies. His publications include: *Le Tribut Foncier urbain* (Paris: Maspéro 1974), *Le Capital et son espace* (Paris: Maspéro 1977, 1983), *Crise et inflation: pourquoi?* (Paris: Maspéro 1979), *Le Monde enchanté* (Paris: Maspéro 1983; London: Verso 1985), *L'Audace ou l'enlisement* (Paris: La Découverte 1984).

Edward J. Malecki was educated at the Ohio State University, receiving his BA degree in international studies in 1971 and a PhD in geography in 1975. Currently Associate Professor of Geography at the University of Florida, he was previously on the faculty at the University of Oklahoma. He is the author of several research reports on federal research and development and has published widely in the journal literature on such topics as regional development, technological change, and corporate location.

Kristin Nelson is currently a lecturer in Social Geography at the University of California, Berkeley, where she received her PhD in geography. She has written articles on office suburbanization and office automation, and is the co-author of *The temporary help supply service and the temporary labor market*, a national study for the Department of Labor. Her current research interests are changes in US female regional labor markets, and the influence of structures of social reproduction on industrial location.

Diane Perrons is a lecturer in the Department of Economics at the City of London Polytechnic. She is a co-author with Michael Dunford of *The arena of capital* (London: Macmillan 1983) and is presently working on the economics of women and work.

David Sadler is research assistant in Geography at the University of Durham. His research interests are centered on traditional industries and communities in decline in northeast England and Western Europe.

313

Contributors

Andrew Sayer is a lecturer in Human Geography in the School of Social Sciences, University of Sussex. His main research interests are the philosophy and methodology of social science and industrial geography. Publications include *Method in social science: a realist approach* (London: Hutchinson 1984). At present he is engaged in research on the electronics industry and regional development.

Allen J. Scott was born in England and educated at Oxford University. He is currently Professor of Geography at the University of California, Los Angeles. He has previously held positions at the Universities of Pennsylvania, London, Toronto, Paris, and Hong Kong. He is the author of various publications on urbanization, regional development, and planning theory. He is the author of *The urban land nexus and the state* (London: Pion 1980) and co-editor of *Urbanization and urban planning in capitalist society* (London: Methuen 1982). He is also editor of the Pion monograph series *Research in Planning and Design*.

Michael Storper is Assistant Professor of Urban Planning at the University of California, Los Angeles. He received his PhD in Geography from the University of California, Berkeley. His current research interests include the role of spatial organization in shaping technological innovation and macro-economic growth in the US during the past 100 years; the role of urbanization in national economic development in the Third World; and the role of territorial organization in social behavior generally, especially in political-economic development paths. He is currently completing a study of the changing organization of the film industry and its implications for understanding the geography of the contemporary metropolis.

John Urry received his PhD from the University of Cambridge. He has taught in the Department of Sociology, University of Lancaster, since 1970. He is currently Professor and Head of Department. His publications include *Reference groups and the theory of revolution* (1973), *Social theory as science* with R. Keat (London: Routledge & Keegan Paul 1975, 1982), *The anatomy of capitalist societies* (London: Macmillan 1981), *Capital, labour and the middle classes* with N. Abercrombie (London/Boston: Allen & Unwin 1983), *Social relations and spatial structures*, co-edited with D. Gregory (1985), and *Localities, class, and gender*, with other members of the Lancaster Regionalism Group (1985).

Michael Webber was educated at the University of Cambridge and the Australian National University. He was a member of the Department of Geography at McMaster University in Canada from 1973 to 1985. He is now Professor of Geography at the University of Melbourne. Author of *Impact of uncertainty on location* (Cambridge, Mass., MIT Press 1971), *Christaller central place structures* with others, (Evanston, Ill.: Dept of Geography, Northwestern University 1977), *Information theory and urban spatial structure* (London: Croom Helm 1979), *Explanation, prediction and planning* (London: Pion 1984) and *Industrial location* (Beverly Hills: Sage 1984), his major research interests are now in the theory and measurement of profit rates and in the processes of regional manufacturing change.

Index

Numbers in italics refer to text figures.

337

341

Watanabe, S. 80, 84, 85, 86, 88, 102
Watertown Arsenal 47
Watkins, A. J. 198
Watts, H. D. 70
Weaver, C. 175, 189
Webb, S. 54
Webber, M. J. xvii, 197–224, 202, 315
Weiss, M. A. 71, 73
Weisskopf, T. 146
welfare policies 201, 248
  in Brazil 282
welfare state 127, 274
  attacks on 8
  in Britain 266
Wells, D. 197
West Germany
  see Germany
Westergaard, J. 267
Western Europe 3, 4–5, 6, 9, 43, 86, 94
  semiconductor production in 111, Table 6.1
  works closures in 172–89
  see also Europe
Wheelwright, S. C. 68–9
Whigham, P. V. 73
White, M. J. 167
whites, families 167
Wickham, H. 261
Wiebe, R. H. 51, 52
Wiener, M. J. 53, 58–9, 60, 61
Wilkinson, F. 80, 87, 91, 92–3, 94, 100, 101
Williams, J. R. 68
Williamson, B. 178
Winnipeg 95
Wisconsin 129
Wolff, G. 73
Wolin, M. L. 81
women 8
  clerical workers 155–66
  exploitation of, in Ireland 254
  homemakers, elasticity of supply of 158
  homeworking 94
  in semiconductor industry 119
  minority 156
    low-income 149
  oppression of 32
  primary-earner, middle class 156
  secondary-earner 158–9
  suburban 157
  see also labor, labor force, workers
Wood, S. 57, 59
work 3, 12, 45, 51, 58, 67, 201, 248, 302
  clerical 153
  day-to-day organization of 45
  dynamics of vii
  habits and experiences of 44
  hours of 128
  locational structure of 304
  nature of 51
  office 149

outwork 80–1, 100
piece work 48, 53
rationalization of 53
relation to fatigue 55
sphere of 52
see also employment, labor, offices
workers 44, 45, 47–8, 49, 51, 54, 55, 59–60,
    71–2, 93, 102, 122, 129, 149, 248, 310
  American 49–50, 88–9
  black 48
  blue-collar 152
  communities of 305, 309
  control of 88
  craft 48
  European, in Brazil 281
  female 48
    clerical 152–75
    in Ireland 254
    minority 149, 166
  in auto industry 131, 132, 139
    wages of 140
  industrial 62
  Japanese 138
  'laws', in Brazil 282
  lay-offs of 90
  mass collective 13, 122
  militant 37, 273
    in Italy 88–9
  mobilization of 310
  'non-production' 140
  non-productive, in Britain and US 62
  organization of 94
  peripheral 38
  primary 74
  production 70
  productive 46, 50
  professional–technical 71, 74, 75
    back office 151–2
  replacement of skilled by unskilled 73
  research and development 72, 122
  semi-skilled 47, 272
  skilled 30, 45, 48, 75, 96, 272–2
    craft 44
    elimination of 71
  specialization of 199
  unskilled 47, 71, 74–5, 96, 166, 272
  see also class, employees, labor, labor force,
      labor market, labor supply, middle
      class, operators, women, working
      class
workers' resistance 94, 135
  in Argentina 30
  in UK 56
workers' struggles 35, 101
working class 29, 32, 38, 50, 51, 58, 122,
    186–7, 189, 199, 249, 309
  competition within 175
  development of 29
  in Britain 30